Firms in the International Economy

CESifo Seminar Series
Edited by Hans-Werner Sinn

See http://mitpress.mit.edu for a complete list of titles in this series.

Firms in the International Economy

Firm Heterogeneity Meets International Business

Edited by Sjoerd Beugelsdijk, Steven Brakman, Hans van Ees, and Harry Garretsen

CESifo Seminar Series

CESifo Seminar Series
The MIT Press
Cambridge, Massachusetts
London, England

MIT Press books may be purchased at special quantity discounts for business or sales promotional use. For information, please email special_sales@mitpress.mit.edu or write to Special Sales Department, The MIT Press, 55 Hayward Street, Cambridge, MA 02142.

This book was set in Palatino LT Std by Toppan Best-set Premedia Limited, Hong Kong. Printed and bound in the United States of America.

Library of Congress Cataloging-in-Publication Data

Firms in the international economy : firm heterogeneity meets international business / edited by Sjoerd Beugelsdijk, Steven Brakman, Hans van Ees, Harry Garretsen.
    pages cm.—(CESifo seminar series)
Includes bibliographical references and index.
ISBN 978-0-262-01974-3 (hardcover : alk. paper)   1. International business enterprises.   2. International trade.   3. International economic relations.
I. Beugelsdijk, Sjoerd, 1976–
HD2755.5.F488 2013
338.8'8—dc23
2013011186

10   9   8   7   6   5   4   3   2   1

Contents

Series Foreword

This book is part of the CESifo Seminar Series. The series aims to cover topical policy issues in economics from a largely European perspective. The books in this series are the products of the papers and intensive debates that took place during the seminars hosted by CESifo, an international research network of renowned economists organized jointly by the Center for Economic Studies at Ludwig-Maximilians-Universität, Munich, and the Ifo Institute for Economic Research. All publications in this series have been carefully selected and refereed by members of the CESifo research network.

Introduction: Firm Heterogeneity, International Economics, and International Business

Despite their common roots and shared interest in globalization, multinationals, and trade and investment patterns, international economics (IE) and international business (IB) have developed as two distinct fields of study. While economists directed their efforts at formalizing the workings of international trade and investment at the macroeconomic level, business scholars attempted to open the black box of the multinational enterprise, relying more on conceptual narratives than mathematical tools. With the advent of new trade theory (Helpman and Krugman 1987; Helpman 2006), the firm was reintroduced as the object of interest in international economics. The recent advancement of the heterogeneous firm in formal models of ("new new") international trade (Melitz 2003) has further spawned an unprecedented amount of theoretical and empirical microeconomic research in international economics (Greenaway and Kneller 2007).

The traditional focus in IE was on the analysis of trade between countries and regions, with the behavior of the internationalizing firm only figuring in the background, but this is no longer true. The modern IE literature has taken a strong microeconomic focus and firm heterogeneity has become a prominent topic in IE. This development naturally leads to questions concerning the behavior and organization of the internationalizing firm. Business strategy and structure of the internationalizing firm has been the natural domain of IB. In fact, it was the specific interest in the role of the multinational firm by international economists such as Ray Vernon, Steve Hymer, Charles Kindleberger, John Dunning, and Richard Caves in the 1960s that gave a major impetus to what later became known as the field of international business. IB scholars have studied the international dimension of firms in great detail over the last decades.

The focus on firms in the international economy in IB versus the macro orientation of IE in the 1960s led to increased divergence and eventually resulted in two self-standing fields of research, each with their own specific journal. The *Journal of International Business Studies* (*JIBS*) saw the light in 1970 and the *Journal of International Economics* (*JIE*) was born in 1971. Apart from the diverging academic interest regarding the role of firms in the international economy, an increased demand for IB education in the same period further pushed the development of IB as a self-standing field of research. As it was put by Vern Terpstra in the very first article published in *JIBS*, "From all evidence that can be gleaned from this study and previous inquiries, university education for international business is indeed a 'going thing.' One reason is undoubtedly the belated recognition by American business schools that internationalism is coming to be a way of life for American business. New business school graduates with a long career ahead of them must be ready for this internationalism" (Terpstra 1970, 96).

With the explicit recognition of the role of firms in contemporary IE research, the potential for knowledge spillovers between IE and IB has increased as well. Both groups of scholars are interested in globalization, the determinants and consequences of international trade, and foreign direct investment (FDI) patterns, and at first sight both groups of scholars now put the firm at the center of their analyses. These thoughts motivated us to release a call for papers to IE and IB scholars to join forces in a CESifo workshop. The workshop took place in July 2011, and this book is the outcome of that initiative. The title of this book marks the ambition to further unravel the role of firms in the international economy and also of our endeavor to bring the two scholarly communities together and see how insights from IB can be used to promote the firm heterogeneity literature in IE.

This volume contains four parts, each consisting of three chapters. This introduction sets the stage and aims to provide a succinct overview of the rest of the book. We briefly discuss the nature of IB research and argue how IB could be a potential source of information for IE scholars to put more flesh on the bones of the firm heterogeneity models. This is not an easy task, as it requires scholars to get out of their scholarly comfort zone. We illustrate the presence of scholarly silos by a cross-citation analysis based on Web of Science data for *JIBS* and *JIE*. We also provide a preview of the chapters in this volume. We conclude our introduction by arguing that despite the central role attributed to firms in the international economy, important differences continue to exist between IE and IB. Having said this, the chapters in this volume make important first steps to what we feel is an interesting and rich research agenda.

What Is the Nature of IB Research?

To see how IB insights may contribute to the firm heterogeneity literature in IE, we first sketch the nature of IB research. International business is about profit-maximizing activities ("business") that cross national borders (Seno-Alday 2010, 19). IB is a field of research that does not constitute a single well-defined discipline (Cantwell and Brannen 2011) but builds upon insights from economics, strategic management, and comparative business systems (Negandhi 1983). It is fair to say that the contemporary IB community consists of scholars with a background and/or interest in economics and scholars with a background and/or interest in strategic management. Historically, IB originated out of the study of FDI but separated from mainstream economics in the 1960s and 1970s by focusing on a more empirical approach in which the multinational firm was not simply a black box. In this period, the works by Raymond Vernon, Steven Hymer, Charles Kindleberger, and Richard Caves are considered to be the most important contributions in IB (Dunning and Lundan 2008; Rugman and Verbeke 2008). As trade theorists directed their efforts at formalizing the workings of international trade and investment at the country or regional level, IB scholars attempted to open the black box of the (multinational) enterprise, relying more on conceptual, data-driven narratives than mathematical tools. IE became increasingly abstract and formal-theoretical during this period (see Leamer 2012 for an account of the formalization of IE since the 1960s).

Centered around firms doing business in a context (the host country) that differs from the one in which they are used to doing business (the home country), IB scholars attribute a central role to the changes in the business environment and a firm's functioning. In order to explore and exploit the location-specific advantages abroad (so far nothing differs from IE and trade theory), firms (and managers) have to overcome the contextual "distance" between the home and the host country, where "distance" should be interpreted in the broadest sense. The distance that firms have to overcome does not relate only to physical distance and the associated transport costs but includes cultural, economic, and institutional (legal) differences (Ghemawat 2001; Slangen and Beugelsdijk 2010). These contextual differences are associated with a liability of foreignness (Hymer 1976; Zaheer 1995), meaning that internationally operating firms incur costs that domestic firms do not have. In general, the assumption in IB research is that the larger the distance that has to be overcome, the more difficult it will be to be successful abroad because the larger the liability of foreignness (Zaheer 1995). The central role ascribed to the liability of foreignness is a distinguishing feature of IB compared to IE. Moreover, IB scholars typically argue that internationally operating firms will have to overcome this liability of foreignness by exploiting their firm-specific advantages (FSAs) abroad in order to be successful (Verbeke 2009). The idea of an FSA is taken from the notion of competitive advantage in economics and has been included in IB from the start. The very first textbook of IB, by John Fayerweather (also the first president of the Academy of International Business in 1960–1961), explicitly built on the notion of unique resources—that is, a competitive advantage—that could be transmitted to host countries by internationalizing firms (Fayerweather 1960). However, in putting these resources to local use, Fayerweather argued that adaptation was required. Contemporary IB scholars refer to this approach as internationalizing firms being confronted with the tension between global integration and standardization on the one hand and local responsiveness on the other hand. This firm-environment interaction is typically studied along two main dimensions (Beugelsdijk 2011). A substantial part of IB research takes a comparative approach because it concerns the comparison of the different ways in which value is added by firms in different (international) contexts. IB also has an interactive dimension in that it concerns firms (and employees) of internationalizing firms of one country that are confronted with firms (and employees) of another country—for example, when engaging in an international joint venture. It is the interaction between people and firms from different countries that is studied in IB. In sum, IB is concerned with the interaction between firms and the new environment in which the firms operate and the comparative analyses of the ways in which firms organize their business activities in different contexts.

Do IE and IB Interact? A Citation Analysis

Given their shared roots and interests, one would expect a certain degree of interaction between IE and IB. Especially given the developments sketched earlier, one would expect IE scholars to borrow insights from IB and vice versa. A simple citation analysis of *JIE* and *JIBS*, using the Web of Science (WoS) database, provides a good test of the actual level of interaction between the two fields. Using a cited reference search in WoS, we selected English-language articles (and hence citations from, for example, conference proceedings are excluded) published in *JIE* and *JIBS* (date of search: September 25, 2012). As mentioned before, *JIBS* was established in 1970 and *JIE* in 1971. Both are considered to be top field journals, which is reflected in their five-year average Social Sciences Citation Index (SSCI) impact scores. *JIBS* holds the seventh position in the business category (with a total of 103 journals) and has a five-year impact factor of 5.5. *JIE* holds the twenty-sixth position of a total of 304 journals in the economics category and has a five-year impact factor of 2.8. Both journals belong to the top 10 percent of their respective fields and are considered the primary outlets for research in international economics and international business.

The WoS data tell us that *JIBS* has been cited 3,704 times, most of which are in the business category. The top ten sources citing *JIBS* are listed in table I.1. The analysis shows that most citations are journal self-citations, followed by common international management and international business journals. The table shows that the articles published in *JIE* have cited *JIBS* only *five* times since both journals came into existence. More than a hundred journals cite more *JIBS* articles than have

Table I.1
Where is the *Journal of International Business Studies* (*JIBS*) cited?

Rank	Journal	No. of citations
1	*Journal of International Business Studies* (self-citations)	439
2	*International Journal of Human Resource Management*	189
3	*International Business Review*	174
4	*Journal of World Business*	138
5	*Journal of Business Research*	133
6	*Journal of International Marketing*	121
7	*Management International Review*	97
8	*International Marketing Review*	93
9	*Strategic Management Journal*	82
10	*Industrial Marketing Management*	73
101	*Journal of International Economics*	5
	Total top ten	1,539
	Total	3,704

Source: Web of Science, September 25, 2012 (own calculations).

Table I.2
Where is the *Journal of International Economics* (*JIE*) cited?

Rank	Journal	No. of citations
1	*Journal of International Economics* (self-citations)	494
2	*Canadian Journal of Economics*	179
3	*Journal of International Money and Finance*	158
4	*World Economy*	147
5	*European Economic Review*	115
6	*Review of International Economics*	106
7	*American Economic Review*	98
8	*Applied Economics*	94
9	*Review of World Economics*	93
10	*Journal of Development Economics*	92
42	*Journal of International Business Studies*	28
	Total top 10	1,576
	Total	5,244

Source: Web of Science, September 25, 2012 (own calculations).

ever been cited in *JIE*, and of all journals that belong to the economics category, *JIE* holds the seventeenth position in citing *JIBS* articles.

In table I.2, we provide an overview of *JIE* citations. The WoS data show 5,244 citations to articles published in *JIE*, most of them in the economics category. Again, self-citations are ranked first, followed by other journals in the field of IE. Just as the *Strategic Management Journal* is included in the top ten journals citing *JIBS* articles, we find the *American Economic Review* (*AER*) in the list of journals citing *JIE*. Thus both *JIBS* and *JIE* find their way to top general-interest journals in economics and management. Articles published in *JIE* have been cited in *JIBS* twenty-eight times, leading to *JIBS* holding the forty-second position in the ranking of journals citing *JIE*.

We end up with thirty-three cross-citations, of a total of 8,948 citations to both journals, implying that only 0.36 percent of all the citations in *JIBS* and *JIE* are cross-citations (for a detailed overview of these thirty-three articles, we refer to the appendix). Given (1) the shared historical roots of both fields, (2) the shared scholarly ambition to understand the process of globalization, the drivers and consequences of trade and FDI, and the role of multinational firms, and (3) the fact that the first generation of IB scholars were typically trained as economists, one would expect the cross-citations to be concentrated in the early years (the 1970s). But this is not the case. A further analysis of the thirty-three cross-citations shows that the five citations from *JIE* to *JIBS* are concentrated in 2004–2013 period. Only one of the five is older than 2004

(1991). A similar observation holds for articles published in *JIBS* citing articles from *JIE*. Of the twenty-eight articles, twenty-four were published in the last decade. The other four were published in 2001, 2000, 1997, and 1994. The good news is that the cross-citations are recent.

The picture that emerges from the cross-citation analysis is clear: international economists rarely cite *JIBS*, and a very limited number of IB scholars cite articles published in *JIE*. Although it is beyond the scope of this introduction to speculate on the reasons for such limited citation, some obvious reasons may be the different formal and informal rules of the publication game in IE and IB, the different language used to express oneself in IE or IB, the differences in methods (although some of the econometrics is similar; e.g., gravity equations are used both in IB and IE), the simple unawareness of what is happening outside one's own community, or the difficulty of translating and integrating insights from another field into one's own field. A more cynical response would be to blame the "publish or perish" research culture in which strategy (to publish) holds over substance (a true scholarly interest in phenomena that are also studied by "others"). Whatever the reason might be for the limited interaction, it is clear that IE and IB can be considered two disciplinary silos.

The Potential Overlap between IB and IE

The low number of citations between IE and IB may suggest that there is no room for combining insights from these parallel fields of research. This claim is easily falsified, though, as a couple of examples will make clear. We discuss how the theory on productivity differences in IE is in fact similar to the notion of firm-specific advantages in IB. We also show how the notion of sequential exporting in IE is strikingly similar to the Uppsala learning model as it is used in IB.

As mentioned before, the recognition of firm heterogeneity in IE has triggered an avalanche of theoretical and empirical studies including firm-specific effects. With the advent of new trade theory—which stressed monopolistic competition—the firm was reintroduced as the object of interest in international economics (Helpman and Krugman 1985). The way in which firm heterogeneity is modeled in many of these firm heterogeneity studies is by means of productivity differences. A key finding is the observation that productivity differences are associated with a certain pecking order (Helpman, Melitz, and Yeaple 2004). For example, Chang and van Marrewijk (2013) analyze firm

heterogeneity in fifteen Latin American countries using data from the
World Bank Enterprise Survey: Argentina, Bolivia, Chile, Colombia,
Ecuador, El Salvador, Guatemala, Honduras, Mexico, Nicaragua,
Panama, Paraguay, Peru, Uruguay, and Venezuela. They investigate the
impact of both export intensity and foreign ownership on productivity
by identifying four types of firms: (1) national domestic firms (nationally owned, producing for the domestic market), (2) national exporting
firms (nationally owned, also exporting), (3) foreign domestic firms
(partly foreign owned, producing for the domestic market), and (4)
foreign exporting firms (partially foreign owned, also exporting).

Figure I.1 illustrates the main findings of their study for the fifteen
countries and thirteen sectors taken together. Although considerable
overlap exists in productivity levels for the different firm types regarding normalized productivity levels (which range from 0 to 1), the
national domestic firms are least productive, and the foreign exporting
firms are the most productive. In between these are the national exporting firms and the foreign domestic firms, in that order of productivity.
A more detailed analysis controlling for factors such as firm size, sector,
and development level further corroborates this main finding. The difference between national exporter and foreign domestic is statistically
significant, as is the productivity difference between national exporters
and foreign exporters. In other words, in terms of productivity the following holds: national domestic < national exporter < foreign domestic

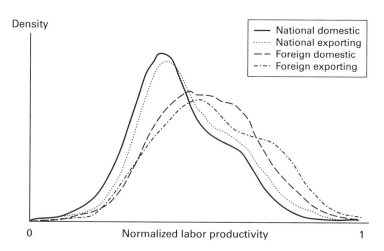

Figure I.1
Productivity and firm type in Latin America, 2006
Source: Chang and Van Marrewijk 2013

= foreign exporter, a finding that has been observed in other studies as well. This finding on productivity differences is perfectly compatible with IB and the literature on FSAs. In order to overcome the liability of foreignness, foreign firms need a competitive—read: firm-specific—advantage, which translates into a higher productivity level than local firms. These two insights, one on the existence of a pecking order and one on the crucial role of firm specific advantages, are crucial building blocks of IE and IB and are perfectly compatible with one another, yet both ideas have been developed in isolation.[1]

Another example of how close IB and IE are is the notion of sequential exporting, which has recently been developed in IE. The essence of these sequential exporting models is that exporters need to learn how to deal with the uncertainty associated with exporting. The risk of entering a new export market can be reduced by delivering small amounts first to test the capacity of the foreign trade partner (Rauch and Watson 2003). Along the same lines, Eaton and colleagues (2007, 2009) argue that firms can learn about export costs only after they actually export; in other words, previous experiences matter. Albornoz and colleagues (2010) suggest that firms do test not only the quality of trading partners but also the conditions of market demand. In their two-period model, uncertainty is resolved after exporting in the first period, leading to export growth and possibly market entry to other markets or market exit decisions. Albornoz and colleagues (2010) stress the importance of recent market entry for export growth and market exit. In IB, the questions of when to enter and in what order over time were first studied by Johanson and Vahlne (1977), two Swedish professors from Uppsala. The internationalization process that they have developed is therefore also referred to as the Uppsala model of internationalization and has become a standard in IB textbooks. Their argument is that firms need to learn and internationalization is a dynamic learning process. Learning is based on experiential knowledge (knowledge gained by experience), on learning-by-doing. The internationalization process is described as a series of small steps in which each step provides a basis for learning about the market. This learning process is important to reduce the liability of foreignness. It not only holds for exports but has been extended to a range of entry modes. To operationalize the liability of foreignness, IB scholars use a variety of constructs among which is a set of distance dimensions. A typical example used in this context is IKEA. The first steps that IKEA took were mainly in western European markets, with the first country entered outside

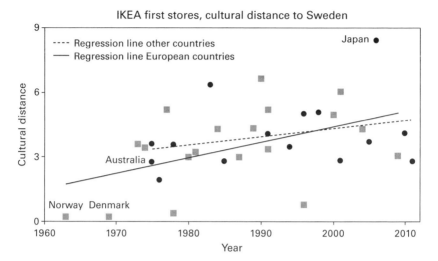

Figure I.2
Cultural distance and dynamic entry decisions
Source: Beugelsdijk et al. 2013

Sweden being Norway and the second Denmark. Both are neighboring countries with a similar culture familiar to the Swedes, thereby reducing the liability of foreignness. This idea—that firms like IKEA expand over time to countries that are increasingly culturally dissimilar—is a typical hypothesis in IB. It is illustrated in figure I.2, showing that over time in the expansion process of IKEA, the cultural distance (measured as a composite index of a set of four culture dimensions as developed by Kogut and Singh 1988) increases. This relationship is significant.

Interestingly, the sequential exporting theory in IE and the Uppsala internationalization model in IB develop a strikingly similar line of reasoning based on experience, learning, and stepwise dynamics. Over the years, IB scholars have developed a fine-grained view on which specific firm factors play a role in these learning processes. There is no reason why IE scholars would not integrate these insights in their models of sequential exporting.

Apart from the productivity (IE)/firm-specific advantage (IB) and sequential exporting (IE)/Uppsala model (IB) issues, other potential for overlap exists. An important contemporary development in economics more broadly, including international economics, concerns the importance attached to the role of institutions and culture (North 2005; Tabellini 2008; Beugelsdijk and Maseland 2011). As a consequence of this interest in culture and institutions, IE also focuses on the contextual differences of the way value added is generated and the way economic activity is organized in different contexts. Differences in legal systems, colonial ties, or other factors that shape institutions turn out to be important for trade relations. This recognition of context specificity is in line with the most fundamental building block of IB research. The shared interest in contextual factors in IE and IB may provide another platform for mutual collaboration.

The Chapters in This Book

The book consists of four parts, with each part made up of three chapters. Part I, "Firm-Specific Advantages," corresponds with a key aspect of IB theory. The first chapter, by Rugman and Nguyen, provides an overview of the historical development of the field of IB. In an accessible way, they explain how the field of IB originated from a pioneering group of scholars in the 1960s and 1970s who took a firm-based approach (versus industry or country) to understand trade and FDI patterns and simultaneously tried to provide empirical support for their theoretical conjectures. As argued before, this interest in firm-level strategic factors, together with the focus on empirical research (versus formal modeling that continued in international economics), was the key factor leading to divergence between IE and IB and resulting in the two fields as we know them today. Despite the recent turn in international economics to focus on the role of the firm and the associated recent wave of empirical studies in international economics, they conclude that the key difference between IE and IB in the end boils down to a difference in the focal unit of analysis. These are provocative statements, and this volume shows that to some extent these observations are no longer valid. As explained in the previous sections in this introduction, IE has moved beyond the country as the main or only unit of observation (Melitz 2003). Chapter 2 is an illustration of this recent turn in IE. Pietrovito, Pozzolo, and Salvatici use aggregate data, though at a very detailed level, to show that heterogeneity and firm size are important determinants of FDI. Empirical work related to Melitz (2003) is still producing interesting results as more microfirm datasets become available. But applications like these show that international trade theory is no longer restricted to the country as the main unit of observation. Sala and Yalcin show in chapter 3 that the effects of variables such as fixed costs and firm productivity are by now well-known variables that determine market entry decisions. This chapter explicitly adds managerial inputs to these two variables typically included in IE. By stressing the role of managerial inputs, Sala and Yalcin's chapter is in line with key insights from IB. The managerial input is subdivided into learning (formal, informal) and manager's international experience. They find evidence that variables like these are important and should stimulate further research. The correlation between the variables is present but a good and convincing story to determine causality and a link between the different types of variables is still work in progress.

Part II deals with the interaction between a firm and its external environment. Chapter 4 takes issue with the relation between foreign firms and their impact on the local environment. The authors of this chapter, Blonigen and O'Fallon, rightfully argue that the study of the effects of multinational enterprises (MNEs) on their host country environment is dominated by possible productivity, growth, and wage effects. They argue that both IB and IE have overlooked the relation between foreign firms and local communities broadly defined. They illustrate this argument by focusing on corporate philanthropy. Based on a unique database, they show that foreign-owned firms differ substantially from domestic-owned firms in their local corporate philanthropy, in that foreign firms are more likely to give less.

The interaction between a firm's external environment and its strategy is further explored in chapter 5. Darby, Desbordes, and Wooton show that the experience of firms with institutions in their home country affects the FDI decision of these firms. Firms coming from institutionally weak countries may have a competitive advantage (an FSA, in IB terms) on which they can capitalize when internationalizing in other developing countries. Mayneris and Poncet put forward a similar experience-based argument in chapter 6. They argue that domestic firms may benefit from the local presence of foreign exporting firms and illustrate their argument using data on Chinese exporters. The presence of exporting experience in the local environment provides a platform from which domestic firms may learn how to internationalize. This local experience is, in Marshallian terms, "in the air" and contributes to the creation of an FSA that can be exploited across borders.

All three chapters in this part complement the first part on the role of FSAs by showing how the interaction between firms and their external environment may provide more insights in the nature of firm heterogeneity. In IB terms, it shows how FSAs originate from and also have an effect on the local external environment.

Part III centers on the boundaries of the firm, a classic topic in both IB and IE. Bombarda (chapter 7) distinguishes between arm's-length trade and intrafirm trade and develops a general equilibrium model leading her to predict that the role of geographical barriers and transportation costs differ between these two types of trade. A test of her argument on the foreign activity of U.S. firms shows that geographical distance has an impact on the organizational choices made by firms, albeit not always in line with the theoretical predictions. Bombarda also shows that strong sector-specific effects exist, and when controlling for these, the empirical evidence converges to her theoretical predictions. The organizational choices made by firms are further explored in chapter 8. Nowak, Schwartz, and Suedekum focus on the global sourcing of complex production processes and link the make-or-buy decision (integrate or outsource) to the baseline model developed by Antràs and Helpman (2004). In line with what is known from IB (Hennart 2009), the make-or-buy decision is driven by the asset specificity, leading Nowak, Schwartz, and Suedekum to predict that sophisticated inputs will be held within the boundaries of the firm. The nature of the transaction determines the optimal organizational structure. Chapter 9 is by Altomonte, Di Mauro, Ottaviano, Rungi, and Vicard. Just like Bombarda in chapter 7 and Nowak, Schwartz, and Suedekum in chapter 8, the authors of this chapter consider the two alternative organizational modes, that is, internalization of activities versus arm's-length contracting. Specifically, Altomonte and colleagues explore how the boundaries of the firm are affected by the recent great trade collapse. They do so by using unique transaction level data on French firms; they show how the different stages in the global value chain respond to the trade collapse. In a global value chain, falling demand leads firms to overreact due to adjustments in the stocks of intermediate inputs, a phenomenon called the "bullwhip effect." The organizational structure (internalize or arm's-length contracting) of the value chain determines the extent to which this phenomenon occurs. Hierarchies of multinational firms in which production stages are internalized are hypothesized to be better able to optimize inventories. The three chapters in this third part complement part I (stressing the role of FSAs) and part II (these FSAs interact with the local environment) by showing that a proper understanding of the organizational structure of multinational firms is necessary to understand the contemporary process of globalization and the role of intrafirm and arm's-length trade.

Given the importance of innovation and technology, the final part of this volume deals with the transfer of technology and the offshoring of innovation. García-Vega and Huergo (chapter 10) investigate whether and how technology transfers from headquarters to their subsidiaries affect the innovative output and labor productivity of these subsidiaries. Their focus on the role of subsidiaries is in line with the contemporary interest of IB scholars in subsidiaries. As described in the first chapter by Rugman and Nguyen, subsidiaries have developed from subordinate units in a hierarchical multinational with headquarters being the center to self-standing units with a more specific role in the overall MNE network, including the role of technology centers. Using data on Spanish firms, García-Vega and Huergo show that the impact of innovation on productivity differs between foreign and domestic firms, arguably because foreign firms—that is, subsidiaries that are part of an overall MNE network—can draw upon crucial resources that domestic firms not part of such a network cannot. Just as in the previous parts, it is argued that a specific organizational structure may provide a firm specific advantage. Smeets and Abramovksy (chapter 11) follow up on the ideas of García-Vega and Huergo and the important role of subsidiaries for innovations by looking at the offshoring of innovations. They do so by investigating the inventor employment decisions of European MNEs. Taking the difference between the extensive margin (the decision whether to employ foreign inventors) and intensive margin (if yes, how many inventors to employ) into account, Smeets and Abramovsky show that foreign inventors substitute for home inventors when wages in the home country increase but also that this mainly holds for the extensive margin, not for the intensive margin. Their results also emphasize the need to distinguish between the two elements of the internationalization decision—that is, go or no go, and if so, how many resources to invest. Finally, Pflüger and Russek (chapter 12) use the Melitz (2003) model that has inspired the literature on firm heterogeneity to develop several general lessons. They show that different business environments—policy induced or not—do not preclude gains of trade and motivate international policy coordination. The chapters in part IV complement the previous parts. MNEs use their network of subsidiaries and the location-specific advantages provided by the local environment in which these subsidiaries operate to strengthen their competitive position in terms of innovation and technology. This is another example of the crucial link between location and firm-specific advantages (see chapter 1) and the way multinational firms leverage the resources within the firm and from the external global environment in which they operate.

In conclusion, this book scratches the surface of a field of research that could be called international economics and business (Beugelsdijk et al. 2013). The book explores the potentially rich opportunities of a fruitful exchange of ideas and insights between IB and IE. The cross-citation analysis suggests virtually no communication, yet the authors of the chapters in this book have made attempts to show otherwise. Against the background of only five citations to *JIBS* articles in *JIE* since 1971, the total number of *JIBS* citations in this book is impressive, as it amounts to thirty-seven (thirty excluding this introduction, and ten excluding the introduction and the first overview chapter on IB theory by Rugman and Nguyen). Is this a reason to expect a full integration of IE and IB in the near future? That would probably be too optimistic. In the end, despite the shared objects of interest and study, the disciplinary differences between IB and IE will remain. These can perhaps best be summarized as IB taking an inside-out perspective versus IE taking an outside-in perspective. Both look at firms in the international economy, but not from the same angle.

Note

1. Interestingly enough, the link between productivity differences and a firm-specific advantage was already made by Dunning and goes back to the 1950s when Dunning was writing his PhD thesis. He studied the U.S. manufacturing industry in the United Kingdom and observed that U.S. subsidiaries in the United Kingdom had higher productivity levels than the UK competitors. This observation triggered a set of related questions that became the core of the framework that has become known as the ownership-location-internalization (OLI) framework. One of the questions was whether this productivity difference was due to the superior resources of the U.S. (versus the UK) economy or whether it was due to the more efficient way of managing these resources by U.S. managers across national borders. The managerial superiority argument was labeled an ownership or firm-specific effect, referring to the fact that these productivity advantages were fundamentally related to non-location-bound, spatially transferable resources—in other words, those resources that belong to a multinational and can be transferred across borders (see also chapter 1).

References

Albornoz, F., H. F. Calvo Pardo, and G. Corcos. 2010. Sequential exporting. CEPR Discussion Paper 8103.

Antràs, P., and E. Helpman. 2004. Global sourcing. *Journal of Political Economy* 112 (3): 552–580.

Beugelsdijk, S. 2011. Location specific advantages and liability of foreignness; time, space and relative advantage. In *Advances in International Management*, ed. C. G. Asmussen, T. Devinney, T. Pedersen, and L. Tihanyi, 181–210. Bingley, UK: Emerald Group.

Beugelsdijk, S., S. Brakman, J. H. Garretsen, and C. Van Marrewijk. 2013. *International Economics and Business*. Cambridge: Cambridge University Press.

Beugelsdijk, S., and R. Maseland. 2011. *Culture in Economics: History, Methodological Reflections and Contemporary Applications*. Cambridge: Cambridge University Press.

Cantwell, J., and M. Y. Brannen. 2011. Positioning *JIBS* as an interdisciplinary journal. *Journal of International Business Studies* 42 (1): 1–9.

Chang, H.-H., and C. van Marrewijk. 2013. Firm heterogeneity and development: Evidence from Latin American countries. Forthcoming in *Journal of International Trade & Economic Development* 22 (1). http://dx.doi.org/10.1080/09638199.2012.704063.

Dunning, J. H., and S. M. Lundan. 2008. *Multinational Enterprises and the Global Economy*. 2nd ed. Cheltenham, UK: Edward Elgar.

Eaton, J., M. Kugler, M. Eslava, and J. Tybout. 2007. Export dynamics in Colombia: Firm-level evidence. NBER Working Paper 13531.

Eaton, J., M. Eslava, C. J. Krizan, M. Kugler, and J. Tybout. 2009. A search and learning model of export dynamics. Mimeo., December.

Fayerweather, J. 1960. *Management of International Operations: Text and Cases*. New York: McGraw-Hill.

Ghemawat, P. 2001. Distance still matters, the hard reality of global expansion. *Harvard Business Review* 79 (8): 137–147.

Greenaway, D., and R. Kneller. 2007. Firm heterogeneity, exporting, and foreign direct investment. *Economic Journal* 117 (517): F134–F161.

Helpman, E. 2006. Trade, FDI, and the organization of firms. *Journal of Economic Literature* 44:589–630.

Helpman, E., and P. R. Krugman. 1987. *Market Structure and Foreign Trade*. Cambridge, MA: MIT Press.

Helpman, E., M. J. Melitz, and S. R. Yeaple. 2004. Export versus FDI with heterogeneous firms. *American Economic Review* 94:300–316.

Hennart, J. F. 2009. Down with MNE centric theories! Market entry and expansion as the bundling of MNE and local assets. *Journal of International Business Studies* 40 (9): 1432–1454.

Hymer, S. H. 1976. *The International Operations of National Firms: A Study of Foreign Direct Investment*. Cambridge, MA: MIT Press.

Johanson, J., and E. Vahlne. 1977. The internationalization process of the firm: A model of knowledge development and increasing market commitments. *Journal of International Business Studies* 8 (1): 23–32.

Kogut, B., and H. Singh. 1988. The effect of national culture on the choice of entry mode. *Journal of International Business Studies* 19 (3): 411–432.

Leamer, E. E. 2012. *The Craft of Economics: Lessons from the Heckscher-Ohlin Framework*. Cambridge, MA: MIT Press.

Melitz, M. 2003. The impact of trade on intra-industry reallocations and aggregate industry productivity. *Econometrica* 71 (6): 1695–1725.

Negandhi, A. R. 1983. Cross cultural management research: Trend and future directions. *Journal of International Business Studies* 14:17–28.

North, D. 2005. *Understanding the Process of Economic Change*. Princeton: Princeton University Press.

Rauch, J. E., and J. Watson. 2003. Starting small in an unfamiliar environment. *International Journal of Industrial Organization* 21:1021–1042.

Rugman, A., and A. Verbeke. 2008. Internalization theory and its impact on the field of international business. In *International Business Scholarship: AIB Fellows on the First 50 Years and Beyond* (Research in Global Strategic Management, vol. 14), ed. J. J. Boddewyn, 155–174. Bradford, UK: Emerald Group.

Seno-Alday, S. 2010. International business thought: A 50 year footprint. *Journal of International Management* 16 (1): 16–31.

Slangen, A. H. L., and S. Beugelsdijk. 2010. The impact of institutional hazards on foreign multinational activity: A contingency perspective. *Journal of International Business Studies* 41 (6): 980–995.

Tabellini, G. 2008. Institutions and culture. *Journal of the European Economic Association* 6 (2/3): 255–294.

Terpstra, V. 1970. University education for international business. *Journal of International Business Studies* 1 (1): 89–96.

Verbeke, A. 2009. *International Business Strategy*. Cambridge: Cambridge University Press.

Zaheer, S. 1995. Overcoming the liability of foreignness. *Academy of Management Journal* 38 (2): 341–363.

Appendix: Detailed Overview of the Thirty-Three Cross-Citations between the *Journal of International Business Studies* (*JIBS*) and the *Journal of International Economics* (*JIE*)

Five Citations from Articles Published in *JIE* to *JIBS*

1. Holger, B. 2008. Trade liberalization and industrial restructuring through mergers and acquisitions. *Journal of International Economics* 76 (2): 254–266.

2. Volpe, M. C., and C. Jeromino. 2008. Is export promotion effective in developing countries? Firm level evidence on the intensive and extensive margins of exports. *Journal of International Economics* 76 (1): 89–106.

3. Branstetter, L. 2006. Is foreign direct investment a channel of knowledge spillovers? Evidence from Japan's FDI in the United States. *Journal of International Economics* 68 (2): 325–344.

4. Ruckman, K. 2004. Modes of entry mode into a foreign market: The case of US mutual funds in Canada. *Journal of International Economics* 62 (2): 417–432.

5. Itagaki, T. 1991. A 2 step decision models of the multinational enterprise under foreign demand uncertainty. *Journal of International Economics* 30 (1–2): 185–190.

Twenty-Eight Citations from Articles Published in *JIBS* to *JIE*

1. Kumaraswamy, A., R. Mudambi, H. Saranga, and A. Tripathy. 2012. Catch-up strategies in the Indian auto components industry: Domestic firms' responses to market liberalization. *Journal of International Business Studies* 43 (4): 368–395.

2. Li, S., J. Qiu, and C. Wan. 2011. Corporate globalization and bank lending. *Journal of International Business Studies* 42 (8): 1016–1042.

3. Golovko, E., and G. Valentini. 2011. Exploring the complementarity between innovation and export for SMEs' growth. *Journal of International Business Studies* 42 (3): 362–380.

4. Gu, Q., and J. W. Lu. 2011. Effects of inward investment on outward investment: The venture capital industry worldwide 1985–2007. *Journal of International Business Studies* 42 (2): 263–284.

5. Cassiman, B., and E. Golovko. 2011. Innovation and internationalization through exports. *Journal of International Business Studies* 42 (1): 56–75.

6. Beugelsdijk, S., J. F. Hennart, A. H. L. Slangen, and R. Smeets. 2010. Why FDI stocks are a biased measure of MNE affiliate activity. *Journal of International Business Studies* 41 (9): 1444–1459.

7. Liu, X., J. Lu, I. Filatotchev, T. Buck, and M. Wright. 2010. Returnee entrepreneurs, knowledge spillovers and innovation in high-tech firms in emerging economies. *Journal of International Business Studies* 41 (7): 1183–1197.

8. Colantone, I., and L. Sleuwaegen. 2010. International trade, exit and entry: A cross-country and industry analysis. *Journal of International Business Studies* 41 (7): 1240–1257.

9. Ito, K., and E. L. Rose. 2010. The implicit return on domestic and international sales: An empirical analysis of US and Japanese firms. *Journal of International Business Studies* 41 (6): 1074–1089.

10. Li, Q., and T. Vashchilko. 2010. Dyadic military conflict, security alliances, and bilateral FDI flows. *Journal of International Business Studies* 41 (5): 765–782.

11. Hejazi, W., and E. Santor. 2010. Foreign asset risk exposure, DOI, and performance: An analysis of Canadian banks. *Journal of International Business Studies* 41 (5): 845–860.

12. Rangan, S., and M. Sengul. 2009. Information technology and transnational integration: Theory and evidence on the evolution of the modern multinational enterprise. *Journal of International Business Studies* 40 (9): 1496–1514.

13. Blalock, G., and D. H. Simon. 2009. Do all firms benefit equally from downstream FDI? The moderating effect of local suppliers' capabilities on productivity gains. *Journal of International Business Studies* 40 (7): 1095–1112.

14. Liu, X., C. Wang, and Y. Wei. 2009. Do local manufacturing firms benefit from transactional linkages with multinational enterprises in China? *Journal of International Business Studies* 40 (7): 1113–1130.

15. Altomonte, C., and E. Pennings. 2009. Domestic plant productivity and incremental spillovers from foreign direct investment. *Journal of International Business Studies* 40 (7): 1131–1148.

16. Fratianni, M., and C. H. Oh. 2009. Expanding RTAs, trade flows, and the multinational enterprise. *Journal of International Business Studies* 40 (7): 1206–1227.

17. Coucke, K., and L. Sleuwaegen. 2008. Offshoring as a survival strategy: Evidence from manufacturing firms in Belgium. *Journal of International Business Studies* 39 (8): 1261–1277.

18. Peng, M. W., D. Y. L. Wang, and Y. Jiang. 2008. An institution-based view of international business strategy: A focus on emerging economies. *Journal of International Business Studies* 39 (5): 920–936.

19. Clougherty, J. A., and M. Grajek. 2008. The impact of ISO 9000 diffusion on trade and FDI: a new institutional analysis. *Journal of International Business Studies* 39 (4): 613–633.

20. Paul, D. L., and R. B. Wooster. 2008. Strategic investments by US firms in transition economies. *Journal of International Business Studies* 39 (2): 249–266.

21. Salomon, R., and B. Jin. 2008. Does knowledge spill to leaders or laggards? Exploring industry heterogeneity in learning by exporting. *Journal of International Business Studies* 39 (1): 132–150.

22. Driffield, N., and J. H. Love. 2007. Linking FDI motivation and host economy productivity effects: conceptual and empirical analysis. *Journal of International Business Studies* 38 (3): 460–473.

23. Tian, X. 2007. Accounting for sources of FDI technology spillovers: Evidence from China. *Journal of International Business Studies* 38 (1): 147–159.

24. Hejazi, W., and P. Pauly. 2003. Motivations for FDI and domestic capital formation. *Journal of International Business Studies* 34 (3): 282–289.

25. Clougherty, J. A. 2001. Globalization and the autonomy of domestic competition policy: an empirical test on the world airline industry. *Journal of International Business Studies* 32 (3): 459–478.

26. Spencer, J. W. 2000. Knowledge flows in the global innovation system: Do US firms share more scientific knowledge than their Japanese rivals? *Journal of International Business Studies* 31 (3): 521–530.

27. Anand, J., and B. Kogut. 1997. Technological capabilities of countries, firm rivalry and foreign direct investment. *Journal of International Business Studies* 28 (3): 445–465.

28. Lenway, S. A., and T. P. Murtha. 1994. The state as strategist in international-business research. *Journal of International Business Studies* 25 (3): 513–535.

I Firm-Specific Advantages

1 International Business Theory for International Economists

Alan M. Rugman and Quyen T. K. Nguyen

1.1 Introduction

The literatures on international business and international economics have diverged over the last fifty years. As shown elsewhere in this volume, research in international business, especially published in the *Journal of International Business Studies* (which now has a one-year ISI impact factor of 4.2) has virtually no impact on international economics—and vice versa. Why is this? We believe the lack of overlap is due to the following four factors:

1. The key unit of analysis in international economics is the country, whereas in international business it is the firm. As a result, international business has developed a vibrant and robust theory of the multinational enterprise (MNE), in which managerial resources and capabilities and other types of firm-specific advantages (FSAs) are explanatory factors rather than country-level attributes, which economists often analyze at industry level. We shall discuss this theme in detail later in this chapter around a discussion of the literature on international business theory.

2. The empirical work in international business uses firm-level data on the activities and performance of MNEs and also analyzes the performance of managers through survey data and other direct observations. In contrast, empirical work in international economics mainly uses country-level data on trade and foreign direct investment (FDI). Although trade data can be disaggregated to three- or even four-digit industry levels, such disaggregation does not capture in an adequate manner the complex activities of MNEs, especially their strategic management decisions.

3. Two key developments in analyzing trade flows have not yet been fully embedded in international business (IB) work. The first

development is the application of the gravity model to international trade and FDI. This focus on geographic distance by economists can usefully relate to the focus on location (L) and country-specific advantages (CSAs) but lacks development in the IB literature (Fratianni, Marchionne, and Oh 2011). In particular, although the work by Hejazi (2007, 2009) on FDI is a useful link to work on trade by Fratianni and Oh (2009) and others, this is a limited exception. Second, the focus on trade in intermediate products in international economics originating in the work by Grubel and Lloyd (1975) relates to the key attributes of MNE activity, namely that the activities of foreign subsidiaries can be just as important as the nature of the home country parent firm. In other words, Grubel and Lloyd found that there was two-way trade (both imports and exports), especially in trade and intermediate (service based) goods. Similarly IB theories have been developed by Dunning (1958, 1981) and Vernon (1966) to explain how MNEs develop two way sets of FDI activities, aligning these in a sequential manner, which leads to inward and outward FDI driven by firm-level strategic behavior. However, these developments have been largely ignored by international economists.

4. In terms of performance, international economists are concerned with the activities of MNEs as they may affect economic welfare (i.e., they examine the efficiency aspects of MNEs). So do scholars in international business, but they test firm performance directly by examination of return on assets (ROA), return on investment (ROI), or by construction of a Tobin Q ratio. MNEs can have large foreign subsidiaries. For example, BP, a European company, has over US$80 billion of sales in North America, making it one of the largest twenty firms in North America. It is necessary to attempt to calculate return on foreign assets (ROFA) as well as the consolidated return on total assets (ROTA) of the parent firm. In general, international economists have been unable, or unwilling, to analyze activities and performance of foreign subsidiaries, treating them separately from the parent firm, possibly due to the difficulties in obtaining data when a complex MNE is decomposed.

In summary, IB scholarship in the last fifty years has made substantial progress in both developing a theory of the MNE and in the implementation of imaginative and constructive new empirical work to test its performance. We shall now develop these points with an historical overview of the literature in international business.

1.2   The Theory of the Multinational Enterprise

Hymer (1960) provides an explanation for the existence of the MNE based on microeconomics foundations by changing the focus from the country level to the firm level. Hymer argues that if the investor directly controls the enterprise, the investment made will be considered to be FDI. Hymer shows that portfolio investment theory (with its simplifying assumptions of lack of risks and uncertainties) can be contrasted with FDI where there are costs of acquiring information and market imperfections exist.

Hymer was the first to consider FDI as an instrument by an MNE to exploit its competitiveness resulting from FSAs, yielding a monopoly position in foreign markets. These FSAs must be sufficient to overcome the liability of foreignness (Hymer 1960; Zaheer 1995)—that is, the additional cost associated with FDI. The FSAs may arise in the product or factor markets. The former includes product differentiation, superior marketing and distribution skills, and trademarks or brand names. The latter may arise from access to raw materials; economies of scale; access to large capital; intangible assets such as knowledge, information, proprietary technology due to research and development activities, patents, and management skills specific to the organizational function of the firm, such as the ability to achieve vertical and horizontal integration and the ability to reduce the transaction costs when replacing an arm's-length transaction in the market by an internal firm transaction. Hence, Hymer argues that FDI will occur in such imperfect markets. In other words, MNEs face location disadvantages compared to domestic firms in the host countries and MNEs overcome these challenges by FSA superiority to create entry barriers in the markets.

Hymer was the first to contrast such firm-level FDI with the prevailing economist orthodoxy that explained FDI as a financial (portfolio) investment decision determined by interest rate differentials across national borders. Hymer recognized that FDI is a firm-level strategy decision rather than a capital-market financial decision, (Dunning and Rugman 1985; Rugman and Verbeke 2008). The Hymer approach thus contrasts with the international economics factor-cost explanation of international trade. Hymer's focus on the firm-level industrial organization approach to FDI is elaborated further by Kindleberger (1969), who identifies imperfections in markets for finished products and for production factors together with scale economies and government regulations of output and entry.

1.2.1   The Product Life Cycle

Vernon (1966) develops the product life cycle (PLC) out of a critique of neoclassical comparative advantage theory, which fails to deal with the role of innovation in trade patterns and lacks attention to the role of economies of scale in determining such patterns. Vernon's product life cycle theory requires imperfections in both the market for products and factors of production. It suggests that FDI is a natural stage in the life cycle of new product from its inception to its maturity and eventual decline. The basic idea is that products tend to have a life that follows a typical pattern. Specifically, a product's life is made up of a finite number of stages encountered in a definite and predictable sequence, from product development through to production at home and eventually abroad. The product cycle predicts that production will initially be carried out in a firm's home country. It is only as the product and production process become more standardized that production can be shifted overseas to U.S. subsidiaries in Canada and Western Europe. Eventually, production goes to a low-cost environment at a time when there are no longer any proprietary FSAs of value to the MNE. Vernon argues that eventually its foreign subsidiaries would replace exports from the home country and export back to it. Furthermore, he also indicates that at the final stages of standardization, labor costs will become a critical consideration in production. Thus, developing markets with low-cost labor will offer a competitive advantage as a production location.

The early works of Hymer, Kindleberger, and Vernon show that despite the perceived risk and additional costs of operating abroad, MNEs must be able to develop production activities that will be competitive in the short or long term compared to the domestic operations of host-country companies. Unfortunately, this economics-based framework is characterized by an absence of managerial considerations and a neglect of the implications of governance costs for the efficiency aspects of FDI decisions (Rugman and D'Cruz 2000).

1.2.2   Horizontal and Vertical Integration

An important extension of market imperfections theory was made by Richard Caves (1971, 1974). Caves studies FDI from the perspective of the economics of industrial organization. He argues that MNEs must possess "unique assets." Caves emphasizes that such FDI occurs mainly in industries characterized by oligopoly market structures. Moreover, he clearly distinguishes among the various types of FDI: horizontal extension, in which a firm produces the same product elsewhere; vertical extension, in which a firm adds a stage in the production process that comes either earlier or later than its principal processing activity; and conglomerate diversification (Caves 1982).

Caves identifies product differentiation as the unique asset that horizontally integrated firms possess. Caves argues that the MNE will have advantages over local competitors because it is protected by trademarks and brand names. Furthermore, the research and marketing process continues to produce a steady stream of new differentiated products. It is difficult and costly for competitors to copy such products, and they face a time lag if they try. Having developed differentiated products for the domestic home market, the firm may decide to market them worldwide, a decision consistent with the desire to maximize return on heavy research and marketing expenditures.

Product differentiation does not necessarily mean that worldwide markets must always be serviced by FDI. Caves classifies differentiated products into three groups. If the costs of a product benefit from economies of scale in production and the product can be marketed without significant adaptation to local market conditions, Caves predicts that exports will be the preferred method of selling. If the product does not enjoy economies of scale, or if the product involves a proprietary process, licensing to foreign firms may occur. However, if the firm's main competitive advantage is embodied in research, marketing, and managerial experience, rather than in any specific existing differentiated products, then expansion may take the form of FDI. Caves also extends the "differentiation" term to include the advantages of managerial, financial, and innovative skills and privileged access to the factors of production. Caves (1982) describes firms possessing these advantages as having "intangible resources." Caves's model helps to explain the expansion of U.S. firms leveraging on their product differentiation.

In addition, Caves argues that the motivation for international production of vertically integrated firms is to avoid oligopoly uncertainty concerning the long-term supply and pricing of its inputs and to erect barriers to entry against new rivals. Other theorists, such as Lall and Streeten (1977) suggest that the firm's privileged access to raw materials or minerals may be the result of the firm's control over final markets or transportation, processing (vertical integration in mining and food processing), or production of the material (mining and plantation). This favored access to raw materials and minerals gives the firms a monopolistic advantage (Barclay 2000). Monopolistic advantage theory is advanced by theorists from the developed world to explain the phenomenon of FDI among industrialized economies. Specifically, it fully explains FDI made by U.S. MNEs during the post–World War II period (Hood and Young 1979).

1.3 Internalization Theory

Internalization theory is a firm-level theory, which explains why the MNE will exert proprietary control (ownership) over intangible knowledge-based assets. The public goods nature of knowledge (an externality) is remedied through the hierarchy of a firm overcoming this situation of market failure. Internalization theory has its origins in the work of various scholars associated with the "Reading School" in England: Buckley and Casson 1976; Casson 1979; Rugman 1980a, 1980b, 1981; Buckley 1987; and Hennart 1982.

Internalization theory is built on the central ideas of Coasian transaction cost theory (Coase 1937) and Penrosian firm theory (Penrose 1959). The first explicit treatment of the relationship between knowledge-based market imperfection and internalization of markets for intermediate goods is in Buckley and Casson (1976) and Casson (1979). Buckley and Casson (1976) state that when markets in intermediate products are imperfect, there is an incentive to bypass them by creating internal markets by bringing interdependent activities under common ownership and control. Therefore, creation of an internal market in the MNE can eliminate problems caused by these market imperfections. Indeed, the internalization of markets across national boundaries generates MNEs. Buckley and Casson (1976) demonstrate that the market for know-how is characterized by imperfections because knowledge is a public good. This characteristic can create complications in its pricing and transfer and consequently increase the associated costs of transacting with a partner. A high transaction cost results in a preference for internalizing the transaction. As a result, a foreign subsidiary is considered more efficient under such circumstances.

Rugman (1981) demonstrates that internalization is a general theory of the MNE because it encompasses within itself the reasons for international (as well as) domestic production. Rugman emphasizes the role of MNEs in overcoming imperfections in various external markets and the public policy implications. Market failure makes it especially difficult for the MNE to appropriate a return on its investment in FSAs from research and development, technology, information and knowledge, and brand and thus lead to the creation of an internal market within a firm. If a firm locates abroad to gain access to foreign markets, it will choose FDI because internalization is a device for keeping FSAs over a worldwide scale. In short, Rugman (1981) shows that MNEs develop in response to market imperfections. The CSAs of a nation leading to trade is replaced by FSAs internal to an MNE, leading to FDI. When there is an advantage specific to a firm, such as knowledge or other special information, it can be transferred between home and host nation within the internal market of the MNE.

Rugman's (1981) concept of the public good characteristics is in some way similar to the Markusen's (1984) general equilibrium model of an MNE that is based on economies of multiplant operation, to explain the allocation and distribution effects of MNE. These economies are modeled as an activity that enters the production function of the firm as a joint input across production facilities. Markusen (1984) develops and compares two cases of the theory. In one version, world production of a good is monopolized by an MNE, and in the other, there is a single independent national enterprise producing the good in each of the two countries. The MNE offers the world increases technical efficiency by eliminating the duplication of the joint input that would occur in independent national firms. Because this technical efficiency may be at the expense of higher exercised market power, the full determinants of home country, host country, and world welfare are explored (Markusen 1984). In a similar manner, Rugman (1981) argues that the MNE is an efficient response to market failure.

Internalization economists acknowledge that country-specific factors might influence the form and extent of market failure. They also accept that location-specific variables largely determine where the value added activities of MNEs would take place. However, the main focus of their attention is directed to identifying and evaluating the kinds of market failure inducing FDI, particularly to the extent to which the internalization of cross-border markets might itself influence these advantages (Dunning 2009a).Thus, internalization theory has been the dominant explanation of the existence and growth of the MNE.

1.3.1 Transaction Cost Economics and MNEs

Transaction cost economics (TCE), developed by Williamson (1975, 1979, 1981, 1985), with its focus on hierarchies and markets, is an extension of Coase's work (1937). Williamson (1975) proposes an "organizational failures framework" that leads to the advantages of hierarchical organization (internalization) instead of markets. In his model, there are human factors such as bounded rationality (the limitations of humans to understand the complex phenomena) and opportunism (the incentive for humans to cheat when such action is expected to improve their position in an economic transaction). These interact with environmental factors, such as uncertainty (due to complexity) and the problem of small numbers such as asset specificity (the fixed costs of an asset and the difficulty of arranging liquidation and recontracting—namely, whether assets are redeployable or salvageable when there are dramatic changes in the business environment). These two sets of factors produce "information impactedness," in which the market fails to function.

Although bounded rationality and opportunism are not transaction costs per se, they affect the cost of transactions (either across markets or within the firm). Williamson discusses three key transaction costs. Information costs are the costs of informing traders. Bargaining costs are the costs of reducing bargaining as to the terms of trade. Enforcement costs are the costs enforcing the terms of trade. These contractual costs make hierarchical organization more favorable than markets. Williamson shows that all three conditions of bounded rationality, opportunism, and asset specificity must hold to meet the conditions necessary for hierarchical organizations to replace market contracting. Organizations can economize on bounded rationality and safeguard against opportunism and asset specificity. When the three contractual costs do not hold simultaneously, then hierarchies will not arise.

In general, TCE is consistent with the basic premises of internalization theory. However, Williamson has not explicitly extended his analysis to the MNE, although there are some hints about such extension in Williamson 1981. Additionally, Williamson has not applied TCE thinking in any substantive manner to explain MNEs; in particular, he fails to examine the parent-subsidiary interaction, as has been achieved by internalization theorists.

Hennart's (1982) approach largely rectifies Williamson's neglect of MNEs. Because it was to a large extent independently developed, Hennart's version of transaction cost theory differs significantly from Williamson's. Specifically, Hennart emphasizes that the concept of asset specificity, which plays a large role in Williamson's theory, is less central as to why an MNE expands abroad. Hennart (1982) shows that for international expansion to take place, setting up facilities abroad must be more efficient than exporting to foreign markets and a firm must find it desirable to own the foreign facilities. Such is the case if the MNE can organize interdependencies between economic actors located in different countries more efficiently than markets. These interdependencies may involve knowhow, raw materials and components, marketing and distribution services, and financial capital. The entry-mode choice decision depends not only on the MNE's extant FSAs but also the complementary resources from foreign actors to make the exploitation of its FSAs feasible and potentially profitably (Hennart 2009).

Both Hennart and McManus (1972) focus on the behavior of MNEs as explained by property rights theory, agency theory, and Williamson's early version of TCE (Williamson 1975). McManus (1972) shows that the essence of the phenomenon of international production is not the transfer of capital but rather the international extension of managerial control over foreign subsidiaries—control that is ownership based and through which management replaces the market as the allocator of resources (Safarian 2003).

There are strong connections between TCE and internalization theory. For example, Rugman (1980b, 1980c) demonstrates the reasons for internalization by MNEs based on market imperfections (transaction costs). There are two types of market imperfection. First, there are Williamson-type natural market imperfections, which occur naturally—for example, the absence of a future market and the firm's inability to exercise discriminatory pricing and information impactedness. Second, there are unnatural market imperfections (Rugman 1981), which are those imposed by government regulations such as government intervention in international markets through the imposition of taxes or restriction of capital movements and foreign exchange controls. Differences in corporate income tax rates between countries would also create internalization of markets through transfer pricing (Rugman 1980c). The MNE would find it difficult to appropriate a return on its FSAs due to market failure (transaction costs), thus leading to the creation of an internal market within the MNE.

1.4 Dunning's Eclectic Paradigm (OLI Framework)

John Dunning (1977, 1988, 1998) develops the eclectic paradigm to explain FDI activities at the country and firm level. Dunning proposes that three types of advantages influence FDI activities: ownership-specific (O) advantages, location-specific (L) advantages, and internalization (I) advantages (the OLI framework). Dunning's OLI framework

(1998) identifies types of FDI: natural resource seeking, market seeking, efficiency seeking, and strategic asset seeking.

Ownership-specific advantage variables can be divided into asset-specific advantages (Oa) and transactional-specific variables (Ot). Ownership asset-specific (Oa) variables include various tangible and intangible assets such as patented technology, management know-how, and brands owned by the investing firms to capture the ownership transactional benefits (Ot) from the common governance of multiple and geographically diverse activities. The degree of possession of various ownership-specific variables influences the degree of ownership chosen in FDI.

Location-specific (L) advantages reflect foreign countries having some CSAs in terms of natural resources, factors of production, and demand conditions. Location advantages include the cultural, legal, political, and institutional environment in which the firm operates. The best geographical location is typically chosen as the result of careful analysis of different sets of relevant costs, such as costs of production, quality control, transportation costs, and so on. Corporate perceptions of environmental factors such as government regulation of MNE activity and political stability are also considered to be important. At the firm level, the location advantages appear to include several "soft" elements such as the firm's experience with foreign involvement, psychic distance variables, attitudes to risk diversification, and attitudes toward the centralization of functions such as research and development (R&D).

Internalization (I) advantages are the advantages that the firm has in transferring assets within its organizations instead of via an outside market. These advantages come from the benefits that the firm gains from the common governance of its value-added activities. Dunning indicates that internalization advantages include not only the lack of search and negotiation costs but also the ability to protect and safeguard the reputation of the firm and engage in practices such as transfer pricing and cross-subsidy. The greater the perceived cost of transactional market failure and the greater the benefits of circumventing the market failure, the more likely it is that the firm will exploit its ownership-specific advantages within the firm. According to Dunning's OLI paradigm, firms decide to invest in foreign countries by considering their O and L advantages. The investment types are decided by the internalization advantages.

From the firm's viewpoint, O and I are really internalization advantages because any O has to be internalized in order to be effective

(Rugman 2010; Casson 1987). Itaki (1991) claims that an O could actually come from an I advantage. Therefore, it is redundant to consider these two separate determinants. Itaki also points out the inseparability of the O advantage from the L advantage. He argues that the O advantage in economic terms is unavoidably influenced by and inseparable from location factors. Hence, the L and the O advantage, consisting of both the "location" and the "ownership" advantages, are simultaneously determined in economic terms. Dunning's paradigm has been called ambiguous regarding the sources of location advantages. However, Dunning (2009b) is not prepared to accept the earlier critics of the paradigm, who tend to focus on an unnecessary distinction between the O and the I components. He emphasizes the interdependence between the OLI variables and the dynamics of the paradigm.

Dunning's OLI framework has also been addressed by international economists such as Ethier (1986). He advances on the economists' traditional country-level focus on location (L) by recognizing the critical importance of the internalization (I) decision in explaining FDI, which is due to MNE activity. Ethier demonstrates that many international trade theorists have failed to consider the I process in their models for FDI. They discuss Dunning's L and O decisions but not internalization. Related work by economists giving attention to some aspects of internalization appears in Ethier and Markusen 1996, Helpman 1985, and Horstmann and Markusen 1987. For example, Horstmann and Markusen (1987) demonstrate that a firm must decide whether to serve a foreign market by exporting, building a foreign branch plant, or licensing to the production to a foreign producer, an issue explored in Rugman 1981. The existence of brand (firm reputation) implies that any licensing agreement must provide the licensee with the incentive to maintain the MNE's reputation. This situation creates a motive for the firm to internalize transactions by building a branch plant (i.e., by becoming a multinational). It reflects the inability of the firm to control the actions of outside agents, which provides an incentive for MNE activity.

Furthermore, international economists also examine some aspects of FSAs, the O in the Dunning OLI framework. For example, Horstmann and Markusen (1989) argue that MNEs arise as the consequence of the existence of knowledge-based FSAs such as superior technology and management know-how, a point made explicitly in Rugman 1981. These assets are much like public goods within the firm, in that they can be supplied without cost to additional plants, thus leading to the efficiency of multiplant production (Markusen 1984). Again, this point is made in Rugman 1981. FDI then consists of supplying the services of the assets to the foreign operations with repatriation of earnings as payments for these services.

Dunning has subsequently extended OLI into five versions (see Eden and Dai 2010 for a comprehensive review), and it has become a big tent. Narula (2010) recommends the simplicity of the "coat hanger" of the original OLI framework rather than the "Swiss Army knife" that the OLI paradigm has become.

Rugman (2010) demonstrates that the OLI framework (Dunning 1977, 1980, 1988, 1998) and four investment motives can be reconciled with the CSA/FSA matrix of Rugman (1981); see figure 1.1. The L advantages in Dunning OLI framework are CSAs, whereas O and I are both components of FSAs in Rugman's CSAs/FSAs matrix. However, the fit is not perfect. The main reason for misalignment is that Dunning's framework focuses mainly on outward FDI by MNEs into host economies, whereas Rugman's matrix is for firm-level strategy covering MNE activity in both home and host countries.

The OLI framework essentially produces a type of comparative statics familiar to economists. Indeed, Dunning and many of the internalization theory scholars discussed here were trained as economists and have built MNE theory on the strong foundation of transaction

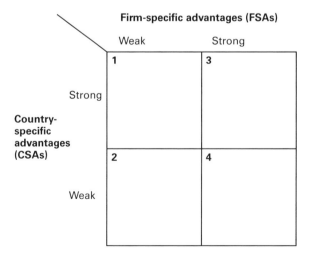

Figure 1.1
The CSA/FSA matrix
Source: Adapted from chapter 8 in Rugman 1981.

costs economics. However, the IB field also incorporates dynamic elements, particularly in the application of real options theory to the choice of location and the entry-mode decisions.

1.4 Dynamics of Internationalization

Drawing upon the classic works of Cyert and March (1963) and Aharoni (1966), this core IB model proposes that internationalization is a sequential and staged process in the incremental international market knowledge and experience (Johanson and Vahlne 1977; Johanson and Wiedersheim-Paul 1975; Luostarinen 1979; Welch and Luostarinen 1988; Eriksson, Majkgird, and Sharma 2000). Johanson and Vahlne (1977) introduce the concept of "psychic distance," which refers to the degree to which a firm is uncertain of the characteristics of a foreign market. These factors prevent or disturb the flow of information between firms and markets and between potential or actual suppliers and customers. They are associated with CSA-type diversities and dissimilarities (Johanson and Wiedersheim-Paul 1975). Thus, the internationalization model suggests that MNEs first enter more proximate countries before penetrating countries with higher psychic distance. In addition, companies increase their resource commitment only incrementally in foreign markets. In short, this literature argues that there is a liability of foreignness (LoF) as firms access the CSAs of host economies. The firms need to learn, over time, how to reduce the LoF.

Though the interests of this group of scholars are largely confined to the market-seeking activities of firms, theirs is one of the first dynamic models of the mode of entry into foreign markets (Dunning 2009a).

More recently, the internationalization model has been extended (Johanson and Vahlne 2009). In the revised model, it is not the liability of foreignness per se that matters, but rather the liability of outsidership, that is, being an outsider to relevant business networks in new local contexts. The key challenge in international expansion is not that a new local context may be foreign in terms of psychic distance with the home country but rather that it may be difficult to becom an insider in local networks.

Li and Rugman (2007), Li (2007), and Rugman and Li (2005) extend applications of real options theory to FDI research regarding choice of location and choice of market entry mode under uncertainty. MNEs are exposed to uncertainty that could be unfavorable conditions or favorable opportunities. These factors play important roles in MNEs' strategic decision making. Real options theory has enriched FDI theory by introducing a new way of thinking—MNEs can strategically benefit from uncertainty because uncertainty is associated not only with downside risks but also with potential future opportunities (Li 2007). To strategically benefit from uncertainty, MNEs must create real options (such as the option to abandon and the option to grow) to maintain flexibility in adjusting decisions, as well as to exercise these options in response to opportunities or challenges. Real options theory, which effectively conceptualizes and quantifies the determinants of real options, has contributed to the development of theories in MNEs' decision making under uncertainty (Buckley and Casson 1998; Buckley, Casson, and Gulamhussen 2002; Chi and McGuire 1996; Kogut 1991; Kogut and Kulatilaka 1994; Tong and Reuer 2007).

1.5   Strategy and the Resource-Based View (RBV) of the Firm

The resource-based view (RBV) was first articulated by Wernerfelt (1984) but is based on Penrose (1959) and her focus on managerial "resources." The RBV argues that a firm's competitive advantages in its markets stem from its unique resources and capabilities, which are all assets, capabilities, organizational processes, firm attributes, information, and firm knowledge under the control of the firm and able to be utilized by the firm to design and implement strategies (Barney 1991). In simple terms, a firm consists of a bundle of productive resources and capabilities. Resources are defined as the stock of available factors owned or controlled by the firm (Amit and Shoemaker 1993), including the tangible and intangible assets that the firm uses to implement its strategies. Resources are assets that can be broadly organized into four categories: financial, physical, technological, and organizational. Resources may include brand name, skilled labor, knowledge of technology, and efficient production processes (Wernerfelt 1984). These are employed in the value-adding activities of the firm in order to establish capabilities.

Capabilities are the firm's capacity to deploy resources, usually in combination, using organization processes to affect a desired end (Amit and Shoemaker 1993). Capabilities can be intangible assets such as skills, relationships, organizational knowledge, innovations, and so on. By holding distinctive capabilities, the firm can gain a competitive advantage over its rivals. It is argued that acquisition and retention of resources that are valuable, rare, in combination, nonimitable, and nonsubstitutable are a source of economic rent and account for the heterogeneity of firms in any industry (Reed and DeFillippi 1990; Barney 1991; Mahoney and Pandian 1992; Oliver 1997).

A firm's competitive advantage derives from its ability to assemble and exploit an appropriate combination of resources. Sustainable competitive advantage is achieved by continuously developing existing resources and capabilities and developing new ones in response to rapidly changing market conditions. Resource-based view theorists such as Grant (1991) and Peteraf (1993) claim that firms can achieve sustainable competitive advantages from resources such as strategic plans, management skills, tacit knowledge, capital, and employment of skilled personnel, among others. The assets and resources owned by the firms may explain the difference in performance. Furthermore, resources may be harnessed in the strength or weakness of firms and can lead to competitive advantage (Barney 1991). The unique resources and capabilities that generate competitive advantages can lead to sustainable superior returns (Rugman and Verbeke 2002).

Competences are the activities and processes through which an organization deploys its resources effectively (Prahalad and Hamel 1990). An organization must achieve at least a threshold level of competence in everything it does. Its core competences underpin its competitive advantage and are difficult for competitors to imitate or obtain (Johnson, Scholes, and Whittington 2005). Hamel and Prahalad (1996) suggest that an important aspect of strategic management is the determination of the competences the company will require in the future in order to provide new benefits to customers.

Tallman and Yip (2009) suggest that international expansion can provide new opportunities to leverage existing valuable resources. The MNEs can also access new resources and generate new capabilities through international diversification (Tallman and Yip 2009). The MNEs strategies require a balance between the deployment and exploitation of existing resources and capabilities and development of new ones.

Mahoney and Pandian (1992) suggest that the resource-based view aligns with the organization economic paradigm. The resources and capabilities can foster and promote organizational learning and knowledge development (Wernerfelt 1984). Teccc, Pisano, and Shuen (1997) find the concept of organizational learning and knowledge development in some way relating to the concept of dynamic capability perspective. They claim that the development of dynamic capabilities can give firms competitive advantages over its rivals. In addition, Madhok (1997) and Amit and Shoemaker (1993) suggest that it is important for a firm to possess a bundle of static and transferable resources that can then be transformed into capabilities through dynamic and interactive firm-specific processes. Furthermore, Birkinshaw and Pedersen (2009) highlight that the resource-based view is now an important concept in strategic management. However, Priem and Butler (2001) have questioned the value of the RBV, as it is tautological and self-verifying and it lacks specificity.

Although the resource-based view has provided a useful insight into the origin and sustainability of the competitive advantages of firms, it has shed little light on understanding the geographical sourcing or exploitation of these advantages. Moreover, the RBV does not show the modality by which these tasks are achieved (Dunning 2009a). In other words, the RBV of strategy is still largely a cell 4 phenomenon in figure 1.1. Clearly, the RBV focus on capabilities is repeating ground covered earlier by internalization theorists and their use of FSAs. Indeed, a capability is a type of FSA.

1.6   Multinational Subsidiaries and Dynamics of Recombinations

Recently, the strategic management research on MNEs has emphasized the study of the subsidiary as a unit of analysis as well as the corporate parent. International business activities and competition occur at the local affiliate level and an MNE is a network of foreign subsidiaries. Subsidiaries can develop their own initiatives (Birkinshaw 1997). Previous research suggests that foreign subsidiaries have entrepreneurial capacity in enhancing their competitive position that in turn depends on their resources and capabilities (Birkinshaw and Hood 1998), their strategies, and their location.

Prahalad and Doz (1987) and Bartlett and Ghoshal (1989) observe that MNEs consist of subsidiaries operating in different host countries. Each subsidiary experiences external conformity pressures from its respective environment. Subsidiaries need to conform to local regulations, business practices, and consumer preferences, among other pressures. Their success in the host country market requires a high level of local adaptation and customization, a strategy called "national responsiveness," when the products need to be adapted to local tastes and preferences or when close ties with local stakeholders are required (Miller and Eden 2006). At the same time, they also experience internal conformity pressures from their MNE parents, namely, the extent to which a subsidiary is integrated into the corporate network of its MNE parents, a strategy called "integration." The parent control of the activities of the subsidiaries, and coordinating these activities with its own activities and with those of its other subsidiaries, realizes synergies in the form of economies of scale and scope. A subsidiary's ability to make independent decisions will be the outcome of a subsidiary trade-off between integration and national responsiveness (Prahalad and Doz 1987; Bartlett and Ghoshal 1989).

However, Birkinshaw and Pedersen (2009) suggest that applying FDI theory and theories of MNE to MNE subsidiary research is troublesome. First, the relevant level of analysis for most theory is the MNE as a whole, not the subsidiary. As a result, there is often a problem in translating or applying the firm-level theory to the subsidiary unit. Second, the theories used in MNE research are eclectic and often incommensurable, with the result that they cannot easily be brought together or compared. It is still valuable to consider how various theories have been applied and their prospects for further development.

Rugman and Verbeke (1992, 2001) have applied internalization theory in the subsidiary context. They argue that FSAs could be developed by both parents and the subsidiaries. On the RBV interpretation of the integration-national responsiveness matrix of strategic management (Prahalad 1976; Prahalad and Doz 1987; Bartlett and Ghoshal 1989), Rugman and Verbeke (1992) show that FSAs can be decomposed by the location specificity, as either location-bound (LB) or non-location-bound (NLB) FSAs. The former reflect strengths that provide a favorable competitive position to a firm in a particular geographical area, such as a country or a limited set of countries, but cannot easily be transferred abroad, whether as an intermediate input (e.g., managerial skills, R&D knowledge) or embodied in a final product. In contrast, the latter represent company strengths that can easily be transferred across locations at low cost and with only limited adaptation. LB FSAs lead to benefits of national responsiveness. NLB FSAS can be deployed worldwide and lead to benefits of integration through the exploitation of national differences. NLB FSAs lead to economies of scale and scope.

Subsidiary-specific advantages (SSAs) are a special kind of LB FSA and a resource and capability that is embedded within a specific subsidiary of the MNE and can be exploited only in the network as an intermediate or end product in the value chain (Rugman and Verbeke 2001). SSAs are related to subsidiary resources (Birkinshaw and Hood

1998) in the context of world product mandate (Rugman and Bennett 1982; D'Cruz 1986) and more sophisticated roles, which emerge through the interaction of FSAs and CSAs. Rugman and Verbeke (2001) present a framework to synthesize ten types of MNE-subsidiary linkages leading to capability development and the process of SSAs development within the organization structure of the MNE when it is a differentiated network of dispersed operations. A more extensive treatment of how these LB FSAs can be recombined into NLB FSAs appears in Verbeke 2009 and Rugman, Verbeke, and Nguyen 2011.

Birkinshaw and Pedersen (2009) also suggest that the RBV of the firm is currently the dominant conceptual paradigm in strategic management. The theory argues that under certain conditions a firm's unique bundle of resources and capabilities can generate competitive advantage (Barney 1991). There are also related schools of thought that focus on the development of dynamic capabilities and knowledge as drivers of competitive advantage (Grant 1991; Teece, Pisano, and Shuen 1997). Birkinshaw and Hood (1998) and Rugman and Verbeke (2001) are among the few scholars who have paid explicit attention to the RBV of the firm. Birkinshaw and Pedersen (2009) offer an explanation that the reason for little attention to RBV is the level of analysis. The RBV implicitly assumes that the resources and capabilities are developed and held in a monolithic firm, whereas in reality in the MNE, some are likely to be held at a MNE firm level and others held at a subsidiary level.

Birkinshaw and Pedersen (2009) argue that if the subsidiary is a valid unit of analysis in its own right, it should be possible to split resources and capabilities up between the subsidiary and the MNE. Considering resources first, most tangible resources (plant, equipment, people) are held primarily in at the subsidiary level, while most intangible resources (financial, organizational, reputation) are held at the firm level. There are plenty of exceptions to this rule, such as employees or equipment that are moved between locations or a reputation that is specific to the local subsidiary. The key point is that it is possible to make such a split in the first place.

Capabilities are much harder to split between firm and subsidiary levels of analysis. Some are clearly held at a firm level and shared across subsidiaries, such as a particular organizational culture. Others are more likely to be specific to a particular subsidiary, such as handling local labor relations or working with government contracts. Most capabilities, however, sit somewhere between the two levels (Birkinshaw and Pedersen 2009). They highlight that the criteria used to evaluate resources in the resource-based view (valuable, rare, nonimitable, non-substitutable) are not really relevant at the subsidiary level. A subsidiary is just one part of the whole; its resources and capabilities need to be complementary to other resources and capabilities elsewhere in the corporation, not necessarily unique. Each building block has a value in itself, but it is the ability to put those building blocks together in a unique, nonimitable way that is the source of advantage, not the independent value of the various blocks. Thus, they suggest that rather than analyzing subsidiary level resources in terms of their potential for competitive advantage, the issue is more one of combining or leveraging them on a global basis. There is a large body of research on subsidiaries' strategies and subsidiaries' roles, the relationship between headquarters and subsidiaries (for an overview of the intensive literature, see Paterson and Brock 2002, Birkinshaw and Morrison 1996, and Taggart 1998). Subsidiary research has several origins.

Scholars in Canada examine the extent to which Canadian subsidiaries of foreign MNEs can act autonomously with world product mandate (Rugman and Bennett 1982; Poynter and Rugman 1982; D'Cruz 1986). They provide public implications on the inefficiency of any arbitrary attempts to boost national R&D expenditures that are always a cost and do not necessarily bring any benefits to the firms and the host country. Rugman's conclusions have been subsequently confirmed by Moore (1996) and Birkinshaw (1997). Birkinshaw (1996, 1997, 2000) and Birkinshaw and Hood (1998, 2001; Birkinshaw, Hood, and Jonsson 1998; Moore 2001; Moore and Birkinshaw 1998) show that subsidiary managers can develop subsidiary initiatives that can be viewed as FSAs. This development is an important driver for the innovations process inside the MNEs.

The research stream on subsidiary role typologies says that an MNE is a network of subsidiaries in which some subsidiaries have strategic roles and therefore have a different mandate beyond the traditional role of exploiting the parent MNEs' FSAs in new markets (Birkinshaw and Morrison 1996). Subsidiaries follow different strategies and obtain different roles in the MNEs. Jarillo and Martinez (1990) identify three generic roles for subsidiaries according to the Bartlett and Ghoshal (1989) multinational types and the Porter (1986) multinational strategies. Recently, using the resource bundling perspective, Rugman, Verbeke, and Yuan (2011) reconceptualized the Bartlett and Ghoshal typology of subsidiary roles in the MNE. They argue that subsidiary

roles can vary dramatically across value chain activities such as innovation, production, sales, and administrative support activities. For each
value chain activity, the subsidiary recombines its bundle sets of internal competences with accessible external location advantages and considers the effects of regional integration on subsidiary roles. Such
schemes may affect substantially the extent to which location advantages of individual countries can be assessed and bundled with internal
competences, thereby typically altering some subsidiaries' roles in
specific value chain activities. However, such substantive changes in
specific value chain activities performed by subsidiaries do not necessarily lead to any move in conventional subsidiary role typologies, such
as the Bartlett and Ghoshal one, as these typologies acknowledge only
aggregate subsidiary role changes, supposedly valid for the entire
value chain.

Similarly, the research stream on the subsidiary's "local embeddedness" (Andersson and Forsgren 1996; Andersson, Forsgren, and Pedersen
2001; Figueiredo 2011), and "multiple/dual embeddedness," namely,
being simultaneously deeply embedded in the MNE corporate internal
network as well as within the external host environment (Narula and
Dunning 2000, 2010; Tavares and Young 2005; Rugman and D'Cruz
2000) also attract large attention. Meyer, Mudambi, and Narula (2011)
argue that MNEs face growing challenges in managing the complexity
of these interactions, because they must manage multiple embeddedness across heterogeneous contexts at two levels. First, at the MNE
level, they must organize their networks to exploit effectively both
the differences and similarities of their multiple host locations. Second,
at the subsidiary level, they must balance internal embeddedness
within the MNE network, with their external embeddedness in the host
countries.

In this context, Rugman and Verbeke (1993, 2009) suggest that CSAs
of other host countries may be used in a "leveraged" way. MNEs make
dual use of host country CSAs, besides those of the home country, and
subsidiaries throughout the MNE network. It is critical in resource
recombination efforts and thus contributes to the development of new
FSAs. This interaction also explains the two-way flows of FDI, parent-
subsidiary relationships, and the nature of network activities of MNEs
as analyzed in the double diamond framework (Rugman and D'Cruz
1993; Rugman and Verbeke 1993; Moon, Rugman, and Verbeke 1998).
As Dunning (1993) observes, there is ample evidence to suggest that
MNEs are influenced in their competitiveness by the configuration of

the diamond other than their home countries, which in turn may impinge on the diamond other than their home countries. Using Rugman and Verbeke's double diamond model, Asmussen, Pedersen, and Dhanaraj (2009) hypothesize the contingencies influencing the links between host country environments and subsidiary competence configuration. They provide empirical evidence from 2,107 MNE subsidiaries in seven European countries (Austria, Denmark, Finland, Germany, Norway, Sweden, and the United Kingdom) and insight into how MNEs can overcome "unbalanced" national diamonds by acquiring complementary capabilities across border. In conclusion, subsidiary level research is all about cell 3 of figure 1.1, discussed later in this chapter.

1.7   Synthesis: The FSA/CSA Matrix

We now synthesize this review of the literature of international business in order to provide a reference base for these statements about the relevance of international business theory for international economists. We now show that the core IB framework for the field of international business is the CSA and FSA matrix in figure 1.1. We then use this framework to synthesize the key literature discussed previously.

The key analytical device we use to bring together the literatures of international economics and international business is shown in figure 1.1 (Rugman 1981). Here, the country factors of interest to international economists are depicted as CSAs on the vertical axis. Orthogonal to these are FSAs. The FSAs are owned and internalized by firms. It is important to distinguish the two units of analysis—country and firm— as different literatures have developed in an international context.

For example, in business schools, cell 3 (see figure 1.1) regarding the RBV became the cornerstone of strategic management thinking after Wernerfelt (1984) rediscovered the Penrose (1959) focus on the limits to growth of the firm due to the inability to grow managerial "resources" in the top management team. A huge literature on the RBV has developed in management arguing that managerial resources in terms of knowledge-based attributes are the key driver of firm-level productivity and growth (Rumelt 1984; Barney 1991). It is immediately obvious that the RBV, with its focus upon competencies and capabilities, is entirely consistent with the earlier internalization theory of Buckley and Casson (1976), with its focus on tacit knowledge-based FSAs (Rugman and Verbeke 2003). Indeed, new internalization theory is based in cell 3, where dynamic capabilities have been considered in the IB literature.

These involve recombinations of FSAs with CSAs in both the home and host countries. Dynamic capabilities are modeled through the interactions by the parent firm in the home country with its subsidiaries in the host country.

There are two elements in the development of dynamic capabilities by MNEs. First, the parent firm develops standalone FSAs through interactions with the home country CSAs, such as in the natural resource sectors. The MNE owns and internalizes these FSAs in cell 3. Other FSAs are tacit knowledge-based ones and are consistent with RBV thinking in cell 4. The MNE can turn these FSAs into knowledge-based dynamic capabilities in cell 3 by recombination with CSAs.

Second, the MNE has foreign subsidiaries that interact with host economies. There is the potential for the MNE subsidiaries to interact with local host country actors, making recombinations of the FSAs of the MNE and other dynamic capabilities in cell 3. Such recombinations may produce LB FSAs (if they are in the form of national responsiveness and adaptation to local cultures). However, they can also be NLB FSAs if the interaction of FSAs and CSAs in cell 3 generates a best practice capability that can be used throughout the MNE network (Rugman and Verbeke 2001; Verbeke 2009; Rugman, Verbeke, and Nguyen 2011).

In contrast to RBV thinking and the FSAs of MNE, cell 1 represents a situation in which CSAs are strong and FSAs are weak. In this cell, successful firms and industries are explained by country factors alone. These can include economic, cultural, political, and governmental activities. For example, strong CSAs in natural resources will explain successful oil and mineral extraction in Canada, offshoring of manufacturing to China, and the development of Singapore. We now discuss these examples in detail.

In Canada, the natural factor endowments give the country a comparative advantage in exports of industries such as oil and petrochemicals, mineral resources, and pulp and paper. The concept of CSAs incorporates country-level factor price arbitrage when it is realized that CSAs can be modeled for both the home and host economies. Techniques in international economics can handle the relative interaction between home and host country CSAs in a highly satisfactory manner. For example, the gravity model, using export data, can focus upon the costs of distance between home and host economies, leading to good analysis of factor price arbitrage (Fratianni, Marchionne, and Oh 2011). However, the gravity model does not handle FDI as well because FDI is undertaken by MNEs that have foreign subsidiaries. Moving to firm-level analysis of the parent MNE and its foreign subsidiaries is more complex than handling exports because ownership matters. The MNE has foreign-owned subsidiaries in the foreign country and any knowledge-based assets in such subsidiaries push the gravity model at the FDI level into cell 3. The literature in international economics mishandles the cell 3 complexities of the gravity model at FDI level (Fratianni 2009; Fratianni, Marchionne, and Oh 2011; Hejazi 2007, 2009).

A similar issue arises in the international economics literature dealing with offshoring to China. International economics goes a long way to explaining this issue in terms of factor price arbitrage and exports. China has a huge comparative advantage in cheap labor relative to North American and European economies, giving an incentive to outsource manufacturing activities to the low cost factor country. But here again, FDI and MNE issues complicate the picture. In this case, the foreign subsidiaries of North American and European firms in China are mainly there to exploit the cheap labor and possibly to develop scale in production and expand their market size. These motivations for FDI in China are mainly driven by host country CSA factors and are entirely based in cell 1. In other words, offshoring is not a cell 3 phenomenon, and here the literature in international economics and international business can coalign, as no convincing literature has developed showing that offshoring to China is primarily explained by knowledge assets of foreign subsidiaries, despite variant attempts by Lewin and Peeters (2006).

Conversely, there is an IB literature, based on asset-seeking FDI that argues that emerging economy MNEs do engage in cell 3 knowledge-seeking activities (Matthews 2002, 2006). In other words, emerging economy MNEs attempt to acquire knowledge-based FSAs from European and North American MNEs. However, this event is highly unlikely to occur, given the basic tenets of internalization theory (Buckley and Casson 1976, 2009). The choice of entry mode literature in international business, derived from Rugman (1980a, 1980b, 1981, 1996, 2005, 2010) argues that MNEs control, monitor, and meter the use of their knowledge-based FSAs, thereby forsaking joint ventures and licensing activity until the risk of dissipation of their FSA is minimized. All of this thinking transforms the offshoring analysis of international economics from cell 1 to cell 3. In other words, although international economists can handle Dunning's L factors quite well in cell 1, they still need to incorporate O and I factors and recognize that all three operate simultaneously in explaining FDI and MNEs. In short, cell 3 matters, and it is time to for international economists to start putting their toes into the swimming pool of international business in cell 3.

Finally, the case of Singapore is partly explained by the cell 1 thinking of international economists. Singapore has few natural resources but has instead strong government support to develop knowledge-based service business, leading to a type of created competitive advantage. This situation has led to rapid economic development and is a type of cell 1 attribute. Indeed, there may be some link between country-level culture and the success of such government policies. Possibly the best approach to this interaction between the country-level infrastructure of physical resources, government policy, supporting service industries, and such created factor conditions is by Porter (1990). However, his single "diamond" model was tested using export data, with some peripheral hand waving about industry-level factors. Most damagingly, Porter (1990) is not aligned with international business theory (Dunning 1993). As a result, a "double diamond" framework, explicitly incorporating MNEs, was developed independently by Rugman and D'Cruz (1993) in a Canadian context and applied more generally by Rugman and Verbeke (1993, 2003). In the double diamond, managers of firms in a resource-based economy such as Canada do two things. First, they build businesses in natural resource sectors according to cell 1 principles, but they simultaneously examine the diamond of their largest trading partner (the United States) in order to market these products. This behavior leads to the development of marketing-type FSAs, shifting Canadian firms from cell 1 to cell 3. Such involvement in the host country diamond means jumping fully clothed into the swimming pool of cell 3.

To summarize, international economists continue to focus upon cell 1 of figure 1.1. In general, they ignore the complexities of the subtle analysis required to be in cell 3. This situation may be partly explained by a traditional focus in economics on the country as the unit of analysis for international economics. In contrast, international business theorists have long ago developed the concept of FSAs (Rugman 1981; Dunning 1981) based upon the principles of internalization theory (Buckley and Casson 1976). They have shown that FSAs are fully consistent with the RBV of cell 4 (Rugman and Verbeke 2003). In other words, international business is now deeply embedded in cell 3. The time has come for international economists to begin the rightward migration from cell 1 to cell 3.

References

Aharoni, Yair. 1966. *The Foreign Investment Decision Process*. Boston: Division of Research, Graduate School of Business Administration, Harvard University.

Amit, Raphael, and Paul J. H. Shoemaker. 1993. Strategic assets and organizational rent. *Strategic Management Journal* 17 (Winter): 155–165.

Andersson, Ulf, and Mats Forsgren. 1996. Subsidiary embeddedness and control in the multinational corporation. *International Business Review* 5 (5): 487–508.

Andersson, Ulf, Mats Forsgren, and Torben Pedersen. 2001. Subsidiary performance in multinational corporations: The importance of technology embeddedness. *International Business Review* 10:3–23.

Asmussen, Christian G., Torben Pedersen, and Charles Dhanaraj. 2009. Host country environment and subsidiary competence: Extending the diamond network model. *Journal of International Business Studies* 40 (1): 42–57.

Barclay, Lou Anne A. 2000. *Foreign Direct Investment in Emerging Economies: Corporate Strategy and Investment Behaviour in the Caribbean* (Studies in International Business and the World Economy Series). London: Routledge.

Barney, Jay B. 1991. Firm resources and sustained competitive advantage. *Journal of Management* 17 (1): 99–120.

Bartlett, Christopher A., and Sumantra Ghoshal. 1989. *Managing Across Borders—The Transnational Solution*. Boston: Harvard Business School Press.

Birkinshaw, Julian M. 1996. How multinational subsidiary mandates are gained and lost. *Journal of International Business Studies* 27 (3): 467–496.

Birkinshaw, Julian M. 1997. Entrepreneurship in multinational corporations: The characteristics of subsidiary initiatives. *Strategic Management Journal* 18 (3): 207–229.

Birkinshaw, Julian M. 2000. The determinants and consequences of subsidiary initiative in multinational corporations. *Entrepreneurship Theory and Practice* 24 (1): 9–35.

Birkinshaw, Julian M., and Neil Hood. 1998. Multinational subsidiary evolution: Capability and charter change in foreign owned subsidiary companies. *Academy of Management Review* 23 (4): 773–795.

Birkinshaw, Julian M., and Neil Hood. 2001. Unleash innovation in foreign subsidiaries. *Harvard Business Review* 79 (3): 131–137.

Birkinshaw, Julian M., Neil Hood, and Stefan Jonsson. 1998. Building firm-specific advantages in multinational corporation: The role of subsidiary initiative. *Strategic Management Journal* 19 (3): 221–241.

Birkinshaw, Julian M., and Allen J. Morrison. 1996. Configuration of strategy and structure in multinational subsidiaries. *Journal of International Business Studies* 26 (4): 729–754.

Birkinshaw, J., and T. Pedersen. 2009. Strategy and management in MNE subsidiaries. In *Oxford Handbook of International Business*, 2nd ed., ed. Alan M. Rugman, 367–388. Oxford: Oxford University Press.

Buckley, Peter J. 1987. *The Theory of the Multinational Enterprise*. Uppsala and Stockholm, Sweden: Uppsala University.

Buckley, Peter J., and Mark C. Casson. 1976. *The Future of the Multinational Enterprise*. Basingstoke, London: Macmillan.

Buckley, Peter J., and Mark C Casson. 1998. Models of the multinational enterprise. *Journal of International Business Studies* 29:539–561.

Buckley, Peter J., and Mark C. Casson. 2009. The internalization theory of the multinational enterprise: A review of the progress of a research agenda after 30 years. *Journal of International Business Studies* 40 (9): 1563–1580.

Buckley, Peter J., Mark C. Casson, and M. A. Gulamhussen. 2002. Internationalisation—real options, knowledge management and the Uppsala approach. In *Critical Perspectives on Internationalisation*, ed. Virpi Havila, Mats Forsgren, and Hakan Hakansson, 229–261. Amsterdam: Elsevier Science Ltd.

Casson, Mark C. 1979. *Alternatives to the Multinational Enterprise*. New York: Holmes & Meier.

Casson, Mark C. 1987. *The Firm and the Market*. Oxford: Basil Blackwell.

Caves, Richard E. 1971. International corporations: The industrial economics of foreign investment. *Economica* 38:1–27.

Caves, Richard E. 1974. Multinational firms, competition and productivity in host-country markets. *Economica* 41 (162): 176–193.

Caves, Richard E. 1982. *Multinational Enterprises and Economic Analysis*. 1st ed. Cambridge: Cambridge University Press.

Coase, Ronald H. 1937. The nature of the firm. *Economica* NS4:386–405.

Chi, Tailan, and Donald J. McGuire. 1996. Collaborative ventures and value of learning: Integrating the transaction cost and strategic option perspectives on the choice of market entry modes. *Journal of International Business Studies* 27 (2): 285–307.

Cyert, Richard M., and James G. March. 1963. *A Behavioural Theory of the Firm*. Englewood Cliffs, NJ Prentice Hall.

D'Cruz, Joseph. 1986. Managing the multinational subsidiaries. In *Managing the Multinational Subsidiary*, ed. Hamid Etemad and Louise S. Dulude, 75–89. London: Croom Helm.

Dunning, John H. 1958. *American Investment in British Manufacturing Industry*. London: Allen & Unwin.

Dunning, John H. 1977. Trade, location of economic activity and the multinational enterprise: A search for an eclectic paradigm. In *The International Allocation of Economic Activity*, ed. P. Wijikman, 395–418. London: Macmillan.

Dunning, John H. 1980. Toward an eclectic theory of international production: Some empirical tests. *Journal of International Business Studies* 11 (1): 9–31.

Dunning, John H. 1981. *International Production and the Multinational Enterprise*. London: Allen & Unwin.

Dunning, John H. 1988. The eclectic paradigm of international production: A restatement and some possible extension. *Journal of International Business Studies* 19 (1): 1–31.

Dunning, John H. 1998. Location and the multinational enterprise: A neglected factor? *Journal of International Business Studies* 29 (1): 45–66.

Dunning, John H. 1993. Internationalizing Porter's diamond. *Management International Review, Special Issue* 33 (2): 7–15.

Dunning, John H. 2009a. The key literature on IB 1960–2006. In *The Oxford Handbook of International Business*, 2nd ed., ed. Alan M. Rugman, 39–71. Oxford: Oxford University Press.

Dunning, John H. 2009b. Location and the multinational enterprise: John Dunning's thoughts on receiving the Journal of International Business Studies 2008 Decade Award. *Journal of International Business Studies* 40 (1):20–34.

Dunning, John H., and Alan M. Rugman. 1985. The influence of Hymer's dissertation on the theory of foreign direct investment. *American Economic Review* 75 (2):228–260.

Eden, Lorraine, and Li Dai. 2010. Rethinking the O in Dunning's OLI paradigm. *Multinational Business Review* 18 (2): 13–34.

Eriksson, Kent, Anders Majkgird, and D. Deo Sharma. 2000. Path dependence and knowledge development in the internationalization process. *Management International Review* 40 (4): 307–328.

Ethier, Wilfred J. 1986. The multinational firm. *Quarterly Journal of Economics* 101:805–833.

Ethier, Wilfred J., and James R. Markusen. 1996. Multinational firms, technology diffusion and trade. *Journal of International Economics* 41 (1–2): 1–28.

Figueiredo, Paulo N. 2011. The role of dual embeddedness in the innovative performance of MNE subsidiaries: Evidence from Brazil. *Journal of Management Studies* 48:417–440.

Fratianni, Michele U. 2009. The gravity equation in international trade. In *The Oxford Handbook of International Business*, 2nd ed., ed. Alan M. Rugman, 72–89. Oxford: Oxford University Press.

Fratianni, Michele U., and Chang H. Oh. 2009. Expanding RTAs, trade flows, and the multinational enterprise. *Journal of International Business Studies* 40 (7): 1206–1227.

Fratianni, Michele U., Franceso Marchionne, and Chang H. Oh. 2011. A commentary on the gravity equation in international business research. *Multinational Business Review* 19 (1): 36–46.

Grant, Robert M. 1991. The resource-based view theory of competitive advantage: Implications for strategy formulation. *California Management Review* 33 (3): 114–135.

Grubel, Herbert G., and P. J. Lloyd. 1975. *Intra-Industry Trade: The Theory and Measurement of International Trade in Differentiated Products*. New York: Wiley.

Hamel, Gary, and C. K. Prahalad. 1996. *Competing for the Future*. Boston: Harvard Business School Press.

Hejazi, Walid. 2007. The regional nature of MNE activities and the gravity model. In *Regional Aspects of Multinationality and Performance* (Research in Global Strategic Management, vol. 13), ed. Alan M. Rugman, 85–109. Boston: Emerald.

Hejazi, Walid. 2009. Does China receive more regional FDI than gravity would suggest? *European Management Journal* 27 (5): 327–335.

Helpman, Elhanan. 1985. Multinational corporations and trade structure. *Review of Economic Studies* 52:443–457.

Hennart, Jean-Francois. 1982. *A Theory of Multinational Enterprise*. Ann Arbor: University of Michigan Press.

Hennart, Jean-Francois. 2009. Down with MNE centric theories! Market entry and expansion as the bundling of MNE and local assets. *Journal of International Business Studies* 40:1432–1454.

Hood, Neil, and Stephen Young. 1979. *The Economics of Multinational Enterprise*. London, New York: Longman.

Horstmann, I., and J. R. Markusen. 1987. Licensing versus direct investment: A model of internalization by the multinational enterprise. *Canadian Journal of Economics. Revue Canadienne d'Economique* 20 (3): 464–481.

Horstmann, Ignatius, and James R. Markusen. 1989. Firm-specific assets and the gains from direct investment. *Economica* 56 (221): 41–48.

Hymer, Stephen H. 1960. The International Operations of National Firms: A Study of Direct Foreign Investment. PhD. thesis. (Published in 1976 by the MIT Press.)

Itaki, Masahiko. 1991. A critical assessment of the eclectic theory of the multinational enterprise. *Journal of International Business Studies* 22:445–460.

Jarillo, J. C., and J. I. Martinez. 1990. Different roles for subsidiaries: The case of multinational corporations in Spain. *Strategic Management Journal* 11 (7): 501–512.

Johanson, Jan, and J-E. Vahlne. 1977. The internationalization process of the firm: A model of knowledge development and increasing foreign market commitments. *Journal of International Business Studies* 8 (1): 23–32.

Johanson, Jan, and Jan-Erik Vahlne. 1990. The mechanism of internationalization. *International Marketing Review* 7 (4): 11–24.

Johanson, Jan, and Jan-Erik Vahlne. 2009. The Uppsala internationalization process model revisited: From liability of foreignness to liability of outsidership. *Journal of International Business Studies* 40 (9): 1411–1431.

Johanson, Jan, and Finn Wiedersheim-Paul. 1975. The internationalization of the firm: The four Swedish cases. *Journal of Management Studies* 12 (3): 305–322.

Johnson, Gerry, Kevan Scholes, and Richard Whittington. 2005. *Exploring Corporate Strategy: Text and Cases*. Harlow, Essex, UK: FT Prentice Hall.

Kindleberger, Charles P. 1969. *American Business Abroad: Six Lectures on Direct Investment*. London: Yale University Press.

Kogut, Bruce. 1991. Joint ventures and the option to expand and acquire. *Management Science* 37 (1): 19–33.

Kogut, Bruce, and Nalin Kulatilaka. 1994. Operating flexibility, global manufacturing and the option value of a multinational network. *Management Science* 40 (1): 123–139.

Lall, Sanjaya, and Paul Streeten. 1977. *Foreign Investment, Transnationals, and Developing Countries*. London: Macmillan.

Lewin, Arie Y., and Carine Peeters. 2006. Offshoring work: Business hype or the onset of fundamental transformation? *Long Range Planning* 39 (3): 221–239.

Li, Jing. 2007. Real options and international strategy: A critical review. *Advances in Strategic Management* 24:67–101.

Li, Jing, and Alan M. Rugman. 2007. Real options and the theory of foreign direct investment. *International Business Review* 16 (6): 687–712.

Luostarinen, Reijo. 1979. *Internationalization of the Firm*. Helsinki: Academie Economicae, Helsinki School of Economics.

Madhok, Anoop. 1997. Cost, value and foreign market entry mode: The transaction cost and the firm. *Strategic Management Journal* 18:39–61.

Mahoney, Joseph T., and J.Rajendran Pandian. 1992. The resource-based view within the conversation of strategic management. *Strategic Management Journal* 13 (5): 363–380.

Markusen, James R. 1984. Multinationals, multi-plant economies and the gains from trade. *Journal of International Economics* 16 (3/4): 205–226.

Matthews, John A. 2002. Competitive advantages of the latecomer firm: A resource-based account of industrial catch-up strategies. *Asia Pacific Journal of Management* 19 (4): 467–488.

Matthews, John A. 2006. Dragon multinationals: New players in 21st century globalization. *Asia Pacific Journal of Management* 23 (1): 5–27.

McManus, John C. 1972. The theory of the multinational firm. In *The Multinational Firm and the Nation State*, ed. G. Paquet, 67–93. Toronto: Collier-Macmillan Ltd.

Meyer, Klaus, Ram Mudambi, and Rajneesh Narula. 2011. Multinational enterprises and local contexts: The opportunities and challenges of multiple embeddedness. *Journal of Management Studies* 48 (2): 235–252.

Miller, Stewart R., and Lorraine Eden. 2006. Local density and foreign subsidiary performance. *Academy of Management Journal* 49 (2): 341–355.

Moon, H. Chang, Alan M. Rugman, and Alain Verbeke. 1998. A generalized double diamond approach to the global competitiveness of Korea and Singapore. *International Business Review* 7:135–150.

Moore, Karl J. 1996. Capturing international responsibilities in the Canadian pharmaceutical industry. Industry Canada Working Paper.

Moore, Karl J. 2001. A strategy for subsidiaries: Centres of excellence to build subsidiary-specific advantages. *Management International Review* 41 (3): 275–290.

Moore, Karl J., and Julian M. Birkinshaw. 1998. Managing knowledge in global service firms: Centres of excellence. *Academy of Management Executive* 12 (4): 81–92.

Narula, Rajneesh. 2010. Keeping the eclectic paradigm simple: A brief commentary and implications for ownership advantages. *Multinational Business Review* 18 (2): 35–50.

Narula, Rajneesh, and John H. Dunning. 2000. Industrial development, globalization and multinational enterprises: New realities for developing countries. *Oxford Development Studies* 28 (2): 141–167.

Narula, Rajneesh, and John H. Dunning. 2010. Multinational enterprises, development and globalization: Some clarifications and a research agenda. *Oxford Development Studies* 38 (3): 263–287.

Oliver, Christine. 1997. Sustainable competitive advantage: Combining institutional and resource based view. *Strategic Management Journal* 18 (9): 697–713.

Paterson, S. L., and D. M. Brock. 2002. The development of subsidiary-management research: Review and theoretical analysis. *International Business Review* 11:139–163.

Penrose, Edith. 1959. *The Theory of the Growth of the Firm*. New York: Wiley.

Peteraf, Margaret A. 1993. The cornerstones of competitive advantage: A resource-based view. *Strategic Management Journal* 14 (3): 179–191.

Porter, Michael E. 1986. *Competition in Global Industries*. Boston: Harvard Business School Press.

Porter, Michael E. 1990. *The Competitive Advantage of Nations*. New York: Free Press.

Poynter, T. A., and Alan M. Rugman. 1982. World product mandates: How will multinationals respond? *Business Quarterly* 47 (3): 54–61.

Prahalad, C. K. 1976. Strategic choices in diversified MNC. *Harvard Business Review* 54 (4): 67.

Prahalad, C. K. and Yves Doz. 1987. *The Multinational Mission: Balancing Local Demands and Global Vision*. New York: The Free Press/ Macmillan.

Prahalad, C. K., and Gary Hamel. 1990. The core competence of the corporation. *Harvard Business Review* 90 (3): 79–91.

Priem, Richard L., and John E. Butler. 2001. Is the resource based view a useful perspective for strategic management research? *Academy of Management Review* 26 (1): 22–40.

Reed, Richard, and Robert J. DeFillippi. 1990. Causal ambiguity, barriers to imitation, and sustainable competitive advantage. *Academy of Management Review* 15:88–102.

Rugman, Alan M. 1980a. A test of internalization theory. *Managerial and Decision Economics* 2 (4): 211–219.

Rugman, Alan M. 1980b. *Multinationals in Canada: Theory, Performance and Economic Impact*. Boston: Martinus Nijhoff.

Rugman, Alan M. 1980c. Internalization theory and corporate international finance. *California Management Review* 23 (2): 73–79.

Rugman, Alan M. 1981. *Inside the Multinationals: The Economics of Internal Markets*. New York: Columbia University Press.

Rugman, Alan M. 1996. *The Theory of Multinational Enterprises* (Selected Scientific Papers of Alan M. Rugman, vol. 1). Cheltenham, UK: Elgar.

Rugman, Alan M. 2005. *The Regional Multinationals: MNEs and "Global" Strategic Management*. Cambridge: Cambridge University Press.

Rugman, Alan M. 2010. Reconciling internalization theory and the eclectic paradigm. *Multinational Business Review* 18 (2): 1–12.

Rugman, Alan M., and J. Bennett. 1982. Technology Transfer and World Product Mandating in Canada. *Columbia Journal of World Business* 17 (4): 58–62.

Rugman, Alan M., and Joseph D'Cruz. 1993. The double diamond model of international competitiveness: The Canadian experience. *Management International Review* 33 (2): 17–40.

Rugman, Alan M., and Joseph D'Cruz. 2000. *Multinationals as Flagship Firm: Regional Business Networks*. Oxford: Oxford University Press.

Rugman, Alan M., and Jing Li, eds. 2005. *Real Options and International Investment*. Cheltenham, UK: Elgar.

Rugman, Alan M., and Alain Verbeke. 1992. A note on the transnational solution and the transaction cost theory of multinational strategic management. *Journal of International Business Studies* 23 (4): 761–771.

Rugman, Alan M., and Alain Verbeke. 1993. Foreign subsidiaries and multinational strategic management. *Management International Review, Special Issue* 33 (2): 71–84.

Rugman, Alan M., and Alain Verbeke. 2001. Subsidiary-specific advantages in multinational enterprises. *Strategic Management Journal* 22 (3): 237–250.

Rugman, Alan M., and Alain Verbeke. 2002. Edith Penrose's contribution to the resource-based views of strategic management. *Strategic Management Journal* 23:769–780.

Rugman, Alan M., and Alain Verbeke. 2003. Extending the theory of the multinational enterprises: Internalization theory and strategic management perspectives. *Journal of International Business Studies* 34 (2): 125–137.

Rugman, Alan M., and Alain Verbeke. 2008. Internalization theory and its impact on the field of international business. In *International Business Scholarship: AIB Fellows on the First 50 Years and Beyond* (Research in Global Strategic Management, vol. 14), ed. J. J. Boddewyn, 155–174. Bradford: Emerald Group.

Rugman, Alan M., and Alain Verbeke. 2009. Location, competitiveness and the multinational enterprises. In *The Oxford Handbook of International Business*, 2nd ed., ed. Alan M. Rugman, 146–180. Oxford: Oxford University Press.

Rugman, Alain M, Alain Verbeke, and Quyen T. K. Nguyen. 2011. Fifty years of international business theory and beyond. *Management International Review, Special Issue* 51 (6): 755–789.

Rugman, Alan M., Alain Verbeke, and Wenlong Yuan. 2011. Re-conceptualizing Bartlett and Ghoshal's classification of national subsidiary roles in the multinational enterprise. *Journal of Management Studies* 48 (2): 253–277.

Rumelt, Richard P. 1984. Towards a strategic theory of the firm. In *Competitive Strategic Management*, ed. R. Lamb, 556–570. Englewood Cliffs, NJ: Prentice-Hall.

Safarian, Edward A. 2003. Internalization and the MNE: A note on the spread of the ideas. *Journal of International Business Studies* 34:116–124.

Taggart, James H. 1998. Strategy shifts in MNC subsidiaries. *Strategic Management Journal* 19:663–681.

Tallman, Stephen B., and George S. Yip. 2009. Strategy and the multinational enterprise. In *The Oxford Handbook of International Business*, 2nd ed., ed. A. M. Rugman, 307–340. Oxford: Oxford University Press.

Tavares, Ana T., and Stephen Young. 2005. FDI and multinationals: Patterns, impacts, and policies. *International Journal of the Economics of Business* 12:3–16.

Teece, David J. 1981. The multinational enterprise: Market failure and market power considerations. *Sloan Management Review* 22 (3): 3–17.

Teece, David J., Gary Pisano, and Amy Shuen. 1997. Dynamic capabilities and strategic management. *Strategic Management Journal* 18 (8): 537–556.

Tong, Tony W., and Jeffrey J. Reuer. 2007. Real options in multinational corporations: Organizational challenges and risk implications. *Journal of International Business Studies* 38 (2): 215–230.

Verbeke, Alain. 2009. *International Business Strategy*. Cambridge: Cambridge University Press.

Vernon, Raymond. 1966. International investment and international trade in the product life cycle. *Quarterly Journal of Economics* 80 (2): 190–207.

Welch, Lawrence S., and Reijo Luostarinen. 1988. Internationalization: Evolution of a concept. *Journal of General Management* 14 (2): 34–55.

Wernerfelt, Birger. 1984. A resource-based view of the firm. *Strategic Management Journal* 5 (2): 171–180.

Williamson, Oliver E. 1975. *Markets and Hierarchies: Analysis and Antitrust Implications: A Study in the Economics of Internal Organizations*. New York: Free Press.

Williamson, Oliver E. 1979. Transaction cost economics: The governance of contractual relations. *Journal of Law & Economics* 22:233–261.

Williamson, Oliver E. 1985. *The Economic Institutions of Capitalism*. New York: Free Press.

Williamson, Oliver E. 1981. The economics of organization: The transaction cost approach. *American Journal of Sociology* 87 (3): 548–577.

Zaheer, Srilata. 1995. Overcoming the liability of foreignness. *Academy of Management Journal* 38 (2): 341–363.

2 Exports versus Foreign Direct Investments: Evidence from Cross-Country Industry Data

Filomena Pietrovito, Alberto Franco Pozzolo, and Luca Salvatici

2.1 Introduction

An interesting feature of the recent process of globalization is the rapid increase of foreign direct investments (FDI), outpacing the simultaneous expansion of arm's-length trade (exporting). At the end of last century, multinational firms accounted for between two-thirds and three-quarters of world exports and more than one-third of world exports were between affiliated firms (UNCTAD 1999). Since then, global FDI have increased even further, with an expected value of FDI inflows in 2011 around US$1.4 trillion (UNCTAD 2010).

The link between trade and FDI is strong, as these are possible modes of entering foreign markets. As a matter of fact, firms can serve foreign consumers through two channels: (1) production at home for exports and (2) production in the destination market through FDI. The trade literature has shown that which is the best mode of foreign entry depends on the characteristics of the products, firms, sectors, and countries involved (Barba Navaretti, and Venables 2004). Similar conclusions have been reached by several strands of firm-level international business research, in which the comparison of the different ways in which value is added has always been a major focus of analysis, including the liabilities and benefits of foreignness and of different entry modes (Slangen, Beugelsdijk, and Hennart 2011).

Although there is a long tradition of studies on the factors underlying specific patterns of foreign expansion through trade or FDI, the literature focusing on measures of relative specialization in trade or FDI, controlling for the common factors affecting both internationalization strategies, is relatively more recent (Brainard 1993, 1997; Yeaple 2003; Helpman, Melitz, and Yeaple 2004; Oldenski 2010). A well-accepted result of these contributions is that FDI become more favorable relative to exports as both the size of the foreign market and the costs of exporting increase and less favorable as costs of setting up foreign production grow (Brainard 1993, 1997; Yeaple 2003). Recent contributions in the international economics field, starting with the seminal paper by Helpman, Melitz, and Yeaple (2004), enrich this "proximity-concentration trade-off" by also taking into account the role of heterogeneities in firm-level productivity.[1] As highlighted in the introduction, the modern international economics literature has focused on a microeconomic perspective by considering firm heterogeneity as a prominent topic: such an interest in the role of the firm and firm-specific differences is closely in line with the focus on firms in international business.

Although it has generated important insights, the empirical validation of these studies is still unconvincing, as it is based almost uniquely on analyses focusing on specific countries, for which data on export and outward foreign investment at a disaggregated level are more readily available. In this chapter, we enlarge the empirical analysis of the trade-off between trade and FDI using a large dataset including twenty-five domestic countries, ninety-one foreign countries, and fifty-seven manufacturing industries between 1994 and 2004. Following Helpman, Melitz, and Yeaple (2004), our main focus is on the role of firm size. In particular, we hypothesize that the presence of a high number of large firms in a sector favors foreign entry through FDI. Our results confirm that sectors with a higher number of large firms are associated with stronger incidence of FDI relative to trade.[2]

Although the main results are not new in the international economics field, our analysis contributes to the existing and rapidly growing literature along three dimensions. First, we explicitly consider the number of large firms in a sector as a determinant of international choice between trade and FDI. Second, we use bilateral flows of trade and FDI at sector level for a large number of countries. Third, we control for several country- and industry-level characteristics, drawn from the specific literature on trade and on FDI, that are likely to affect not only the single modes of internationalization but also their relative incidence. The value added in incorporating industry-level insights in macro-level studies is particularly high because both international economics and international business literature have examined internationalization modes separately at the country and firm levels, respectively, and hence there is a keen interest in the links between the two (Slangen, Beugelsdijk, and Hennart 2011).

In this respect, our analysis could be seen as part of the "migration" away from the country as the unit of analysis for international economics mentioned by Rugman and Nguyen (chapter 1, this volume). The perspective of analysis of this chapter lies between international economics, in which the key unit of analysis is the country, and international business, in which the unit of observation is the firm. Even if the results of this chapter cannot be imputed directly to firms, moving from the country to the industry perspective allows us to draw some indirect implications for single firms. Indeed, although our unit of analysis is not the single firm, we focus our analysis on firm size, a characteristic that the international business literature classifies among firm-specific advantages, not among country-specific advantages. We therefore analyze the sector-level implications of firm-specific advantages while controlling for the impact of location- and country-specific advantages (see chapter 1, this volume).

To overcome the limitations of data on bilateral FDI at the sector level, we use information on the value of mergers and acquisitions (M&A) as a proxy for FDI. Although this is a limitation of our analysis, we believe that it should not affect the qualitative results of our analysis, because cross-border M&A are by and large the most widely used mode of operating a foreign firm (Herger, Kostoggiannis, and McCorriston 2008). Moreover, in our robustness checks we provide some evidence that our results are confirmed, controlling for the potential impact of greenfield investment.

The rest of the chapter is organized as follows. Section 2.2 briefly discusses the theoretical background and the hypothesis to be tested. Section 2.3 describes the data used in the analysis. Section 2.4 presents the empirical model used to test the main hypothesis. The main results of the analysis are presented in section 2.5; section 2.6 presents the results of a number of robustness checks. Section 2.7 draws some conclusions.

2.2 Theory and Hypothesis

The link between exports and FDI has long been studied in the international economics field; we can trace it back to the eclectic paradigm of Dunning (1993). More recently, in the international economics literature, Helpman, Melitz, and Yeaple (2004) have developed an influential theoretical model to study the impact on the choice between trade and FDI of a selection mechanism based on productivity, such as that of Melitz (2003).[3]

In this framework, firm heterogeneity leads to self-selection in the mode of internationalization, with the most productive firms finding it profitable to meet the higher costs associated with FDI, firms with an intermediate level of productivity serving foreign markets through exports, and lower productivity firms selling only in the domestic market. In the model, a higher within-industry heterogeneity in firm sales is associated with a higher incidence of sales by foreign affiliates relative to exports, because with greater dispersion there is a larger share of firms with a sufficiently high level of productivity to find it profitable to invest abroad.

Using data on exports and on foreign sales of U.S. manufacturing firms in thirty countries and fifty-two industries, Helpman, Melitz, and Yeaple (2004) also find direct firm-level evidence supporting their theoretical prediction (i.e., multinational firms are more productive than non-multinational exporters) as well as indirect industry-level evidence, because higher firm size dispersion, expressing a higher productivity dispersion, is associated with more foreign affiliates' sales relative to exports. In the same vein, Tomiura (2007) finds that foreign outsourcers and exporters tend to be less productive than the firms active in FDI or in multiple globalization modes, but more productive than domestic firms, and shows that this productivity ordering is robust when firm size, factor intensity, and sector of economic activity are controlled for. Moreover, Oldenski (2010) extends the analysis of Helpman, Melitz, and Yeaple (2004), showing that greater firm-level heterogeneity in firm size significantly increases FDI relative to exports also in service industries.

The prediction of Helpman, Melitz, and Yeaple (2004) of a negative relationship between firm heterogeneity and the incidence of trade relative to FDI critically hinges on two crucial assumptions: (1) that fixed costs to export are lower than those to invest abroad, and (2) that variable costs of producing abroad are not (much) different from those of producing domestically. In fact, if foreign production were less efficient than domestic production for all firms, for example because of a less skilled labor force, even the most productive firms would find it optimal to export their products rather than to produce them locally. On the other hand, if foreign production costs were lower than the domestic ones for only a subset of the firms population, just the least productive firms would find it optimal to pay the FDI sunk costs and locate abroad, while the most productive firms would prefer to export

(Greenaway and Kneller 2007). Indeed, Head and Ries (2003) demonstrate that when there are factor price and market size differentials, the ordering of the productivity distribution between multinationals and non-multinationals can be the opposite of that obtained from the Helpman, Melitz, and Yeaple (2004) framework.

In light of the different forces at work, we believe that what effects prevail in shaping the relationship between the level of productivity and the relative incidence of trade and FDI is an empirical issue. An important difference between our empirical framework and that of Helpman, Melitz, and Yeaple (2004) is that their key explanatory variable is within-industry firm heterogeneity, measured by sales dispersion, and ours is the number of large firms in each country and sector. The choice of Helpman, Melitz, and Yeaple (2004) is a direct consequence of the assumptions made in their theoretical model, namely that firm size depends on the level of productivity, which in turn follows a Pareto distribution. In this setting, the share of large (and highly productive) firms is an increasing function of within-industry firm heterogeneity. However, if firm size followed a different distribution across sectors—for example, because of technological factors or economies of scale (Bartelsman, Scarpetta, and Schivardi 2005) the relationship between dispersion and number of highly productive (large) firms could be nonlinear (or even nonmonotonic), as sectors presenting similar dispersion measures could feature a different number of large firms. For this reason, we prefer to focus on firm size. Moreover, to focus more explicitly on the role of fixed costs and firm size, we single out the effect of productivity, including a measure of sector-level total factor productivity (TFP) as an additional exogenous control in our empirical specification.

Our main hypothesis relates therefore the number of large firms in a sector and the relative specialization in trade or FDI and can be stated as follows: *a higher number of large firms in a given sector of a given country is associated with a higher incidence of FDI relative to trade.*

2.3   Data and Sample

2.3.1   Dependent Variable
A first issue in testing our hypothesis is how to measure the relative specialization in exports or FDI at the country-sector level. Because we measure FDI through the value of M&A, we cannot compute the ratio

of the value of exports to that of the sales of foreign affiliates, as is customary in the literature (Brainard 1997; Helpman, Melitz, and Yeaple 2004; Oldenski 2010).

We therefore build a measure of the relative importance of exports on FDI in the spirit of the literature on revealed comparative advantages (Michaely 1967; Laursen 1998), expressed as the difference between the share of exports in a given sector of a given country with respect to total country exports and the same share for M&A, our proxy for FDI:

$$Index_{ij}^{h} = \frac{X_{ij}^{h}}{\sum_{h} X_{ij}^{h}} - \frac{M\&A_{ij}^{h}}{\sum_{h} M\&A_{ij}^{h}}. \tag{2.1}$$

The first term of our index is the share of exports from country i to country j in sector h with respect to total exports between the two countries; the second term is the share value of M&A from country i to country j of sector h with respect to total value of M&A between the two countries. By construction, the index ranges between -1 and $+1$: it is -1 when sector h of country i is fully specialized in M&A to country j; it is $+1$ when sector h of country i is fully specialized in exports to country j; the index is equal to 0 if sector h of country i shows the same relative degree of specialization in exports and M&A to country j. The index can also be interpreted in terms of similarities between two different entry market modes: 0 indicates the maximum level of similarity (as is the case in the few instances in which the share of exports is equal to the share of M&A); -1 and $+1$ are opposite cases indicating maximum differences, with M&A prevailing on trade and trade prevailing on M&A, respectively.

Working at a disaggregated level implies the presence of many zero-value trade and/or investment flows. The index we construct is undefined in the following two cases: (1) if total exports (across all sectors) between two countries are equal to zero and/or (2) if total M&A between two countries are equal to zero. In both cases, the denominator of at least one of the two building blocks of our index is equal to zero. To avoid any loss of information, we replace these observations with a value of 0. This choice implies that for couples of countries with no trade or M&A flows across all sectors, the index is not centered on zero; that is, the sum of the indices across h is not equal to zero.[4]

By construction, the index in equation (2.1) ranges between -1 and $+1$. To avoid being forced to use a truncated regression model, we normalize it taking the following transformation:

$$Index\_norm^h_{ij} = \ln \frac{\dfrac{Index^h_{ij}+1}{2}}{1-\dfrac{Index^h_{ij}+1}{2}}. \tag{2.2}$$

The normalized index ranges by construction between $-\infty$ and $+\infty$ and is always defined when the original index is defined (including the 0 values).

To construct the index of specialization, we need data on both exports and on the value of M&A operations.[5] The main statistical source of data on exports is the database UN Comtrade, managed by the statistical division of the United Nations (UN), which reports data on the bilateral flows in several industrial sectors. In particular, it contains annual international trade statistics for many countries, detailed by commodity and partner country from 1962 to 2009. Commodities are classified according to different recognized classifications, such as the standard international trade classification (SITC) and the Harmonized Commodity Description and Coding System (HS). We use the International Standard Industrial Classification (ISIC), Revision 3, at the four-digit level, which is an aggregation level comparable with other data used in the empirical analysis.

Data on M&A are sourced from the SDC Platinum Global Mergers and Acquisitions, a database provided by Thomson Financial Securities Data that records all deals involving a change in ownership of at least 5 percent of total equity and exceeding US$1 million over the period 1985–2009. The Thomson dataset allows analysis of M&A for a large range of countries and years. This source records two related aspects of cross-border acquisitions: the number of acquisitions and their value.[6] For the purpose of our analysis, and consistently with the literature on M&A, we focus on the value of M&A, and therefore we do not consider undisclosed and incomplete deals for which the value of transaction is not available.

The database also contains information on target and acquirer profiles, such as primary industry and location, that are used in our empirical analysis. In particular, we identify cross-border deals in manufacturing Standard Industrial Classification (SIC) codes at the four-digit level.[7]

2.3.2   Key Independent Variable

The second issue when testing our hypothesis is how to measure the presence of large firms. First, for each sector we divide the world distribution of firms by total sales in ten deciles. Then, for each sector of each domestic country, we count the number of firms in the first decile of the world distribution of firms by total sales. This indicator proxies for the incidence in each country and sector of those firms that are large enough to overcome the higher fixed costs of expanding abroad through FDI rather than exports (Helpman, Melitz, and Yeaple 2004).[8] Although our dependent variable is the incidence of trade and FDI at the country and sector levels, our main focus is on the impact of a firm-specific advantage, firm size, rather than on a location- or country-specific advantage.

Data on firm's sales are drawn from the Worldscope database, which includes financial statements of about 29,000 companies listed in developed and emerging markets, representing approximately 95 percent of the global market capitalization. Because we focus on large firms, excluding nonlisted companies is unlikely to introduce a relevant bias in our measure of each sector's ability to internationalize. Data are classified according to the SIC classification at the four-digit level.

2.3.3   Control Variables

To avoid omitted-variable bias, we add to the main variable of interest three sets of controls that have been shown in the international economics and international business literatures to affect the scope and the relative incidence of different internationalization modes. First, we control for some relevant sector characteristics in the country of origin (country-specific advantages, in the international business literature). Second, we control for a set of characteristics of the bilateral relationship between each couple of countries (location-specific advantage). Finally, we control for some sector characteristics that are specific of each pair of countries and might have an impact on the trade-off between exports and FDI.

Country of Origin Sector-Level Variables   First, we control for average sector wages (expressed in U.S. dollars deflated by using the U.S. consumer price index, with base year in 2000), obtained from UNIDO (Indstat4 2008 version). Second, following Helpman, Melitz, and Yeaple (2004), who show that capital intensity is a useful predictor of the incidence of exports relative to FDI, we use data from UNIDO to construct a measure of capital intensity defined as the ratio between capital and number of employees at sector level. Third, again following Helpman, Melitz, and Yeaple (2004), who show that technological intensity favors FDI relative to exports, we include the number of utility patents granted by the U.S. Patent Office that have been produced worldwide in each sector, provided by the national bureau of economic research (NBER).[9] Finally, as discussed previously, we include the average industry TFP, calculated under the assumption of constant returns to scale Cobb-Douglas production function:

$$TFP_i^h = \frac{Y_i^h}{(K_i^h)^\alpha (L_i^h)^{1-\alpha}} \qquad (2.3)$$

where (omitting indices): Y is the sector value added, K is the stock of capital at the sector level, and L is the number of employees in the sector, assuming a capital share of one-third and a labor share of two-thirds.

Total factor productivity at the national sector level was calculated from data on investment and labor from UNIDO (Indstat4 2008 version) and estimating each sector's capital stock with the inventory method (Bernanke and Gurkaynak 2002; Isaksson 2009). In particular: (1) for each country, we calculated the sector's share of investment using flow information for the first five years of data available; (2) we used investment shares to divide information on each country's total capital provided by UNIDO's World Productivity Database across sectors; (3) we used the estimates of the country- and sector-specific initial stock of capital obtained as described previously as the starting point to apply the inventory method, that is, adding each year's value of real-term investment and applying a sector-specific rate of depreciation to account for obsolescence.

Bilateral Country-Level Variables The empirical literature has identified a large set of variables that influence foreign markets entry modes, though the magnitudes and even the signs of the impact on either trade or FDI are not always consistent (see, e.g., Blonigen 2005; Disdier and Head 2008; Helpman, Melitz, and Rubinstein 2008; Herger, Kostoggiannis, and McCorriston 2008; Oldenski 2010; Slangen and Beugelsdijk 2010; Wang, Wei, and Liu 2010; Slangen, Beugelsdijk, and Hennart 2011).

These variables include both physical distance (Zaheer 1995) and the location advantages described in by Rugman and Nguyen (chapter 1, this volume). Distance directly increases transaction costs because of the transportation costs of shipping products, the cost of acquiring information about other economies, and the cost of finding a partner and contracting at a distance. The view that firms (and, indirectly, sectors in a country) have to overcome the "distance" between the home and the host country (where distance should be interpreted in the broadest sense) in order to explore the location-specific advantage, is common to both international business (see, e.g., Slangen, and Beugelsdijk 2010) and international economic scholars, as highlighted in the introduction.

Similarly, common legal systems, common languages, common religions, common borders, and colonial ties are expected to affect bilateral relationships, through both trade and investment. It is worth noting that the relevance of this type of variable is confirmed by the analysis carried out by Darby, Desbordes, and Wooton (chapter 5, this volume), who show that a firm with experience of poor institutions in its home market may have a competitive advantage over firms from less risky countries with respect to investing in developing countries.

Our data on bilateral characteristics (distance, number of islands and landlocked countries in a pair, common language, contiguity and colonial ties) are drawn from the dataset provided by the Center d'Etudes Prospectives et d'Informations Internationales (CEPII).[10] The only exception are the data on common legal systems that are from Djankov et al. 2002.

Bilateral Sector-Level Variables   We consider two bilateral sector-level variables. First, bilateral trade tariffs with an expected negative sign, because firms shift to FDI according to the well-known "tariff jumping" effect pointed out in the literature (Brainard 1997; Carr, Markusen, and Maskus 2001; Markusen, and Maskus 2002; Yeaple 2003; Helpman, Melitz, and Yeaple 2004). To make data comparable to other data used in the analysis, we aggregate HS six-digit level data on tariffs from Trade Analysis and Information System (TRAINS) to the four-digit ISIC classification through simple averages.

Second, building on the results of Chaney (2011)—who shows that the existing contacts of a firm can be used to find new ones—we include in our specification two "network indexes," calculated as the number of common partners in trade and in M&A of each couple of countries (Francois 2010). We expect that a higher number of common partners in exports (or in M&A) between two countries increases trade (or M&A) specialization between those same countries. This argument is in line with the reasoning presented by Mayneris and Poncet (chapter

6, this volume) that exposure to foreign exporters helps reduce the fixed cost of creating new international linkages. Data on the number of common partners is built from our information on trade and FDI.

Table 2.1 lists all variables used in our analysis and their sources.

2.3.4   Sample and Summary Statistics

Matching our different sources, we construct an original database that associates bilateral trade and FDI flows at sector level in a common classification, for a sample of developed as well as developing countries. Ideally, the full set of industries should be included, with the extent of tradability reflected in transport costs (Brainard 1997). In practice, however, data on transport costs are available only for industries in which trade exists.

As a consequence, industries including finance and utilities were excluded, along with wholesale and retail trade, because of the nontradable nature of these activities. We also excluded agriculture and primary sectors (i.e., mining and oil and gas extraction) due to the lack of data on productivity. As a result, we focus on manufacturing sectors, namely, sectors with an ISIC code between 1511 and 3720.

Because our measures of M&A and sales are available with the SIC classification, we made a connection between the manufacturing sectors identified by the SIC code and data classified according to the ISIC code, both at the four-digit level, using the concordances produced by Statistics Canada, as in Brakman, Garretsen, and Van Marrewjk (2005).[11] To take into account that at the four-digit level of disaggregation we have a large number of empty cells, both in exports and in M&A, we aggregate data available at three digits of ISIC classification. Matching different datasets yields data on twenty-five domestic countries and ninety-one foreign countries, covering fifty-seven manufacturing industries at the three-digit ISIC level from 1994 to 2004.

As shown by many theoretical and empirical studies (e.g., Caballero and Engel 1999), investment dynamics are lumpy. This statement is even truer in the case of FDI and M&A (e.g., Brakman, Garretsen, and Van Marrewjk 2005). For these reasons, although our sample covers eleven years, we estimate our empirical model on data averaged over the entire sample to smooth time-series variability.

Table 2.2 presents the descriptive statistics for the variables used in the estimations. It shows substantial variation in all our key variables.

Table 2.1
Variables description and sources: Description and sources of variables used in the empirical analysis

Definition	Description and source
Exports	Value of exports from country i to country j in sector h. *Source:* UN Comtrade
FDI	Value of mergers and acquisitions from country i to country j in sector h. *Source:* SDC Platinum
Index_norm	Difference between the share of exports from country i to country j in sector h, with respect to total exports between the two countries, and the share value of M&A from country i to country j of sector h, with respect to total value of M&A between the two countries, normalized so that it takes values between $-\infty$ and $+\infty$. *Sources:* UN Comtrade and SDC Platinum
Num. of large firms[a]	Number of firms in country i in the first decile of the world distribution of firm sales in a given sector h. *Source:* Worldscope Database
Num. of large firms in other countries	Number of large firms in a sector h, in all countries except for country i. *Source:* Worldscope Database
Num. of large firms in other sectors	Number of large firms in a country i, in all sectors except for sector h. *Source:* Worldscope Database
TFP[b]	Average level of total factor productivity in sector h in country i. *Source:* UNIDO (Indstat4 2008 version)
Wage[b]	Average wages in sector h in country i. *Source:* UNIDO (Indstat4 2008 version)
Capital intensity	Ratio between capital and number of employees in sector h in country i. *Source:* UNIDO (Indstat4 2008 version)
Patents	Number of patents produced in a country i and in a given sector h and granted by the U.S. Patent Office. *Source:* NBER
Distance[b]	Average distance between countries i and j calculated through the great circle formula that uses latitudes and longitudes of the most important cities (in terms of population). *Source:* CEPII; available at http://www.cepii.fr/anglaisgraph/bdd/distances.htm
Islands	Number of countries that are islands in the pair of countries i and j. *Source:* CEPII; available at http://www.cepii.fr/anglaisgraph/bdd/distances.htm
Landlocked	Number of countries that are landlocked in the pair of countries i and j. *Source:* CEPII; available at http://www.cepii.fr/anglaisgraph/bdd/distances.htm

Table 2.1
(continued)

Definition	Description and source
Common legal system	Dummy variable equal to 1 if country i and j share the same legal system. *Source:* CEPII; available at http://www.cepii.fr/anglaisgraph/bdd/distances.htm
Common language	Dummy variable equal to 1 if country i and j share the same language. *Source:* CEPII; available at http://www.cepii.fr/anglaisgraph/bdd/distances.htm
Common religion	Dummy variable equal to 1 if country i and j share the same religion. *Source:* CEPII; available at http://www.cepii.fr/anglaisgraph/bdd/distances.htm
Contiguity	Dummy variable equal to 1 if country i and j share common borders. *Source:* CEPII; available at http://www.cepii.fr/anglaisgraph/bdd/distances.htm
Colonial ties	Dummy variable equal to 1 if country i and j have ever been in colonial relationship. *Source:* CEPII; available at http://www.cepii.fr/anglaisgraph/bdd/distances.htm
Tariffs	Tariffs applied from country j to country i in sector h. *Source:* TRAINS
Common partners in trade	Number of partners in trade common to country i and j in sector h. *Source:* UN Comtrade
Common partners in FDI	Number of partners in FDI common to country i and j in sector h. *Source:* SDC Platinum
Share greenfield	Number of greenfield investments realized in a given destination country j relative to total number of greenfield investments in the world. *Source:* UNCTAD

[a]This variable is included as ln(1 + variable).
[b]This variable is included as ln(variable).

Table 2.2
Summary statistics

Variable	Mean	Median	Standard deviation	Min	Max
Index_Norm	0.051	0.008	0.188	−0.884	7.058
Num. of large firms[a]	0.571	0	0.897	0	3.965
Num. of large firms in other countries	44	38	32	1	167
Num. of large firms in other sectors	120	25	232	0	763
TFP[b]	5.073	5.174	0.705	1.614	7.785
Wage[b]	10.054	10.294	1.230	6.279	12.559
Capital intensity	1.681	1.664	0.178	1.309	2.468
Patents	17	0	89	0	1,465
Distance[b]	8.826	9.052	0.742	5.371	9.892
Islands	0.417	0	0.570	0	2
Landlocked	0.164	0	0.383	0	2
Common legal system	0.277	0	0.447	0	1
Common language	0.108	0	0.310	0	1
Common religion	0.197	0	0.291	0	1
Contiguity	0.021	0	0.143	0	1
Colonial ties	0.039	0	0.194	0	1
Tariffs	11.734	9.295	10.770	0	58.235
Common partners in trade	58	58	37	0	117
Common partners in FDI	0	0	1	0	30
Share greenfield	1.124	0.464	2.376	0.000	17.608

Notes: Variable descriptions and sources are provided in table 2.1. Summary statistics are computed after excluding observations in the 1st and the 99th percentile of the distribution of the dependent variable. Summary statistics are calculated on 67,911 observations for all variables.
[a]This variable is included as ln(1 + variable).
[b]This variable is included as ln(variable).

The dependent variable (*Index_norm*) has an average value of 0.051 and a standard deviation of 0.188, with values ranging from −0.884 to 7.058. Positive values are associated with couples of countries presenting higher exports share than M&A share in a given sector; negative values are for country pairs presenting higher M&A shares than exports shares in a given sector.

Considering our explanatory variables, the number of firms in the first decile (taking the natural logarithm of 1 plus the number of firms) of the world distribution of firms by total sales is 0.571 with a high within-sample variability (values range from 0 to 3.965). The TFP levels (in natural logarithm) range from 1.614 to 7.785 (average value: 5.073), and the sectors presenting (on average) the highest values are: refined petroleum products, tobacco products, and motor vehicles and automobiles. The number of patents, reflecting the level of technological development, shows an average value of 17 and a high variability, in that it ranges between 0 and 1,465.

Concerning bilateral characteristics, tariffs show a high variability, with values ranging between 0 and 58.2 percent and an average level of 11.7 percent. The average number of common partners in trade is 58, with values ranging between 0 and 117, whereas the average number of common partners in FDI is much lower and the range narrower (between 0 and 30). This difference highlights that the two "networks" are quite different and the former is much larger than the latter (consistently with the lower fixed costs assumption, again).

In table 2.3, we report simple correlations among the variables used in the empirical model. The correlation between the normalized index and the number of firms in the first decile of the world distribution of sales is negative, suggesting that having a larger share of world large firms favors FDI relative to trade. Further, TFP levels are positively correlated with the relative importance of exports: higher levels of TFP in a given sector determine higher trade compared to M&A flows between two countries. Higher wages in the domestic country are also positively associated with the incidence of exports, and the contrary is true for capital intensity and patents.

Bilateral correlations are suggestive, but they do not control for potentially confounding factors. For this reason, in the following methodology section we perform a more refined econometric analysis.

2.4   Methodology

To analyze the underlying motives of the composition of international commerce between trade and FDI, we have designed two sets of regression models. The first set is used to test our hypothesis considering the full set of information available (67,911 observations), including all 0 values. Using the normalized index and the three sets of controls defined earlier in this chapter, we estimate the following model:

$$Index\_norm_{ij}^{h} = \alpha + \beta_1 Number\_large\_firms_i^{h} + \beta_2 Z_i^{h} + \beta_3 T_{ij} + \beta_4 X_{ij}^{h} + \quad (2.4)$$
$$\beta_5 DU_i + \beta_6 DU_j + \beta_7 DU^{h} + \varepsilon_{ij}^{h}$$

Table 2.3
Correlation matrix

	(1)	(2)	(3)	(4)	(5)	(6)	(7)	(8)	(9)	(10)	(11)	(12)	(13)	(14)	(15)	(16)	(17)	(18)	(19)	(20)
(1) Index_Norm	1																			
(2) Num. of large firms[a]	-0.004	1																		
(3) Num. of large firms in other countries	0.076	0.032	1																	
(4) Num. of large firms in other sectors	-0.054	0.792	-0.189	1																
(5) TFP[b]	0.073	0.340	-0.113	0.359	1															
(6) Wage[b]	0.062	0.352	0.082	0.292	0.678	1														
(7) Capital intensity	-0.055	-0.157	-0.103	-0.137	0.384	0.365	1													
(8) Patents	-0.025	0.422	-0.043	0.459	0.117	0.146	0.108	1												
(9) Distance[b]	0.014	0.065	-0.015	0.088	-0.065	-0.098	-0.098	0.029	1											
(10) Islands	-0.042	0.153	-0.054	0.163	0.181	0.146	0.094	-0.001	0.067	1										
(11) Landlocked	0.013	-0.029	0.027	-0.039	0.029	0.075	0.070	-0.014	-0.105	-0.137	1									
(12) Common legal system	0.011	-0.087	0.006	-0.082	-0.110	-0.130	-0.084	-0.010	-0.043	0.021	-0.071	1								

Table 2.3
(continued)

	(1)	(2)	(3)	(4)	(5)	(6)	(7)	(8)	(9)	(10)	(11)	(12)	(13)	(14)	(15)	(16)	(17)	(18)	(19)	(20)
(13) Common language	-0.011	0.022	-0.018	0.050	-0.014	-0.056	-0.071	0.059	-0.102	0.113	-0.024	0.409	1							
(14) Common religion	0.030	-0.116	0.004	-0.112	-0.045	-0.059	-0.013	-0.029	-0.064	-0.073	0.041	0.279	0.103	1						
(15) Contiguity	-0.006	-0.039	-0.002	-0.032	-0.033	-0.047	-0.015	-0.006	-0.394	-0.089	0.054	0.123	0.146	0.122	1					
(16) Colonial ties	-0.018	0.036	-0.030	0.021	0.047	0.070	-0.025	0.005	-0.031	0.212	-0.047	0.236	0.323	-0.028	0.015	1				
(17) Tariffs	-0.003	0.007	-0.124	0.037	0.028	0.031	-0.018	0.011	0.018	-0.062	0.016	0.031	0.021	-0.144	-0.038	-0.005	1			
(18) Common partners in trade	0.005	0.013	0.091	-0.008	-0.068	0.021	-0.122	0.019	-0.074	-0.022	-0.109	-0.108	-0.071	-0.010	0.055	0.022	-0.230	1		
(19) Common partners in FDI	-0.028	0.218	0.148	0.150	0.091	0.146	-0.019	0.117	-0.036	0.024	0.077	-0.054	0.000	0.140	0.087	0.015	-0.171	0.334	1	
(20) Share greenfield	-0.021	-0.025	-0.015	-0.022	-0.009	-0.017	0.012	-0.011	-0.031	-0.092	-0.113	-0.095	-0.004	-0.127	0.043	0.007	0.048	0.342	0.096	1

Notes: Variable definitions and sources are provided in table 2.1. Correlations are computed after excluding observations in the 1st and the 99th percentile of the distribution of the dependent variable. Correlations are calculated on 67,911 observations for all variables.

[a]This variable is included as ln(1 + variable).

[b]This variable is included as ln(variable).

where (omitting indices): *Index_norm* is the measure defined earlier of the relative incidence of trade relative to FDI in sector h and countries i and j; *Number_large_firms* is the number of country i firms in the first decile of the world firms distribution of total sales in sector h; Z is the set of sector-specific control variables for the exporting country in each sector (i.e., TFP, wage levels, capital, and technological intensity); T is the set of control variables describing the bilateral relationship between countries (e.g., distance, common language, and common religion); X is the set of control variables describing the bilateral relationship between countries in a given sector (i.e., tariffs, number of common partners in trade, or FDI); and DU are three sets of dummies controlling for the domestic country, the foreign country, and the sector-specific fixed effects.

In our specification, we test the impact of firm size on foreign market entry modes. However, a potential reverse causality problem emerges if the entry mode affects firm size. As a matter of fact, M&A can lead to an increase in the productivity of the bidder and therefore in its production and sales.[12] In the same vein, foreign trade could increase firm productivity— for example, if it allows the exploitation of economies of scale. We address this potential endogeneity problem by instrumenting the number of large firms in each country and sector with two variables: the number of large firms in a given sector h in all countries, except for country i; and the number of large firms in a given country i in all sectors, except for sector h.

As a robustness check, in a second set of regressions, we estimate two Heckman correction models (Helpman, Melitz, and Rubinstein 2008) to separately account for the cases in which there is no trade and/or no M&A in any sector between a couple of countries. In this way, we transform the selection bias problem into an omitted variable problem, which can be solved by including an additional variable: the inverse Mills ratio between the regressors. The Heckman two-step approach allows us to distinguish the impact of preferences on the extensive as well as the intensive margins.

In the first Heckman model, the extensive margin is represented by the probability of any form of internationalization. Accordingly, we estimate the impact of the independent variables included in equation (2.4) on a binary variable that is equal to 1 if trade and/or M&A exist and 0 otherwise. In the second step (intensive margin), we estimate the same regression in equation (2.4), but on a reduced sample of 60,298 observations, excluding all cases in which both trade and M&A are 0 and including among the independent variables the inverse Mills ratio from the first stage.

Because our database includes only a relatively small number of cases with positive flows of both trade and FDI, it is also interesting to assess the impact of the presence of large firms on the probability of internationalization through both trade and M&A. Accordingly, in the second Heckman model, the first step estimates the impact of the number of large firms on the probability to enter foreign markets using both trade and FDI, and the second stage focuses on those cases in which both exports and M&A are present (3,755 observations).

In both Heckman models, identification of the first stage is obtained through the exclusion of the measures of contiguity and colonial ties from the second-step estimates.

2.5 Results[13]

2.5.1 Baseline Regression and Sample Splits

The first step of our empirical analysis is the estimation of the model described in equation (2.4), in which the dependent variable is the index of relative specialization in trade or FDI. We estimate this specification on a sample that includes all 67,911 cases.

Results in column (1) of table 2.4 show that sectors with a higher number of large firms have a stronger incidence of FDI relative to trade. The negative coefficient of the number of firms in the first decile of the world distribution by total sales, statistically significant at the 99 percent level, confirms our main hypothesis that when the distribution of firms in a given sector country is shifted toward large firms, it is more likely that the prevailing internationalization mode is direct investment rather than trade.[14] It therefore provides further support to the evidence of Helpman, Melitz, and Yeaple (2004) that larger firms are more likely to be able to afford the higher fixed costs required to invest abroad. Reassuringly, in a number of unreported regressions we have verified that this result is also confirmed using the number of firms in the first quintile of the world distribution by total sales as a threshold to define large firms.[15]

To analyze whether the relationship of interest is affected by some structural features of the domestic sectors, we then split our sample according to (1) the average wage level and (2) the average capital intensity.

Table 2.4
Baseline regression and sample splits

	(1)		(2)		(3)		(4)		(5)	
	All sample		Wages				Capital intensity			
			Above the median		Below the median		Above the median		Below the median	
Num. of large firms[a]	-0.012	***	-0.021	***	0.003	*	-0.047	***	0.015	***
	(0.003)		(0.005)		(0.002)		(0.005)		(0.003)	
TFP[b]	0.060	***	0.064	***	0.046	***	0.017	***	0.109	***
	(0.004)		(0.005)		(0.004)		(0.003)		(0.008)	
Wage[b]	-0.007	*	0.009	**	-0.018	***	0.016	***	-0.018	***
	(0.004)		(0.004)		(0.005)		(0.003)		(0.006)	
Capital intensity	-0.117	***	-0.213	***	-0.063	***	-0.065	***	-0.429	***
	(0.006)		(0.012)		(0.007)		(0.007)		(0.025)	
Patents[c]	0.016	***	0.027	***	-0.006	*	0.145	***	0.004	
	(0.003)		(0.006)		(0.003)		(0.027)		(0.004)	
Distance[b]	0.008	***	0.009	***	0.005	***	0.001		0.014	***
	(0.001)		(0.002)		(0.002)		(0.001)		(0.002)	
Islands	0.029		0.026		0.029	**	-0.005		0.058	***
	(0.018)		(0.030)		(0.014)		(0.020)		(0.017)	
Landlocked	0.025	*	0.053	**	-0.013		-0.003		0.052	
	(0.015)		(0.025)		(0.012)		(0.021)		(0.033)	
Common legal system	0.001		-0.002		0.005	*	-0.004	**	0.005	
	(0.002)		(0.003)		(0.003)		(0.002)		(0.004)	
Common language	-0.011	***	-0.010	**	-0.011	***	-0.007	**	-0.014	***
	(0.003)		(0.005)		(0.004)		(0.003)		(0.005)	

Table 2.4
(continued)

	(1)		(2)		(3)		(4)		(5)	
	All sample		Wages				Capital intensity			
			Above the median		Below the median		Above the median		Below the median	
Common religion	-0.020	***	-0.018	**	-0.017		0.006		-0.037	***
	(0.006)		(0.009)		(0.007)		(0.006)		(0.010)	
Contiguity	-0.007		-0.007		-0.008		0.002		-0.015	**
	(0.005)		(0.008)		(0.005)		(0.005)		(0.008)	
Colonial ties	0.001		-0.005		0.006		0.002		0.000	
	(0.003)		(0.005)		(0.004)		(0.005)		(0.005)	
Tariffs[d]	-0.077	***	-0.061	***	-0.057	***	-0.039	***	-0.127	***
	(0.014)		(0.017)		(0.019)		(0.012)		(0.028)	
Common partners in trade[c]	0.931	***	0.970	***	0.664	***	0.500	***	1.264	***
	(0.066)		(0.101)		(0.077)		(0.059)		(0.114)	
Common partners in FDI[c]	-2.598	***	-2.400	***	-3.240	***	-2.380	***	-2.962	***
	(0.417)		(0.618)		(0.473)		(0.665)		(0.567)	
Observations	67,911		35,528		32,383		32,473		35,438	
Adjusted R^2	0.141		0.174		0.247		0.113		0.185	

Notes: Variables description and sources are provided in table 2.1. The dependent variable is *Index_Norm*. All columns report two-stage least-squares estimates, instrumenting *Num. of large firms* with *Num. of large firms in other countries* and *Num. of large firms in other sectors*. Column (1) reports estimates on the whole sample. Columns (2) and (3) report estimates on the subsamples of sectors with wages above and below the median level, respectively. Columns (4) and (5) report estimates on the subsamples of sectors with capital intensity above and below the median level, respectively. All estimates include unreported domestic country, foreign country and sector-specific fixed effects. Standard errors, robust to heteroskedasticity, are reported in parentheses. ***, **, and * indicate statistical significance at the 1%, 5%, and 10% level, respectively.
[a]This variable is included as ln(1 + variable).
[b]This variable is included as ln(variable).
[c]This coefficient is multiplied by 1,000.
[d]This coefficient is multiplied by 100.

Columns (2) and (3) report the results obtained splitting the sample between countries and sectors with average wages above and below the median. In the former sectors, the coefficient of the number of large firms is negative and statistically significant; in those below the median, it is positive. Our general result of a preference for FDI over trade when the presence of large firms is higher is therefore driven by the sectors paying wages above the median. Apparently, large firms in sectors paying high wages try to find abroad cheaper labor inputs, consistent with a cost-minimization strategy. On the contrary, those in sectors paying low wages may find it optimal to internationalize only through trade: this effect determines an increase in the positive value of our index leading to the positive coefficient of column (3).[16]

Along a similar vein, the preference of large firms for an FDI-driven internationalization is due to the firms with a capital intensity ratio above the median, that is, by more productive sectors (columns [4] and [5]).[17] These conclusions are reinforced when we look at the sign of the coefficients of the control variables. Sectors with higher average wages show a lower relative specialization on trade, except for sectors with wages and capital intensity above the median. Moreover, firms in capital-intensive industries have a stronger incentive to invest abroad.

The fact that sectors with higher average productivity have a higher relative incidence of trade may come as a surprise even if it is quite consistent with the findings of Sala and Yalcin (chapter 3, this volume). However, it should be noted that the impact is quite small: a 10 percent increase in productivity leads to a trade share only 0.2 percentage points larger than the corresponding M&A share.[18] Moreover, in an unreported regression, substituting the continuous measure of TFP with a set of four dummies for each quartile level, we verify the presence of nonlinear effects of productivity on our index of specialization. The positive and statistically significant coefficient of the dummy for sectors in the top quartiles of the within-country distribution shows that only very high levels of productivity influence the choice between trade and FDI. In other words, only the most productive sectors tend to favor exports with respect to foreign investment, while in all the other groups the opposite is true. Such a finding is confirmed by the fact that the number of patents produced in a sector show a positive and significant impact on the preference on trade over foreign investment. As a matter of fact, sectors with a high technological intensity, which are likely to be the most productive, prefer to produce at home and then export, instead of producing in foreign countries. This result is only apparently in contrast with the hypothesis that sectors with a higher presence of more productive and therefore larger firms are relatively more likely to invest abroad than to export. Indeed, it is possible that in some sectors, technological constraints make it difficult for even highly productive firms to reach the size that allows them to overcome the fixed costs of FDI, forcing these firms to internationalize through trade.

Regarding country-level bilateral characteristics, most of the control variables related to trade and investment costs (e.g., common language and religion) present a negative and statistically significant coefficient, providing evidence that these factors favor FDI with respect to trade. The opposite is true as far as the distance variable is concerned, which flies in the face of traditional gravity models predicting that trade costs increasing with distance should promote investment. More recent papers focusing on FDI, though, provide a set of explanations pointing in a different direction. In Head and Ries 2008, for instance, monitoring requires costs that are increasing in distance between head office and subsidiary. Slangen, Beugelsdijk, and Hennart (2011) argue that arm's-length affiliate sales are likely to decline with cultural distance, but this is not necessarily the case with arm's-length exports, which may in fact increase with cultural distance.

Concerning sector-level bilateral characteristics, the coefficient of applied tariffs is negative and statistically significant, providing evidence of the "tariff jumping" effect: higher tariffs provide an incentive to switch from trade to investment abroad. The coefficients associated with the number of common partners in trade or in FDI confirm the relevance of the network effects. Apparently, firms in sectors with a higher number of foreign contacts are more likely to enter an additional market, and sectors benefit from the contacts of their contacts. In other words, if a firm k has a contact in country i', which itself has a contact in country j, then firm k is more likely to enter country j. Furthermore, our results show that the trade and investment contacts form different networks and have opposite impacts on the internationalization choices.

In table 2.5, we present the findings obtained considering different samples of countries. First, we consider the choice between different entry market modes made by firms operating in developed countries, distinguishing G-10 (Belgium, Canada, France, Germany, Italy, Japan, Sweden, Switzerland, United Kingdom, and United States) and Organisation for Economic Co-operation and Development (OECD) countries. In this respect, we consider G-10 and OECD as origin countries

Table 2.5
Groups of countries

	(1) G-10 (origin)		(2) OECD (origin)		(3) OECD (origin and destination)		(4) Developing (destination)		Share of greenfield investment			
									(5) Above the median		(6) Below the median	
Num. of large firms[a]	-0.041	***	-0.022	***	-0.014	***	-0.010	***	-0.015	***	-0.008	**
	(0.003)		(0.003)		(0.004)		(0.004)		(0.003)		(0.004)	
TFP[b]	0.084	***	0.077	***	0.053	***	0.070	***	0.052	***	0.071	***
	(0.008)		(0.005)		(0.010)		(0.006)		(0.005)		(0.006)	
Wage[b]	0.064	***	0.044	***	0.038	***	-0.004		-0.005		-0.000	*
	(0.006)		(0.004)		(0.006)		(0.005)		(0.004)		(0.006)	
Capital intensity	-0.153	***	-0.085	***	-0.098	***	-0.108	***	-0.136	***	-0.117	***
	(0.012)		(0.009)		(0.014)		(0.009)		(0.009)		(0.030)	
Patents[c]	0.014	***	0.012	***	0.005		0.010	**	0.024	***	0.006	
	(0.005)		(0.003)		(0.006)		(0.004)		(0.004)		(0.005)	
Distance[b]	0.004	**	0.006	***	0.003	***	0.010	***	0.007	***	0.008	***
	(0.002)		(0.001)		(0.003)		(0.002)		(0.002)		(0.002)	
Islands	-0.003		0.002		0.005		-0.035	***	-0.001		-0.031	***
	(0.014)		(0.010)		(0.011)		(0.011)		(0.009)		(0.011)	
Landlocked	-0.008		-0.002		-0.123	***	0.024		0.189	***	0.087	***
	(0.017)		(0.011)		(0.030)		(0.015)		(0.018)		(0.008)	
Common legal system	-0.005	*	-0.003		-0.010	**	0.004		0.001		0.000	
	(0.003)		(0.002)		(0.004)		(0.003)		(0.003)		(0.003)	
Common language	0.000		-0.002		0.010		-0.019	***	-0.012	***	-0.009	**
	(0.004)		(0.003)		(0.006)		(0.006)		(0.004)		(0.005)	
Common religion	-0.006		-0.005		0.008		-0.018	**	-0.015	*	-0.026	***
	(0.008)		(0.005)		(0.009)		(0.007)		(0.009)		(0.008)	

Table 2.5
(continued)

	(1)	(2)	(3)	(4)	(5)	(6)
					Share of greenfield investment	
					Above the median	Below the median
	G-10 (origin)	OECD (origin)	OECD (origin and destination)	Developing (destination)		
Contiguity	-0.001	-0.001	-0.004	-0.018 **	-0.006	-0.013
	(0.008)	(0.005)	(0.006)	(0.008)	(0.006)	(0.008)
Colonial ties	-0.001	0.001	0.001	0.002	-0.002	0.009 *
	(0.005)	(0.004)	(0.007)	(0.005)	(0.004)	(0.005)
Tariffs[d]	-0.087 ***	-0.077 ***	0.016 ***	-0.117 ***	-0.056 ***	-0.082 ***
	(0.018)	(0.013)	(0.037)	(0.018)	(0.016)	(0.021)
Common partners in trade[c]	0.388 ***	0.396 ***	0.270 **	0.482 ***	1.361 ***	0.690 ***
	(0.071)	(0.055)	(0.132)	(0.084)	(0.102)	(0.091)
Common partners in FDI[c]	-3.177 ***	-3.281 ***	-1.833 ***	-13.899 ***	-1.903 ***	-2.792 **
	(0.473)	(0.422)	(0.514)	(4.464)	(0.446)	(1.205)
Observations	23,430	41,631	10,453	37,843	34,687	33,060
Adjusted R²	0.175	0.173	0.175	0.143	0.162	0.131

Notes: Variables description and sources are provided in table 2.1. The dependent variable is *Index_Norm*. All columns report two-stage least-squares estimates, instrumenting *Num. of large firms* with *Num. of large firms in other countries* and *Num. of large firms in other sectors*. Column (1) reports estimates on the subsample of origin countries belonging to the group of G-10 countries. Column (2) reports estimates on the subsamples of origin countries belonging to the group of OECD countries. Column (3) reports estimates on the subsample of origin and destination countries belonging to the group of OECD countries. Column (4) reports estimates on the subsample of destination countries belonging to the group of developing countries. Columns (5) and (6) report estimates on the subsamples of destination countries belonging to the group of countries with the share of greenfield investment above and below the median level, respectively. All estimates include unreported domestic country, foreign country, and sector-specific fixed effects. Standard errors, robust to heteroskedasticity, are reported in parentheses. ***, **, and * indicate statistical significance at the 1%, 5%, and 10% level, respectively.
[a]This variable is included as ln(1 + variable).
[b]This variable is included as ln(variable).
[c]This coefficient is multiplied by 1,000.
[d]This coefficient is multiplied by 100.

and then consider the group of OECD countries as both origin and destination countries. Next, we test our main hypothesis limiting the sample to the developing countries as destination markets.

Columns (1) and (2) refer to the internationalization strategies of firms based in G-10 and OECD countries, respectively. The preference of large firms for FDI is higher with respect to the baseline specification, and the sign and the significance of the other coefficients remains by and large unchanged with a few exceptions. The first exception is represented by the wage coefficient, as firms' trading in developed countries is not negatively affected by labor costs (higher wages actually have a positive impact on trade choices). The second exception is because trade between most developed countries and their partners is not impaired by common language and religion.

In column (3) we analyze the determinants of foreign market entry modes for the subsample of OECD countries toward other OECD members. Restricting the sample of origin and destination countries does not change the overall picture, but trade costs in terms of both distance and tariffs—are not significant in explaining the internationalization choices among developed countries.

Considering the group of developing countries as destinations of foreign investment, the overall results are confirmed. Indeed, the coefficient of our variable of interest that is, the number of large firms is still negative and significant. In other terms, for internationalization toward developing countries, large firms still prefer M&A relative to trade, though with a lower intensity with respect to the baseline estimation.

Finally, we control for the possibility that M&A flows are influenced by the existence of other types of FDI. In particular, we assess the sensitivity of the results to the presence of greenfield investments, splitting the sample of destination countries according to their ability to attract this type of investments. In practice, we consider the share of the number of greenfields in each destination country over the world's greenfield investment and separate the countries with a share of world greenfield investment above the median from those that follow.[19]

The rightmost two columns of table 2.5 report the results for the two groups of countries depending on whether they show a share of world greenfield investment above or below the median. Our baseline result holds in both cases. More interestingly, results for the group of countries attracting a high share of greenfield investment are similar to those for developing countries. This finding confirms the observation that developing countries tend to attract a relatively large number of green-field investments (UNCTAD 2010).[20]

2.5.2   Robustness Checks: Heckman Models

In table 2.6, we provide some robustness tests of our previous results by estimating the two Heckman models described in section 2.4.

The first step of the first Heckman model consists in estimating the probit model, in which the dependent variable is the probability of internationalization through trade and/or FDI.[21] Results, reported in column (1) of table 2.6, show that the number of large firms in a given sector exerts a positive impact on the extensive margin, that is, on the probability of accessing foreign markets through trade and/or FDI. This result confirms the key prediction of selection models à la Melitz (2003), namely the existence of a productivity ordering of firms according to their participation in international markets.

In the second step of the Heckman model, we estimate an instrumental variable regression to account for the incidence of our key independent variable on the relative importance of trade on FDI by excluding all cases in which both trade and FDI flows are zero. We include among the regressors the Heckman correction term, calculated from the previous probit regression, to account for the restriction of the sample.

Column (2) of table 2.6 shows the results. In terms of our main hypothesis, it is confirmed that a higher number of large firms is associated with a higher incidence of FDI. This finding implies that our main results are confirmed also excluding observations with both trade and FDI flows equal to 0. Comparing coefficients of our key explanatory variable in column (1) of table 2.4 and in column (2) of table 2.6, it can be inferred that among internationalized firms, the preference of large firms for FDI is lower (–0.010) than in the overall sample (–0.012). This finding is consistent with the fact that in the second stage we drop the least productive firms. The positive and statistically significant coefficient of the inverse Mills ratio confirms that the characteristics of sectors featuring positive trade or FDI bilateral flows show a higher incidence of trade.[22]

Results on the extensive margin for the second Heckman model, reported in column (3) of table 2.6, show that the probability of accessing foreign markets with both exports and FDI increases when the number of large firms is higher. In the second stage, we analyze the effect of our key explanatory variables on relative trade specialization,

Table 2.6
Heckman models

	(1)	(2)	(3)	(4)
	Heckman model 1		Heckman model 2	
	Probit	Two-stage least-squares	Probit	Two-stage least-squares
Num. of large firms[a]	0.240 ***	−0.010 ***	0.192 ***	−0.020 ***
	(0.040)	(0.003)	(0.028)	(0.005)
TFP[b]	0.139 ***	0.072 ***	−0.040	0.041 ***
	(0.039)	(0.005)	(0.058)	(0.010)
Wage	0.094 **	−0.013 ***	0.109 *	0.022 **
	(0.042)	(0.004)	(0.061)	(0.010)
Capital intensity	−0.871 ***	−0.126 ***	−0.058	−0.111 ***
	(0.114)	(0.007)	(0.160)	(0.028)
Patents[c]	0.527	0.016 ***	−0.060	0.002
	(0.383)	(0.003)	(0.092)	(0.009)
Distance[b]	−0.840 ***	0.010 ***	−0.454 ***	−0.001
	(0.061)	(0.002)	(0.042)	(0.004)
Islands	0.030	−0.001	−0.489	0.005
	(0.298)	(0.010)	(0.302)	(0.017)
Landlocked	−1.010 ***	0.094 ***	−1.180 ***	0.002
	(0.195)	(0.012)	(0.441)	(0.031)
Common legal system	0.048	0.002	−0.010	0.003
	(0.066)	(0.003)	(0.089)	(0.006)
Common language	0.649 ***	−0.015 ***	0.420 ***	−0.002
	(0.100)	(0.004)	(0.119)	(0.008)
Common religion	0.206 **	−0.026 ***	0.492 *	0.027
	(0.098)	(0.008)	(0.263)	(0.030)
Contiguity	−0.586 ***		0.174	
	(0.207)		(0.132)	

Table 2.6
(continued)

	(1)	(2)	(3)	(4)
	Heckman model 1		Heckman model 2	
	Probit	Two-stage least-squares	Probit	Two-stage least-squares
Colonial ties	0.657 **		0.205 *	-0.006
	(0.269)		(0.116)	(0.037)
Tariffs[d]	-0.490 ***	-0.092 ***	0.583 **	-0.165
	(0.184)	(0.013)	(0.272)	(0.201)
Common partners in trade[c]	16.403 ***	1.025 ***	11.832 ***	
	(1.430)	(0.074)	(1.464)	
Common partners in FDI[c]	159.839 **	-2.392 ***	136.190 ***	-1.600 ***
	(66.738)	(0.390)	(12.998)	(0.560)
Mills ratio		0.052 ***		-0.005
		(0.012)		(0.010)
Observations	63,176	60,298	48,167	3,755
Adjusted R²		0.164		0.259

Notes: Variables description and sources are provided in table 2.1. Column (1) reports estimates of the first probit model. The dependent variable in column (1) takes the value of 1 if sector h of country i exports and/or invests in country j; and the value of 0 if both exports and FDI are 0 for a sector h of country i. Column (2) reports two-stage least-squares estimates on the subsample, including all cases in which sector h of country i exports and/or invests in country j; instrumenting *Num. of large firms* with *Num. of large firms in other countries* and *Num. of large firms in other sectors*. Column (3) reports estimates of the second probit model. The dependent variable in column (3) takes the value of one if sector h of country i exports and invests in country j, and the value of zero otherwise. Column (4) reports two-stage least-squares estimates on the subsample, including all cases in which sector h of country i exports and invests in country j, instrumenting *Num. of large firms in other countries* and *Num. of large firms in other sectors*. All estimates include domestic country, foreign country, and sector-specific fixed effects (not reported). In columns (1) and (3), standard errors, are clustered by country pairs. In columns (2) and (4), standard errors, reported in parentheses, are reported in parentheses. In columns (1) and (3), standard errors, reported in parentheses, are bootstrapped with 100 replications. ***, **, and * indicate statistical significance at the 1%, 5%, and 10% level, respectively.

[a]This variable is included as ln(1 + variable).
[b]This variable is included as ln(variable).
[c]This coefficient is multiplied by 1,000.
[d]This coefficient is multiplied by 100.

focusing on those 3,755 cases with positive flows of both exports and FDI (column [4] of table 2.6). In the restricted sample of the most internationalized sectors, the incidence of large firms still augments the preference for FDI over trade. Interestingly, the exclusion of country pairs with no trade or no M&A does not cause a sample selection bias, as it is confirmed by the statistically insignificant coefficient of the inverse Mills ratio.

2.6   Conclusions

The firm choice between exporting at arms' length and FDI, traditionally modeled as a proximity-concentration trade-off (Brainard 1993, 1997), has been enriched in more recent contributions (Yeaple 2003; Helpman, Melitz, and Yeaple 2004; Oldenski 2010) taking into account heterogeneity in firm productivity. Although they have generated important insights, these studies have generally focused on single-country analysis.

In this chapter, we study the determinants of the composition of international commerce between exports and FDI across sectors and countries, explicitly considering the number of large firms in a sector instead of the heterogeneity in firm productivity. We test the hypothesis that a higher number of large firms leads to a specialization on foreign investment using a novel dataset including twenty-five domestic countries, ninety-one foreign countries, and fifty-seven manufacturing industries covering the period 1994–2004. We found sound and convincing evidence in favor of this hypothesis, consistent with the predictions of Helpman, Melitz, and Yeaple (2004). Although we are aware that "trade data can be disaggregated to three or even four digit industry levels, such disaggregation does not capture in an adequate manner the complex activities of MNEs, especially their strategic management decision" (Rugman and Nguyen, chapter 1, this volume) our analysis is nonetheless a first step in the direction of studying the impact of firm characteristics (a firm-specific advantage, in the international business jargon) on the trade-off between exports and FDI. In this sense, our analysis can be seen as an attempt to build a bridge between the international economics and the international business perspective of analysis.

In addition, we are able to shed some light on the empirical linkages between internationalization choices and a rich set of economic variables. First, we confirm the relevance of the well-known tariff-jumping rationale for FDI. Second, although most of the literature studies the role of the host country wages in attracting/repelling FDI, we focus on the role of the domestic country wages, showing that they encourage outbound FDI—but this is true only for sectors paying lower wages and characterized by low capital intensity. As far as capital intensity is concerned, our results confirm the findings of Helpman, Melitz, and Yeaple (2004) for the United States: more capital-intensive sectors export less relative to FDI. Finally, we provide empirical support to the predictions of the most recent network models (Chaney 2011) providing a theory of the distribution of entry into foreign markets without any assumptions on firms' productivity distribution. Our results show that export and investment contacts are substitutes rather than complements: being part of a trade network increases the likelihood of using the same mode of internationalization when entering into another foreign market.

Investigating in more detail the characteristics of sectors that are likely to drive our results, we discover that the preference of sectors characterized by a high presence of large firms for an FDI-driven internationalization is due to a specific group of sectors, namely those with an average level of wages and a capital intensity ratio above the world median. Moreover, our results are robust to different country group splits as well as to the exclusion of different sets of zero trade and/or FDI flows. In this perspective, the treatment of the zero values through the Heckman selection model allows to distinguish the impact on both the extensive as well as the intensive margin. This finding suggests a future extension of the present analysis to explain the distribution of the number and the geographic location of foreign markets, with an emphasis on the extensive margin of trade and FDI.

Notes

We are extremely grateful to participants at the CESifo Workshop on Globalisation, Trade, FDI and the Multinational Firm (2011) for helpful comments. We would also thank participants at the XVI International Economic Association World Congress 2011, at the seminar organized by the Department of Economics of University Roma Tre, and at the 12th European Trade Study Group Annual Conference 2010. We thank the editors and two anonymous reviewers for their useful suggestions on previous versions of this chapter. A special thanks to the Electronic Resources Area of Bocconi University's library for providing the access to the Worldscope Database. We acknowledge financial support from the "New Issues in Agricultural, Food and Bio-energy Trade (AGFOODTRADE)" (Small and Medium-scale Focused Research Project, Grant Agreement no. 212036) research project funded by the European Commission. The views expressed in this chapter are the sole responsibility of the authors and do not necessarily reflect those of the European Commission.

1. A related issue is the traditional distinction between horizontal and vertical FDI (see, e.g., Carr, Markusen, and Maskus 2001). However, this issue is out of the scope of the analysis in this chapter.

2. Pietrovito, Pozzolo, and Salvatici (2012) test the impact of these sector characteristics on the extensive margin between exports and FDI, finding that the higher the number of large firms in a sector, the higher the probability of internationalize—especially through FDI.

3. In the seminal theoretical model by Melitz (2003), monopolistically competitive firms have different level of productivity, depending on a draw from an exogenous distribution. With fixed costs to export, only the most productive firms reach a sufficient scale to find it profitable to export. The model is therefore capable of explaining the positive link between productivity and export status, with a causality nexus running from the former to the latter.

4. For a couple of countries that have both trade and M&A in at least one sector, the sum of the index across h is by construction equal to zero; to maintain the symmetry of our index we could therefore have assumed a uniform (i.e., $1/h$) trade or M&A distribution. However, because our estimates are not sensitive to this choice, we opted for the more intuitive option of substituting undefined ratios with zeroes.

5. Both trade and M&A are expressed in current U.S. dollars; it is not necessary to deflate them because our index is constructed as a difference between two shares.

6. The main sources of information of data on M&A are financial newspapers and specialized agencies such as Bloomberg and Reuters. It should be kept in mind that until the mid-1980s, Thomson focused very much on M&A for the United States only, and for only the last twenty years or so that (systematic) M&A data gathering took place for other countries (Brakman, Garretsen, and Van Marrewjk 2005).

7. Domestic M&A—that is, acquisitions with acquirer and target located in the same country could still provide access to foreign markets if the target firm is active abroad or if the acquirer is controlled by a foreign firm. However, in the former case we do not know what foreign markets are (possibly) involved, and in the latter case we have no information about foreign controls: as a consequence, we exclude domestic M&A from our sample.

8. By considering the world rather than the national distribution(s), we avoid the risk of a country-specific definition of "large firms." On the other hand, the total number of firms in each sector may be influenced by technological peculiarities, such as the existence of economies of scale. To account for this issue, it is possible to either use the share rather than the absolute number of large firms or, as we do in this chapter, account for all sector-specific features through the use of sector dummies.

9. Because the original data on patents are classified according to the U.S. Patent Classification, we combined them with other information, adopting the correspondence scheme between the U.S. Patent Classification and the International Patent Classification and between the latter and the ISIC Revision 3 provided by Johnson (2002).

10. The CEPII follows the great circle formula and uses latitudes and longitudes of the most important cities (in terms of population) to calculate the average of distances between city pairs. Data on distances are available at http://www.cepii.fr/anglaisgraph/bdd/distances.htm. We also adopted distances between capitals as an alternative measure and the results remain unchanged.

11. The concordances used are available at http://www.macalester.edu/research/economics.

12. We are indebted to an anonymous referee for pointing out this issue.

13. All estimates reported in this section include three sets of dummies controlling for the domestic country, the foreign country, and the sector-specific fixed effects, as described in section 2.4.

14. The coefficient of 0.012 reported in column (1) of table 2.4 implies that an increase of 1 percent in the number of large firms in a given national sector determines a reduction of the value of our normalized index of specialization (*Index_norm*) by 0.012 percent. In turn, starting from a value of the index of 0 (i.e., symmetry between trade and FDI) and from the average number of large firms (3), it implies that one additional large firm determines an increase in the value of the non-normalized index of specialization (*Index*) of 0.19 percent.

15. Results are available upon request.

16. Recall that the second term in our index takes a value of 0 for country pairs with no bilateral M&A flows. To control for this undesired consequence of our index, in an unreported regression (available upon request) we have estimated equation (2.4) on the reduced sample that includes only nonzero observations for both trade and FDI, controlling for potential sample selection bias through the inclusion of a Heckman correction term (see also section 5.3). Reassuringly, we find a negative coefficient for the number of large firms also in the subsample of low wage sectors.

17. Also in these cases, results (available on request) are robust when we use as a threshold the number of firms in the first quintile of the world distribution.

18. Starting from a value of the index of 0 (i.e., symmetry between trade and FDI) and from the average level of *TFP*. In fact, the coefficient of 0.060 for *TFP* in column (1) of table 2.4 implies that a 10 percent increase in the average level of sector TFP determines an increase of our dependent variable (*Index_norm*) of 0.6 percent and an increase in the value of the non-normalized index of specialization (*Index*) of 0.2 percent.

19. Data on the incidence of greenfield investment is obtained from UNCTAD (available at http://unctad.org).

20. We are indebted to an anonymous referee for pointing out this issue.

21. The estimates are in this case obtained from a smaller sample of 63,176 observations because observations are dropped when country or sector dummies perfectly predict the absence of FDI.

22. Because the inverse Mills ratio is an estimated regressor obtained from the probit estimates, we have used bootstrapped standard errors with one hundred replications, as in Helpman, Melitz, and Rubinstein 2008.

References

Barba Navaretti, Giorgio, and Anthony J. Venables. 2004. *Multinational Firms in the World Economy*. Princeton: Princeton University Press.

Bartelsman, Eric, Stefano Scarpetta, and Fabiano Schivardi. 2005. Comparative analysis of firm demographics and survival: Evidence from micro-level sources in OECD countries. *Industrial and Corporate Change* 14 (3): 365–391. doi:10.1093/icc/dth057.

Bernanke, Ben S., and Refet S. Gurkaynak. 2002. "Is growth exogenous? Taking Mankiw, Romer and Weil seriously." *NBER Macroeconomics Annual 2001* 16:62–70. http://www.nber.org/chapters/c11063.

Blonigen, Bruce A. 2005. A review of the empirical literature on FDI determinants. *Atlantic Economic Journal* 33:383–403. doi:10.1007/s11293-005-2868-9.

Brakman, Steven, Harry Garretsen, and Charlie Van Marrewjk. 2005. "Cross-border mergers and acquisitions: On revealed comparative advantage and merger waves." CESifo Working Paper 1602. http://www.cesifo-group.de/portal/pls/portal/docs/1/1188428.

Brainard, S. Lael. 1993. "A simple theory of multinational corporations and trade with a trade-off between proximity and concentration." NBER Working Paper 4269. http://www.nber.org/papers/w4269.

Brainard, S. Lael. 1997. An empirical assessment of the proximity-concentration trade-off between multinational sales and trade. *American Economic Review* 87 (4): 520–544.

Caballero, Ricardo J., and Eduardo M.R.A. Engel. 1999. Explaining investment dynamics in US manufacturing: a generalized (S, s) approach. *Econometrica* 67 (4): 783–826. doi:10.1111/1468-0262.00053.

Carr, David L., James R. Markusen, and Keith E. Maskus. 2001. Estimating the knowledge capital model of the multinational enterprises. *American Economic Review* 91 (3): 693–708.

Chaney, Thomas. 2011. "The network structure of international trade." NBER Working Paper 16753. http://www.nber.org/papers/w16753.

Disdier, Anne C., and Keith Head. 2008. The puzzling persistence of the distance effect on bilateral trade. *Review of Economics and Statistics* 90:37–48. doi:10.1162/rest.90.1.37.

Djankov, Simeon, Raphael La Porta, Florencio Lopez-de-Silanes, and Andrei Shleifer. 2002. The regulation of entry. *Quarterly Journal of Economics* 117:1–37. doi:10.1162/003355302753399436.

Dunning, John. 1993. Trade, location of economic activity and the multinational enterprise: A search for an eclectic approach. *The Theory of Transnational Corporations* 1:183–218.

Francois, Joseph F. 2010. Who trades with whom. Paper presented at the 12th European Trade Study Group, Lausanne, September 9–11, 2010.

Greenaway, David, and Richard Kneller. 2007. Firm heterogeneity, exporting and foreign direct investment. *Economic Journal* 117 (517): 134–161. doi:10.1111/j.1468-0297.2007.02018.x.

Head, Keith, and John Ries. 2003. Heterogeneity and the FDI versus export decisions of Japanese manufacturers. *Journal of the Japanese and International Economies* 17:448–467.

Head, Keith, and John Ries. 2008. FDI as an outcome of the market for corporate control: Theory and evidence. *Journal of International Economics* 74:2–20.

Helpman, Elhanan, Mark J. Melitz, and Yona Rubinstein. 2008. Estimating trade flows: Trading partners and trading volumes. *Quarterly Journal of Economics* 123 (2): 441–487. doi:10.1162/qjec.2008.123.2.441.

Helpman, Elhanan, Mark J. Melitz, and Stephen R. Yeaple. 2004. Export versus FDI with heterogeneous firms. *American Economic Review* 94:300–316. doi:10.1257/000282804322 970814.

Herger, Nils, Christos Kostoggiannis, and Steve McCorriston. 2008. Cross-border acquisitions in the global food sector. *European Review of Agriculture Economics* 35 (4): 563–587. doi:10.1093/erae/jbn033.

Isaksson, Anders. 2009. The UNIDO world productivity database: An overview. *International Productivity Monitor* 18 (Spring): 38–50.

Johnson, Daniel K.N. 2002. "The OECD Technology Concordance (OTC): Patents by industry of manufacture and sector of use." OECD Science, Technology and Industry Working Paper 2002/5. http://ideas.repec.org/p/oec/stiaaa/2002-5-en.html.

Laursen, Keld. 1998. "Revealed comparative advantage and the alternatives as measures of international specialization." Danish Research Unit for Industrial Dynamics Working Paper 98-30. http://www3.druid.dk/wp/19980030.

Markusen, James R., and Keith E. Maskus. 2002. Discriminating among alternative theories of the multinational enterprise. *Review of International Economics* 10 (4): 694–707. doi:10.1111/1467-9396.00359.

Melitz, Mark J. 2003. The impact of trade on intra-industry reallocation and aggregate industry productivity. *Econometrica* 71 (6): 1695–1725.

Michaely, Michael. 1967. *Concentration in International Trade: Contributions to Economic Analysis.* Amsterdam: North-Holland Publishing Company.

Oldenski, Lindsay. 2010. Export versus FDI: A task based approach. Working Paper, Georgetown University.

Pietrovito, Filomena, Alberto F. Pozzolo, and Luca Salvatici. 2012. Internationalization choices: A multinomial probit analysis. Paper presented at the Italian Trade Study Group, Catania, June 15–16, 2012.

Slangen, Arjen H.L., and Sjoerd Beugelsdijk. 2010. The impact of institutional hazards on foreign multinational activity: A contingency perspective. *Journal of International Business Studies* 41:980–995. doi:10.1057/jibs.2010.1.

Slangen, Arjen H.L, Sjoerd Beugelsdijk, and Jean F. Hennart. 2011. The impact of cultural distance on bilateral arm's length exports: An international business perspective. *Management International Review* 51 (6): 875–896. doi:10.1007/s11575-011-0103-2.

Tomiura, Eiichi. 2007. Foreign outsourcing, exporting, and FDI: A productivity comparison at the firm level. *Journal of International Economics* 72 (1): 113–127. doi:10.1016/j.jinteco.2006.11.003.

UNCTAD. 1999. World Investment Report 1999. United Nations Conference on Trade and Development, Geneva.

UNCTAD. 2010. World Investment Report 2010. United Nations Conference on Trade and Development, Geneva.

Wang, Chengang, Yingqi Wei, and Xiaming Liu. 2010. Determinants of bilateral trade flows in OECD countries: Evidence from gravity panel data models. *World Economy* 33:894–915. doi:10.1111/j.1467-9701.2009.01245.x.

Yeaple, Stephen R. 2003. The role of skill endowments in the structure of US outward foreign investments. *Review of Economics and Statistics* 85 (3): 726–734. doi:10.1162/003465303322369849.

Zaheer, Srilata. 1995. Overcoming the liability of foreignness. *Academy of Management Journal* 38 (2): 341–363.

3 Managerial Characteristics and the Export Decision of Firms

Davide Sala and Erdal Yalcin

3.1 Introduction

As micro data have become increasingly accessible in recent years, the focus of the analysis in the trade literature has gradually shifted from trade patterns between countries or industries to the engagement of firms into international markets. Several studies (e.g., Bernard and Jensen 1999) have uncovered that even in narrowly defined industries exporters and nonexporters are different along a number of dimensions, namely the productivity level, the turnover, the number of employees, the wages paid, and the value added. The challenge of explaining these pervasive differences between exporters and nonexporters has culminated in what has become known as the *new trade theory*. The core element of this theory is the recognition that exporting involves sizable fixed costs—product customization, sales, or distribution networks—and that firms are not homogenous production units (Melitz 2003). These two elements coupled together determine the self-selection of firms into international markets: only the most productive firms are in the position to overcome the fixed costs of exporting and expand into foreign markets, seizing the opportunity to enlarge their scale of production offered by trade; the least productive firms can produce only for the domestic market, suffering competitive pressure from trade. Therefore, factors that foster trade opportunities have also distinct and asymmetric implications for exporters and nonexporters, implying that exporters will typically expand and domestic firms will either shrink or exit the market. This argument, the *self-selection hypothesis*, is finding growing empirical evidence: Bernard and Jensen 1999 and 2004, Wagner 2007, and other recent studies have confirmed that more productive firms are more likely to engage in trade. However, these studies, despite confirming the exporters' advantage, leave out many of the determinants that have been broadly discussed in the international business literature—in particular, managerial characteristics. This chapter brings these insights from the international business studies into an otherwise standard empirical model of international trade.

International business studies have emphasized that firms, particularly multinational enterprises, command an idiosyncratic set of firm-specific advantages (FSAs) that, together with country-specific advantages (CSAs), confer to firms their competitive advantage (chapter 1, this volume). When the firm is viewed as a complex structure, "a differentiated network rather than a monolithic hierarchy," its governance, "the mechanism that leads the firm," becomes "a critical feature of internationalization theory" and a prerogative up to the top management (Rugman et al. 2011).

The logical consequence is that elements of the management structure may contribute to the critical capability of a firm to have an FSA. In particular, within this strand of literature, a firm's export decision is considered to be a highly complex process evolving over time (Dicken 1992). Given the relevance of fixed costs associated with exporting, it is natural to regard the internationalization process of a firm as a strategic investment commanded by the management's business plan. In this context, managerial experiences represent a valid proxy for executives' skills and hence represent powerful explanations for the variation in their strategic choices (Datta and Herrmann 2006).

Theoretically, Lucas (1978) discusses the importance of management as a specific input factor. However, an embedment into the recent trade literature has not followed. Equivalently, the empirical literature on the self-selection hypothesis, using the terminology of international business studies, accounts for a broad range of CSAs (e.g., availability of high-skill workers, capital, etc.); the relevance of managerial characteristics (FSAs) remains relatively unexplored, partly due to the unavailability of suitable data.[1]

Considered properly, the insights from the international business literature raise the interesting question of whether the inclusion of managerial characteristics into the analysis strengthens and is complementary to, or weakens and is therefore substitutable with, the self-selection hypothesis. On the one hand, management skills and inputs are just one element of the firm's set of FSAs. On the other hand, productivity, as measured by total factor productivity (TFP), remains a "residual" measure. It is therefore possible that the importance of firm productivity may appear in a different light once the analysis controls for managerial skills and export experience.

To this purpose, we have assembled Danish firm-level data in the manufacturing sector from1995 to 2006, for a total of about 6,000 firms in each period—an unprecedented number of firms for international business studies.[2] To ease the comparison of the results obtained with and without managerial characteristics, our empirical strategy deliberately follows the analysis of Bernard and Wagner (2001). We have or can construct employment, wage bill, the share of highly skilled and white-collar workers, and all other variables typically included in Wagner 2007. We can also identify the top five chief executives and observe their personal characteristics as nationality, education, age, and gender. Moreover, we can track these people in the years and investigate whether they possess exporting experiences from previous occupations. These characteristics are objectively measured based on registry data and do not involve any form of self-assessment as would data sources such as survey data.

Our results seem inclined to the "complementary" hypothesis. Productivity remains a strong and robust predictor of the probability of whether a company exports. In addition, our estimates indicate a systematic relationship between management characteristics and Danish firms' export decision: the export experience of newly hired managers and their education play an important role for the firm's internationalization process.

The self-selection issue that arises with the firm's hiring decision of managers hinders establishing a proper causal link in our analysis. Establishing the causality of these types of variables is not without problems and poses several challenges that should be addressed in future research. But what our results establish is a correlation between managerial inputs and firm's performance.

The remainder of this article is structured as follows: section 3.2 presents a discussion of the factors that international economic theories and the management literature alike have identified as drivers for the internationalization of firms. We then sketch a theoretical partial equilibrium model in which these factors coexist to guide us in the formulation of our empirical strategy presented in section 3.3. In section 3.4, we briefly describe the dataset and how we measure these factors empirically. Section 3.5 presents and discusses our results. Section 3.6 concludes.

3.2   Theoretical Framework for the Export Decision

Albeit simple and stylized, a model sketching the export decision of the firm should contain and possibly integrate some prominent elements stemming from the recent economic and business literature.

First, exporting involves substantial fixed costs and productivity greatly varies across firms, even in narrowly defined industries (Roberts and Tybout 1997; Bernard and Jonson 1999). These two elements substantially imply that firms sort into the exporting activity and some firms exclusively target the domestic market (Melitz 2003). Second, productivity evolves during the firm's life span as a consequence of technology adoption and learning by exporting. In such a dynamic context, fixed and sunk costs shape the value of action and inaction of firms, a clear lesson of the investment literature of the last decades, implying that the timing of entry into a foreign market can also vary across firms (Bertola 2010). In Peng's words, multinational corporations (MNCs) "have to figure out (1) when to enter, (2) how to enter" (2001, 816). The final element is the identification of international knowledge and experience as a valuable, unique, and hard-to-imitate resource that differentiates firms in global competition (Peng and York 2001).

To simplify, each "firm" consists of a single manager (or entrepreneur), l homogeneous employees, and k homogeneous units of capital, as in Lucas 1978. The manager manages resources l and k to produce output:

$$y = ca^{1-b} [f(k,l)]^{b} \tag{3.1}$$

where the function f is homogeneous of degree one.[3] The parameter c is common to all firms, representing therefore the countrywide productivity or a CSA, in the terminology of international business studies (Rugman et al. 2011). The term a is idiosyncratic to the firm and captures in Lucas's (1978) formulation managerial input, and b is the degree of diminishing returns at the plant level.[4] It is assumed that a is growing deterministically (i.e., evolving productivity).

Although it is mathematically simple, this formulation is a shallow one, stating only that some firms have better management than others; it is silent both on the nature of the tasks performed by the managers and the source of heterogeneity. Atkeson and Kehoe (2005) qualify the "managerial input" as organizational capital; Garicano (2000) interprets it as "know-how." The international business literature and the "resource base view" of the firm offer richer interpretations for a. In a top-down organization, headquarters transfer the capability to subsidiaries to exploit knowledge effectively (Caves 1996; Dunning 1993). With respect to organizational capital, Hamel (1991) advocates organizational learning as a tacit resource underlying a firm's competitive advantage, so alliances are designed to exploit relationship-specific assets. In particular, Mitchell et al. (2000) argue that firms contribute asymmetric knowledge in "link-alliance." Undeniably, part of the know-how emphasized by Garicano (2000) originates from international experience, an attribute representing firm-specific tacit knowledge that is difficult to access or copy by other firms whose top managers do not possess the same background, thus leading to higher firm's performances (Carpenter et al. 2001). Daily et al. (2000) confirm that executives' international experience is attractive to other firms that are interested in acquiring tacit knowledge. Finally, exporting is the outcome of a dynamic and longitudinal process in which firms build on capabilities and experience from previous entries or multiple entries (Kogut 1997).

Capitalizing on our dataset, we shall concentrate in our analysis on the following factors as the main drivers of internationalization:

- organizational learning
- know-how of managers, plausibly originated by their background (education, tenure, nationality, past working experience, international experience)
- "link-alliances" or informal networking

To relate these factors to the internationalization of the firm, we have to show how a affects export initiation of the firm. Doing so is the first step toward outlining our empirical strategy in the next section.

Let s be time and let y be the potential sales on the foreign market.[5] The firm's variable profit at time s is defined as

$$v_s \equiv v(a_s) = pca_s^{1-b}\left[f(k(a_s),l(a_s))\right]^b - qk(a_s) - wl(a_s) \tag{3.2}$$

where q and w are the rental prices of the input factors, p is the free on board (f.o.b.) price of output, and $k(a)$ and $l(a)$ are the factor-demand derived from the profit maximization problem.[6] Because the idiosyncratic term a is the only growing term, the variable profit is also growing: we assume, without loss of generality, that units are such that v grows at a constant rate g, that is, $dv_s = gv_s ds$. Let also $s = 0$ be the initial period (the founding year of the company), and t be the time of entry into the export market.

The value of the firm V evaluated in the founding year 0 is the stream of discounted variable profits from t on, or

$$V(v_0,t) = \int_t^\infty v_0 e^{-(r-g)s} ds, \quad r > g \tag{3.3}$$

where r is the discount rate equal to the return of a safe bond on the capital market. Entry entails the fixed cost I_E to be paid once, in the first period when the firm starts exporting. In this context, the firm faces a fundamental trade-off in determining the timing of entry, as the real-option framework exemplifies.[7] Delaying entry allows also saving on the entry cost I_E, which, if invested alternatively on a safe bond, gives a periodical yield of rI_E. Consequently, as a nonarbitrage condition, the real investment of expanding the economic activity into a foreign market should not yield an inferior return. Formally,

$$v_t = rI_E \tag{3.4}$$

which well exemplifies the firm's trade-off by equating the per-period variable profit to the user cost of capital, which is Jorgenson's investment rule.[8] Higher values of a make the LHS of the equation above higher and therefore increase the likelihood that a firm will start exporting.

We proceed to substantiate our empirical strategy in the next section.

3.3   Empirical Strategy

The theory outlined in the previous section suggests that a firm will be exporting if

$$ex = \Gamma(ex^* \equiv v_t - Ir_E \geq 0) \tag{3.5}$$

where Γ [.] denotes an indicator function taking value 1 if the expression in brackets is true. Therefore, ex is a unity indicator for the export status of the firm. We assume

$$ex_{ijt}^* = X_{ijt}B = b_1 m_{it} + b_2 x_{it} + b_3 z_{jt} + \gamma_j + \gamma_t + u_i + e_{ijt} \tag{3.6}$$

where B is the vector of parameters to be estimated and X is a row vector of regressors. The vector m is managerial input, and its element will capture organizational learning, managers' know-how, and international experience as discussed previously. We describe each element comprehensively in the next section when we describe the data. The vector x_{it} contains firm characteristics; the vector z_{jt} comprises time-varying industry characteristics; γ_t and γ_j are, respectively, time and industry effects; u_i is unobserved heterogeneity; and finally, e_{ijt} is the continuously distributed error term around zero and is independent of all explanatory variables. If G is the cumulative distribution function (cdf) of e_{ijt}, then

$$P(ex = 1 \mid X) = G(b_1 m_{it} + b_2 x_{it} + b_3 z_{jt} + \gamma_j + \gamma_t + u_i) \tag{3.7}$$

and the probit model is simply the special case with G being the cdf of a standard normal distribution, and the linear probability model is the special case with G being the identity function.[9]

Clearly, our major interest is in the parameter b_1. Although we generally expect a positive impact of "managerial inputs," we remain agnostic about the sign of specific variables. For instance, the tenure and education of managers can be conceived as factors pertaining to the managers' international experience. Distinct studies emphasize that the effect of these factors on strategic decisions is mediated by team dynamics and the work environments. The working hypothesis of Barkema and Shvyrkov 2007 is that education and tenure diversity among managers increase foreign market participation if task conflicts orient the team toward a wider range of strategic options. On the other hand, if task conflict exacerbates emotional conflict, this can induce the team communication to break down and decrease the likelihood that novel strategic options are considered. Environments where team diversity is coupled with age, race, or gender diversity may be more prone to the formation of hardened subgroups and therefore to this eventuality. Nevertheless, the interaction over time between the same team members diminishes the cognitive diversity, attenuating the effect of the group dynamics. Indeed, team members learn to avoid or resolve conflicts, attenuating emotional conflict hindering novel strategies but also reducing knowledge asymmetries and thus reducing the potential for wider strategy options.

When first evaluating quantitatively the relation between "management processes" and the internationalization process of a firm, it is useful to have a benchmark as a reference. Because it is well rooted in the recent "new trade theory," we choose Bernard and Wagner 2001 as our ideal benchmark.[10] To follow their empirical strategy closely, we center our analysis on the linear probability model and the random-effect probit model, and to enhance the comparability of our results, vector x is similarly specified as in Bernard and Wagner 2001. Yet although our benchmark relies on a dynamic formulation of the linear probability model and of the random probit model to account for the fixed and sunk costs of entry into exporting markets, our preferable strategy entails a different approach. Because a lagged dependent variable among the explanatory variables notoriously introduces substantial econometric challenges and further complexity, we exploit a theoretical proposition by Krautheim (2007) and proxy the fixed cost of exporting, I_E, with the share of exporting firms within the same industry. The idea is that such a fixed cost is decreasing with higher export shares within an industry, as information about destination markets and distributors are diffused (network effect). Hence, the higher the export share within an industry, the lower will be the fixed costs incurred by a firm that starts exporting.[11] This approach has also the advantage to capture to some extent link-alliances, as some of our firms may have formal partnerships that extend beyond the informal exchange of information allowing firms to share knowledge more systematically or possibly asymmetrically.

Unobserved heterogeneity, u_i, is considered to be a random component in the random-effect probit model and, as part of the error term, it should not be correlated with any of the explicative variables to obtain consistent estimates. As some of the FSA are plausibly determining the firm's observed export performances yet are unobservable to the econometrician, we regard as a more interesting approach a scenario that allows unobserved heterogeneity to be potentially correlated with some explanatory variables. In this regard, we corroborate our analysis with a fixed effect estimator (FE) and a first difference estimator (FD) for our linear probability model.

These estimators, however, cannot alone resolve the potential endogeneity of some of the managerial inputs, such as managers' international experience. The direction of the causality remains undetermined: it is equally plausible that a company may internalize because a manager with a sound experience on international markets is hired or promoted, the channel of interest, or that a manager with exporting experience is appointed as a consequence of the company's intention to export (conscious self-selection). Unfortunately, the proper identification of this channel is hardly attainable, as we are lacking a variable that affects a hiring policy without affecting participation into foreign markets. We remain skeptical that a short lag to this variable can successfully address the issue, but it can nevertheless address the issue of simultaneity between some of the explanatory variables and the export status.

In spite of these open issues, we advocate that establishing a relation between managerial inputs and the internationalization process of a firm within a large dataset represents an opportunity both for the international economic literature and for the management literature. Indeed, from the perspective of the international economic literature, the self-selection hypothesis can be reinforced and the empirical workhorse model enriched. From the perspective of the management litera-ture, the factors underlying the internationalization of firms are tested on the population of Danish manufacturing firms observed for a decade on the basis of registry data. If the results are encouraging, future research should investigate the causality of this link.

3.4   Data Description

Our dataset comprises a large fraction of Danish manufacturing firms for the period from 1995–2006. First, we use registers of Statistics Denmark to merge the firms' data with the firms' employee-specific data and assess CEOs' background characteristics.[12] Second, we use firm's accounting statistics (*Regnskabsstatistikken*) to assess balance sheet information.

We then proceed to eliminate firms with inconsistent figures, such as firms showing total or foreign negative turnover, export revenue greater than total revenue, negative physical capital, or a year of foun-dation subsequent to when the firm is first observed. We end up with a panel containing about 73,000 observations.

A positive export turnover defines our export status. To measure organizational learning, we construct, on the basis of a five-digit indus-try code, the share of Danish firms within the same industry already exporting to some destinations. As argued previously, our intention for the inclusion of this variable is twofold: to proxy for the fixed cost of exporting (informal information sharing) as well as for link-alliances (asymmetrical but formal information sharing).[13] Even if it is done imperfectly, we believe it is important to account for link-alliances, as we cannot observe firm ownership.

Productivity is a key variable in the analysis: we use both labor productivity (value added per employees) and TFP, our preferred measure, which we construct from firms' accounting statistics (*Regnsk-absstatistikken*) following Olley and Pakes (1996).

The dataset consists of matched employer-employee data allowing us to identify managers (CEOs) on the basis of annual salaries, where the employee with the highest salary is assumed to be the chief execu-tive officer, as in Bell 2005.[14] Once a manager is identified, her or his years of education, degree of education (e.g., MBA) as well as national-ity and age can be determined.

CEOs are usually tiered and companies can be led by team manage-ment. The narrow definition of a CEO includes the single person with the highest wage (CEO-1); the broader definition of a CEO aims at capturing team leadership, our preferred definition, and includes vice-presidents, identified as the top five ranked persons in the firm's wage distribution (CEO-5).[15] In this case, "education" refers to the person with the longest education or the highest academic degree, "national-ity" indicates whether at least one member of the board is a foreigner, and "age" is the average age of the CEO-5 team. Finally, we determine the share of women among the top five earners.[16] These variables capture team diversity along age, gender, or race attributes that affect social processes and can be associated with distrust and emotional conflict (Jehn 1997; Jehn et al. 1999). As discussed previously, the impli-cations of these group dynamics repeated over time on the interna-tionalization process remain unpredictable, and therefore we remain agnostic about the sign of these coefficients.

Because we can follow people along the years and workplaces, we track whether new people, either within the company or externally to the company, are promoted into CEO-5 offices. Unfortunately, we can observe managers' tenure only starting from 1995 or the first year in which the company appears in the dataset (which is not necessarily the year in which the firm was founded or when the managers have started in the company). Such imperfect measure is likely to introduce biases in our analysis and therefore we do not pursue this avenue further. But we can investigate whether externally promoted people have export experience, defined as having held positions within exporting compa-nies. We label these promoted managers as "externally promoted man-agers with exporting experience." These managers possess international experience, which is the embedded tacit knowledge that companies are interested in acquiring. This fundamental asset distinguishes them from the "externally promoted managers," which includes all people promoted to executive offices regardless of whether they have had previous export-ing experiences. To sum up, managers' background comprises educa-tion and international experience. One advantage of the measures we are introducing over those derived from survey data is that they are based on registry data and preclude any form of self-assessment. The disadvantage is that they are confined to characteristics objectively mea-surable. In particular, in the scheme adopted by Leonidou et al. (1998), they include objective-general and objective-specific characteristics but necessarily exclude subjective-general and subjective-specific factors such as the manager's risk tolerance, flexibility, commitment, dyna-mism, profit perception, growth perception, and complexity perception.

Table 3.1
Domestic and exporting Danish firms

Year	Domestic	Exporter	Total		Year	Domestic	Exporter	Total
1995	2,331	3,743	6,074		2001	2,271	4,194	6,465
%	38.38	61.62	100		%	35.13	64.87	100
1996	2,304	3,876	6,180		2002	2,198	4,060	6,258
%	37.28	62.72	100		%	35.12	64.88	100
1997	2,321	3,878	6,199		2003	2,084	3,965	6,049
%	37.44	62.56	100		%	34.45	65.55	100
1998	2,347	3,945	6,292		2004	1,994	3,864	5,858
%	37.3	62.7	100		%	34.04	65.96	100
1999	2,368	4,293	6,661		2005	1,829	3,722	5,551
%	35.55	64.45	100		%	32.95	67.05	100
2000	2,382	4,206	6,588		2006	1,706	3,581	5,287
%	36.16	63.84	100		%	32.27	67.73	100
		Total	26,135	47,327	73,462			
		%	35.58	64.42	100			

Information at the workplace is aggregated at the firm level to construct a precise measure of employment and human capital. These measures include the proportion of white-collar workers and the share of highly skilled workers.[17] Finally, from the firm's statistics we take the total capital of the firm, our measure of size. Table 3.1 presents the total number and the share of Danish manufacturing companies that are serving solely the domestic market or are involved into international trade. Denmark is a fairly open economy, which is also reflected in these descriptive statistics; each year, the share of domestic firms is far smaller than the share of exporting firms. During the period considered, more than 60 percent of all firms in our sample were exporting, which is a high degree of openness compared to other countries. Furthermore, with some exceptions, the share of exporting firms has steadily increased over the years.

In line with general empirical findings in the related literature (see, e.g., Roberts and Tybout 1997; Bernard and Wagner 2001), the average productivity of Danish exporters—regardless of whether it is measured as TFP or as labor productivity—outperforms the domestic firms' productivity in every year, as shown in figure 3.1. This dominance of exporting firms also prevails if average wages are compared, as shown in figure 3.2. Average wages in exporting firms exhibit a steady nominal

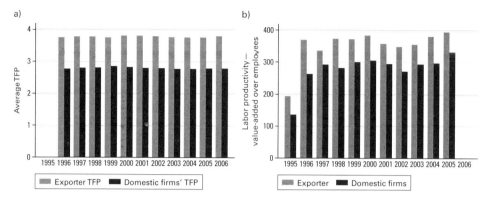

Figure 3.1a,b
Average TFP and labor productivity for exporting and domestic firms. *Notes:* Average TFP across all domestic and exporting firm is calculated following Olley and Pakes 1996. Average labor productivity across all firms is calculated as value added over employees.

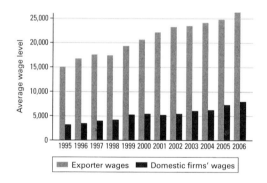

Figure 3.2
Average wage levels in exporting and domestic firms.

increase over the considered period, accompanied by a steady increase in the share of exporting firms (except in the year 2000) as shown in table 3.1.

In figure 3A.1 we present average TFP patterns for exporting and domestic firms within different industries. Although the superiority of exporting firms is persistent over all industries, the productivity premium highly differs across industries. For instance, the productivity difference between exporters and domestic firms for the chemical industry is twice as large as for the beverage industry.

Figure 3.3 presents the age distribution of domestic and exporting firms. Clearly, exporting firms exhibit on average a higher age compared to domestic firms. Finally, figure 3.4 shows that women are underrepresented in the top management positions and more so among only exporters. About 60 percent of domestic firms don't have a woman among the top five executives, and this percentage increases to 65 percent for the exporting companies. Therefore, gender is of little or no concern as a cause of "behavioral disintegration" or "emotional conflict" within CEO groups in our data (Hambrick 1994).

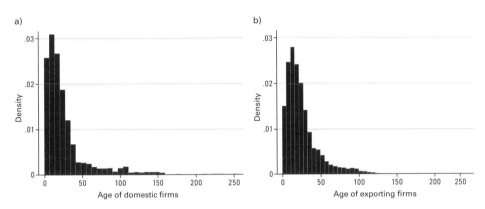

Figure 3.3a,b
Age distribution of exporting and domestic firms. *Note:* The age of a firm is measured in years.

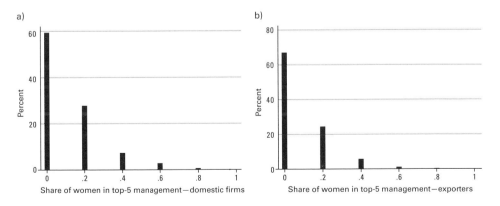

Figure 3.4a,b
Share of women in top five management positions. *Note:* The share of women among the top five executives is measured based on the top five earners in each company.

3.5. Results

We present the main results of our analysis in two tables. Both tables are figuratively divided into an upper part and a lower part by a horizontal line. Above the divide we list the control variables, referred to in equation (3.7) as the vector x; below the divide we include our measures for "managerial inputs," referred to in equation (3.7) as the vector m.

In the control variables in table 3.2, we have included *employment* as a measure of size, *labor productivity* as a measure of efficiency and *employees' wages* and the *share of white-collar workers* as measures of the quality of the labor forces. These are the same control variables used in our benchmark model by Bernard and Wagner (2001). In this model, the one- and two-period lagged export status (*L.Export* and *L2.Export*) proxy for export fixed cost.

Partly to avoid the econometric complexity of a lagged dependent variable and partly to root our analysis in the theory outlined previously, we prefer to proxy these fixed costs using the share of firms that within the same five-digit industry classification are also exporting (*industry export share*). Recall the interpretation of this variable as "organizational learning." Taking advantage of our accounting statistics (to which Bernard and Wagner [2001] did not have access), we prefer to use a TFP measure for productivity (*TFP_Olley_Pakes*). Finally, to alleviate collinearity between employment and wages, we use the *total capital* as a measure of size. These changes differentiate columns (3) and (4) from columns (1) and (2).

We augment this set of explicative variables that are commonly included in the workhorse empirical trade model with managerial inputs. These inputs, as argued previously, are the managers' international experience (*external promoted manager with export experience*) and the managers' education (*MBA Degree*); the *average age of managers* and the *share of foreign managers* measure the diversity of the management team and control for group dynamics.

Adding managerial inputs is the value added of our analysis, and these variables result generally positive and statistically significant: hiring or promoting a manager with exporting experience raises the probability for export of about 2 percent. We find that the effect of having an MBA education is slightly larger, but our interpretation is that these variables together are part of the manager's experience and form the firm's tacit knowledge.

To this point, it is interesting to note that international experience is the asset valued by firms. Mere managerial recruitment from other firms (*external promoted manager*) is unimportant, in line with Daily et al. 2000.

We expected that managers' education and international experience had a positive impact on the likelihood of exporting, given the tacit knowledge that these characteristics embed, but we are agnostic about the effect of age and nationality attributes. Their positive signs may indicate that on average, diversity is a contributing factor to strategic novelty for Danish manufacturing firms or, alternatively, that emotional conflict can resolve with time through iterative interactions. In terms of Barkema and Shvyrkov 2007, the results seem to offer support for hypothesis 1 or, otherwise stated, that the effects implied by their hypothesis 1 seems to prevail on the effects implied by their hypothesis 2.

These results are robust across the specifications presented: the coefficients preserve their sign and statistical significance regardless of whether the linear probability model or the probit model is used as estimation method and of whether the fixed costs are approximated following the Bernard and Wagner (2001) approach or our approach. The latter fact is probably not surprising if we briefly examine table 3A.1. In the first two columns of this table we present our benchmark model as estimated by Bernard and Wagner (2001) (column [1] and compare it with our approach (column [2]). The two approaches deliver remarkably similar results, implying that our strategy to measure fixed costs is equally effective. But their approach has the merit to reveal persistency of export behavior: the point estimate for *L.Export* is above 0.5, suggesting that the probability of exporting next year is 50 percent higher if the firm is already currently exporting. This probability drops to 22 percent in the pooled probit estimation and ranges and, depending on the specification, between 12 percent and 23 percent if the firm was exporting two years before. We conclude that Danish firms are confronted with substantial fixed costs for exporting and furthermore that these cost are depreciating over time. These numbers could be similarly interpreted in light of Kogut's (1997) suggestion that multiple entries concur to build up experience. The numerical interpretation of the coefficient of the *industry export share* is not as easy because the variable is a continuous variable and the coefficient, as it is specified in our regression, cannot be interpreted as an elasticity or as a semi-elasticity. Nevertheless, its effect in both table 3.2 and table 3A.1 is positive and statistically significant, confirming the importance of fixed costs and the exchange of information, formally through link-alliances

Table 3.2
Estimating the probability of exporting with manager characteristics, no firm-specific effects

Variables	(1) LP-OLS Export	(2) LP-OLS Export	(3) LP-OLS Export	(4) LP-OLS Export	(5) Probit marginal effects Export	(6) Probit marginal effects Export	(7) Probit marginal effects Export
L.Export	0.532***	0.532***			0.22***		
	(0.00905)	(0.00906)			(0.003)		
L2.Export	0.232***	0.232***			0.12***		
	(0.00889)	(0.00890)			(0.003)		
Log Total Employment	0.0200***	0.0207***			0.021***		
	(0.00151)	(0.00153)			(0.0016)		
Log Labor Productivity	0.0135***	0.0134***			0.013***		
	(0.00254)	(0.00255)			(0.002)		
Log Wage p. Worker	0.0216***	0.0198***	0.0641***	0.0607***	0.017***	0.044***	0.0378***
	(0.00637)	(0.00638)	(0.0063)	(0.0063)	(0.005)	(0.006)	(0.006)
White-collar	0.00066***	0.000717***	0.0009***	0.0009***	0.001***	0.003***	0.0033***
	(0.000148)	(0.000149)	(0.0002)	(0.000200)	(0.0001)	(0.0002)	(0.0001)
Industry export share			0.490***	0.490***		0.787***	0.79***
			(0.0595)	(0.0594)		(0.046)	(0.0458)
TFP Olley_Pakes			0.0810***	0.0827***		0.0457***	0.0474***
			(0.00541)	(0.00542)		(0.004)	(0.004)
Log total capital			0.0279***	0.0276***		0.0815***	0.082***
			(0.00410)	(0.00411)		(0.003)	(0.003)

Table 3.2
(continued)

Variables	(1) LP-OLS Export	(2) LP-OLS Export	(3) LP-OLS Export	(4) LP-OLS Export	(5) Probit marginal effects Export	(6) Probit marginal effects Export	(7) Probit marginal effects Export
External promoted manager with export experience	0.0209*** (0.00311)		0.0187*** (0.00278)		0.02*** (0.003)	0.0475*** (0.0039)	
Average age of top 5 managers	0.00110*** (0.0003)	0.000889*** (0.0003)	0.00176*** (0.0004)	0.00149*** (0.0004)	0.001*** (0.0003)	0.004*** (0.0003)	0.0034*** (0.0002)
MBA degree—manager	0.0902*** (0.00712)		0.0775*** (0.00468)	0.0580*** (0.00463)	–		
Share of foreigners in top 5	0.00614 (0.00394)	0.00566 (0.00394)	0.0188*** (0.00577)	0.0182*** (0.00578)	0.006 (0.004)	0.052*** (0.005)	0.052*** (0.005)
External Promoted Manager		0.00399 (0.00305)		−0.00392 (0.00272)			−0.003 (0.004)
Constant	−0.134*** (0.0345)	−0.111*** (0.0346)	−0.831*** (0.0715)	−0.792*** (0.0716)			
Year dummies	yes	yes	yes	yes	yes	yes	yes
Industry dummies	yes	yes	yes	yes	yes	yes	yes
Observations	32,480	32,480	54,676	54,676	32,479	54,674	54,674
Number of firms	6,063	6,063	6,761	6,761			
R^2	0.670	0.67	0.207	0.205	0.604 (pseudo)	0.204 (pseudo)	0.202 (pseudo)

Notes: Robust standard errors are given in parentheses and the statistical significance denoted with stars: *** = $p < 0.01$, ** = $p < 0.05$, * = $p < 0.1$. Coefficients represent change in probability of becoming an exporter, due to a one standard deviation increase in the explanatory variable.. In case of dummy variables, coefficients represent probability for a change from 0 to 1.

or informally through networking, for the internationalization process of the firm. We can also notice that its magnitude remain similar across the two tables as well as for the coefficient on *TFP*. These results are consistent with the predictions of the "new new trade theory," which emphasizes the productivity of the firm and the fixed costs as the main drivers to firms' internationalization.

A specification issue we have touched upon is the plausible endogeneity of *external promoted manager with export experience*. Although we have already admitted to have no cure for it, it is likely that lagging the explicative variables one period may attenuate this issue. As table 3A.3 shows, the results are generally confirmed, especially in terms of statistical significance. The coefficient of *external promoted manager with export experience* is almost halved, possibly confirming our suspicion about the endogeneity of this variable but also indicating that international experience may have persistent effects. In comparison, the magnitude of the coefficient of *TFP* is preserved, in congress with what we know from the studies on the "self-selection" hypothesis—that *TFP* antecedent to the years of exporting is important for selection into foreign markets. Finally, the significance of the lagged *industry export share* is consistent with our prediction that this variable may be suitable to capture, to a partial extent, firms' exchange of knowledge, which does not vanish rapidly in the years.

Perhaps more relevant to a causal analysis in this context is controlling for unobserved heterogeneity, allowing managerial inputs and the other explicative variables to be correlated with unobserved characteristics. Table 3.3 extends the estimations in table 3.2, including firms' fixed effects in columns (1) and (2) and using the first-difference transformation in column (3).

These are our preferred specifications, and the general figures are confirmed: both productivity and fixed costs on one side and international experience and education on the other side have a positive impact on the likelihood that firms export, regardless of the type of estimator used (fixed effect or first difference). Note how the point estimates of *TFP*, *export industry share*, and *external promotion with exporting experience*, all statistically significant, drop compared to those in table 3.2. If we interpret these time-invariant unobservables to be factors such as business culture or formal institution regulations (laws and regulations), presumably fairly constant over our time span, the positive difference between the ordinary least squares (OLS) estimator and the FE estimator indicate that these factors are likely to be positively correlated with some of our explicative variables (such as international experience), a plausible scenario in our view.[18]

On the contrary, the variables capturing group dynamics (the *average age of the management team* and the *share of foreign in the team*) confirm their statistically positive sign only for the fixed effect estimator and are insignificant with the first difference estimator. There are a number of reasons for this result. One possible argument is related to the nature of the error term: if the error term is serially correlated rather than following a random walk, the FE estimator result is more efficient than the FD estimator.[19]

Attributes that we have referred to as "quality" of the labor force, namely, the *share of white-collar* and *highly skilled* employees, lose significance. This finding indicates that part of the unobserved heterogeneity is related to these characteristics of the workforce. This is also the case when we compare columns (1) and (2) in table 3A.2 with column (2) in table 3A.1. Continuing with the comparison of table 3A.2 with table 3.3, note how similar the coefficients are on *TFP* and *export industry share*. The fact that their magnitude does not respond to the inclusion or exclusion of managerial characteristics just strengthens the findings of the literature on the self-selection hypothesis.

We mentioned that gender differences in the management team was of little concern in our analysis as a possible driver of emotional conflict or other group dynamics, mostly because of the scarce presence of women in the top positions (itself an interesting topic!). Table 3A.4 includes *the share of women* in the management team but no result is quantitatively or qualitatively affected.

In this section, we have commented only on the results from our linear probability model. The reason lies on the possibility of comparing all results with the specifications for which we can account explicitly for unobservable heterogeneity. However, for completeness of the analysis, we present in all tables maximum likelihood estimation (either a probit or a logit model, fixed or random effects): it is comforting that the estimates from these models confirm all our findings while properly dealing with the discrete nature of our dependent variable. Overall, the fact that our results do not depend on the choice of the estimation method make us also comfortable that they are not attributable to a particular distribution assumption underlying the maximum likelihood estimators.

We interpret our results in favor of what in the introduction we have called the *complementary hypothesis*. The findings from the self-selection

Table 3.3
Export market entry probability with managerial characteristics and firm-specific effects

Variables	(1) FE Export	(2) FE Export	(3) FD D.Export	(4) IV-FD D.Export	(5) Logit marginal effects Export	(6) RE-probit marginal effects Export
L.Export				0.103** (0.0494)		
L2.Export				– (–)		
Log total capital	0.01** (0.0045)	0.0102** (0.004)	0.00581 (0.005)	−0.00406 (0.00420)	0.034** (0.0155)	0.0394*** (0.0055)
TFP Olley_Pakes	0.0821*** (0.007)	0.0839*** (0.007)	0.0415*** (0.007)	0.0429*** (0.00790)	0.09** (0.04)	0.1029*** (0.011)
Log wages p. worker	0.0613*** (0.006)	0.0583*** (0.007)	0.0334*** (0.006)	0.0260*** (0.00679)	0.067** (0.03)	0.0761*** (0.0097)
White-collar worker	0.000296 (0.0002)	0.000329 (0.0002)	−0.000309 (0.0002)	−4.55e−05 (0.000201)	0.001** (0.0004)	0.0011*** (0.0002)
Highly skilled worker	0.0002** (0.0001)	−0.0001 (0.0002)	−0.000134 (0.000)	−4.21e−05 (0.000)	0.0002* (0.0001)	0.0003*** (0.0001)
Industry export share	0.369*** (0.066)	0.368*** (0.066)	0.304*** (0.0500)		0.6187** (0.2817)	0.7041*** (0.0986)
External promoted manager with export experience	0.0152*** (0.00281)		0.0106*** (0.00253)	0.003 (0.00226)	0.020** (0.0096)	0.023*** (0.004)

Table 3.3
(continued)

Variables	(1) FE Export	(2) FE Export	(3) FD D.Export	(4) IV-FD D.Export	(5) Logit marginal effects Export	(6) RE-probit marginal effects Export
Average age of top 5 managers	0.0011*** (0.0004)	0.0009** (0.0004)	0.0002 (0.0003)	-0.0003 (0.0003)	0.002** (0.001)	0.0025*** (0.0004)
MBA degree—manager	0.0198*** (0.005)	0.00145 (0.004)	0.0178*** (0.005)	– (–)	0.08 (0.004)	0.0822 (0.005)
Share of foreigners in top 5	0.0141** (0.006)	0.0136** (0.006)	0.00701 (0.005)	0.0136*** (0.005)	0.019* (0.009)	0.0213*** (0.006)
External promoted manager		-0.00428 (0.00275)				
Constant	-0.319*** (0.0932)	-0.286*** (0.0930)	-0.00354 (0.00442)	-0.0114*** (0.00204)		
Year dummies	yes	yes	yes	yes	yes	yes
Industry dummies	yes	yes	yes	yes	yes	yes
Observations	54,676	54,676	47,254	19,357	54,676	54,676
Number of senr	6,761	6,761	6,404	3,672	6,761	6,761
R^2	0.017	0.017	0.0111	0.0507		

Notes: Robust standard errors a given in parentheses and the statistical significance denoted with stars: *** $= p < 0.01$, ** $= p < 0.05$, * $= p < 0.1$ Coefficients represent change in probability of becoming an exporter, due to a one standard deviation increase in the explanatory variable. In case of dummy variables, coefficients represent probability for a change from 0 to 1.

hypothesis are confirmed, as productivity and the fixed cost of exporting prove to be strong predictors of the likelihood of the start of exporting, even controlling for managerial inputs. At the same time, and
despite the highlighted weakness of our approach, some of the channels
advocated by the management literature find support across a considerable number of observations and a relative long period of time, indicating the desirability of more empirical research in this direction as well.

3.6. Conclusion

Although it is empirically successful and important, the self-selection
hypothesis—that only a "happy few" firms successfully export—
proves to be shallow for the understanding of the factors underlying
the capacity of the firm to expand the range of its activities into foreign
markets.[20] To enrich the standard workhorse empirical model of international trade, this article draws on the richness of international business studies and the resource-based view of the firm as to the drivers
of this internationalization process.

The working hypothesis is that exporting is, from the firm's perspective, a complex investment involving sunk and fixed costs and therefore commands substantial managerial inputs in terms of business and
financial planning. In particular, we identify two inputs that we can
also measure empirically: the formal and informal information exchange
and managers' international experience. Empirically, our effort was
directed at measuring these distinct elements. We believe our biggest
achievement to be the reconstruction of the managers' personal records,
which traced their international experience. We have in addition gath-
ered data on managers' education, on their age, on their gender, and
on their nationality—all attributes that influence social processes and
group dynamics.

Our results suggest that managerial inputs are important to the
internationalization process of the firm and that they also indicate that
the selection arising from the firms' hiring process of managers should
be properly modeled to discern the causal impact of management.
Given that the self-selection hypothesis is, once more, strongly confirmed, our results suggest complementarity and reciprocal strengthen-
ing between the factors that underlay the internationalization of firms
in the two strands of the literature. The challenge for future research is
to link these aspects together, hopefully into a sound causality frame-

work. We foresee this challenge as an opportunity to go beyond the self-selection hypothesis and to deepen the understanding of the drivers of this selection mechanism.

The difficulty of introducing managerial inputs into the analysis is represented by the fact that managers' international experience is a highly valuable tacit resource for the firm and is difficult to acquire without hiring new managers with those prerequisites. The econometrician, however, cannot observe firms' intentions and therefore cannot discern whether a firm is starting to export because it has promoted new managers or because it has hired new managers for the reason that it intended to export. The discernibility of these two equally plausible events hinder our analysis from establishing a causal link between managerial input and the internationalization process of the firm. Such discernibility represents the challenge of future research. What one would need to address this issue is some policy discontinuity that affects the hiring process but not the export opportunity. As an example of a quasi experimental event, let us just imagine that several countries (unexpectedly) block expatriates of managers toward Denmark or that Denmark restricts border access to foreign managers or MBA students, so that the Danish firms' ability to acquire international knowledge is restricted but their export potential is not.

Lacking such an experimental value, we present our results with lagged regressors that, if not solved, attenuate this problem—a strategy followed by our benchmark model as well. The results prove to be robust to this change, which is encouraging for future research on this topic.

As trade economists, we hope that this empirical study can be appreciated, from the perspective of the management literature, with regard to the scope of the analysis, which comprises the population of the Danish manufacturing firms. Thereby, our dataset is larger than the one typically characterizing empirical contributions in the management literature but compromises, for some aspects, the available set of specific variables. Yet we judge our data as innovatively rich from the perspective of the empirical trade literature.

Generally, we regard the richness of international business studies and the resource-based view of the firm as both an asset and an opportunity for empirical work in international economics, as both disciplines seem to converge toward interest about the motives of firms' internationalization.

Appendix

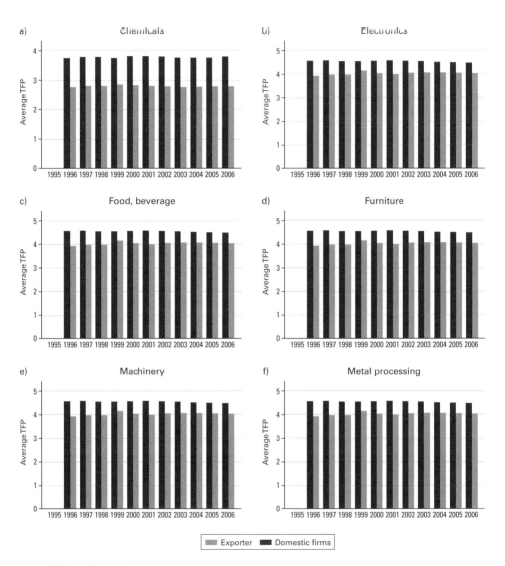

Figure 3A.1a–m
Average TFP in different industries. *Note:* Average TFP in each sector is measured following Olley and Pakes 1996.

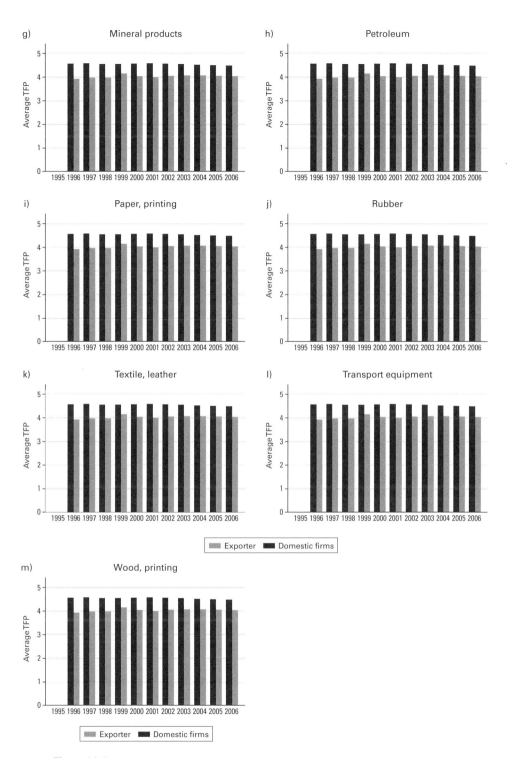

Figure 3A.1
(continued)

Table 3A.1
Estimating the probability of exporting, without firm-specific effects

Variables	(1) LP-OLS	(2) LP-OLS	(3) Pooled probit marginal effects	(4) Pooled probit marginal effects
	Export	Export	Export	Export
L.Export	0.533***		0.222***	
	(0.00906)		(0.0032)	
L2.Export	0.232***		0.121***	
	(0.00889)		(0.0036)	
Log total employment	0.0216***		0.0220***	
	(0.00149)		(0.0016)	
Log labor productivity	0.0134***		0.0168***	
	(0.00255)		(0.0052)	
Log wage p. worker	0.0211***	0.0626***	0.0127***	0.044***
	(0.00635)	(0.00625)	(0.00219	0.005
White-collar worker	0.00074***	0.00093***	0.0008***	0.0033***
	(0.000148)	(0.000200)	(0.0002)	0.0001
Log total capital		0.0281***		0.085***
		(0.00411)		0.003
TFP_Olley_Pakes		0.0820***		0.0445***
		(0.00542)		0.0038
Industry export share		0.491***		0.818***
		(0.0594)		0.046
Constant	−0.0802**	−0.739***		
	(0.0330)	(0.0703)		
Year dummies	yes	yes	yes	yes
Industry dummies	yes	yes	yes	yes
Observations	32,480	54,676	32,480	54,676
Number of firms	6,063	6,761		
R^2	0.669	0.202	0.603 pseudo	0.199 pseudo

Notes: Robust standard errors are given in parentheses and the statistical significance denoted with stars: *** = $p < 0.01$, ** = $p < 0.05$, * = $p < 0.1$. Coefficients represent change in probability of becoming an exporter, due to a one standard deviation increase in the explanatory variable. In case of dummy variables coefficients represent probability for a change from 0 to 1.

Table 3A.2
Export market entry probability with firm-specific effects

Variables	(1) FE Export	(2) FD D.Export	(3) IV-FD D.Export	(4) Logit marginal effects Export	(5) RE-probit marginal effects Export
L.Export			0.102**		
			(0.0495)		
L2.Export			–		
			(–)		
Log total capital	0.0107**	0.00559	−0.00278	0.0343***	0.0395***
	(0.00456)	(0.00457)	(0.00417)	(0.00376)	0.00436
TFP_Olley_Pakes	0.0816***	0.0440***	0.0389***	0.0907***	0.1034***
	(0.00742)	(0.00764)	(0.00771)	(0.00596)	0.00696
Log wage p. worker	0.0583***	0.0325***	0.0229***	0.0650***	0.0738***
	(0.00689)	(0.00675)	(0.00673)	(0.00627)	0.00722
White-collar worker	0.000440*	−0.000280	−5.09e−05	0.0011***	0.0012***
	(0.000225)	(0.000206)	(0.000199)	(0.00018)	0.00021
Highly skilled worker	0.000265**	−0.000122	−6.29e−05	0.0002***	0.0002***
	(0.000104)	(9.63e−05)	(9.28e−05)	(0.00008)	0.00009
Industry export share	0.367***	0.305***		0.6236***	0.7075***
	(0.0667)	(0.0500)		(0.06791)	0.07839
Constant	−0.261***	−0.00309	−0.0113***		
	(0.0917)	(0.00441)	(0.00203)		
Year dummies	yes	yes	yes	yes	yes
Industry dummies	yes	yes	yes	yes	yes
Observations	54,676	47,254	19,357	54,676	54,676
Number of firms	6,761	6,404	3,672	6,761	6,761
R^2	0.016	0.00357	0.0746		

Notes: Robust standard errors are given in parentheses and the statistical significance denoted with stars: *** = $p < 0.01$, ** = $p < 0.05$, * = $p < 0.1$. Coefficients represent change in probability of becoming an exporter, due to a one standard deviation increase in the explanatory variable. In case of dummy variables, coefficients represent probability for a change from 0 to 1.

Table 3A.3
Lagged estimation for probability of exporting with manager variables, no firm-specific effects

Variables	(1) LP-OLS Export	(2) LP-OLS Export	(3) LP-OLS Export	(4) LP-OLS Export	(5) Probit Export	(6) Probit Export
L.Export	0.530***					
	(0.00857)					
L2.Export	0.225***					
	(0.00845)					
L.Log total employment	0.0231***					
	(0.00150)					
L.Log labor productivity	0.0118***					
	(0.00244)					
L.Log wage p. worker	0.00756	0.0341***	0.0325***	0.0340***	0.0863***	0.104***
	(0.00673)	(0.00666)	(0.00667)	(0.00667)	(0.0224)	(0.0227)
L.white collar	0.000856***	0.00119***	0.00120***	0.00119***	0.0121***	0.0120***
	(0.000141)	(0.000226)	(0.000226)	(0.000226)	(0.000707)	(0.000707)
L.Industry Export Share		0.242***	0.242***	0.242***	2.239***	2.246***
		(0.0456)	(0.0455)	(0.0456)	(0.148)	(0.148)
L.TFP Olley_Pakes		0.0804***	0.0811***	0.0802***	0.161***	0.170***
		(0.00584)	(0.00585)	(0.00590)	(0.0146)	(0.0148)
L.Log total capital		0.0282***	0.0281***	0.0282***	0.291***	0.296***
		(0.00430)	(0.00430)	(0.00430)	(0.0128)	(0.0129)
L.External promoted manager with export experience	0.00819***	0.0102***	0.0102***	0.0102***	0.155***	0.159***
	(0.00287)	(0.00284)	(0.00285)	(0.00285)	(0.0149)	(0.0149)

Table 3A.3
(continued)

Variables	(1) LP-OLS Export	(2) LP-OLS Export	(3) LP-OLS Export	(4) LP-OLS Export	(5) Probit Export	(6) Probit Export
L.Average age of top 5 managers	0.00103***	0.00184***	0.00172***	0.00184***	0.0124***	0.0120***
	(0.000272)	(0.000418)	(0.000420)	(0.000418)	(0.00108)	(0.00108)
L.MBA degree—manager	0.0860***	0.0901***	0.0811***	0.0898***	—	—
	(0.00602)	(0.00531)	(0.00530)	(0.00558)		
L.Share of foreigners in top 5	0.00338	0.00295	0.00270	0.00296	0.154***	0.150***
	(0.00395)	(0.00587)	(0.00587)	(0.00587)	(0.0197)	(0.0197)
L.Share of women in top 5				-0.00291	—	0.240***
				(0.0148)		(0.0364)
Constant	-0.0487	-0.471***	-0.454***	-0.470***	-7.394***	-7.626***
	(0.0353)	(0.0680)	(0.0682)	(0.0683)	(0.199)	(0.203)
Year dummies	yes	yes	yes	yes	yes	yes
Industry dummies	yes	yes	yes	yes	yes	yes
Observations	36,984	47,585	47,585	47,585	47,583	47,583
Number of firms	6,477	6,432	6,432	6,432		
R^2	0.676	0.206	0.205	0.206	0.205 (pseudo)	0.206 (pseudo)

Notes: Robust standard errors are given in parentheses and the statistical significance denoted with stars: *** $= p < 0.01$, ** $= p < 0.05$, * $= p < 0.1$. Standard errors are denoted in parentheses. Coefficients represent change in probability of becoming an exporter, due to a one standard deviation increase in the explanatory variable. Marginal effects are not denoted.

Table 3A.4
Export market entry probability with managerial characteristics and firm-specific effects

Variables	(1) FE Export	(2) FE Export	(3) FD Export	(4) Logit Export	(5) RE-probit Export
L.Export		0.205***			
		(0.0127)			
L2.Export		0.0117			
		(0.00983)			
Log total employment		0.0377***			
		(0.00888)			
Log labor productivity		0.00771			
		(0.00480)			
Industry export share	0.368***		0.304***	8.397***	4.636***
	(0.0668)		(0.0500)	(0.836)	(0.467)
Log total capital	0.0104**		0.00579	0.462***	0.259***
	(0.00456)		(0.00457)	(0.0457)	(0.0255)
TFP Olley_Pakes	0.0815***		0.0411***	1.222***	0.676***
	(0.00743)		(0.00763)	(0.0611)	(0.0338)
Log wages p. worker	0.0611***	0.0336***	0.0333***	0.909***	0.501***
	(0.00689)	(0.00961)	(0.00675)	(0.0758)	(0.0422)
White-collar worker	0.000301	0.000258	−0.000308	0.0140***	0.00769***
	(0.000220)	(0.000286)	(0.000205)	(0.00239)	(0.00133)
Highly skilled worker			−0.000135	0.00293***	0.00165***
			(9.63e−05)	(0.00108)	(0.000610)
External promoted manager with export experience	0.0151***	0.0123***	0.0105***	0.288***	0.161***
	(−0.00282)	(0.00327)	(0.00254)	(0.0432)	(0.0243)
Average age of top 5 managers	0.00115***	0.00124**	0.000216	0.0301***	0.0168***
	(0.000420)	(0.000505)	(0.000383)	(0.00457)	(0.00258)
MBA degree—manager	0.0173***		0.0163***	17.62	5.570
	(0.00508)		(0.00494)	(14,395)	(1,681)
Share of foreigners in top 5	0.0141**		0.00697	0.279***	0.152***
	(0.00611)		(0.00498)	(0.0761)	(0.0431)
Share of women in top 5	−0.0175		−0.0134	−0.0857	−0.0439
	(0.0157)		(0.0140)	(0.157)	(0.0890)
Constant	−0.313***	0.146*	−0.00348	−21.49***	−11.92***
	(0.0934)	(0.0836)	(0.00442)	(0.930)	(0.519)
Year dummies	yes	yes	yes	yes	yes
Industry dummies	yes	yes	yes	yes	yes
Observations	54,676	32,480	47,254	54,676	54,676
Number of firms	6,761	6,063	6,404	6,761	6,761
R^2	0.017	0.050	0.0112		

Notes: Robust standard errors are given in parentheses and the statistical significance denoted with stars: *** = $p < 0.01$, ** = $p < 0.05$, * = $p < 0.1$ Standard errors are denoted in parentheses. Coefficients represent change in probability of becoming an exporter, due to a one standard deviation increase in the explanatory variable. Marginal effects are not denoted.

Notes

The authors acknowledge CESifo's financial sponsorship. Erdal Yalcin thanks Aarhus University for hosting him while working on this paper. The authors thank an anonymous referee for his or her thorough and inspiring comments.

1. In chapter 1, Rugman and Nguyen discuss other causes on the "distance" between the fields of international economics and international business. However, in the introduction of this book emerges an increasing effort in international economics to incorporate insights from the international business.

2. See Mion and Opromolla 2011 for evidence on Portugal.

3. This formulation follows Atkeson and Kehoe 2005.

4. In Lucas 1978, this is the *span of control parameter*, so that when the allocation of managers to firms is endogenously determined, one manager—even the most talented one—cannot manage all companies simultaneously.

5. For simplicity, we abstain from considering the domestic activity of the firm, as our purpose is to analyze the forces that determine selection into an export market.

6. The variable profit v is also the manager's income in this formulation.

7. See Dixit and Pindiyck 1994. See also Li and Rugman 2007 for an application of the real option theory to FDI.

8. See Jorgenson 1963. Mathematically, this condition expresses the first order condition to the optimal entry time, $t = argmax[V(v_0, t) - I_E e^{-rt}]$. See Sala et al. 2010 for more details.

9. The logit model is a special case with $G(z) = \Lambda(z) = \exp(z)/[1 + \exp(z)]$.

10. Bernard and Jensen (2004) follow also Bernard and Wagner 2001.

11. The reader may note the similarity of this argument with the one proposed in chapter 6 by Mayneris and Poncet.

12. We are grateful to Smith et al. (2008), who first compiled data on CEO boards and shared this information with us.

13. In Krautheim 2007, the return to networking among domestic exporters is the reduced fixed cost of exporting and the higher this return, the larger the network, as measured by the fraction of exporting companies.

14. We prefer this option to using the occupational code, also available, as Smith et al. (2008) cast some doubts on its reliability. Nevertheless, the two strategies yield highly correlated definitions.

15. Hambrick and Mason (1984) think of management as a shared effort of the management team as a whole, rather than solely the experience of the CEO of the company.

16. We opt for the highest education as a measure of the team's education because we observe the years of education, not the type of education, most reliably and extensively. Therefore, a proper measure of education diversity is hard to build.

17. We define a worker to be highly skilled if his or her codified occupational status falls into a specified range.

18. See Peng and Heath 1996 for a discussion on formal institutional constraints versus informal constitutional constraints and their impact on firms' performance.

19. Another argument, which is negative for our estimates, would be related to the violation of the strict exogeneity assumption for these variables, but in our view, the point estimates are rather close to support this conjecture.

20. Mayer and Ottaviano (2007) refer to successfully exporting firms as the "happy few."

References

Atkeson, A., and P. J. Kehoe. 2005. Modeling and measuring organizational capital. *Journal of Political Economy* 113 (5): 1026–1053.

Barkema, H., and O. Shvyrkov. 2007. Does top management team diversity promote or hamper foreign expansion? *Strategic Management Journal* 28 (7):663–680.

Bell, L. 2005. Women-led firms and the gender wage gap in top executive jobs. IZA Discussion Paper, no. 1689.

Bernard, A. B., and J. B. Jensen. 1999. Exceptional exporter performance: Cause, effect, or both? *Journal of International Economics* 47:1–25.

Bernard, A. B., and J. B. Jensen. 2004. Why some firms export. *Review of Economics and Statistics* 86 (2): 561–569.

Bernard, A. B., and J. Wagner. 2001. Export entry and exit by German firms. *Review of World Economics* 137 (1): 105–123.

Bertola, G. 2010. Options, inaction and uncertainty. *Scottish Journal of Political Economy* 52 (3): 1268–1290.

Carpenter, M., W. G. Sanders, and H. Gregersen. 2001. Building human capital with organizational context: The impact of international assignment experience on multinational firm performance and CEO pay. *Academy of Management Journal* 44 (3): 493–511.

Caves, R. 1996. *Multinational Enterprise and Economic Analysis*. 2nd ed. New York: Cambridge University Press.

Daily, C., S. Certo, and D. Dalton. 2000. International experience in the executive suite: The path to prosperity? *Strategic Management Journal* 21 (4): 515–523.

Datta, D. K., and P. Herrmann. 2006. CEO experiences: Effects on the choice of FDI entry mode. *Journal of Management Studies* 43 (4): 756–778.

Dicken, P. 1992. *Global Shift: The Internationalization of Economic Activity*. London: Paul Chapman.

Dixit, A. K., and R. S. Pindyck. 1994. *Investment under Uncertainty*. Princeton: Princeton University Press.

Dunning, J. 1993. *Multinational Enterprises and the Global Economy*. Wokingham, UK: Addison-Wesley.

Garicano, L. 2000. Hierarchies and the organization of knowledge in production. *Journal of Political Economy* 108 (5): 874–904.

Hambrick, D. C. 1994. Top management groups: A conceptual integration and reconsideration of the "team" label. In *Research in Organizational Behavior*, vol. 16, ed. B. M. Staw and L. L. Cummings, 171–213. Greenwich, CT: JAI Press.

Hambrick, D. C., and P. A. Mason. 1984. Upper echelons: The organization as a reflection of its top managers. *Academy of Management Review* 9 (2): 193–206.

Hamel, G. 1991. Competition for competence and interpartner learning within international strategic alliances. *Strategic Management Journal* 12 (S1): 83–103.

Jehn, K. A. 1997. A qualitative analysis of conflict types and dimensions in organizational groups. *Administrative Science Quarterly* 42:530–557.

Jehn, K. A., G. B. Northcraft, and M. A. Neale. 1999. Why differences make difference: A field study of diversity, conflict, and performance in workgroups. *Administrative Science Quarterly* 44:741–763.

Jorgenson, D. W. 1963. Capital theory and investment behavior. *American Economic Review* 53 (2): 247–259.

Kogut, B. 1997. The evolutionary theory of the multinational corporation. In *International Business: An Emerging Vision*, ed. B. Toyne and D. Nigh, 470–488. Columbia, SC: University of South Carolina Press.

Krautheim, S. 2007. Gravity and information: Heterogeneous firms, exporter networks and the distance puzzle. EUI Working Paper 2007/51.

Leonidou, L. C., C. S. Katsikeas, and N. F. Piercy. 1998. Identifying managerial influences on exporting: past research and future directions. *Journal of International Marketing* 6 (2): 74–102.

Li, J., and A. M. Rugman. 2007. Real options and the theory of foreign direct investment. *International Business Review* 16 (6): 687–712.

Lucas, R. E., Jr. 1978. On the size distribution of business firms. *Bell Journal of Economics* 9 (2): 508–523.

Mayer, T. and Ottaviano, G. 2007. The happy few: New facts about the internationalization of European firms. CEPR Policy Insight No. 15.

Melitz, M. J. 2003. The impact of trade on intra-industry reallocations and aggregate industry productivity. *Econometrica* 71 (6): 1695–1725.

Mion, G., and L. Opromolla. 2011. Managers' mobility, trade status, and wages. Banco de Portugal working paper.

Mitchell, R., B. Smith, K. Seawright, and E. Morse. 2000. Cross-cultural cognitions and the venture creation decision. *Academy of Management Journal* 43 (5): 974–993.

Olley, S. J., and A. Pakes. 1996. The dynamics of productivity in the telecommunications equipment industry. *Econometrica* 64 (6): 1263–1297.

Peng, M. W. 2001. The resource-based view and international business. *Journal of Management* 27:803–829.

Peng, M. W., and P. Heath. 1996. The growth of the firm in planned economies in transition: Institutions, organizations, and strategic choice. *Academy of Management Review* 21 (2): 492–528.

Peng, M. W., and A. York. 2001. Behind intermediary performance in export trade: Transactions, agents, and resources. *Journal of International Business Studies* 32 (2): 327–346.

Roberts, M., and J. Tybout. 1997. The decision to export in Colombia: an empirical model of entry with sunk costs. *American Economic Review* 87 (4): 545–564.

Rugman, A. M., A. Verbeke, and Q. Nguyen. 2011. Fifty years of international business theory and beyond. *Management International Review* 51 (6): 755–786.

Sala, D., P. Schröder, and E. Yalcin. 2010. Market access through bound tariffs. *Scottish Journal of Political Economy* 57 (3): 272–289.

Smith, N., V. Smith, and M. Verner. 2008. Gender differences in promotion into top-management jobs. Aarhus Business School Working Paper, 08–21.

Wagner, J. 2007. Exports and productivity: A survey of the evidence from firm-level data. *The World Economy* 30 (1): 60–82.

II Firm-Environment Interaction

4   Foreign Firms and Local Communities

Bruce Blonigen and Cheyney O'Fallon

Toyota has been reluctant to start its own manufacturing facility in the United States. Its biggest concern is whether it can transplant its highly efficient manufacturing system into a different cultural context.
—Steve Lohr, *New York Times*, March 9, 1982

4.1   Introduction

The effect of foreign direct investment (FDI) on host countries is a topic of much interest to both the academic community and policymakers. FDI has been growing faster than trade over the past couple decades, and multinational enterprises (MNEs) are often seen as potential drivers of innovation and growth not only for the world economy, but especially for the locations where MNE affiliates reside. Indeed, locations often compete for FDI through lowered tax rates and other incentives.[1]

In this chapter, we first provide an overview of the main topics covered by prior literature on the effects of FDI on host countries, which have primarily examined the effects on host country productivity, growth, and wages.[2] An important focus in this literature is the extent to which foreign-owned firms differ in their impacts relative to domestic-owned firms. If there are no significant differences in the behavior and impacts of foreign-owned firms, then there is little reason to separately examine FDI from total private corporate investment. What is interesting to us is that although this topic seems to be very ripe for firm-level international business (IB) work, it has mainly been addressed by the international economics (IE) literature using country- and industry-level data.

We then discuss how many topics connected with FDI and host countries have been left unexplored to this point by both the IE and IB literature, particularly ones that examine how foreign firms and local communities interact, and how these interactions may vary from those between domestic firms and local communities. For example, foreign firms may have different political goals than domestic firms, leading to differences in behavior. Relatedly, investment by foreign firms can be polarizing for a local community, which may affect optimal behavior by both the MNE and the local government.[3] As another example, cultural differences may matter across many various dimensions. Firms may face more difficult challenges to finding suitable workers because of such cultural differences and, relatedly, may request different worker training incentives from local governments. They may also differ in the way they organize production due to corporate management differences and therefore request different local infrastructure from governments as well. All of these differences can then lead to quite different impacts of foreign-owned firms on local communities versus those of domestic-owned firms.

As an illustration, we provide an analysis of differences in local corporate philanthropy using data on corporate gifts to local chapters of the United Way (UW) organization, a predominant charity organization in the United States whose local chapters coordinate giving to other charities in their communities. Our analysis finds statistically significant evidence that foreign-owned firms differ substantially from domestic-owned firms in their local corporate philanthropy. Foreign-owned firms are less likely to give. However, the non-European foreign-owned firms in our sample give proportionately more when they do give to local charities, and this is particularly true for the larger plants. The overall pattern is consistent with the notion that foreign firms are less interested in giving to local charities, but some of them do so when they have a high profile in the community and must overcome local polarization.

4.2   A Brief Review of the Literature on the Effects of FDI on Host Countries

The earliest empirical literature on the effect of FDI on host countries primarily consists of a more macroeconomic focus on how FDI affects GDP growth of the countries hosting the FDI. This type of approach, as discussed in chapter 1, is very much an IE approach to these topics.

However, this focus naturally brought about both theoretical and empirical analysis to understand microeconomic foundations of how

FDI could affect country-level growth. The theoretical side provided models about how foreign firms bring technology that could ultimately spill over and diffuse through the host country (e.g., see Findlay 1978). As richer data—particularly plant-level data—became available, empirical analyses of productivity spillovers became feasible, leading to a virtual cottage industry analyzing this topic over the past two decades. Availability of plant-level data also allowed researchers to examine differences in wages across foreign- and domestic-owned firms, with ever more sophisticated work to understand whether foreign firms pay higher wages even when controlling for firm and worker characteristics. A major empirical hurdle inherent in all of these topics is endogeneity: are foreign-owned firms affecting host countries in these dimensions or are they simply drawn to countries with these attributes? Interestingly, this evolution of the literature into firm- and plant-level data should naturally interface nicely with comparative IB approaches, which hasn't yet happened. Thus, we think establishment-level analysis is an important area of study that would naturally be an intersection point for the IB and IE literatures.

Lipsey (2004) provides an excellent review of the effects of FDI and economic activity of MNEs on host countries from an IE perspective. In the rest of this chapter, we characterize his summary of the literature at the time he wrote and highlight important developments since 2004, with an eye toward where IB approaches would be quite useful.

4.2.1   FDI Effects on Host Country Growth

Initial work to estimate the effect of FDI and host country growth using country-level data found mixed evidence at best for a significant relationship. However, more recent evidence has found positive effects of FDI on growth for particular circumstances, including when the country has a high enough level of development (Borensztein et al. 1998) or well-developed financial markets and institutions (Durham 2004 and Alfaro et al. 2004). However, there has also been recent studies by Carkovic and Levine (2005), Chowdhury and Mavrotas (2006), Hansen and Rand (2006), and Herzer et al. (2008), which used advanced econometric techniques to control for endogeneity and find no robust evidence for FDI effects on growth, even under these more particular circumstances. In general, this literature seems to have run out of steam, perhaps because the endogeneity issues make it difficult to draw strong conclusions.

4.2.2   FDI Productivity Spillovers in Host Countries

The inconclusiveness of FDI growth studies is a main reason why the recent literature has turned its focus to productivity of foreign-owned firms and the possibility that their productivity spills over to domestic firms in the host country. Often, turning to micro-level data can help alleviate or eliminate endogeneity concerns that exist with macro-level data, but not in this case. A finding that there is a positive correlation between foreign firm presence in a host country and productivity of domestically owned firms can still suffer from endogeneity bias that is difficult to eliminate—for instance, the foreign firm may have been attracted to that country because of some third factor that is driving higher productivity for all firms in the country.

One clear fact that has been verified by the literature is that foreign firms are generally more productive than the average domestic firm. However, when one controls for other firm characteristics, it is no longer as clear that foreign firms are different from domestic firms. In fact, the evidence suggests that it is the attributes of MNEs in general, not ownership nationality, that leads them to be more productive than other firms. This is another issue that is not always fully considered by previous literature—identifying whether MNEs have differing impacts on the host country because they are from a different country (i.e., due to country-level attributes) or because they have firm-level attributes that led them to be an MNE in the first place. This issue obviously matters for policy. Should a host country encourage foreign-owned companies to locate in their economy or encourage MNE presence, including their own domestic-based MNEs?

Although there are clear productivity differences with MNEs, the evidence for positive spillovers from foreign firms to domestic firms has been very mixed, despite hundreds of studies on the topic, particularly for what are termed horizontal spillovers—those between firms in the same industry. A meta-analysis by Görg and Greenaway (2004, 23) concludes that "only limited evidence in support of positive spillovers has been reported. Most work fails to find positive spillovers, with some even reporting negative spillovers, at the aggregate level."

A resuscitation of the literature came with Javorcik 2004, which finds strong evidence for a vertical backward linkage spillover effect, that is, a positive impact of foreign firms on domestic-owned upstream suppliers to foreign firms in the host country. There have been many follow-up studies estimating both vertical backward and forward linkage spillovers using different countries and settings. Havranek and

Irsova (2010) perform a meta-analysis of these many estimates in the literature and conclude that there is evidence for a significant positive vertical backward linkage spillover, a statistically significant but trivial effect for a vertical forward linkage, and no evidence for horizontal spillovers.

This literature seems to be reaching serious diminishing marginal returns as well, though there have been some recent work that looks at new avenues to understand the micro-level foundations for spillovers via foreign firms. For example, Branstetter (2006) uses patent data to examine the flows of knowledge to and from Japanese-owned firms in the United States.

4.2.3   FDI Effects on Wages in Host Countries

Initial work in this area was empirical and established that foreign firms pay substantially higher wages than domestic-owned firms (see, e.g., Aitken et al. 1996). These "foreign premiums" for wages fall some but are still substantial when controlling for firm characteristics, which contrasts with productivity spillover differences that are insignificant once one controls for firm characteristics, as discussed previously. More recent work has examined the next question of whether the wage premium exists, controlling for the same worker attributes—or even the same worker. OECD 2008 provides a more recent review of literature in this area.

An interesting innovation is the use of matched firm-employee data to examine wage changes for individuals after a domestic-owned firm is acquired by a foreign-owned firm or when a worker switches between a domestic-owned and foreign-owned firm (see, e.g., Heyman, Sjöholm, and Tingvall 2007). Although they are not ideal natural experiments, these studies get much closer than previous ones to truly identifying a treatment effect of foreign ownership on wages. The wage premium found in these studies is much smaller and often not significantly different from zero.

4.3   New Directions for Examining the Impact of Foreign Firms on Host Countries

Although much has been learned from the examination of FDI and MNEs on growth, productivity, and wages in host countries, it is surprising how deeply the literature has investigated these issues without branching out into other possible ways in which FDI and MNEs can affect host countries. From our perspective, there are quite a few new directions to explore, particularly with respect to how foreign firms interact with the local communities in which they locate. As pointed out in the introduction and chapter 1, this is precisely where an IB approach has obvious advantages over an IE approach.

There are some general tensions that underlie this topic. The first is that foreign-owned firms have cultural differences with new local communities, which may affect not only how a foreign firm chooses locations but also how it operates in that location. Thus the foreign firm, and particularly its (foreign) managers, may not consider the welfare of its employees and local community in its decision making in the same way that a domestic-owned firm would. At the same time, local communities may view foreign-owned firms differently than domestic-owned firms. These inherent differences (and potential biases) may significantly alter the important interactions that take place between local communities and foreign-owned firms, from the bidding and concessions local communities make to attract and retain firm investment to the outcomes of local political elections. We next enumerate a few different topics in this area that are relatively unexplored but potentially quite important.

Local communities often bid with special incentive packages to attract investment by larger industrial establishments. For example, it is easy to find media accounts describing incentives provided to new automobile or semiconductor manufacturing plants. Foreign-owned firms may systematically differ from domestic-owned firms in the types of incentives they request and how local endowments and policies affect their location decision. Although there is a substantial body of literature examining the bidding for investment, these issues have rarely been seriously considered to our knowledge. One exception is Figlio and Blonigen 2000, which examines the differential impacts not only on wages by foreign-owned firms but also on local public expenditures. Using data on foreign and domestic firm investment into South Carolina counties, Figlio and Blonigen find that unlike domestic investment, new foreign firm investment is associated with lower county-level per-pupil expenditures on public education but higher expenditures on public safety and transportation infrastructure. Another exception is Gemmell, Kneller, and Sanz (2008), which looks at how the size and composition of public expenditures in OECD countries respond to globalization forces, including inbound FDI. They find that FDI does not correlate with any change in the public sector but is associated with greater social spending. A final paper related to this issue is by List, McHone, and Millimet (2004), who find that foreign firms are not affected in their location decisions in the United States by local environmental regulations, as are domestic firms.

A second area that we feel has significant potential for future research is the interaction of foreign investment and local political economy. There is strong anecdotal evidence that FDI can affect local politics—the size of incentives given to foreign-owned automobile manufacturers had a significant impact on U.S. gubernatorial elections in Alabama, Indiana, and Kentucky in the early 1990s (Chappell 1994). It is quite possible that these political ramifications would not have occurred had the investment in question been by domestic-owned firms, although this has not been systematically investigated. But foreign firms may also actively pursue policy changes in local communities that domestic firms would not. An example of this is the concept of quid pro quo FDI, hypothesized by Bhagwati, Dinopoulos, and Wong (1992), in which foreign firms invest in a country to lower import barriers or the threat of import barriers. Blonigen and Feenstra (1997) find some evidence for this hypothesis using U.S. data on FDI and trade protection; Blonigen and Figlio (1998) find a more nuanced result when examining FDI into regions and votes by national legislative representatives from those regions. FDI appears to strengthen politicians' prior trade protection stances, with increased FDI associated with free traders more likely to vote for free trade in the future and protectionists becoming more protectionist in their stance. A related paper is Grether et al. 2001, which finds that FDI-intensive sectors in Mexico tend to have greater trade protection, ceteris paribus.

There are very likely many other local and national policies that foreign firms may systematically try to influence once located in the host country, yet there has been little done in this area. Likewise, little has been done to examine how local politics may affect incentive packages given to foreign firms. Articles by Janeba (2004) and Branstetter and Feenstra (2002) are notable exceptions. Janeba provides a model in which voters balance FDI incentives with redistributive policies, and Branstetter and Feenstra examine and estimate how much the Chinese government balances the gains from trade and FDI with its preferences favoring state-owned enterprises.

A final general topic area concerns the cultural and human dimensions of foreign firm interactions with local communities. Do these firms operate in an isolated manner or do they have a significant impact on cultural and international awareness of the communities in which they operate. Likewise, how much does adaptation of a foreign firm to a new culture affect the firm's own corporate culture? The IB literature has started to address this last question through studies that compare and find differences in management practices across subsidiaries of the same firm. (see, e.g., Fenton-O'Creevy, Gooderham, and Nordhaug 2008). This works shows that MNEs adapt practices to local conditions but does not address the extent to which this adaptation feeds back to operations of headquarters.

In summary, these are areas that both the IE and IB literatures have largely ignored. Rodriguez et al. (2006) point out that although the IB literature is more naturally sensitive to how businesses interact with society, MNEs interactions with (local) politics, corruption, and social responsibility have received little attention in the IB literature. Some recent exceptions in the IB literature include Martin et al. 2007, Chen et al. 2010, and Galang 2012, which investigate MNE responses to local corruption.

Again, these are suggestions of topics that we think are potentially quite important but have not been explored. It is not meant to be an exhaustive list and we certainly have not provided many details. As such, we next provide a more specific (and detailed) example of a type of interaction between foreign firms and local communities—local corporate philanthropy decisions—which demonstrates that foreign firms are surprisingly different in their approach than domestic firms. The analysis shows how such interactions are not necessarily straightforward to analyze yet can clearly have important economic and policy implications.

4.4   An Example: Differences in Corporate Giving Based on Ownership Nationality

In this section, we use data collected from local charitable organizations—United Way chapters—to examine whether foreign-owned firms differ from domestic-owned firms in their decision about whether, and how much, to give to charities in the local community. We first provide a brief overview of the literature on corporate social responsibility (CSR), which includes charitable giving by firms. We then present some hypotheses about how foreign-owned firms may differ in their charitable giving to local charities and examine these hypotheses empirically.

4.4.1 Corporate Social Responsibility Literature

There is a growing literature on firm motivations for engaging in CSR activities such as charitable donations.[4] One school of thought is that it is inefficient for firms to engage in CSR. Because all individuals in a firm (workers and owners) are free to personally donate from the income they gain from the firm, some question why the enterprise itself should be involved in giving from the firms' profits. Indeed, Friedman (1970) argues that firms are organized to maximize profits for their shareholders and that there is thus no role for CSR. Firm resources spent to make CSR decisions could be better used to maximize profits, providing greater income for the workers and owners to donate, should they so choose. As Friedman concludes, "There is one and only one social responsibility of business—to use its resources and engage in activities designed to increase its profits so long as it stays within the rules of the game, which is to say, engages in open and free competition without deception or fraud" (1970, 124).

An alternative view is that CSR may be a strategy used by firms to maximize profits. For example, consumers' demand for a firm's product may be positively related to whether the firm engages in CSR. Additionally, CSR may be used as a strategy to boost employee morale, creating a more energized workforce that leads to greater profitability of the firm. Porter and Kramer 2002 is a well-known recent piece advocating this view that provides a number of examples of the interdependence of CSR and the firm's own economic objectives. One example: "Apple Computer has long donated computers to schools as a means of introducing its products to young people. This provides a clear social benefit to the schools while expanding Apple's potential market and turning students and teachers into more sophisticated purchasers" (Porter and Kramer 2002, 61). Even more cynically, they note that Philip Morris spent $100 million publicizing a charitable gift of $75 million. In summary, this alternative view is that firms use charitable donations in a strategic manner to increase their profits.

A number of studies have statistically examined the observable factors that affect whether a firm engages in CSR and the level of their CSR activity. These studies invariably examine data on national-level CSR activities by firms and have generally found that giving (even on a per-employee basis) typically goes up with firm size (e.g., see Brammer and Millington 2006 and Muller and Whiteman 2009), though Amato and Amato (2007) find evidence that this holds mainly for small and large firms but not medium-sized firms. Studies have hypothesized that firms give more when profits and cash flow are high but have not found conclusive statistical evidence for this hypothesis (e.g., see Seifert, Morris, and Bartkus 2003). Some have also found that characteristics of the industry in which a firm operates matters. For example, Zhang et al. (2010) find that Chinese firms in industries where advertising is important were more likely to donate to the 2008 Sichuan earthquake efforts in China, especially in industries where the market was very competitive for customers. This finding suggests that CSR can be motivated by the possibility of increasing market share and profits of the firm.

4.4.2   Giving to Local United Way Organizations

Unlike these prior studies, we provide a statistical analysis of local (not national) corporate giving. We focus on direct corporate giving to local UW organizations and have collected a sample of establishment-level observations from three UW organizations on the U.S. West Coast. Our presumption is that corporate gifts to the local UW organization are a good measure of overall local CSR by a firm, as UW organizations in the United States are often the primary agency in a local area that coordinates fundraising and volunteer efforts for local social services.[5] UW organizations work with community leaders, government agencies, schools, and local nonprofit organizations to identify community needs and then direct funding to the various local agencies and charitable organizations to address these needs. There are presently over one thousand local UW chapters in the United States; they have well-recognized and publicized local fundraising campaigns each year.

A significant share of UW contributions comes from direct corporate donations. By "direct corporate donations," we refer to donations given by corporations from their profits, not the contributions from their employees. The 2009 Annual Report of the United Way provides a number of examples in which firms gave millions of dollars directly for various UW programs, and many firms also provide direct corporate gifts by matching their employees' giving to UW.[6] The UW of Greater Knoxville website reports that 30 percent of their donations come from direct corporate gifts, and it is not unreasonable to think that this is representative of other UW organizations.[7]

4.4.3   Hypotheses on the Effect of Foreign Ownership

Our main interest is the extent to which foreign-owned firms may differ from domestic-owned firms in terms of their giving behavior to the local UW organization, ceteris paribus. Our null hypothesis is that foreign-owned firms do not differ in this way, on the assumptions that firms make CSR decisions from a strict profit-maximization perspective and that ownership does not influence the profit-maximization environment of a firm. However, both of these assumptions may be violated and lead to alternative hypotheses.

An alternative hypothesis is that foreign firms are less likely to give and/or give less than domestic-owned firms. There are a couple reasons why this may be true. First, a larger portion of final demand for a foreign-owned firms' product may be nonlocal and local consumers are less familiar with their brand because it is foreign. Thus, the firm prefers to direct their CSR toward their nonlocal consumers. This behavior stems from a profit-maximizing motive in which charitable giving is part of a firm's marketing efforts but foreign ownership is systematically correlated with different final markets for the firms' products. A different justification for this alternative hypothesis is that foreign-owned firms often have foreign managers, who—due to home-biased personal preferences—may be more likely to direct corporate CSR back to their home country. This justification views corporate CSR as motivated more by managers' utility maximization than profit-maximization considerations. Although these two justifications are quite different, they both stem from the "foreignness" of the foreign-owned firm, not other attributes of the firm connected with its MNE status. Thus, these effects should be present statistically, even after controlling for size and other firm attributes.

A second alternative hypothesis is that foreign firms are more likely to give and/or give more than domestic-owned firms. One reason this may be true is that the foreign firms' corporate culture differs from domestic-owned firms toward engaging in more CSR.[8] A second, more intriguing, reason is that foreign firms may have more political and cultural barriers to overcome in a local community than domestic firms and therefore use local philanthropy as a means to mitigate these barriers. This motive is compatible with a profit-maximization view of CSR in which philanthropy is used as part of a firm's public relations strategy.[9] Goyal (2006) provides a game theoretic model in which MNEs may use CSR to signal that they are an accommodating firm to a host region and thereby receive more favorable location incentive packages. Importantly, the reasons supporting this alternative hypothesis are again connected with the "foreignness" of the firm, not attributes that would be common to all MNEs, regardless of ownership.

4.4.4 Empirical Specifications

To examine our hypotheses, we employ the following empirical specification:

$$Donation_{ijt} = \alpha + \beta \times ForeignOwnership_{it} + X_{ijt}\gamma + \theta_j + \varepsilon_{ijt}$$

where $Donation_{ijt}$ is a variable measuring the local corporate donation activity of establishment i to the local UW chapter j in year t; $Foreign Ownership_{it}$ is an indicator variable of foreign ownership of establishment i in year t; X_{ijt} is a matrix of other control variables; θ_j is a set of indicator variables of the local UW chapters to reflect differences in how well each chapter is able to raise charitable donations; and ε_{ijt} is an error term assumed to have a mean of 0. The parameters α, β, and γ are coefficients to be estimated.

We explore our hypotheses using two different but related measures of corporate donations to local charities. The first is an indicator variable of whether establishment i donates any nonzero amount to its local UW chapter j in year t. This variable allows us to estimate the factors affecting the probability of local corporate giving using probit maximum likelihood estimation techniques. Our second measure is the amount of donation given by establishment i to its local UW chapter j in year t, which we log due to skewness in the variable. We estimate the specification with this dependent variable using ordinary least squares estimation on only the sample of establishments that gave a nonzero amount. Thus, these estimates provide evidence on the magnitude of local corporate donations conditional on the firm deciding to give locally.

To avoid omitted variable bias, we include a number of control variables. We note that estimates of the effect of these variables may be of interest in their own right because the factors affecting local corporate giving may be quite different than what motivates national- and international-level corporate giving, which has been the only focus of the prior literature. First, we include the number of employees of the establishment ($Employees_{it}$) as an observable measure of its size. Although prior studies find that total (national and international) corporate philanthropy goes up with firm size, this may not be true when examining the corporate philanthropy patterns of a local establishment. For example, it may be more profitable for larger firms to engage in CSR at a national level than to coordinate local giving in the many markets where their consumers may be located. Thus, larger firms may actually give less in a given location because they are more likely serving national, not local, markets.

These considerations suggest a couple of additional control variables. Establishments that are locally owned and sell primarily to the local market should be more likely to give locally, everything else equal. While we do not have direct information on whether an establishment is locally-owned, we expect that single location establishments (*Single Plant$_{it}$*) are more likely to be locally owned and thus more likely to give locally than a branch plant that is part of a multiplant firm. We also include a variable indicating whether a local establishment is headquarters (*Headquarters$_{it}$*) for a firm. This attribute implies that the establishment is part of a multiplant firm, which suggests less local corporate philanthropy, given the previous discussion. However, a firm may be more likely to give to the local community in which it is headquartered. Thus, we have no clear prediction for the sign of the coefficient on this variable. We also include a set of Standard Industrial Classification (SIC) one-digit industry variables because the industry in which it operates may also influence whether an establishment is more likely to sell to local markets or to national and international markets.[10] Many nonmanufacturing sectors are nontradable (personal services, utilities, local transportation, etc.) and will be oriented only to the local market. For example, manufacturing firms that send their goods around the world may be less likely to give locally than homeowners insurance firms that rely on their agents developing relationships with local consumers. Similarly, we include indicator variables for the local UW organization, as these organizations may differ in their general fundraising skills. Finally, we include a time trend, as there has been a national trend of lower giving to UW chapters over the past decade, but inflation contributes to higher nominal donation amounts.[11]

4.5   Data

The focus variable of our analysis is corporate giving to the local UW. Although corporations may give to a number of local organizations, the local UW serves as an "umbrella" agency to fund raise and distribute funds to local charities. Thus, we expect UW donations to capture a representative pattern of corporate giving to local charities and community. We were able to collect records of all business enterprise donations to three of the UW organizations located on the West Coast of the United States, one covering a large metropolitan area and its outlying suburbs and two covering smaller metropolitan areas under 500,000 in population. The records are for a number of years in the 2000s and provide firm names, addresses, corporate donations, and employment numbers in some circumstances. As we are interested only in philanthropy motives of the manager and owners of the firm, the corporate donation amount excludes the money given by a firm's employees. When a firm had multiple plants in the local area, we combined these into one observation.

We use Dun and Bradstreet (DB) corporate directories to supplement the information we have from the UW organizations. First, we gather employment data on the enterprises in our sample from the DB directories when missing in the original UW data. Second, the DB directories provide information on whether the enterprise is domestic- or foreign-owned, as well as whether it is a single-enterprise firm or an affiliate of a multilocation firm. We also can distinguish from the DB data whether the enterprise is a headquarters for a multilocation firm. Third, the DB directories provide the main four-digit SIC code for each enterprise. Fourth, we use the DB directories to randomly sample other enterprises in the same area as the enterprises in our UW data in order to get a control set of enterprises that did not give to the local UW. Finally, our focus is on whether foreign-owned firms differ in their corporate donation behavior from domestic-owned firms. We were able to obtain the nationality of ownership for various plants using the online directory service of Uniworld Online (http://uniworldbp.com). We verified these data through corporate websites.[12]

We end up with 7,990 usable observations; 2,890 (or about 36 percent) of the 7,990 enterprises gave to the UW organizations we sample. We did not collect data on all nongiving enterprises, only a random sample of nongivers; thus the true percentage of giving enterprises is much lower. Of the 7,990 enterprise-year observations in our sample, 282 are connected with foreign-owned enterprises, of which 31 observations have nonzero donations to the local UW. Of course, this lower giving rate by foreign-owned firms may be due to other reasons, such as the industry to which they belong. Our regression analyses were able to determine to what extent these various factors affect giving by foreign-owned firms.

4.6   Results

As mentioned earlier, we examine two different dependent variables. The first is the "giving probability"—the likelihood that a firm gives any nonzero corporate gift to its local UW. The second is the "giving level"—how much a firm gives to the UW. We examine the donation level only for the sample of enterprises that give some nonzero amount. We next provide results for each of these analyses in turn, before exploring a few extensions.

4.6.1   What Determines the Probability of Giving?

Our first analysis examines the factors that affect the probability of an enterprise giving to the local UW. We use probit maximum likelihood techniques to estimate coefficients but report the marginal effects of each independent variable on the giving probability to easily interpret the magnitude of our estimated effects. Thus, each marginal effect indicates the percentage point change in the corporate giving probability (in decimal form) for a one-unit change of a variable. This result can be compared to our sample average of about a 36 percent probability of an establishment donating to the local UW.

The results of our statistical analysis on local corporate giving probabilities are given in table 4.1. In the first column, we provide results from a specification where we only include the $ForeignOwnership_{ijt}$ variable. The sign of the effect is clearly negative and statistically significant at the 1 percent level. The magnitude is also large, indicating that foreign-owned establishments have a local giving probability that is 29 percentage points less than domestic-owned establishments.

In the next two columns of table 4.1, we sequentially add control variables. Column (2) adds our vector of control variables and local UW organization indicator variables; column (3) adds these plus a set of one-digit SIC industry indicator variables. Inclusion of controls clearly increases the fit of the empirical specification, with the pseudo-R^2 measure rising from 0.02 to 0.18. The magnitude of the effect of foreign ownership falls in half but is still highly statistically significant and indicates that a foreign-owned establishment is about 16 percentage points less likely to engage in corporate giving to the local UW chapter than a domestic-owned enterprise, even after controlling for size, industry, and other attributes.

Many of the marginal effects of the control variables are statistically significant and provide results that are new to the CSR literature. First, firm size is actually negatively correlated with local corporate giving, in contrast to prior results showing that total firm CSR is positively associated with size. Our estimates indicate that each additional 100 employees decreases an establishment's probability of local corporate

Table 4.1
Effect on giving probability (marginal effects)

Foreign ownership	–0.291**	0.162**	0.156**
	(0.015)	(0.018)	(0.019)
Employee size (hundreds)		–0.024**	–0.022**
		(0.001)	(0.001)
Single plant		0.125**	0.134**
		(0.011)	(0.011)
Headquarters		–0.059**	–0.047**
		(0.013)	(0.013)
Trend		–0.025**	–0.026**
		(0.001)	(0.001)
United Way effects	No	Yes	Yes
Industry effects	No	No	Yes
Likelihood ratio test: chi-squared	167.07	1663.43	1848.23
statistic (*p*-value)	(0.000)	(0.000)	(0.000)
Pseudo R²	0.02	0.16	0.18
Observations	8115	7990	7990

Notes: Table reports marginal effects and their standard errors from a standard maximum likelihood probit specification on a dependent variable indicating whether a firm donated to their local United Way chapter in a given year. United Way effects are a set of binary variables to indicate different local United Way organizations; industry effects are binary variables to indicate one-digit SIC industry of the firm. ** denotes statistical significance at the 1% level; * denotes statistical significance at the 5% level.

giving by 2.2 percentage points. Relatedly, single-plant firms (which are likely locally owned and focused) have local giving probabilities that are 13.4 percentage points higher than other establishments. And finally, establishments that are headquarters actually have lower giving probabilities, by about 4.7 percentage points.

4.6.2 What Determines Giving Amounts for Those Enterprises that Give?

We now turn our focus to examining how various factors affect the amount given for the enterprises that choose to give to the UW. The average annual donation amount from a donating enterprise in our sample is $1,224.57 and ranges from $5 to $90,000. We use the same regressor set as for our regressions examining the probability of local corporate giving, though we log the donation amount and the employee size variable.

Table 4.2 provides results from these statistical analyses, displaying the same sequential inclusion of controls as in table 4.1. The first column

Table 4.2
Effect on giving level (in gogs) for those firms that give

Foreign ownership	1.060**	0.382*	0.378*
	(0.217)	(0.161)	(0.161)
Log employee size		0.259**	0.266**
		(0.011)	(0.012)
Single plant		−0.042	−0.048
		(0.035)	(0.036)
Headquarters		0.120*	0.110*
		(0.050)	(0.051)
Trend		0.022**	0.021**
		(0.005)	(0.005)
United Way effects	No	Yes	Yes
Industry effects	No	No	Yes
Likelihood ratio test: chi-squared	23.89	462.25	254.94
statistic (*p*-value)	(0.000)	(0.000)	(0.000)
Pseudo R^2	0.01	0.50	0.51
Observations	2902	2738	2738

Notes: Table reports coefficients and their standard errors from a standard ordinary least squares specification for the sample of firms that donated to their local United Way chapter in a given year. United Way effects are a set of binary variables to indicate different local United Way organizations; industry effects are binary variables to indicate one-digit SIC industry of the firm. ** denotes statistical significance at the 1% level; * denotes statistical significance at the 5% level.

shows that foreign ownership has a statistically positive impact on the local corporate donation level for the sample of establishments that give to their local UW chapter, with a coefficient that suggests that foreign-owned establishments donate 106 percent more than domestic-owned establishments. After including a full set of controls (column [3] estimates), this difference goes down to about a 38 percent difference in giving levels but is statistically significant and obviously economically significant as well. Putting this together with earlier results, foreign-owned firms are much less likely to engage in local philanthropy, but when they do, it is at giving levels that are quite high. One reason for this may be that foreign firms give locally only when their presence is obvious to the community, and they then face cultural hurdles and bias. This finding suggests that there may be interactions with foreign ownership and establishment size, which we explore in the next subsection.

A similar result obtains for establishment employee size. Although larger firms are less likely to give, our results in table 4.2 suggest that local corporate giving levels for those firms that give are positively associated with the establishment's size—a 10 percent increase in an establishment's number of employees is associated with a 2.7 percent increase in local corporate donation levels. The coefficient on single-plant establishments and headquarters are likewise of opposite sign. Putting these effects together with the estimates in the prior sections, our general results are that larger multiplant firms are less likely to give to the local UW, but when they do give, it is significantly more than smaller, single-plant firms. These results are intriguing, as they suggest that there are two very different types of large, multiplant firms when it comes to local giving.[13] One type does not give to local UW organizations at all, perhaps choosing instead to focus their CSR at the national or international level. The other type gives quite generously at the local level. These differences remain even when we control for the type of industry with which the firm is connected. Thus, our analysis here cannot uncover why there are these two types of large, multiplant firms, but future research efforts should consider examination of this question.

4.6.3   Foreign Ownership Interactions with Establishment Size

Larger establishments likely receive much greater attention and scrutiny by their local communities. For example, it is common to see local media report any significant changes in employment at larger employers in their communities. This extra scrutiny may accentuate any local bias against foreign-owned firms, and increased use of local corporate philanthropy as a way to generate positive public relations may be one way of mitigating these effects. This finding suggests that the probability of giving locally and/or the amount donated to the local UW chapter may increase as the size of the foreign-owned firms increases. To examine this possibility, we add to our specifications a variable that combines our indicator for foreign ownership with the establishment's number of employees. Our expectations were that the coefficient on this variable would be positive.

Columns (1) and (2) of table 4.3 provide these results. The coefficient on the interaction variable is positive and statistically significant for both our empirical specifications. With respect to the probability of giving, the results suggest that although the probability of giving goes down 2.3 percentage points with each additional 100 employees for domestic firms, there is essentially zero change in the probability of

Table 4.3
Firm size and country source effects

	Firm size effects		Country source effects	
	Who gives?	How much?	Who gives?	How much?
Foreign ownership	−0.177**	0.346*		
	(0.018)	(0.161)		
Asian-owned			−0.118**	0.906**
			(0.040)	(0.288)
European-owned			−0.163**	−0.122
			(0.024)	(0.231)
Other foreign-owned			−0.246**	0.756*
			(0.076)	(0.350)
Employee size	−0.023**	0.264**	−0.022**	0.266**
(hundreds)	(0.002)	(0.012)	(0.001)	(0.012)
Foreign ownership ×	0.021**	0.339**		
Employee size	(0.006)	(0.104)		
Single plant	0.133**	−0.047	0.133**	−0.045
	(0.011)	(0.036)	(0.011)	(0.036)
Headquarters	−0.048**	0.111*	−0.046**	0.119*
	(0.013)	(0.051)	(0.013)	(0.051)
Trend	−0.026**	0.021**	−0.026**	0.022**
	(0.001)	(0.005)	(0.001)	(0.005)
United Way effects	Yes	Yes	Yes	Yes
Industry effects	Yes	Yes	Yes	Yes
Likelihood ratio test:	1854.29	235.40	1849.64	217.01
chi-squared statistic	(0.000)	(0.000)	(0.000)	(0.000)
(p-value)				
Pseudo R^2	0.18	0.51	0.18	0.51
Observations	7990	2738	7990	2738

Notes: Columns (1) and (3) of the results report marginal effects and their standard errors from a standard maximum likelihood probit specification on a dependent variable indicating whether a firm donated to their local United Way chapter in a given year. Columns (2) and (4) report coefficients and their standard errors from a standard ordinary least squares specification for the sample of firms that donated to their local United Way chapter in a given year. United Way effects are a set of binary variables to indicate different local United Way organizations; industry effects are binary variables to indicate one-digit SIC industry of the firm. ** denotes statistical significance at the 1% level; * denotes statistical significance at the 5% level.

giving by foreign firms as employee size increases.[14] In contrast, the effect of establishment size on the size of contribution (column [2] results) is quite sizable. The elasticity of donation with respect to additional employees is 0.264 for domestic firms but 0.603 for foreign-owned firms. In other words, a one-unit log change in employment at an establishment essentially doubles the amount by which foreign-owned establishments' local giving exceeds that of domestic-owned establishments.

Although this work is obviously far from a direct test, these results are consistent with the hypothesis that larger foreign-owned establishments receive greater local scrutiny, leading them to strategically use local corporate philanthropy to mitigate these effects. Data collection of local media stories on establishments in the sample would allow one to get a measure of local community scrutiny and examine this hypothesis more directly. However, we leave this arduous task for future work.

4.6.4 Heterogeneous Foreign Ownership Interactions by Country Source

One final issue we examine is whether there is heterogeneity in the foreign ownership effect across different MNE nationalities. For example, Pinkston and Carrol (1994) and Bennett (1998) survey MNEs regarding their CSR activities and find that corporate procedures and decisions regarding CSR activities vary systematically according to the nationality of the MNE. The vast majority of foreign investors on the West Coast of the United States are from Asia, Canada, and Europe. Therefore, in our sample, 47 percent of the foreign-owned establishments have European owners, 29 percent are from Asian countries (primarily Japan), and 24 percent are from other countries (primarily Canada). To examine whether there are any systematic cultural differences across these types of foreign investors, we provide specifications in columns (3) and (4) of table 4.3 that include indicator variables for whether an establishment is Asian-owned, European-owned, or owned by any other foreign nationalities. As the results in column (3) show, all three nationalities show significantly lower probabilities of giving relative to domestic-owned firms, though there are no statistical differences across these different types of foreign owners.

Column (4) results, however, suggest that non-European firms who donate to the local UW chapters give significantly more than their European or domestic counterparts.

4.7 Conclusion

Prior literature on the effect of FDI and MNEs on host countries has primarily focused on the effects for growth, productivity, and wages. This chapter first discusses new possibilities for future research in this area that center on the interactions between the local community and foreign firms. We discuss the many ways in which the IB approach could strongly benefit our understanding of these issues, which have been studied mainly by IE scholars only. As an example, we take an IB-inspired approach to analyze why and how corporate philanthropy by foreign firms to local charities may differ in important ways from domestic firms. Using data on corporate giving to local UW chapters, we find that foreign-owned enterprises are less likely to give, but when they do give, it is substantially more in the amount given than domestic firms, ceteris paribus. This evidence is consistent with the hypothesis that foreign-owned firms prefer to use CSR on a more international scale but strategically use CSR for public relation motives when the MNE faces greater local scrutiny and/or bias.

We think examination of interactions between foreign firms and local communities is not only interesting but also important, as it has the potential to affect location of FDI, infrastructure development of local communities, and local and national politics. Our chapter's discussion and analysis has been centered mainly on issues for local communities in a developed economy, but the stakes and range of issues may be even greater for less-developed areas of the world. Calvano (2008) provides examples of conflicts between MNEs and local communities in the less-developed countries and discussion of the factors that contribute to such conflict.

Notes

This chapter benefited from the many comments of the participants of the 2011 CESifo Venice Summer Workshop on Globalisation, Trade, FDI, and the Multinational Firm, as well as anonymous referees. Any errors or omissions are our own.

1. Oman (1999) provides evidence of the incentives governments offer MNEs across various countries, particularly for industries locating large plants, such as in the automobile sector. Wilson (1999) provides an overview of the literature on tax competition for investment, and the literature on this topic in recent years has been quite strong.

2. This literature has primarily been examined by the international economics literature, whereas the international business literature has been more focused on where MNEs locate and the form of their organizations.

3. For example, there is evidence that high-profile foreign investments in the United States had significant impacts on state-level gubernatorial elections.

4. "CSR" is a general term that covers everything from firm-based community volunteering initiatives to simple corporate philanthropy of the arts, sciences, or various public goods.

5. Importantly, each region has only one UW organization, as UW boundaries do not overlap.

6. See page 15 of http://unway.3cdn.net/04b58dce33919e32fb_alqm6v8jg.pdf.

7. See http://www.unitedwayknox.org/ways-to-give.shtml.

8. Of course, they may differ with foreign firms systematically less inclined to engage in CSR as well.

9. This finding is consistent with Findlay's (1978, 9) seminal model of foreign investment and technology transfer assumes that foreign firms pay higher wages "for purposes of good public relations."

10. We get qualitatively identical results when we use two-digit SIC indicator variables, though many of these are dropped due to multicollinearity issues. Use of industry indicator variables at even finer levels of disaggregation introduces severe multicollinearity issues and related convergence issues in our probit estimates.

11. We get qualitatively identical results when using year indicator variables.

12. There were eight firms that the Uniworld Online database indicated were foreign-owned but that we could not verify through other sources. Thus, we excluded these observations.

13. We note that we can make this statement about two types of firms, as we observe that nearly all firms either give in all the years they are sampled or never give.

14. This result is seen by adding the coefficient on "Employee size (hundreds)" with the coefficient on the interaction of this variable with the "Foreign ownership" indicator variable.

References

Aitken, Brian, Ann Harrison, and Robert E. Lipsey. 1996. Wages and foreign ownership: A comparative study of Mexico, Venezuela, and the United States. *Journal of International Economics* 40 (3–4): 345–371.

Alfaro, Laura, Areendam Chanda, Sebnem Kalemli-Ozcan, and Selin Sayek. 2004. FDI and economic growth: The role of local financial markets. *Journal of International Economics* 64 (1): 89–112.

Amato, Louis H., and Christie H. Amato. 2007. The effects of firm size and industry on corporate giving. *Journal of Business Ethics* 72 (3): 229–241.

Bennett, Roger. 1998. Corporate philanthropy in France, Germany, and the UK: International comparisons of commercial orientation towards company giving in European nations. *International Marketing Review* 15 (6): 458–475.

Bhagwati, Jagdish N., Elias Dinopoulos, and Kar-Yiu Wong. 1992. Quid pro quo foreign investment. *American Economic Review* 82 (2): 186–190.

Blonigen, Bruce A., and Robert C. Feenstra. 1997. Protectionist threats and foreign direct investment. In *Effects of U.S. Trade Protection and Promotion Policies*, ed. R. C. Feenstra, 55–80. Chicago: University of Chicago Press for the National Bureau of Economic Research.

Blonigen, Bruce A., and David N. Figlio. 1998. Voting for protection: does direct foreign investment influence legislator behavior? *American Economic Review* 88 (4): 1002–1014.

Borensztein, E., J. De Gregorio, and J.-W. Lee. 1998. How does foreign direct investment affect growth? *Journal of International Economics* 45 (1): 115–135.

Brammer, Stephen J., and Andrew Millington. 2006. Firm size, organizational ability, and corporate philanthropy: an empirical analysis. *Business Ethics (Oxford, England)* 15 (1): 6–18.

Branstetter, Lee G. 2006. Is foreign direct investment a channel of knowledge spillovers? Evidence from Japan's FDI in the United States. *Journal of International Economics* 68 (1): 325–344.

Branstetter, Lee G., and Robert C. Feenstra. 2002. Trade and foreign direct investment in China: a political economy approach. *Journal of International Economics* 58 (2): 335–358.

Calvano, Lisa. 2008. Multinational corporations and local communities: a critical analysis of conflict. *Journal of Business Ethics* 82 (4): 793–805.

Carkovic, Maria, and Ross Levine. 2005. Does foreign direct investment accelerate economic growth? In *Does Foreign Direct Investment Promote Development?* ed. T. Moran, E. Graham, and M. Blomstrom, 195–220. Washington, DC: Institute for International Economics.

Chappell, Lindsay. 1994. Alabama politics ensnare Mercedes project. *Automotive News* 68 (5540): 8.

Chen, Charles J. P., Yuan Ding, and Chansog Kim. 2010. High-level politically connected firms, corruption, and analyst accuracy around the world. *Journal of International Business Studies* 41 (9): 1505–1524.

Chowdhury, Abdur, and George Mavrotas. 2006. FDI and growth: What causes what? *World Economy* 29 (1): 9–19.

Durham, J. B., and J. Benson. 2004. Absorptive capacity and the effects of foreign direct investment and equity portfolio investment on economic growth. *European Economic Review* 48 (2): 285–306.

Fenton-O'Creevy, Mark, Paul Gooderham, and Odd Nordhaug. 2008. Human resource management in US subsidiaries in Europe and Australia: centralisation or autonomy. *Journal of International Business Studies* 39 (January/February): 151–166.

Figlio, David N., and Bruce A. Blonigen. 2000. The effects of foreign direct investment on local communities. *Journal of Urban Economics* 48 (2): 338–363.

Findlay, Ronald. 1978. Relative backwardness, direct foreign investment, and the transfer of technology: A simple dynamic model. *Quarterly Journal of Economics* 92 (1): 1–16.

Friedman, Milton. 1970. The social responsibility of business is to increase its profits. *The New York Times Magazine*, September 13.

Galang, Roberto Martin N. 2012. Victim or victimizer: Firm responses to government corruption. *Journal of Management Studies* 49 (2): 429–462.

Gemmell, Norman, Richard Kneller, and Ismael Sanz. 2008. Foreign investment, international trade and the size and structure of public expenditures. *European Journal of Political Economy* 24 (1): 151–171.

Görg, H., and D. Greenaway. 2004. Much ado about nothing? Do domestic firms really benefit from foreign direct investment? *World Bank Research Observer* 19 (2): 171–197.

Goyal, Ashima. 2006. Corporate social responsibility as a signaling device for foreign direct investment. *International Journal of the Economics of Business* 13 (1): 145–163.

Grether, J. M., Jaime de Melo, and M. Olarreaga. 2001. Who determines Mexican trade policy? *Journal of Development Economics* 64 (2): 343–370.

Hansen, Henrik, and John Rand. 2006. On the causal links between FDI and growth in developing countries. *World Economy* 29 (1): 21–41.

Havranek, Tomas, and Zuzana Irsova. 2010. Estimating vertical spillovers from FDI: Why results vary and what the true effect is. Mimeo.

Herzer, Dierk, Stephen Klasen, and Nowak-Lehmann D. Felicitas. 2008. In search of FDI-led growth in developing countries: The way forward. *Economic Modelling* 25 (5): 793–810.

Fredrik, Heyman, Fredrik Sjöholm, and Patrik Gustavsson Tingvall. 2007. Is there really a foreign ownership wage premium? Evidence from matched employer-employee data. *Journal of International Economics* 73 (2): 355–376.

Janeba, Eckhard. 2004. Global corporations and local politics: Income redistribution vs. FDI subsidies. *Journal of Development Economics* 74 (2): 367–391.

Javorcik, Beata Smarzynska. 2004. Does foreign direct investment increase the productivity of domestic firms? In search of spillovers through backward linkages. *American Economic Review* 94 (3): 605–627.

Lipsey, Robert E. 2004. Home- and host-country effects of foreign direct investment. In *Challenges to Globalization: Analyzing the Economics*, ed. Robert E. Baldwin and L. Alan Winters, 332–382. Chicago: University of Chicago Press for the National Bureau of Economic Research.

List, John A., W. W. McHone, and Daniel L. Millimet. 2004. Effects of environmental regulation on foreign and domestic plant births: Is there a home field advantage? *Journal of Urban Economics* 56 (2): 303–326.

Lohr, Steve. 1982.Toyota and G.M. study joint plant. *The New York Times*, March 9.

Martin, Kelly D., John B. Cullen, Jean L. Johnson, and K. Praveen Parboteeah. 2007. Deciding to bribe: A cross-level analysis of firm and home country influences on bribery activity. *Academy of Management Journal* 50 (6): 1401–1422.

Muller, Alan, and Gail Whiteman. 2009. Exploring the geography of corporate philanthropic disaster response: A study of global fortune 500 firms. *Journal of Business Ethics* 84 (4): 589–603.

Oman, Charles P. 1999. *Policy competition for foreign direct investment: a study of competition among governments to attract FDI.* Paris: Organisation for Economic Co-operation and Development.

Organisation for Economic Co-operation and Development. 2008. The impact of foreign direct investment on wages and working conditions. Mimeo.

Pinkston, Tammie S., and Archie B. Carrol. 1994. Corporate citizenship perspectives and foreign direct investment in the U.S. *Journal of Business Ethics* 13 (2): 157–169.

Porter, Michael E., and Mark R. Kramer. 2002. The competitive advantage of corporate philanthropy. *Harvard Business Review* 80 (12): 57–68.

Rodriguez, Peter, Donald S. Siegel, Amy Hillman, and Lorraine Eden. 2006. Three lenses on the multinational enterprise: Politics, corruption, and corporate social responsibility. *Journal of International Business Studies* 37 (November): 733–746.

Seifert, Bruce, Sara A. Morris, and Barbara R. Bartkus. 2003. Comparing big givers and small givers: Financial correlates of corporate philanthropy. *Journal of Business Ethics* 45 (3): 195–211.

Wilson, J. D. 1999. Theories of tax competition. *National Tax Journal* 52 (2): 269–304.

Zhang, Ran, Jigao Zhu, Heng Yue, and Chunyan Zhu. 2010. Corporate philanthropic giving, advertising intensity, and industry competition level. *Journal of Business Ethics* 94 (1): 39–52.

5 Institutional Quality and FDI to the South

Julia Darby, Rodolphe Desbordes, and Ian Wooton

5.1 Introduction

Foreign direct investment (FDI) was for a long period considered to be a phenomenon of developed, industrialized countries (the "North"). This was especially the case with respect to the nationality of the investing firms, which were almost entirely based in the North, with developing countries (the "South") being hosts to a significant share of inward FDI flows but investing little themselves in overseas markets. Our research was sparked by the fact that this picture of global FDI flows is no longer accurate. It remains true that the South attracts a significant share of the world's FDI. Figure 5.1 illustrates that the South's share of global FDI inflows, although widely fluctuating, has risen over the past forty years from around 20 percent to nearly 40 percent of total FDI.

Perhaps more significantly, the South has also become an established source of FDI. Figure 5.2 shows the global share of FDI outflows attributable to firms from the South over the past forty years. In 1970, the South did indeed provide a negligible amount of the world's FDI flows, but its share has steadily risen. At the end of the first decade of the twenty-first century, the South contributed over 20 percent of global FDI flows. If we consider developing and transition economies as a group, the latest available data suggest that more than 50 percent of FDI flows originate from that group (UNCTAD 2011b). The changing pattern of FDI flows is also confirmed in UNCTAD's global rankings of the largest FDI recipients and investors: six developing and transition source economies were among the top twenty global investors in 2010, yet there were none in 1990. Similarly, half of the top twenty host economies are now developing or transition countries (UNCTAD 2011b).

Alongside these broad trends, available data indicate that the lion's share of FDI flows from the South are directed to host countries that

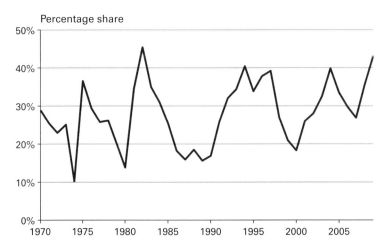

Figure 5.1
South's share of global FDI inflows
Source: UNCTAD 2011a.

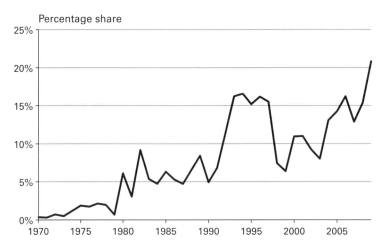

Figure 5.2
South's share of global FDI outflow.
Source: UNCTAD 2011a.

are also located in the South. For example, in 2010, 63 percent of cross-border mergers and acquisitions and greenfield FDI projects from developing and transition economies were invested within other developing economies and a further 7 percent in transition economies. In contrast, in the same period 49 percent of FDI from the developed North was directed to developing and transition economies (UNCTAD 2011b).

The combination of the fast increasing FDI flows from the South and the greater extent to which these flows are invested within the other developing countries has generated a changing picture of global FDI. Although in the early 1990s FDI flows to developing countries originated almost entirely in the North, even by the late 1990s estimates from Aykut and Ratha (2005) suggest that the share of South-South FDI in total FDI flows to the South was approaching 40 percent. Moreover, for some of the lowest-income recipients, FDI inflows were almost entirely from other developing countries.[1]

These aggregates mask some notable shifts in investment patterns. In 1995, Latin American countries such as Brazil, Argentina, and Mexico featured strongly in the outward flows from developing and emerging economies, with their investments being largely concentrated within the same region. By 2005, this picture had changed such that the flows were dominated by intraregional investments from Asian newly industrialized economies, Russia and to a lesser extent Kazakhstan (Goldstein 2009; Goldstein and Pusterla 2008; UNCTAD 2006, 2007). In the past decade, there has been increasing evidence of these economies investing in some of the poorest least-developed countries (LDCs). For example, Africa's share of inflows from Brazil, China, India, Malaysia, and particularly South Africa have been increasing strongly, albeit from a low base (UNCTAD 2011c).

Although there is a wealth of theoretical and empirical literature that models FDI, this work has focused on FDI coming from the North. There is a lack of literature that examines both FDI originating from the North and the FDI flows from the emerging and developing MNEs in the South. Furthermore, most theoretical studies fail to incorporate mechanisms that could explain the circumstances in which emerging MNEs might have an advantage in developing countries. In addition, the vast majority of empirical studies still employ data sets that omit flows emanating from the South, and consequently can investigate only North-North and perhaps North-South FDI flows. Finally, the established literature on outward FDI from the South is predominantly descriptive in nature and as such can offer only suggestions as to possible drivers of the outward FDI flows or sometimes present evidence from specific case studies. In short, to date there is very limited use of theoretical and econometric analysis that both proposes and tests specific hypotheses of how North-South and South-South flows differ or that seeks to identify and quantify the strongest and most significant determinants of South-South FDI flows.

Existing studies in international economics have progressively given more weight to political and institutional determinants of FDI flows and emphasize the importance of "good" institutions. However, to the extent that these studies have confronted data, they have primarily been directed at explaining why some South countries may find it hard to attract inward FDI flows. Among others, Wei (2000), Globerman and Shapiro (2002, 2003), and Azémar and Desbordes (2009) find a strong statistical and substantial positive impact of good public governance on FDI. Similarly, Daude and Stein (2007) find that better institutions have a positive and economically significant effect on FDI, with the unpredictability of laws, regulations and policies, excessive regulatory burden, government instability, and lack of commitment playing major roles in deterring FDI. That FDI flows into some low-income, high-risk South countries have increased—despite risks that are associated with poor institutions and public governance—is something of a paradox in this context.

However, a smaller set of studies, largely in international business, have claimed that there may be a divergence in the impact of these risk factors on different investors. In a sense, this notion dates back to the work of Lecraw (1977) and Kumar (1982), who suggest that South multinational enterprises (MNEs) may be relatively less sensitive to poor institutional quality. Aykut and Goldstein (2007) assert that experience with conditions similar to those in the chosen host country can result in lower risk aversion. This effect may make emerging MNEs more willing to invest in countries that might be ignored by investors from the North. In addition, Cuervo-Cazurra (2006), Cuervo-Cazurra, Maloney, and Manrakhan (2007), and Cuervo-Cazurra and Genc (2008) have suggested that superior knowledge of how to operate in "challenging environments" is among the potential advantages of emerging MNEs relative to those from the North. They assert that some emerging MNEs may have acquired the ability to operate in a particular institutional environment over time in a learning-by-doing manner, while their counterparts in the North are likely to lack this experience and to have to overcome deep-seated assumptions about operating in particular unfamiliar international environments.[2] Factors such as experience with technology better adapted for poor governance, experience of the importance of contacts and relationships in navigating regulatory obstacles, and being more used to dealing with bribery are all cited in the overview provided by Dixit (2011). However, these arguments have not been incorporated into a formal model and comprehensively tested using appropriate data.

The present chapter can be seen as filling this gap. We model explicitly how MNEs' experience of institutional quality and political risk within their "home" business environments influences their decisions to enter a given country. Our particular interest is in determining whether the increasing role played by MNEs from the South is reflected in FDI in different investment environments. We ask whether the experience gained by such MNEs of poorer institutional environments has resulted in their being more prepared to invest in other countries with correspondingly weak institutions as compared to MNEs from the North. Put simply, we ask whether investors from countries that have experienced poor domestic institutional quality are less deterred by country risk abroad.

Javorcik and Wei (2009) propose an alternative analytical model, but their focus is on the entry mode adopted by an MNE in the face of corruption in the host country, finding that corruption tilts the choice toward joint ventures. They argue that having a local partner cuts through the bureaucratic maze associated with a corrupt environment. In this chapter, we construct a model to analyze the choice of location for MNEs, taking into account the quality of institutions in both the firms' home countries and the potential destinations for their FDI. This broader perspective suggests that the specific advantages of firms from the North are less valuable in the South because they require better developed markets and a stable, low-risk, contracting environment. To the best of our knowledge, these arguments have not previously been formalized in a model.

In the next section, we set out a simple analytical model of FDI flows in which an MNE makes its choice of host based upon a comparison of the expected present value of profit achievable in each potential host country, taking into account institutional quality in both source and host nations. We quickly extend this model to incorporate the risk that the production facility in the host country will cease to return a profit to its owners. Importantly, we allow the source country's previous experience with institutional risk at home to influence its perception of risks inherent in investing in other nations. Thus we explicitly allow for the likelihood that a firm that has faced institutional difficulties in its home country will have developed the skills that render similar problems overseas less problematic, relative to investors from other nations who have not been exposed to such risks. We show that poorer institutions in a potential host country make the expected return from FDI in that location less attractive. However, the greater the source country's past experience of poor performance at home, the better able it is to cope with the risk to its FDI.

Having demonstrated the inherent trade-offs that cause some firms to abandon a particular destination but allow that destination to continue to attract more experienced investors, we investigate whether our prediction has empirical support and find strong evidence in its favor. The final section concludes.

5.2   A Simple Analytical Model

We develop a simple model of FDI in which an MNE operating in a particular industry and based in source country s chooses among a number of countries as potential hosts for its overseas production facilities. It will make its choice based upon a comparison of the expected present value of profits from production in each potential host, taking into account institutional quality in both source and host nations.

We assume that if a firm from source country s establishes a production facility in host country h, the factory will generate a flow of after-tax profits in each period equal to Π_{sh}. When faced with the choice of locating in either host country i or host country j, the firm from country s will take into account the difference in profitability of the two plants. We define Γ_{sij} to be country i's geographical advantage:

$$\Gamma_{sij} \equiv \Pi_{si} - \Pi_{sj}. \tag{5.1}$$

A broad range of factors may account for one country having a geographic advantage over another nation as the host for a firm's FDI. Differences in the economic environments of host nations may arise with respect to their rates of corporate taxation, the costs of local inputs into production such as labor, the sizes of their domestic markets, their levels of development (and resulting ability to assimilate the firm's technology), and so on. We do not model the reason behind these differences but merely accept that firms will find some investment locations more attractive than others. Clearly, the geographic advantage enjoyed by a potential host in one industry may not carry over to all sectors of the economy.

The investment made by the MNE is expected to be productive and to last into the future. Consequently, the firm will look at the present value of the expected stream of current and future profits. Assume, for now, that there is no risk involved in the FDI and that the plant is expected to maintain production (and profitability) indefinitely. The present values of the terms in equation (5.1) are

$$PV\left(\Pi_{sh}\right) = \frac{\Pi_{sh}}{1-\delta} \tag{5.2}$$

$$PV\left(\Gamma_{sij}\right) = \frac{\Pi_{si} - \Pi_{sj}}{1-\delta} \tag{5.3}$$

where δ is the discount rate of the firm.[3] When investments have the same expected longevity, accounting for the future leaves the firm's optimal choice of location for its FDI unchanged. We now consider the implications of international differences in the future profitability of foreign production facilities, modeling these as differences in expected lifetimes of the investments.

5.2.1 Institutional Risk

The life of the MNE's overseas plant may be cut short for many reasons. We focus on problems with respect to the institutions in the host country. We suppose that there is a risk r_h in every period that the production facility in host country h will cease to return a profit to its owners in source country s. This event may arise because of some breakdown in the host country's business environment such that the firm is unable to continue producing. Alternatively, production may carry on but ownership of the firm be expropriated by the host country's government.[4]

We are particularly interested in determining whether the source country's exposure to poor institutions at home has an influence on its perceptions of the risk inherent in investing in other nations and whether this effect can explain why MNEs from countries with differing past records of institutional quality may choose different recipients of their FDI. It may be the case that a firm that has faced institutional difficulties at home has developed skills that render similar problems overseas less problematic relative to investors from other nations who have never been exposed to such risks. Thus, we incorporate an experience effect to capture the impact of past exposure to institutional risk on a source country's willingness to engage in FDI in a less-than-secure investment environment.

We define ε_{sh} as the subjective probability of investing country s that FDI in country h will shut down in the current period. This can be modeled as

$$\varepsilon_{sh} \equiv \left(1 - e_s^{\alpha}\right) r_h \tag{5.4}$$

where e_s is the source country's experience of past, domestic institutional risk ($e_s < 1$) and $\alpha > 0$. For a host that is perceived to be free of risk ($r_h = 0$), the firm's experience of dealing with poor institutions is irrelevant. Should the potential host be seen to have an uncertain investment climate ($r_h > 0$), an investing firm with relatively more experience of institutional risk will have greater confidence in FDI in country h than a firm based in a country with a less checkered past. Thus source country experience of poor institutions mitigates the institutional risk in the host country.

We can rewrite equation (5.2) using equation (5.4) to incorporate risk such that the expected present value of the profit stream to a firm from country s arising from FDI in country h is

$$EPV\left(\Pi_{sh}\right) = \frac{\Pi_{sh}}{1 - \delta + \delta\varepsilon_{sh}} \tag{5.5}$$

The partial derivatives of equation (5.5) are

$$\frac{dEPV\left(\Pi_{sh}\right)}{dr_h} = \frac{-\delta\left(1 - e_s^{\alpha}\right)\Pi_{sh}}{\left[1 - \delta + \delta\varepsilon_{sh}\right]^2} < 0$$

$$\frac{dEPV\left(\Pi_{sh}\right)}{de_s} = \frac{\delta\alpha e_s^{\alpha-1} r_h \Pi_{sh}}{\left[1 - \delta + \delta\varepsilon_{sh}\right]^2} > 0$$

Thus, poorer institutions in the potential host country lower the expected stream of profits, making FDI in that location less attractive. The greater the source country's experience of poor institutions at home, the better it perceives it will be able to cope with risk to its FDI.

Now consider, once again, a firm's investment choice between two potential host countries, 1 and 2. The firm will consider the expected present values of the two locations and will choose country 1 over country 2 if

$$EPV(\Gamma_{s12}) = \frac{\Pi_{s1}}{1-\delta+\delta\varepsilon_{s1}} - \frac{\Pi_{s2}}{1-\delta+\delta\varepsilon_{s2}} > 0 \tag{5.6}$$

Rewriting equation (5.6), separating the risk elements, yields

$$EPV(\Gamma_{s12}) = PV(\Gamma_s) + \frac{\delta[(1-\delta+\delta\varepsilon_{s1})\varepsilon_{s2}\Pi_{s2} - (1-\delta+\delta\varepsilon_{s2})\varepsilon_{s1}\Pi_{s1}]}{(1-\delta)(1-\delta+\delta\varepsilon_{s1})(1-\delta+\delta\varepsilon_{s2})} \tag{5.7}$$

This decomposition indicates that any geographic advantage that country 1 might enjoy is mitigated if country 2 is perceived to be a relatively safer investment environment.

5.2.2 Different Hosts for Different Sources?

We have already established that source country experience of poor institutional quality can be beneficial for FDI in hosts with poor institutions, but such experience is of no value for FDI in risk-free host countries. Thus there is the potential for firms that are in all other respects identical save for their institutional experience, to perceive potential FDI returns differently when the hosts differ in institutional quality.

Suppose that two potential hosts differ in that country 2 is completely safe while FDI in country 1 carries some risk, that is, $r_1 > r_2 = 0$. We might therefore categorize country 2 as being in the North while riskier country 1 is located in the South. We further assume that source country B has had a more turbulent past than has rock-solid country A, that is $e_B > e_A = 0$. Thus we may think of the relatively inexperienced country A as being located in the North with country B located in the South.[5] This assumption allows us to rank the perceived levels of risks associated with source and host pairs of nations:

$$r_1 = \varepsilon_{A1} > \varepsilon_{B1} > \varepsilon_{A2} = \varepsilon_{B2} = r_2 = 0$$

We can then rewrite equation (5.7) as

$$EPV(\Gamma_{A12}) = PV(\Gamma_{A12}) - \frac{\delta r_1 \Pi_{A1}}{(1-\delta)(1-\delta+\delta r_1)}$$

$$EPV(\Gamma_{B12}) = PV(\Gamma_{B12}) - \frac{\delta \varepsilon_{B1} \Pi_{B1}}{(1-\delta)(1-\delta+\delta\varepsilon_{B1})} \tag{5.8}$$

Suppose that in the absence of uncertainty, the two firms would be equally profitable in the same host nation, that is, $\Pi_h = \Pi_{Ah} = \Pi_{Bh}$ for $h = \{1, 2\}$. Assume also that country 1 has a geographic advantage, such that $PV(\Gamma_{A12}) = PV(\Gamma_{B12}) > 0$. The second terms of the expressions in equation (5.8) are positive; thus the risk associated with FDI in country

1 will always offset its geographic advantage to some degree. Indeed, if FDI in country 1 is particularly risky, the relative stability of country 2's institutions might be sufficiently large that it attracts FDI from both firms. However, country B's firm has been exposed to poor institutions, making it better able to deal with any problems in country 1. Thus it may choose to invest in that location if geographic advantage is large enough to offset the increased risk of closure, while country A's firm opts for the more secure environment of country 2.

Maintaining our assumptions regarding the institutional experiences of the four countries in question, we illustrate the circumstances under which each source country would choose FDI in the lower-profit, risk-free host over investing in the riskier but potentially more profitable nation.[6] Consider first how varying the experience with risk on the part of the firm changes the relative attractiveness of the two locations. This is illustrated in figure 5.3, which traces $EPV(\Gamma_{s12})$ as the experience of the source country changes. When $EPV(\Gamma_{s12}) > 0$, the higher return in host country 1 more that offsets the greater risk associated with investing in that country. The less experience a firm has of dealing with investment risk, the less able it is to deal with the poor institutional framework in the higher return country, and the more likely it is that the firm would choose low-risk country 2 instead.

Effectively, a country with greater experience of host country institutional problems is more willing to invest in a risky climate relative

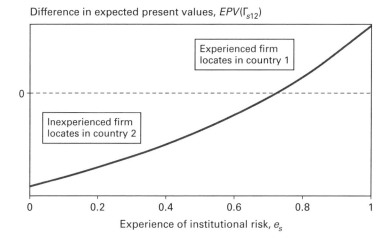

Figure 5.3
Impact of experience on firm's location choice between lower-risk, lower-profit country 2 and higher-risk, higher-profit country 1.

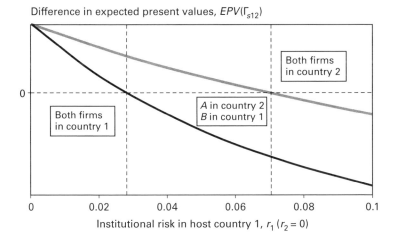

Figure 5.4
Interaction between risk and experience where the more experienced firm from country B is more tolerant of the higher risk in host country 1.

to placing its FDI in a safer host that has a lower return. In figure 5.4, we illustrate the cases under which each source country may choose a different host for its investment and when they co-locate. The lower line represents $EPV(\Gamma_{B12})$ and the upper line shows $EPV(\Gamma_{A12})$. When country 1 is as safe as its rival location for FDI, both firms will choose to invest there to take advantage of the higher profitability. The benefits for both firms from investing in country 1 begin to be eroded as that country's riskiness increases, but the impact will be more severe for the firm from country A, which has no experience of dealing with poor institutions. Thus higher risk in country 1 will eventually make country 2 the preferred location for the FDI of both firms. There will, however, be a range of levels of risk in country 1, at which the more experienced firm from source country B will choose to invest there, while country A's firm, with little experience of poor institutions, will abandon country 1 for the security of investing in the less risky location of country 2.

5.3   Empirical Investigation

We also conducted an empirical investigation that focuses on testing the hypothesis that the relationship between FDI and the quality of host countries' public governance is influenced significantly by the host countries' experience of risk.[7]

We first describe our key variables, the dependent variable, and our measures of public governance quality and then briefly discuss the control variables included in our regressions. We then turn to the econometric methods, which are fundamentally related to the modeling of overdispersed count data with a preponderance of zero values. Finally, we provide a graphical presentation of our key results.

5.3.1   Dependent Variable

We model bilateral count data on the total number of majority-owned foreign affiliates located in each developing country host by MNEs located in each source country (Dun and Bradstreet 2007).

There are a number of advantages to these data, a primary one being their breadth of coverage: we have bilateral counts for 144 source countries (developed and developing) and 104 destination developing countries. Figure 5.5 depicts the frequencies with which source and recipient countries of FDI to the South are recorded in the data. Unsurprisingly, the main sources tend to be the G8 countries and the regional economic powers, such as Brazil, South Africa, Russia, India, and China. Given that we are interested in investigating how the sensitivity of MNEs to destination governance is shaped by governance conditions at home, we omit from the final sample all tax haven countries, as these are likely to be the sources and destinations of large volumes of "roundtripping" and "trans-shipping" FDI flows. The cross-sectional nature of the data does not permit us to investigate the trends discussed in the introduction, but the snap shot taken in November 2007 is sufficient to focus on modeling the features of the data that we are most interested in. Moreover, serious limitations remain with older time-series data on FDI from the South, which are best described as patchy and of dubious quality.

5.3.2   Explanatory Variables

Our explanatory variables include indicators of the quality of host countries' public governance and source countries' experience of risk, together with control variables.

Data on the current quality of host countries' public governance come from Kaufmann, Kraay, and Mastruzzi (2008). These authors evaluated six dimensions of public governance for the period 1996–2007 on the basis of polls of experts or surveys of businessmen/citizens. These are Voice and Accountability (VA), Political Stability (PS), Government Effectiveness (GE), Regulatory Quality (RQ), Rule of Law

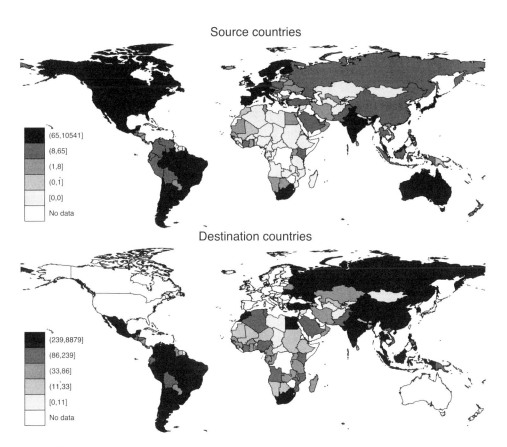

Figure 5.5
Sources and hosts of South FDI in 2007. *Note:* Class breaks correspond to quantiles of number of distinct foreign parent companies owning majority-owned foreign affiliates. *Source:* Dun and Bradstreet 2007.

(RL) and Control of Corruption (CC). VA and PS attempt to capture the process by which those in authority are selected and replaced, GE and RQ are related to the ability of the government to formulate and implement sound policies, and RL and CC assess the respect of citizens and the state for the institutions which govern their interactions. These indicators have been widely used in the FDI literature, as in Globerman and Shapiro 2003 and Daude and Stein 2007. The data are available over the period 1996–2004.

Our primary measure of each source country's past experience of risk is the average of the risk ratings given for that country in the International Country Risk Guide (ICRG) over the period 1983–1990 (Political

Risk Services Group 2009). The ICRG rating aggregates evaluations of twelve dimensions of political risk.[8] The indicator ranges from 0 (high political risk) to 100 (no political risk). Our second measure, reflecting the strong correlation between institutional quality and total factor productivity (TFP), is the logarithm of the average TFP for the years 1980 and 1990, as computed by Baier, Dwyer, and Tamura (2006). Both indicators are closely correlated ($t = 0.56$) and show that two decades ago, a median developing country was much more risky than a developed country. As illustrated in figure 5.6, source countries' past institutional quality is not necessarily indicative of current domestic institutional quality, suggesting that experience of risk, corresponding to low past institutional quality, could not readily be inferred from the latter.

We also include a number of control variables. The particular choice of control variables reflects the widespread use of gravity-type models in the FDI literature. Specifically, we include log GDP and log GDP per capita of the host and source countries and two "Doing Business" variables capturing the differences between corporate tax rates in the source and host countries and the difference in the ease of firing workers in source and host countries, along with a number of dummy variables identifying shared borders, use of a common language, landlocked

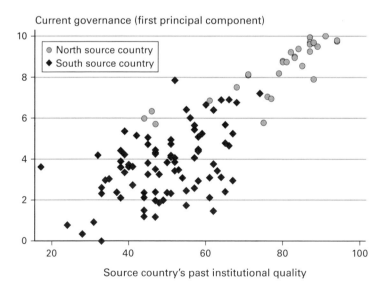

Figure 5.6
Evolving institutional experience.
Data source: Kaufman, Kraay, and Mastruzzi 2008, Political Risk Services Group 2009.

source or host, (past) colonial links, tax havens, involvement in currency unions, regional trade agreements, generalized system of preferences programs, and secondary and tertiary sector dummies, such that the primary sector is the omitted category.

As noted earlier, our dependent variable consists of cross-sectional data for 2007, which can be seen as the cumulative outcome of past FDI decisions shaped by the perceived values of the determinants at the times the decisions were made. Given this setup, and restrictions of data availability, we use the average of the 2000–2004 values of the public governance and income variables and averages over 2004–2008 for the Doing Business variables.[9]

5.3.3 Econometric Approach

By construction, the dependent variable consists only of zero or positive counts of foreign affiliates. Ninety-five percent of the bilateral counts are zero, as a direct result of FDI being concentrated in a small number of South countries. In view of this characteristic in the data, our modeling approach relaxes the assumption that zero and positive counts come from the same data generating process. We consider a two-stage process in which MNEs from a source country first decide which potential host countries to reject for investment and, after this initial screening, decide how many affiliates to establish in the remaining set of eligible countries. Specifically, in our model the probability that FDI never occurs between two countries is determined through a logit binary model; the second part is captured by a negative binomial regression model.

5.3.4 Empirical Results

For the sake of brevity, we report only our results for Regulatory Quality (RQ). Our key findings are, however, robust across all six measures of host country public governance.[10]

Given the relative complexity of the interaction effects in our zero-inflated model, we follow the simulation-based approach of King, Tomz, and Wittenberg (2000) in using graphical representations to draw out the key features in the results. Figure 5.7 illustrates how the size and significance of the impact of host country's RQ on FDI is estimated to change with the source countries' experience of risk, measured by source countries' past institutional quality. The semi-elasticity of FDI with respect to host countries' RQ is shown on the vertical axis (that is, the estimated impact on the number of foreign affiliates resulting

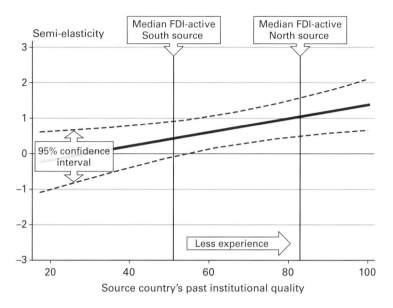

Figure 5.7
The estimated impact of host RQ on FDI, as a function of experience.

from a unit discrete change in the host's RQ). Source countries' past institutional quality is shown on the horizontal axis.[11] The dark solid line shown in the figure is the estimated semi-elasticity; the dotted lines on either side represent the upper and lower bounds of a 95 percent confidence interval.

Starting at the right-hand side of the figure, the estimated semi-elasticity indicates that host country regulatory quality has a positive impact on FDI for source countries with little experience of risk: the estimate is positive and, because the lower bound of the 95 percent confidence interval is also positive, significantly different from zero. This positive and significant impact persists as we consider source countries that have had more experience of risk (moving from right to left along the horizontal axis), but the size of the estimated semi-elasticity declines. The figure also shows that there is a threshold level of past experience of risk beyond which host country regulatory quality no longer has a significant impact.

The two vertical lines shown in the figure play no part in the estimation but are there to aid interpretation. They show the level of past institutional quality for both the median, FDI-active, South country and the median, FDI-active, North country. Although host country RQ clearly exerts a significant positive effect on FDI for the median North country, the estimated impact on the median South country is smaller and statistically insignificant.

In our analytical model, we argue that an MNE's experience of poor institutions at home may influence its willingness to invest in risky locations. Our empirical results offer strong support for this hypothesis, in that the sensitivity of FDI to host countries' RQ is heterogeneous and depends on an MNE's experience of risk in its source country. Indeed, this finding extends across all six measures of host country public governance. Hence, we can conclude that the effects on inflows of FDI resulting from an improvement in the quality of a host country's public governance depend on the origin of the FDI.

5.4   Discussion and Conclusion

This chapter addresses a gap in the existing literature in international economics by providing an explicit theoretical model that encompasses key determinants of North-South and South-South FDI. Although a number of authors in international business have discussed the possibility that experience with risk may be a feature of emerging MNEs' firm-specific advantage, to the best of our knowledge our chapter is the first to formalize this hypothesis within an explicit theoretical framework. Specifically, we have developed a model that allows for the possibility that firms from South source countries may, by virtue of their experience with poor institutional quality, derive a competitive advantage over firms from North countries with respect to investing in destinations in the South.

Our chapter addresses the paradox that although existing studies having found that the existence of good institutions in a host country is a strong, positive determinant of its ability to attract FDI, there is nevertheless clear evidence of increasing FDI flows into developing countries, despite many of these nations having poor institutions and public governance. We model how a firm's exposure to poor institutions in its home country mitigates its attitude to risk in potential host nations. We predict that a firm from a poor institutional background will be better prepared to override hurdles overseas and will show greater willingness to invest in a risky foreign environment compared to a firm that has not had to deal with domestic governance problems. Our empirical results offer strong support for this hypothesis, confirming our prediction that South MNEs are less deterred by risk than North

MNEs. Firms from the South may even deliberately choose to locate in a risky, but potentially profitable, environment if their competitive advantage resides largely in their resilience in the face of risk.

Notes

1. These have at times exceeded 90 percent of the inflow in a given year and are estimated to exceed 70 percent of stock of inward FDI in Cambodia, Ethiopia, and Laos (UNCTAD 2011c, 12).

2. For a related discussion, see Battat and Aykut 2005.

3. We ignore international differences in discount rates.

4. Modeling host country risk as having an impact on the life span of an investment is convenient analytically. Alternatively, this risk might be reflected in a reduction in the profitability of a plant in every period. Given that the results would be qualitatively the same, we have chosen the more convenient analytical route.

5. The labeling convention that we have adopted captures an important stylized fact: the more established industrialized economies of the North tend to have better institutions and have had this high institutional quality for some time as compared to newly industrializing nations of the South.

6. Without loss of generality, we use the following parameter values: $\Pi_{s1} = 1.0$, $\Pi_{s2} = 0.8$, $\delta = 0.9$, $r_1 = 0.1$, $r_2 = 0$, $e_A = 0$, $e_B = 0.8$, and $\alpha = 1$ in the simulations. The relatively lower risk in country 2 mitigates the lower profitability of investing in that nation; a firm from source country B has greater experience of poor institutions, making it more willing to invest in a riskier environment.

7. Complete specification of the empirical model, with a more extensive discussion of the data and the complete results, can be found in our working paper (Darby, Desbordes, and Wooton 2009).

8. These dimensions are government stability, socioeconomic conditions, investment profile, internal conflict, external conflict, corruption, military in politics, religion in politics, law and order, ethnic tensions, democratic accountability, and bureaucracy quality.

9. The Doing Business project is an initiative of the World Bank begun in 2002. The indicators we use were first included in the 2004 report. Each annual report relates to the previous year. See http://www.doingbusiness.org.

10. We provide full details in Darby, Desbordes, and Wooton 2009.

11. Experience of risk is assumed to be inversely related to past institutional quality, so experience of risk is lowest for those with high past institutional quality and experience of risk increases as we move from right to left along the horizontal axis.

References

Aykut, Dilek, and Dilip Ratha. 2005. South-South FDI flows: How big are they? *Transnational Corporations* 13:149–176.

Aykut, Dilek, and Andrea Goldstein. 2007. Developing country multinationals: South–South investment comes of age. In *Industrial Development for the 21st Century: Sustainable Development Perspectives*, ed. United Nations Department of Economic and Social Affairs, 85–116. New York: United Nations.

Azémar, Céline, and Rodolphe Desbordes. 2009. Public governance, health and foreign direct investment in Sub-Saharan Africa. *Journal of African Economies* 18 (4): 667–709.

Baier, Scott L., Gerald P. Dwyer, and Robert Tamura. 2006. How important are capital and total factor productivity for economic growth? *Economic Inquiry* 44:23–49.

Battat, Joseph, and Dilek Aykut. 2005. Southern multinationals: A growing phenomenon. World Bank Working Paper 7425807.

Cuervo-Cazurra, Alvaro. 2006. Who cares about corruption? *Journal of International Business Studies* 37:807–822.

Cuervo-Cazurra, Alvaro, Mary M. Maloney, and Shalini Manrakhan. 2007. Causes of the difficulties in internationalization. *Journal of International Business Studies* 38:709–725.

Cuervo-Cazurra, Alvaro, and Mehmey Genc. 2008. Transforming disadvantages into advantages: developing-country MNEs in the least developed countries. *Journal of International Business Studies* 39:957–979.

Darby, Julia, Rodolphe Desbordes, and Ian Wooton. 2009. Does public governance always matter? How experience of poor institutional quality influences FDI to the South. CEPR Working Paper 7533, November.

Daude, Christian, and Ernesto Stein. 2007. The quality of institutions and foreign direct investment. *Economics and Politics* 19:317–344.

Dixit, Avinash. 2011. Foreign direct investment—from the South. Presentation at NHH Vårkonferansen (Norwegian School of Economics and Business Administration Spring conference). http://www.nhh.no/Files/Billeder/forskningogfagmiljo/Konferanser/Vaarkonferanse%202011/Dixit.pdf.

Dun and Bradstreet. 2007. Global reference solution. November. https://solutions.dnb.com/grs/.

Goldstein, Andrea, and Fazia Pusterla. 2008. Emerging economies' multinationals: General features and specificities of the Brazilian and Chinese cases. KITeS Working Papers 223, KITeS, Centre for Knowledge, Internationalization and Technology Studies, Università Bocconi, Milano, Italy.

Goldstein, Andrea. 2009. *Multinational Companies from Emerging Economies*. Basingstoke, UK: Palgrave Macmillan.

Globerman, Steven, and Daniel Shapiro. 2002. Global foreign direct investment flows: The role of governance infrastructure. *World Development* 30:1899–1919.

Globerman, Steven, and Daniel Shapiro. 2003. Governance infrastructure and US foreign direct investment. *Journal of International Business Studies* 34:19–39.

Javorcik, Beata S., and Shang-Jin Wei. 2009. Corruption and cross-border investment in emerging markets: Firm-level evidence. *Journal of International Money and Finance* 28:605–624.

Kaufmann, Daniel, Aart Kraay, and Massimo Mastruzzi. 2008. Governance matters VII: Aggregate and individual governance indicators 1996–2007. World Bank Policy Research Working Paper 4654.

King, Gary, Michael Tomz, and Jason Wittenberg. 2000. Making the most of statistical analyses: Improving interpretation and presentation. *American Journal of Political Science* 44:341–355.

Kumar, Krishna. 1982. Third world multinationals: A growing force in international relations. *International Studies Quarterly* 26 (3): 397–424.

Lecraw, Donald J. 1977. Direct investment by firms from less developed countries. *Oxford Economic Papers* 29 (3): 442–457.

Political Risk Services Group. 2009. International Country Risk Guide. http://www.prsgroup.com/ICRG.aspx.

UNCTAD. 2006. *World Investment Report 2006: FDI from Developing and Transition Economies: Implications for Development*. New York and Geneva: United Nations.

UNCTAD. 2007. *World Investment Report 2007:Transnational Corporations, Extractive Industries and Development*. New York and Geneva: United Nations.

UNCTAD. 2011a. Inward and outward foreign direct investment flows, annual, 1970–2009. UNCTADstat. http://unctadstat.unctad.org.

UNCTAD. 2011b. *World Investment Report 2011: Non-Equity Modes of International Production and Development*. New York and Geneva: United Nations.

UNCTAD. 2011c. Foreign Direct Investment in LDCs: Lessons Learned from the Decade 2001–2010 and the Way Forward. UNCTAD/DIAE/IA/2011/1. http://www.unctad.org/en/docs/diaeia2011d1_en.pdf.

Wei, Shang-Jin. 2000. How taxing is corruption on international investors? *Review of Economics and Statistics* 82:1–11.

6 Heterogeneous Export Spillovers to Chinese Domestic Firms: The Role of the Difficulty to Enter the Destination Market

Florian Mayneris and Sandra Poncet

6.1 Introduction

Recent studies have focused on the role of foreign firms in the surge of Chinese exports over the past twenty years. From a pure quantitative point of view, the analysis of Chinese statistical yearbooks shows that the share of foreign firms in total Chinese exports has grown from 26 percent in 1992 to 57 percent in 2007. From a more qualitative perspective, it is clear that Chinese exports have upgraded in the past few years. Rodrik (2006) finds that the sophistication of Chinese exports is disproportionately high: three times higher than the level predicted by Chinese average income per capita. Schott (2008) shows that the overlap between Chinese exports and exports from OECD countries is high and growing over time. A consensus has emerged on the fact that foreign firms played an important part in this evolution. Amiti and Freund (2010) show for example that once processing trade is excluded, the skill content of Chinese exports remains unchanged. Because processing trade activities are mainly conducted by foreign firms, this finding suggests that no upgrading occurs for domestic exports. Xu and Lu (2009) show that FDI has a positive impact on Chinese export upgrading when it emanates from fully foreign-owned firms from OECD. They also find export sophistication within an industry to be positively related to the share of processing trade realized by foreign firms and negatively related to the share of processing exports realized by domestic firms.

These results suggest that foreign firms account for most of the quantitative and qualitative growth of Chinese exports. However, they might also exert an indirect impact on domestic ones through export spillovers. Very few theoretical studies exist on export spillovers. Krautheim (2012) builds a model in which the fixed export cost decreases in the number of firms already exporting to a given destination. The rationale for this assumption is information spillovers or cost mutualization. Exporting firms might diffuse specific information on foreign consumers' tastes or on export administrative procedures that might help domestic firms located in the same neighborhood to enter export markets. Exporting firms might also mutualize some costs linked to the participation to international fares or to the transport of their commodities, which reduces the individual cost to conquer new markets. It might also be the case that foreign firms, by exporting to some countries where domestic firms do not export, show to the latter firms that some business opportunities exist in those specific markets. However, conflicting results exist in the empirical literature on the topic: Aitken, Hanson, and Harrison (1997) find a positive impact of export activities conducted by multinationals on the export status of Mexican domestic firms. Kneller and Pisu (2007) confirm this result on UK data. Evidence is much less clear for Barrios, Gorg, and Strobl (2003) on Spanish firms, and Ruane and Sutherland (2005) find a negative impact of foreign exports on entry of Irish domestic firms into export markets.

Recent studies are more encouraging for the specific case of China. Swenson (2008) finds a positive impact of foreign exports on the creation of new trade linkages by Chinese domestic firms, and Chen and Swenson (2013) show that foreign exports increase the unit value and the durability of new transactions created by domestic firms. Mayneris and Poncet (2013) investigate the nature and the specificity of these spillovers. They show that foreign export spillovers are specific to product and destintation: the probability that Chinese domestic firms start exporting a given product to a given country responds positively to the presence of foreign firms in the same province exporting, the year before, the same product to the same country. Foreign export activities considered at a more general level (same product/other countries, other countries/same product or other products/other countries) are much weaker or insignificant.[1] They find moreover that these export spillovers derive mainly from ordinary trade activities and are driven by both the presence of foreign exporters and the extent of their export activities, measured by the value of their exports.

In this chapter, we strongly build on Mayneris and Poncet (2013) to explore another dimension of foreign export spillovers in China. We investigate the possible heterogeneity of export spillovers depending on the difficulty of entering the foreign markets. All destination countries are not equally easy to enter. In particular, administrative documents to fill in, corruption, and political or economic uncertainty might necessitate more specific knowledge from potential exporters; this knowledge will increase the fixed export cost, which has been shown to determine firm-level decision to enter export markets (Melitz 2003). For example, Crozet, Koenig, and Rebeyrol (2008) develop a theoretical model in which insecurity on foreign markets acts as a random additional sunk cost, which disrupts the usual selection of firms on foreign markets based on productivity. Araujo, Mion, and Ornelas (2011) investigate the role of institutional quality of the destination markets on firm-level export dynamics. In their model, firms learn from their own experience on destination markets, with this learning effect being more important for more difficult countries. As a consequence, firms start exporting smaller quantities on risky markets and, conditioning on survival, the growth of firm-level exports decreases with the quality of institutions in the destination country.

The approach we adopt in this work is rooted in the international economics literature but borrows many concepts and questions from the international business literature. As mentioned in the introduction to this book, the international business literature focuses on the interactions between firms and their environment, which is exactly the point of this chapter on foreign export spillovers in China. Export spillovers can be seen as a local advantage that helps Chinese firms to overcome the distance between China and foreign partners. Concerning distance, while international economics mainly focuses on geographic distance, the quality of institutions or the toughness of import procedures in the destination country can make export activities to this country more difficult, increasing the "actual distance" between this country and China; export spillovers might become more decisive in this case. These many dimensions of "distance" are much emphasized in the international business literature, less in international economics studies (see the introduction). Hence, we try to relate the importance of foreign export spillovers to the specific institutional context in the destination country by asking whether foreign export spillovers are stronger for more difficult, and thus more distant, destination countries. This question is somehow symmetric to the question asked in chapter 5, which studies the heterogeneous impact of host country regulatory quality on FDI depending on the institutional quality in the source country.

We consider three dimensions of the access difficulty of a given destination market: the GDP per capita, which is itself linked to a second dimension, the institutional quality or degree of risk of a country. This second dimension is measured by the International Country Risk Guide (ICRG) index, which combines political, economic, and financial risk measures (defined in detail later in this chapter and also used in chapter 5). A third dimension is related to the complexity of import procedures in a given country, measured by the number of days and the number of documents needed to deliver products in this country (measured in the Doing Business databases of the World Bank, as discussed shortly). Thanks to these measures, we thus capture elements that are linked both to the general climate of business in a given country and to the specific procedures required for imports. They are good proxies to account for sources of the differences in the fixed export costs across markets that have been pointed at in the theoretical literature cited previously. However, we must also acknowledge that these dimensions are empirically highly correlated. As shown at the end of this chapter, isolating the one that is the most important driving force of heterogeneous export spillovers is consequently difficult.

Preliminary statistics on the geographic presence of Chinese domestic firms stress the improvement of their capacity to reach difficult destinations. Between 1998 and 2007, the share of domestic export flows to the top decile countries in terms of average time required to import[2] rose from 8.5 to 12.3 percent. When focusing on domestic export starts, the share is not only higher but also increasing faster; it jumped from 11.3 to 17.9 percent, attesting to the enhanced capacity of Chinese domestic firms to penetrate difficult markets over the past years. One can wonder whether the increasing presence of multinational[3] firms appears to influence this evolution in the orientation of China's integration with the world economy.

If we think of institutional quality or administrative duties as a fixed export cost, the marginal impact of export spillovers might be more important for more difficult countries. The diffusion of specific information will be more valuable in this case. Koenig, Mayneris, and Poncet (2010b) investigate this issue on French firm-level data. They show that the probability of entering a given market is positively affected by the number of surrounding firms exporting the same product to the same country, especially for more difficult destinations. In this chapter, we follow the same kind of analysis. We use data on Chinese exports by province, product, destination country, and type of firm (foreign or domestic firm). We merge these data with indicators taken from the

ICRG and the Doing Business databases edited by the World Bank. These indicators are informative on institutional quality and toughness of administrative procedures linked to imports in a given destination country. We are then able to investigate potential heterogeneity of export spillovers on the probability that Chinese domestic firms start exporting a given product to a given country, depending on the difficulty of entry on the considered export market. We actually find that foreign export spillovers are more important for more difficult markets, pointing at a possible role of foreign firms in the geographic diversification of Chinese domestic exports toward more risky markets.

We present the data we use and our empirical methodology in section 6.2. Section 6.3 discusses our results and section 6.4 concludes.

6.2 Data and Empirical Strategy

We study the impact of exposure to foreign exporters on the extensive margin of trade of Chinese domestic firms. In line with Koenig, Mayneris, and Poncet (2010a, 2010b) and Mayneris and Poncet (2013), we explain why domestic firms from province i export product k to country j at time $t + 1$, although they did not at time t. To do so, we use a gravity framework applied to the decision to start exporting. We restrict our analysis to ordinary trade activities for both the dependent and the spillover variables, as Mayneris and Poncet (2013) have shown that foreign export spillovers in China are mainly limited to this sphere of export activities.[4]

6.2.1 Data

We use customs data on Chinese exports by province, HS6 product,[5] destination country, and type of exporting firms (domestic and foreign[6]) for the period 1997–2007. We reaggregate the data in terms of product activity at the HS4 level, which is a fairly detailed level. For example, the HS2 product category "clocks and watches and parts thereof" comprises fourteen different four-digit products, from wristwatches in precious metal to time registers, passing by wristwatches in base metal. We thus consider big product lines, because working at a more detailed level in terms of nomenclature would have implied in some cases to deal with varieties of the same product.

Thanks to this information, we can build a database recording all domestic entries on foreign export markets at the province-product-destination country level. Our dependent variable takes the value 1

if domestic firms from a given province export a given product to
a given country in $t + 1$ and they did not in t. For a specific province,
we consider as potential alternatives all product-country pairs for
which we observe at least one positive export flow over the period. We
focus on export starts and consequently eliminate from the sample
observations corresponding to continuing and ceasing export flows.
Because we have ten years of observations, we can observe, over the
period, multiple domestic starts for the same province-product-
destination country triad. For example, the sequence 00011001111
becomes in our sample .001..01..., with a period denoting a missing
value. In the end, only triads with at least one export start remain in
the sample. The estimation sample covers 220 countries and 1,213 HS4
products.

Regarding data on institutional quality and on toughness of import
procedures in destination countries, we use two databases. The first
one is the International Risk Country Guide dataset (ICRG), edited
since 1980 by an independent American institute, the PRS Group. A
composite index is computed, based on three subindices, measuring
respectively the political, the economic, and the financial risks of a
country. The second data source is the Doing Business database published by the World Bank. Several variables related to country-level
regulations of economic activities are recorded in this database. We use
in our empirical work two of them: the number of documents and the
number of days that are needed to import in a given country the commodities transported by a standard cargo. The number of documents
is calculated from the signature of the contract to the delivery of goods;
the time needed is calculated from the arrival of the cargo in the harbor.
Both variables appear to be good proxies for the toughness of procedures that an exporter has to face to sell its goods to a given foreign
country.

We provide some descriptive statistics on these indices of institutional quality and administrative procedure for the different trade partners of China in the appendix.

6.2.2 Estimated Equation

We estimate a gravity equation on the decision to start exporting. More
precisely, we assume that the probability that domestic firms from
province i start exporting product k to country j at time $t + 1$ can be
written as follows:

$$Prob\left(domestic\ start_{ikjt+1}\right)$$
$$= Prob\left(\alpha\ foreign\ spill._{ikjt} + \beta_1 Z_t + \beta_2 Z_{t-1} + \eta_{ikj} + \mu_t + \varepsilon_{ikjt+1} > 0\right)$$

where foreign spill.$_{ikjt}$ is a proxy for foreign export spillovers that measures the intensity of exports of product k to country j by foreign firms in province i at time t (described shortly), Z is a group of time-varying controls specific to destination country j and/or to province i from which the export flow emanates, η_{ikj} is a province-product-destination country fixed effects, μ_t is a year fixed effect, and ε_{ikjt+1} is the error term, distributed logistically. We estimate the determinants of this probability thanks to a conditional logit estimation. Given the presence of province-product-destination country fixed effects, the impact of our explanatory variables is estimated in the time dimension. We test the heterogeneity of export spillovers depending on the difficulty of entering export markets by splitting the sample into groups of countries, using as a threshold the mean of different country-specific measures of institutional quality and toughness of import procedures. We show that results also hold when using interaction terms.

Several remarks follow about the implications of our estimation strategy. We use a logit estimation with province-product-destination country fixed effects. From a technical point of view, this approach implies that triads for which we observe positive export flows, or on the opposite null export flows, all over the period, cannot participate to the estimation. In this case, the fixed effect would perfectly predict the outcome. This legitimates ex post the limitation of our sample to triads for which we observe at least one export start over the period.

From a more conceptual point of view, the use of such fixed effects means that what we really explain is the timing of entry. We relate the year of entry of domestic firms on specific export markets to the presence of foreign firms exporting the same product to the same country the year before. If such an issue can be apprehended through a continuous time duration model, we still prefer using a discrete time model. According to Hess and Persson (2010, 2011), continuous-time methods perform poorly with large annual trade datasets with many short-lived trade relationships such as ours. Because our sample is at the product and destination country level, it contains many entries and exits of domestic firms into/from export markets. Discrete-time specifications with adequate controls are preferable in this case, which is why we use a logit estimation with triadic (province-product-destination country) fixed effects.

This estimation strategy implies that our effects are estimated in the time dimension only. We thus capture short-run determinants of the entry of domestic firms into export markets. The fact that we observe, for a given product and a given destination country, many variations over the period in the export status of domestic firms suggests the existence of such short-run determinants of entry. It is true that the nature of spillovers could be different in the short and in the long run: foreign firms might facilitate the entry of domestic firms but could make, due to competition effects, their trade relationships less durable. However, such does not seem to be the case in China: Mayneris and Poncet (2013) show that their assessment of foreign export spillovers holds when they consider durable starts only,[7] and Chen and Swenson (2013) find that the presence of foreign exports increases the durability of new export transactions created by domestic firms.

6.2.3 Spillover Variables

Export spillovers have often been studied at a quite aggregated level. Swenson (2008) and Chen and Swenson (2013) explore foreign export spillovers within a given HS2 category. They thus consider fewer than one hundred sectors of activities. We think it is worth investigating export spillovers at a finer level in terms of product nomenclature. Many export regulations are actually defined at a very fine level in terms of product, and it is likely that specific tastes of foreign consumers also vary at a detailed level of product. In the same vein, the destination-country dimension has generally been overlooked, often because of the lack of data, while many trade impediments or many peculiarities in consumers' demand are specific to the destination country.

Koenig, Mayneris, and Poncet (2010a) confirm the interest of this detailed assessment of export spillovers. They show, on French firm-level data, that export spillovers are much stronger when product and destination specific. What matters for domestic starts is being surrounded by firms exporting the same product to the same country. Mayneris and Poncet (2013) find the same result for foreign export spillovers in China: the probability that Chinese domestic firms start exporting product k to country j is positively related to the presence in the same province of foreign firms exporting the same product k to the same country j the year before. We thus focus here on the product and destination country specific spillover.

Another issue is related to the way in which we measure foreign export activities. Less than 10 percent of domestic starts in our estimation sample are associated to the presence, the year before, of positive foreign exports for the same product and same country. Using the value of foreign exports as only a proxy for spillovers would be problematic for the interpretation of our results: are export spillovers linked to the intensity of foreign exports, or to the mere presence of foreign exporters in the province? As in Mayneris and Poncet (2013), we deal with this issue by introducing both a dummy equal to 1 in the case of positive exports and the value of foreign exports.

Note that in addition the positive externalities they might bring to domestic firms, foreign firms may also generate competition effects on foreign markets or congestion effects at the local level. For example, Hale and Long (2011) show that the presence of foreign firms puts pressure on local labor markets and increases the wages of skilled workers, which could be detrimental to domestic firms' export activities. Lu, Ni, and Tao (2010) find that the net externalities generated by horizontal FDI on Chinese domestic firms in terms of output and productivity depend on distance: foreign firms have a positive impact on domestic ones when they are close enough. Consequently, the coefficient we obtain on our proxies for foreign export spillovers must be interpreted as the net effect of positive and negative externalities generated by foreign firms' export activities, but we cannot separate both types of externalities.[8]

Finally, one might worry that Chinese provinces are too large to investigate spillovers linked to information and knowledge spillovers between proximate foreign and domestic firms. However, we provide evidence that export activities of foreign firms located in contiguous provinces have a lower marginal impact on export starts of domestic firms located in province i than export activities of foreign firms within this same province i. We thus observe the spatial decay that we expect to measure in case of export spillovers. Moreover, although the surface area of some provinces (especially those in the western part of China) is rather large, the economic activity is very concentrated. Data for 2000 indicate that roughly one-third of industrial production is generated in the capital city of those provinces. It even rises to 37 percent in the province of Gansu, 45 percent in Shaanxi, and 49 percent in Heilongjiang. Hence the actual internal distance between economic players is much smaller than the geographic size of the province suggests. This feature is also true for smaller provinces. For example, in the coastal province of Jilin, 46 percent of the industrial activity takes place in the capital city.

6.2.4 Time-Invariant and Time-Variant Control Variables

Many other determinants can explain why we observe exports of product k to country j by both foreign and domestic firms from the same province i. Some of them are time invariant and province specific; provinces with better infrastructure or a more educated workforce might attract FDI and facilitate exports, regardless of the nationality of the firm. Some others are also time invariant but province and destination country specific; some provinces might have, for example, specific relationships with particular countries due to migrants' networks, geographic contiguity, or history. These bilateral characteristics ij can explain why we observe exports to country j from both foreign and domestic firms located in province i. Third, there might exist time-invariant province and product-specific determinants of export performance: province i might have developed specific know-how for product k that could explain the good export performance of both foreign and domestic firms producing product k in that location. All of these time-invariant determinants are controlled for by the triadic (province-product-destination country) fixed effect ikj we finally introduce in our regression.

Our estimations also account for time-varying determinants of domestic and foreign firms' exports activities. For example, comparative advantages of provinces might have changed over the fast growing period 1997–2007. We consequently introduce total exports of product k by province i, total exports of province i, and total Chinese exports of product k at time t. Because we control for time fixed effects, total Chinese exports are also controlled for, so that all the elements of a Balassa index of "revealed comparative advantage" at the province-product level are taken into account. We also include the bilateral export values to country j for China and for province i to control for the possible changes in bilateral commercial relationships with country j over the period. We finally introduce the GDP per capita of province i to account for supply side determinants of exports. The evolution of demand in the destination country must also be taken into account. We consequently introduce total world imports of product k by country j

in year t, taken from the BACI (Base pour l'Analyse du Commerce International) database,[9] and destination country GDP per capita.[10]

The value in $t-1$ of provincial and Chinese exports and of destination country imports is also introduced to control for specific dynamics in local comparative advantages and demand.

Last, we want to be sure that foreign exports do not proxy for domestic firms' own experience into export markets. It could be the case that positive foreign export flows of product k to country j are more often observed in provinces where domestic firms also export product k or export to country j at time t. Foreign exports would in this case partly capture spillovers among domestic firms or scope economies in domestic export activities. We thus introduce domestic exports of product k (to countries other than j by definition since we focus on domestic starts) and domestic exports to country j (of products other than k) at time t.

6.3   Results

We first replicate the results on the assessment of foreign export spillovers in China obtained by Mayneris and Poncet (2013). We then investigate several dimensions along which foreign export spillovers might vary depending on destination countries. All regressions are clustered at the province level (Moulton 1990). To split the whole sample, we use as a threshold the mean of the variable used to measure access difficulty of the destination country. Results generally hold when using the median.[11]

6.3.1   Product- and Destination-Specific Foreign Export Spillovers

We focus on ordinary trade (ODT) export starts, as most export starts of Chinese domestic firms occur in ODT rather than in processing trade (PCS). Moreover, foreign export spillovers are found to apply mainly to domestic ordinary trade activities (Mayneris and Poncet 2013). Results presented in column (1) of table 6.1 clearly show that foreign export spillovers exist in China and that they are product and destination specific. The mere presence in province i of foreign firms exporting product k to country j increases the probability that domestic firms from the same province start exporting product k to country j the year after by 10.96 percent,[12] that is, by 2.40 percentage point. A 10 percent increase in the value of foreign exports of product k to country j

Table 6.1
Nature of foreign export spillovers

Explained variable; ODT domestic new export link in $t + 1$	Specification			
	(1)	(2)	(3)	(4)
Same product/country foreign export	0.011**			
	(0.004)			
0/1 same product/country foreign export	0.104***			
	(0.042)			
Other country/same product foreign export	0.003**			
	(0.002)			
Same country/other products foreign export	−0.0001			
	(0.003)			
Other country/product foreign export	−0.288			
	(0.209)			
Same product/country ODT foreign export		0.017***	0.017***	0.014***
		(0.003)	(0.003)	(0.003)
0/1 same product/country ODT foreign export		0.062**	0.062**	0.079***
		(0.027)	(0.027)	(0.028)
Other country/same product ODT foreign export		0.009**	0.009**	0.008***
		(0.002)	(0.002)	(0.002)
Same country/other product ODT foreign export		0.003	0.002	0.002
		(0.002)	(0.002)	(0.002)
Other country/product ODT foreign export		0.082	0.084	0.081
		(0.110)	(0.107)	(0.107)
Neighboring ODT same product/country foreign export				0.009***
				(0.032)
Same product/country PCS foreign export		0.002		
		(0.007)		
0/1 same product/country PCS foreign export		0.098*		
		(0.056)		
Other country/same product PCS foreign export		0.004**		
		(0.002)		
Same country/other product PCS foreign export		−0.002		
		(0.002)		
Other country/product PCS Foreign export		−0.007		
		(0.068)		
Controls for domestic own experience into export markets	Yes			

Table 6.1
(continued)

Explained variable: ODT domestic new export link in $t+1$	Specification			
	(1)	(2)	(3)	(4)
Controls for demand (country-product imports and country GDP per capita)	Yes			
Controls for Macro export (Balassa, bilateral exports of China and of province, province GDP per capita)	Yes			
Control for demand and macro export lags	Yes			
Observations	4161535			4161535
R^2	0.13	0.13	0.13	0.13
Share of domestic starts	0.22			
Province-product-destination country FE	Yes			
Year fixed effects	Yes			

Notes: Heteroskedasticity-robust standard errors are reported in parentheses. Standard errors are clustered at the province level. ***, **, and * indicate significance at the 1%, 5%, and 10% confidence level. Conditional logit estimations in all columns.

increases this same probability by 0.10 percent,[13] that is, by 0.02 percentage point. The impact of other foreign export activities is insignificant or very small in magnitude (for foreign exports of product k to countries other than j). This result suggests that information that foreign firms provide to domestic ones is both product and destination specific. This finding is not surprising because consumers' tastes or quality norms and requirements imposed on imports are often both product and destination specific.

We then distinguish in column (2) ODT foreign exports from PCS foreign exports. Both the presence and the value of ODT foreign exports of product k to country j at time t have a positive and significant impact on the probability that Chinese domestic firms start exporting product k to country j in $t+1$. For PCS trade, the value of foreign exports has no significant impact, and the dummy accounting for the presence of foreign exporters is only weakly significant. Again, foreign exports that are not product and destination specific are either insignificant or very small in magnitude for both ODT and PCS activities.

These results suggest that foreign export spillovers mainly derive from ODT foreign exports and that they are product and destination country specific. We hence focus in column (3) and in the remaining of

this study on product- and destination-specific foreign export spillovers from ODT to ODT export activities. Finally, in column (4), we
also control for ODT export activities of foreign firms in surrounding
(contiguous) provinces. The marginal impact of these firms is much
lower, suggesting that they matter less to explain domestic starts than
foreign firms within the province. We take this spatial decay as a confirmation that we actually capture externalities between proximate
foreign and domestic firms.

6.3.2 Foreign Export Spillovers and GDP per Capita of the Destination Country

We first investigate the potential heterogeneity of foreign export spillovers depending on the destination country GDP per capita. Because
rich countries have better institutions than poor countries on average,
they might be easier targets for Chinese domestic firms. Moreover, rich
countries import more varieties than poor countries (Hummels and
Klenow 2005), which could make them more accessible for Chinese
domestic firms. In this particular case, the specific information that surrounding foreign exporters could provide would be less valuable for
prospective domestic exporters. Overall, foreign export spillovers might
be less important for these destination countries. This conjecture is confirmed by results presented in table 6.2. In this table, we run separate
regressions for low and high GDP per capita destination countries. A
country is considered high GDP per capita if its GDP per capita is higher
than US\$9,059 (the mean value for our sample); otherwise, it is classified
as a low GDP per capita country. The comparison of columns (2) and (3)
shows that the impact of foreign export spillovers (measured by the
presence of surrounding foreign exporters) is significantly different
between these two groups. The mere presence of foreign exports of
product k to country j has a positive and significant impact on domestic
starts only for countries in which GDP per capita is below the average.
Hence when the destination country is poor, the presence of foreign
firms increases the probability of a domestic start by around 13.2 percent
(i.e., by 2.88 percentage point). No strong differences emerge regarding
the impact of the value of foreign exports. As shown in the final column,
the result is confirmed when we interact the dummy identifying countries with a GDP per capita above the average with the spillover variable: the coefficient on the interaction term is negative and significant.
This last column is obtained thanks to a linear probability model to
interpret the coefficients as marginal impacts directly.

Table 6.2
Export spillovers and destination country GDP per capita

Explained variable: domestic ODT new export link in $t + 1$	Heterogeneity indicator			
	Destination country GDP per capita			
	$\neq$	$\leq$ mean	> mean	Interaction
	(1)	(2)	(3)	(4)
Same product/country ODT foreign export	0.015***	0.015***	0.015***	0.005***
	(0.003)	(0.005)	(0.005)	(0.001)
Same product/country ODT foreign export * Above threshold dummy				−0.001
				(0.001)
0/1 same product/country ODT foreign export	0.079***	0.124***	0.036	0.033***
	(0.028)	(0.043)	(0.040)	(0.008)
0/1 same product/country ODT foreign export * above threshold dummy				−0.025**
				(0.009)
Other country/same product ODT foreign export	0.008***	0.007***	0.008***	0.001***
	(0.002)	(0.002)	(0.002)	(0.0004)
Same country/other product ODT foreign export	0.002	−0.001	0.006	−0.0004***
	(0.002)	(0.002)	(0.005)	(0.00008)
Other country/product ODT foreign export	0.084	0.108	0.047	0.017***
	(0.107)	(0.117)	(0.100)	(0.001)
Controls for domestic own experience into export markets	Yes			
Controls for demand	Yes			
Controls for macro export	Yes			
Control for demand and macro export lags	Yes			
Observations	4161535	2350003	1311532	4161535
R^2	0.125	0.139	0.097	0.087
Share of domestic starts	0.217	0.209	0.235	0.217
Province-product-destination country fixed effects	Yes			
Year fixed effects	Yes			

Notes: Heteroskedasticity-robust standard errors are reported in parentheses. Standard errors are clustered at the province level. ***, **, and * indicate significance at the 1%, 5%, and 10% confidence level. Conditional logit estimations in all columns but the last column, where a linear probability model is used.

However, it is difficult to figure out what is really at play with this heterogeneity of foreign export spillovers depending on GDP per capita. We use ICRG and Doing Business indexes to investigate this question further.

6.3.3 Foreign Export Spillovers and Institutional Quality of the Destination Country

One novel contribution of our chapter is to investigate the possibility that the relationship between foreign export spillovers and domestic creation of new trade linkages depends on destination countries' institutional quality.

We use the ICRG composite index, which is a weighted average of the political, financial, and economic risks indexes (which respective weights are 50%, 25%, and 25%) as calculated by the PRS group. The higher this index, the less risky the countries. Because the entry on risky markets is more difficult, we expect foreign export spillovers to be stronger for those destination countries, which is exactly what we observe in table 6.3.

In table 6.3, the regressions are run separately for countries with a low/high ICRG composite index (defined as being below/above the sample average of 70) in columns (2) and (3), respectively.

The presence of foreign firms exporting product k to country j at time t is positively associated with a rise in the probability that domestic firms start exporting the same product to the same country in $t + 1$ for countries with a low ICRG composite index only, that is, for more risky markets. We can compute that the mere presence of foreign exporters increases the probability of a domestic start the year after by 15.1 percent (3.32 percentage points) when considering countries with a low value of the ICRG index; a 10 percent increase in the value of these exports raises this same probability by 0.11 percent (0.02 percentage point). For less risky market, no significant impact of foreign presence is detected; a 10 percent increase of the value of foreign exports of product k to country j increases the probability of domestic starts by 0.16 percent (0.04 percentage point). The difference between both samples in terms of "intensive margin" of spillovers is thus negligible. Again, results are qualitatively similar when capturing heterogeneity through an interaction term, as shown in column (4). These results suggest that domestic exporters penetrating countries with poor institutional quality are likely to benefit more from exposure to multinational firms because they are confronted to greater risks and probably informational asymmetries. Hence our

Table 6.3
Export spillovers and destination country institutional quality

	Heterogeneity indicator			
	Destination country ICRG composite index			
Explained variable: domestic ODT new export link in $t + 1$	$\neq$.	$\leq$ mean	$>$ mean	Interaction
	(1)	(2)	(3)	(4)
Same product/country ODT foreign export	0.015***	0.012**	0.017***	0.004***
	(0.003)	(0.006)	(0.005)	(0.001)
Same product/country ODT foreign export * above threshold dummy				0.001
				(0.001)
0/1 same product/country ODT foreign export	0.068**	0.141***	0.037	0.039***
	(0.029)	(0.045)	(0.038)	(0.009)
0/1 same product/country ODT foreign export * above threshold dummy				−0.030***
				(0.001)
Other country/same product ODT foreign export	0.007***	0.006***	0.008***	0.0009***
	(0.002)	(0.002)	(0.002)	(0.00007)
Same country/other product ODT foreign export	0.002	−0.002	0.003	−0.0004***
	(0.003)	(0.003)	(0.004)	(0.00009)
Other country/product ODT foreign export	0.095	0.094	0.091	0.019***
	(0.108)	(0.123)	(0.101)	(0.001)
Controls for domestic own experience into export markets	yes			
Controls for demand	yes			
Controls for macro export	yes			
Control for demand and macro export lags	yes			
Observations	3850193	1904098	1946095	3850193
R^2	0.126	0.145	0.108	0.083
Share of domestic starts	0.219	0.210	0.228	0.219
Province-product-destination country fixed effects	yes			
Year fixed effects	yes			

Notes: Heteroskedasticity-robust standard errors are reported in parentheses. Standard errors are clustered at the province level. ***, **, and * indicate significance at the 1%, 5%, and 10% confidence level. Conditional logit estimations in all columns but the last column, where a linear probability model is used.

findings also support the hypothesis that proximity to foreign exporters reduces informational barriers to trade.

6.3.4   Foreign Export Spillovers and Import Procedures in the Destination Country

Finally, we study another dimension of the difficulty of entry on a given market using two measures of the restrictive effect of administrative procedures imposed by countries on their imports: the number of documents needed between the signature of the contract and the delivery of the goods, and the number of days between the arrival of commodities in the harbor and their delivery. The higher the values of these two variables, the more difficult the entry in the destination country.

Results presented in table 6.4 indicate that the presence in the province of foreign exports of product k to country j increases the probability that domestic firms start exporting k to j by 10.63 percent (2.41 percentage points) when the number of documents required by the destination country is high and by 13.66 percent (2.84 percentage points) when the number of days between the arrival in the harbor and the delivery of the commodities is high.

No significant impact of foreign exporter presence is detected when administrative procedures in the destination country are lighter. The impact of the value of foreign exports is not significantly different across countries. Results are qualitatively the same when measuring heterogeneity, thanks to an interactive term.

We have conducted a number of robustness checks. In table 6A.2, we show in particular that the results we obtain for our four indices of access difficulty are qualitatively the same if we exclude the top and bottom 5 percent of countries for each index. Outlier countries do thus not drive the heterogeneity we capture in terms of foreign export spillovers. We would have also liked to disentangle which dimension of access difficulty of destination country, GDP per capita, institutions or import administrative procedures—matters most likely to account for this heterogeneity. This step proved to be impossible. Indeed, all dimensions are highly correlated: correlation between GDP per capita and ICRG composite index is equal to more than 80 percent, and the correlation between GDP per capita and both measures of import administrative procedures is slightly higher than 60 percent. Consequently, when we try to introduce interactions of spillovers with all the different dimensions of access difficulty, results are poorly significant (results available upon request).

6.4   Conclusion

In this study, we explore how the intensity of foreign export spillovers in China varies depending on the difficulty of entering export markets. This approach allows us to shed light on the way the increasing presence of multinational firms influences the orientation of Chinese domestic firms' integration with the world economy. Several studies show that the presence of foreign firms in Chinese provinces and cities has a positive impact on the entry of domestic firms into export markets. If the externality provided by the exposure to foreign exporters partially acts through information spillovers, thereby helping the prospective domestic exporter to reduce the fixed cost of creating new trade linkages, we expect the effect to be particularly important for more difficult countries. This result is what we find, using different proxies to define a "difficult" country. Our results indicate that the presence of surrounding foreign exporting firms helps domestic ones to start exporting, especially when destination countries have a lower GDP per capita, are risky as measured by the ICRG index, or impose tough administrative procedures for the import of commodities. However, we cannot disentangle these to learn which dimension matters most.

Our results suggest that the increasing presence of foreign exporting firms in China might contribute to the diversification of domestic firms' exports toward more difficult and previously inaccessible destinations. Although on average, exposure to foreign exporters is associated with a 10 percent increase in the probability that domestic firms start exporting the year after, the figure is around 30 to 50 percent higher when the targeted destination country is identified as difficult. This finding does not mean that Chinese domestic firms export to easier markets than their foreign counterparts and that the gap between the two types of firms decreases over time thanks to foreign export spillovers. By contrast, Chinese domestic firms actually export on average to more risky markets or to countries where the administrative procedures imposed on imports are tougher (by roughly 10%) compared to foreign exporters located in China. Nevertheless, our results show that when domestic firms in a province do not yet export a given product to a given country, the more difficult the entry on this market is, the stronger the beneficial effect of exposure to foreign exporters is on the probability that Chinese domestic firms will start exporting this product to this new destination.

Table 6.4
Export spillovers and destination country administrative procedures

	Heterogeneity indicator						
	≠	Nb of documents			Nb of days		
Explained variable: domestic ODT new export link in $t + 1$		≤ mean	> mean	Interaction	≤ mean	> mean	Interaction
	(1)	(2)	(3)	(4)	(5)	(6)	(7)
Same product/country ODT foreign export	0.016*** (0.003)	0.016*** (0.005)	0.016** (0.006)	0.006*** (0.001)	0.017*** (0.005)	0.014*** (0.004)	0.006*** (0.001)
Same product/country ODT foreign export * above threshold dummy				0.001 (0.001)			-0.0004 (0.001)
0/1 same product/country ODT foreign export	0.069** (0.031)	0.052 (0.045)	0.101* (0.056)	0.008 (0.006)	0.041 (0.040)	0.128*** (0.038)	0.008 (0.006)
0/1 same product/country ODT foreign export * above threshold dummy				0.019* (0.010)			0.025** (0.012)
Other country/same product ODT foreign export	0.008*** (0.002)	0.008*** (0.002)	0.007*** (0.002)	0.001*** (0.00007)	0.008*** (0.002)	0.007*** (0.002)	0.001*** (0.00007)
Same country/other product ODT foreign export	0.001 (0.002)	0.001 (0.003)	0.001 (0.002)	-0.0005*** (0.00009)	0.006 (0.004)	-0.002 (0.002)	-0.001*** (0.00009)
Other country/product ODT foreign export	0.101 (0.122)	0.069 (0.097)	0.101 (0.122)	0.018*** (0.001)	0.070 (0.097)	0.097 (0.120)	0.017*** (0.001)

Table 6.4
(continued)

Explained variable: domestic ODT new export link in $t + 1$	Heterogeneity indicator						
	$\neq$	Nb of documents			Nb of days		
		$\leq$ mean	> mean	Interaction	$\leq$ mean	> mean	Interaction
	(1)	(2)	(3)	(4)	(5)	(6)	(7)
Controls for domestic own experience into export markets	Yes						
Controls for demand	Yes						
Controls for Macro export	Yes						
Control for demand and macro export lags	Yes						
Observations	4041770	1747070	2294700	4041770	1743238	2298532	4041770
R^2	0.124	0.105	0.140	0.086	0.104	0.141	0.086
Share of Domestic starts	0.218	0.227	0.211	0.218	0.230	0.208	0.218

Notes: Heteroskedasticity-robust standard errors are reported in parentheses. Standard errors are clustered at the province level. ***, **, and * indicate significance at the 1%, 5%, and 10% confidence level. Conditional logit estimations in all columns but columns 4 and 7, where a linear probability model is used.

Appendix

Table 6A.1
Descriptive statistics (average values for period 1997–2006)

Country	Nb of doc.	Nb of days	Composite ICRG	GDP per cap.	Share in China's exp.
United States	5.0	5.0	81	41,890	20.93
Hong Kong	5.3	8.7	81	25,604	14.71
Japan	5.0	11.0	85	35,484	11.71
Korea Rep	7.3	11.3	79	16,388	4.88
Germany	5.0	7.0	83	33,890	4.22
United Kingdom	4.0	14.0	83	36,555	2.66
Netherlands	5.0	6.0	87	38,248	2.28
Russia	13.0	36.0	63	5,342	2.23
Taiwan	7.0	12.0	83	15,270	2.17
Singapore	4.0	3.0	90	26,877	1.94
Italy	5.0	18.0	80	30,073	1.74
Canada	5.0	11.3	84	34,484	1.68
France	7.7	15.7	81	34,936	1.57
Australia	7.7	13.3	82	36,046	1.55
India	13.0	35.0	66	736	1.34
United Arab Emirates	8.0	13.0	79	28,612	1.32
Malaysia	7.0	14.0	76	5,159	1.29
Spain	8.0	10.0	79	25,914	1.26
Indonesia	8.0	29.0	58	1,301	1.18
Thailand	11.0	19.3	74	2,743	1.06
Mexico	5.0	23.0	70	7,447	0.80
Vietnam	8.0	23.0	67	637	0.76
Brazil	7.0	23.3	64	4,734	0.72
Kazakhstan	14.0	76.0	70	3,771	0.68
Turkey	11.3	21.7	55	5,042	0.65
Philippines	8.0	18.0	70	1,184	0.61
Saudi Arabia	7.7	29.3	74	13,399	0.61
S. Africa	9.0	35.0	71	5,162	0.60
Iran	10.0	42.0	68	2,781	0.53
Pakistan	9.3	25.7	58	714	0.52
Denmark	3.0	5.0	87	47,769	0.47
Panama	4.0	9.0	71	4,791	0.46
Finland	5.0	8.0	87	36,820	0.44
Sweden	3.0	6.0	84	39,637	0.42

Table 6A.1
(continued)

Country	Nb of doc.	Nb of days	Composite ICRG	GDP per cap.	Share in China's exp.
Poland	5.0	27.0	78	7,943	0.40
Bangladesh	11.7	48.7	63	423	0.40
Ukraine	10.0	39.0	64	1,830	0.39
Nigeria	10.3	48.3	55	686	0.38
Hungary	7.0	17.0	77	10,941	0.36
Chile	7.0	21.0	77	7,297	0.33
Greece	6.0	25.0	76	20,282	0.31
Egypt	8.0	24.0	69	1,211	0.31
Switzerland	5.0	9.0	89	49,351	0.30
Israel	4.0	12.0	68	17,828	0.29
Macau				25,162	0.23
Romania	9.0	18.0	64	4,569	0.23
Norway	4.0	7.0	90	63,918	0.22
Algeria	9.0	22.3	59	3,098	0.21
Argentina	7.0	20.0	67	4,728	0.20
New Zealand	5.0	9.0	80	26,664	0.20
Morocco	11.0	26.3	71	1,713	0.19
Ireland	4.0	12.0	87	48,524	0.19
Sudan	11.0	73.3	45	770	0.18
Korea DPR			46		0.17
Czech Rep	7.0	18.0	78	12,115	0.16
Benin	7.0	41.0		508	0.16
Kirghizia	13.0	75.0		478	0.15
Syrian	12.0	36.3	70	1,493	0.15
Colombia	10.0	34.3	60	2,735	0.14
Sri Lanka	10.0	25.0	63	1,199	0.14
Myanmar			59		0.14
Venezuela	11.3	58.0	64	5,449	0.14
Portugal	7.0	16.7	81	17,376	0.13
Jordan	8.7	24.0	72	2,349	0.12
Austria	5.0	8.7	85	37,175	0.12
Ghana	9.7	42.0	61	485	0.11
Kuwait	11.0	20.0	80	31,861	0.10
Cuba			62		0.10
Peru	8.0	31.0	67	2,838	0.09
Croatia Rep	10.3	23.7	72	8,754	0.09
Togo	9.0	33.7	59	343	0.09

Table 6A.1
(continued)

Country	Nb of doc.	Nb of days	Composite ICRG	GDP per cap.	Share in China's exp.
Rep Yemen	9.0	31.0	65	798	0.09
Guatemala	8.3	29.0	68	2,517	0.07
Lebanon	9.7	35.3	58	5,366	0.07
Kampuchea	11.3	49.0		440	0.07
Ecuador	8.0	44.0	59	2,758	0.07
Kenya	9.7	45.3	62	560	0.07
Bulgaria	9.0	23.7	69	3,513	0.07
Iraq	10.0	101.0	42		0.06
Angola	9.0	58.0	49	2,058	0.06
Libyan Arab Jamahiriya			67	7,118	0.06
Lithuania	6.0	13.0	74	7,513	0.06
Malta			81	13,803	0.05
Marshall Is. Rep	5.0	33.0		2,282	0.05
Estonia	4.0	5.0	74	10,213	0.05
Mongolia	10.0	59.0	65	821	0.05
Ethiopia	8.0	42.0	61	160	0.04
Slovak Rep	8.0	25.0	75	8,803	0.04
Tanzania	9.0	37.0	60	327	0.04
Latvia	5.3	12.0	74	6,973	0.04
Dominican Rep	9.0	15.7	71	3,073	0.04
Azerbaijan	14.0	56.0	62	1,579	0.04
Slovenia Rep	8.0	21.0	79	17,173	0.04
Afghanistan	10.7	79.7			0.01
Netherlands Antilles					0.01
Suriname	7.0	25.0	64	2,989	0.01
Zambia	11.0	64.0	57	623	0.01
Niger	10.0	68.0	57	243	0.01
Georgia	9.7	26.7		1,433	0.01
Belize	6.0	26.0		3,786	0.00
Sierra Leone	7.0	34.0	42	220	0.00
Haiti	10.0	53.0	54	518	0.00
Guyana	8.0	35.0	65	1,057	0.00
Er Virgin Is.					0.00
Macedonia Rep	7.0	23.7		2,835	0.00
Armenia	6.7	32.7	59	1,625	0.00
Barbados				11,465	0.00

Table 6A.1
(continued)

Country	Nb of doc.	Nb of days	Composite ICRG	GDP per cap.	Share in China's exp.
Equitorial Guinea	7.0	46.0		14,936	0.00
French Polynesia					0.00
Burkina Faso	11.0	54.0	61	431	0.00
Bosnia & Herzegovina	7.0	22.7		2,540	0.00
Maldives	9.0	20.0		2,296	0.00
Chad	9.0	102.0		604	0.00
Malawi	10.0	54.0	60	161	0.00
New Caledonia			64		0.00
Burundi	10.0	71.0		105	0.00
Somalia			38		0.00
Rwanda	16.0	85.3		237	0.00
St Vincent & Grenadines	6.0	16.0		3,612	0.00
Central African Republic	18.0	66.0		339	0.00
Vanuatu	9.0	30.0		1,741	0.00
Eritrea	14.3	69.0		220	0.00
Tuvalu					0.00
Samoa	7.0	31.0		2,184	0.00
Cape Verde	5.0	21.0		1,972	0.00
Guinea Bissau	3.5	26.0	46	190	0.00
Solomon Is.	4.0	21.0		624	0.00
Tonga	6.0	25.0		2,097	0.00
Seychelles	5.0	19.0		8,551	0.00
Micronesia FS	6.0	30.0		2,145	0.00
Cayman Islands					0.00
Comoros	10.0	21.0		645	0.00
East Timor				359	0.00
Gibraltar					0.00
St Kitts–Nevis	6.0	17.0		9,438	0.00
Bhutan	11.0	38.0		1,299	0.00
Greenland					0.00
Sao Tome Principe	9.0	29.0		719	0.00
Cook Is.					0.00
Norfolk Is.					0.00
Montserrat					0.00

Table 6A.2
Heterogeneity investigation of export spillovers: without extreme observations (top and bottom 5%)

Criteria	Specification			
	(1)	(2)	(3)	(4)
	GDP per capita	ICRG	Nb of doc	Nb of days
Same product/country foreign ODT export	0.006*** (0.001)	0.005*** (0.001)	0.006*** (0.001)	0.006*** (0.001)
Interaction with above threshold dummy	−0.001 (0.001)	0.001 (0.001)	−0.001 (0.001)	−0.001 (0.001)
0/1 same product/country foreign ODT export	0.027*** (0.007)	0.037*** (0.009)	0.007 (0.006)	0.006 (0.006)
Interaction with above threshold dummy	−0.014 (0.010)	−0.030*** (0.011)	0.023** (0.011)	0.026** (0.011)
Controls for domestic own experience into export markets	Yes			
Controls for demand (country-product imports and country GDP per capita)	Yes			
Controls for Macro export (Balassa, bilateral exports of China and of province, province GDP per capita)	Yes			
Control for demand and macro export lags	Yes			
Observations	4004570	3722207	3985811	3906476
R^2	0.08			
Share of domestic starts	0.20			
Province-product-destination country FE	Yes			
Year fixed effects	Yes			

Notes: Heteroskedasticity-robust standard errors are reported in parentheses. Standard errors are clustered at the province level. ***, **, and * indicate significance at the 1%, 5%, and 10% confidence level. Linear probability model in all regressions.

Notes

1. Koenig, Mayneris, and Poncet (2010a) obtain a similar result on export spillovers in France, even though in this case the authors do not distinguish between foreign and domestic firms.

2. Although the average world duration is 27 days, at least 44 days are required to clear the customs in the top decile countries. See section 6.2.1 for more details on this indicator, taken from the World Bank Doing Business databases.

3. We use the terms "multinational" and "foreign" interchangeably throughout the chapter.

4. Ordinary trade activities refer to exports of products that are produced with local inputs mainly; processing trade activities refer to trade flows of products that have been assembled in China but for which components have been produced abroad and then imported.

5. Six-digit level of the Harmonized System nomenclature.

6. The data are separately reported by firm type, including foreign-owned enterprises, equity joint ventures and Sino-foreign joint ventures, collective enterprises, private enterprises, and state-owned enterprises. We consider the first three categories as foreign and the three latter as domestic.

7. Defined as exports for at least two consecutive years.

8. However, our strategy to introduce both a dummy for foreign presence and the value of foreign exports allows to assess the shape of export spillovers: if the dummy turns out to be positive and significant while the value is insignificant, this means that export spillovers are entirely driven by the sole presence of foreign firms; a positive and significant coefficient on the value of exports only would mean that the intensity of spillovers increases log linearly with the value of foreign exports. Finally, a negative (resp. positive) and significant coefficient on the dummy and a positive (resp. negative) and significant coefficient on the value of exports indicate that export spillovers impact positively on domestic starts for high (resp. low) enough value of foreign exports only.

9. This dataset, which is constructed using COMTRADE original data, provides bilateral trade flows at the six-digit product level (Gaulier and Zignago 2010). BACI is downloadable from http://www.cepii.fr/anglaisgraph/bdd/baci.htm.

10. World countries' real GDP per capita in PPP are taken from the World Development Indicators database (World Bank).

11. These results are available from the authors upon request.

12. Given the form of the logistic function, the increase in probability generated by the sole presence of foreign firms exporting product k to country j is equal to $[e^{0.104} - 1]\%$. The increase expressed in percentage points of probability is found by multiplying this expression by the probability of starting to export at the point at which the marginal impact is estimated.

13. If we consider a reference value x_i for variable x, the increase in probability generated by a 10 percent increase in x is equal to $(1.1^{\beta_x} - 1)$, β_x being the coefficient on x. The increase expressed in percentage points of probability is equal to $(1.1^{\beta_x} - 1)P_{xi}$.

References

Aitken, Brian J., Gordon H. Hanson, and Ann E. Harrison. 1997. Spillovers, foreign investment, and export behavior. *Journal of International Economics* 43:103–132.

Amiti, Mary, and Caroline Freund. 2010. An anatomy of China's export growth. In *China's Growing Role in World Trade*, ed. Robert Feenstra and Shang-Jin Wei, 35–56. Chicago: University of Chicago Press.

Araujo, Luis, Giordano Mion, and Emanuel Ornelas. 2011. Institutions and export dynamics. Mimeo.

Barrios, Salvador, Holger Gorg, and Eric Strobl. 2003. Explaining firms' export behaviour: R&D, spillovers and the destination market. *Oxford Bulletin of Economics and Statistics* 65 (4): 475–496.

Chen, Huiya, and Deborah Swenson. 2013. Multinational exposure and the quality of new Chinese exports. Forthcoming in *Oxford Bulletin of Economics and Statistics*.

Crozet, Matthieu, Pamina Koenig and Vincent Rebeyrol 2008. Exporting to insecure markets: A firm-level analysis. CEPII DP 2008-13.

Gaulier, Guillaume, and Soledad Zignago. 2010. BACI: A world database of international trade at the product level, The 1994–2007 version. CEPII Working Paper 2010-23.

Hale, Galina, and Cheryl Long. 2011. Did foreign direct investment put an upward pressure on wages in China? *IMF Economic Review* 59: 404–430.

Hess, Wolfgang and Maria Persson 2010, The duration of trade revisited: Continuous-time vs. discrete-time hazards. IFN WP 829.

Hess, Wolfgang, and Maria Persson. 2011. Exploring the duration of EU imports. *Review of World Economics* 147 (4): 665–692.

Hummels, David, and Pete Klenow. 2005. The variety and quality of a nation's exports. *American Economic Review* 95 (3): 704–723.

Kneller, Richard, and Mauro Pisu. 2007. Industrial linkages and export spillovers from FDI. *World Economy* 30 (1): 105–134.

Koenig, Pamina, Florian Mayneris, and Sandra Poncet. 2010a. Local export spillovers in France. *European Economic Review* 54:622–641.

Koenig, Pamina, Florian Mayneris, and Sandra Poncet. 2010b. Economies d'agglomération à l'exportation et difficulté d'accès aux marchés. *Economie & Statistique* 435–436:85–103.

Krautheim, Sebastian. 2012. Heterogeneous firms, exporter networks and the effect of distance on international trade. *Journal of International Economics* 87 (1): 27–35.

Lu, Yi, Joyce Ni, and Zhigang Tao. 2010. Hold your enemies closer: in search of positive impacts of horizontal foreign direct investment on domestic firms. Mimeo.

Mayneris, Florian and Sandra Poncet. 2013. Export performance of Chinese domestic firms: the role of foreign export spillovers. Forthcoming in *World Bank Economic Review*.

Melitz, Marc. 2003. The impact of trade on intra-industry reallocations and aggregate industry productivity. *Econometrica* 71 (6): 1695–1725.

Moulton, Brent R. 1990. An illustration of a pitfall in estimating the effects of aggregate variables on micro unit. *Review of Economics and Statistics* 72 (2): 334–338.

Rodrik, Dani. 2006. What is so special about China's exports? *China & World Economy* 14 (5): 1–19.

Ruane, Frances, and Julie Sutherland. 2005, Foreign direct investment and export spillovers: How do export platforms fare? IIIS Discussion Paper 58.

Schott, Peter K. 2008. The relative sophistication of Chinese exports. *Economic Policy* 53:5–49.

Swenson, Deborah. 2008. Multinationals and the creation of Chinese trade linkages. *Canadian Journal of Economics. Revue Canadienne d'Economique* 41 (2): 596–618.

Xu, Bin, and Jiangyong Lu. 2009. Foreign direct investment, processing trade, and the sophistication of China's exports. *China Economic Review* 20:425–439.

III Boundaries of the Firm

7 Intrafirm and Arm's-Length Trade: How Distance Matters

Pamela Bombarda

7.1 Introduction

Intrafirm trade and arm's-length trade play an important role in trade arena.[1] Dunning (1994) shows that a large part of international trade is conducted by multinational firms (MNFs). He estimated that MNFs together with their subsidiaries are responsible for 75 percent of the world's trade commodity. UNCTAD (2001) reports that one-third of world trade is intrafirm trade (trade between MNF headquarters and subsidiaries or among subsidiaries). More recently, Bernard et al. (2007) documented that 90 percent of U.S. exports and imports occurs through multinational firms. Recent studies try to analyze the different behavior of related-party versus arm's-length trade (Irarrazabal, Moxnes, and Opromolla 2013; Corcos et al. 2009; Bernard et al. 2010, among others). The notion of openness should therefore include trade as well as multinational production.

This chapter develops a model of trade that features heterogeneous firms, multinational firms, exporters, and intrafirm trade in a general equilibrium framework. Its main contribution is to explain the different impact of geographical distance on related-party versus arm's-length trade. It also provides stylized facts to support the model's main predictions using 1999–2004 data from the Bureau of Economic Analysis (BEA) and the Center for International Data (CID) at the University of California–Davis.[2]

The theoretical framework offers a possible explanation of the puzzling larger effect of distance on trade rather than on intrafirm trade and on complementarity versus substitutability debate. Globalization boosts both export and affiliate revenues. However, certain intermediate goods are closer complements than others. In these sectors, foreign affiliates take advantage from globalization and thus the effect of distance should be important.

In this chapter, a trade policy intervention affects the trading activity of firms that occurs both within and outside the boundaries of the firm and across different sectors. Globalization should increase the volume of trade. Measuring the response of arm's-length and related-party trade to globalization pressures is important to define specific policy intervention. For example, a reduction in trade barriers increases multinational activity more rapidly with a higher share of intrafirm trade between the headquarters and the affiliate.

To provide a more appealing explanation for the coexistence of national and multinational firms, we extend the Melitz (2003) model to allow for intra-industry firm heterogeneity in productivity, which avoids the coexistence of different types of firms only as a knife-edge case. This extended model can explain the within-industry variation across firms in their decisions about export and foreign direct investment (FDI).

To accounts for intrafirm trade, we claim that each foreign affiliate must import an intermediate input from the home headquarters. Thus, in a departure from Helpman, Melitz, and Yeaple (2004), trade costs apply to both exports and multinational production because both involve transportation (the first of a finished good, the second of an intermediate good). The model suggests that the more productive firms enter a larger number of markets, undertake a large part of intrafirm trade, and sell more in each market that they enter than do less productive firms. In a similar way, countries with characteristics that are more attractive to U.S. multinationals should attract relatively less productive firms.

In this model, heightening of trade barriers affects in two opposite ways the FDI mode of supply. First, it increases the threshold productivity cutoff: the need to import intermediate goods from headquarters makes it more difficult to enter as a foreign affiliate when trade costs increase. This result is opposite to Helpman, Melitz, and Yeaple (2004), for whom an increase in trade costs makes FDI strategy easier. Second, sales of the existing foreign affiliates decrease (new margin of adjustment for MNFs). By contrast, in absence of traded intermediates a change in trade costs translate into a change in the number of MNFs entering the market, while the profit of the already existing foreign affiliates is left unaffected.

To consider the different behavior of related-party and arm's-length trade, we try to connect the model to the data. The empirical section studies the gravity equations for U.S. intrafirm exports (aggregated at the sectoral level) and U.S. arm's-length exports (aggregated at the sectoral level) to quantify the different role of geographical distance. This part describes how the model can deliver the features of the data related to foreign sales which are observed for U.S. multinational and exporting firms. Using BEA and CID data at the sectoral level, we are able to confirm that geographical distance is more important for arm's-length trade than for intrafirm trade.

This chapter contributes to the growing literature on intrafirm trade by focusing on the boundaries of the firm, an important topic for both international business (IB) and international economics (IE) literature. As Rugman and Nguyen suggest in chapter 1, the aspects related to a IB understanding of trade and FDI patterns differ. Although this chapter has a more IE orientation, it is also connected to IB literature in terms of the focal unit of analysis and the determinance of firms' boundaries.

Trade and FDI literature has grown over time. Hanson, Mataloni, and Slaughter (2001), using detailed data on U.S. multinationals, find that vertical FDI is common and that affiliates respond to policies and foreign countries' characteristics in different ways. Keller and Yeaple (2008) embody in a trade model two crucial elements: product's technological complexity and distance between the buyer and the seller. In their model, the interaction of these elements determines the size of the costs of reaching foreign markets. Their empirical results confirm the existence of gravity for weightless goods (complex technology products). Irarrazabal, Moxnes, and Opromolla (2013) structurally estimate a model of trade and multinational production with firms' heterogeneity. Their results reject the proximity versus concentration hypothesis, which did not consider intrafirm trade. Corcos et al. (2009), using French firm-level data, investigate the main determinants of the internalization choice. Their findings highlight the roles of capital, skill, and productivity in explaining the choice of intrafirm trade.

Although we do not consider the choice of whether to internalize the production process, it is important to remember that intrafirm versus arm's-length trade strategies are at the heart of the classical "make or buy" decision literature. This literature combines elements from international trade theory and the theory of the firm. The issues of where to locate the different stages of the value chain as well as the control exerted on these processes have being studied by, among others, Ethier (1986), Grossman and Helpman (2002), Antràs (2003, 2005), and Antràs and Helpman (2004)

The goal of this chapter is to shed new light on firms' global sourcing strategies, focusing more on the role of distance and trade costs while omitting the issue of incomplete contracts. In the present framework, geographical distances are crucial in explaining how firms reshape their global sourcing strategies.

The rest of the chapter is organized as follows. Section 7.2 provides a description of facts on U.S. multinational firms. Section 7.3 describes the theoretical framework that rationalizes the main features of the data. Section 7.4 characterizes the equilibrium. Section 7.5 presents the empirical analysis. Section 7.6 concludes.

7.2   Data on U.S. Multinational Firms

Data on U.S. multinational firms are obtained from the direct investment data set accessible from the BEA website.[3] Among different types of information provided by BEA, this chapter focuses on the following data: number of U.S. foreign affiliates in different destination countries; local affiliate sales; volume of U.S. intrafirm trade, that is, U.S. exports of goods shipped to affiliates by U.S. parents, by country of affiliate.

7.2.1   U.S. Affiliates and Market Entry

Figures 7.1 and 7.2 plot the number of U.S. affiliates selling to a market across 200 destination markets in 2004. More precisely, figure 7.1 plots the number of U.S. affiliates against total absorption in that market. Because the data are matched with production data, the sample is here restricted to less than fifty countries. The number of firms selling to a market tends clearly to increase with the size of the market.

In figure 7.2, the relationship is neater: here the number of U.S. affiliates is normalized by the U.S. market share in a destination. Following Eaton, Kortum, and Kramarz (2008), the x-axis of figure 7.2 reports market size across different destinations. The y-axis replaces the number of U.S. affiliates in a market with that number divided by U.S. market share. U.S. market share is defined as total U.S. affiliate sales to that market, $X_{us,j}^M$, divided by the market's total absorption, X_j,

$$\pi_{us,j} = \frac{X_{us,j}^M}{X_j}$$

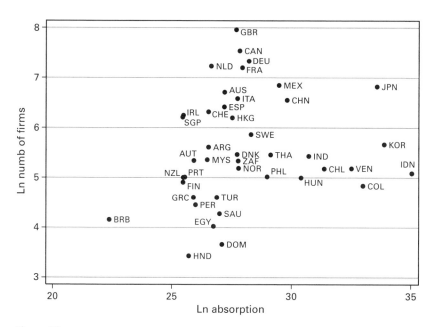

Figure 7.1
Number of U.S. affiliates. *Note:* Author calculations based on BEA dataset for 2004.

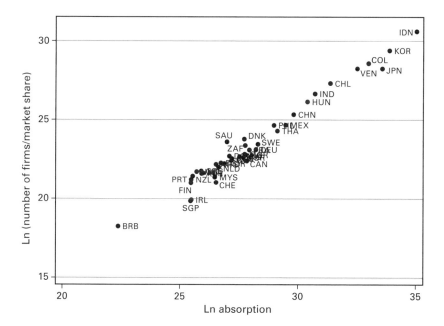

Figure 7.2
Number of U.S. affiliates. *Note:* Author calculations based on BEA dataset for 2004.

The relationship in figure 7.2 is tight. Canada is pulled from the position of a positive outlier to a negative one. A regression line is a slope of 0.93. Figures 7.1 and 7.2 confirm that the number of sellers in a market varies with market size.[4]

7.2.2   Intrafirm Trade and Affiliate Sales

Figure 7.3 plots the relationship between U.S. exports of goods shipped to affiliates by U.S. parents, by country of affiliate against total affiliate sales in a market. Figure 7.4 shows the increase in the value of the good sold by the U.S. affiliate in j: all points lie below the 45° line.

7.3   Theoretical Framework

In what follows we propose a model of export and FDI as well as intrafirm trade. Following Chaney (2008), we do not assume free entry.[5] This setup allows us to study the supply mode decision between FDI and export in a multicountry framework.

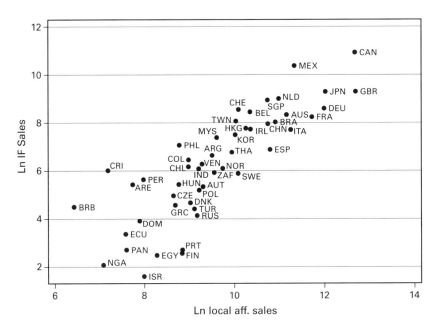

Figure 7.3
Intrafirm trade and local affiliate sales in 2004. *Note:* Data on local sales in the destination market from BEA (majority-owned nonbank foreign affiliates of nonbank U.S. parents).

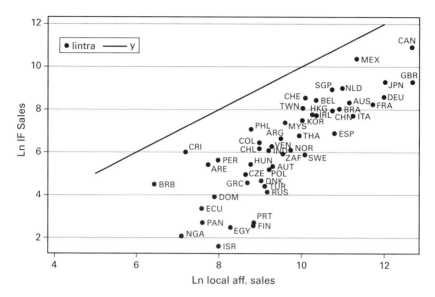

Figure 7.4
Intrafirm trade and local affiliate sales in 2004. *Note:* Data on local sales in the destination market from BEA (Majority-owned nonbank foreign affiliates of nonbank U.S. parents).

7.3.1 Preferences

Consumers in each country share the same preferences over the final good. The preferences of a representative consumer are given by constant elasticity of substitution (CES) utility function over a continuum of goods indexed by v,

$$U = \left[\int_{v \in V} c(v)^{(\sigma-1)/\sigma} \, dv \right]^{\frac{\sigma}{\sigma-1}}$$

where $\sigma > 1$ represents the elasticity of substitution between any two products within the group and V is the set of available varieties.

7.3.2 Supply

In the following setup, we have one final good, two intermediate goods, and one factor. Each country is endowed with labor, L, which is supplied inelastically. There are N potentially asymmetric countries that produce goods using only labor. Country n has a population L_n.

There is one differentiated sector that produces a continuum of horizontally differentiated varieties, $q(v)$, from two intermediate goods (or tasks), y_1 and y_2. Both y_1 and y_2 are produced with one unit of labor, but y_1 can be made only at home, due to technological appropriability issues. Each variety is supplied by a Dixit-Stiglitz monopolistically competitive firm that produces under increasing returns to scale that arise from a fixed cost. We assume that the fixed cost is paid in units of labor in the country where the good is produced.

We consider three modes of supply in the differentiated sector: firms that sell only domestically (D-mode); firms that export (X-mode), and firms that supply the foreign market via FDI (M-mode). Hence when a firm decides to serve the foreign market, it chooses whether to export domestically produced goods or to produce in a foreign country via affiliate production. In making those decisions, they consider the net profits from selling in a given market and they compare the profits from exports and from FDI.

As in Helpman, Melitz, and Yeaple (2004), this choice is affected by the classical scale versus proximity trade-off.[6] Nevertheless, in our model, the introduction of intrafirm trade makes the M-mode of supply sensitive to geographical distance between countries. The fact that y_1 can be made only at home plays an important role. If a firm chooses to supply the foreign market via local sales of its affiliates, the affiliate must import the intermediate good y_1 from the home nation. This intrafirm trade relationship implies that the M-mode does not entirely avoid trade costs. The trade link between the home parent and the affiliate captures the complementary relationship between trade and FDI. In this model, the existence of asymmetric countries implies that there is not a one-to-one mapping between the productivity of a firm and the scale of its production.

Upon drawing its own parameter a from a cumulative density function $G(a)$ that is common to every country, each firm decides to exit (which happens if it has a low productivity draw) or to produce. In this case, the firm must face additional fixed costs linked to the mode of supply chosen. If it chooses to produce for its own domestic market, it pays the additional fixed market entry cost, f_{ii}. If the firm chooses to export, it bears the additional costs f_{ij} of meeting different market-specific standards (for example, the cost of creating a distribution network in a new country). Finally, if the firm chooses to serve foreign markets through FDI, there would be two types of fixed costs: a fixed cost of creating a distribution network and a fixed cost of building up new capacities in the foreign country.[7] We call these fixed costs $f_{M,ij}$.

7.3.3   Intermediate Results

Demand   Given preferences across varieties have the standard CES form, the demand of a representative consumer from country i for a type a good is given by

$$c_i(a) = A_i p_i(a)^{-\sigma} \text{ where } A_i \equiv \frac{Y_i}{P_i^{1-\sigma}}$$

where the subscript i indicates the country, a is the unit labor coefficient, A_i is the demand shifter, and $p_i(a)$ is the consumer price index paid to a firm with marginal cost a. A_i is exogenous from the perspective of the firm and composed by the aggregate level of spending on the differentiated good, Y_i divided by the CES price index, $P_i^{1-\sigma}$.

Organization and Product Variety   We assume that the production of the final good combines the two intermediates, y_1 and y_2, in the following Cobb-Douglas function,

$$q_i(a) = \frac{1}{a}\left(\frac{y_1}{\eta}\right)^{\eta}\left(\frac{y_2}{1-\eta}\right)^{1-\eta}, 0 < \eta < 1 \tag{7.1}$$

where $1/a$ represents the firm-specific productivity parameter and η is the Cobb-Douglas cost share of y_1, common across all nations. When trade is possible, firms that produce decide whether to sell to a particular market and how—that is, via export or FDI strategies. This decision depends on their own productivity, on trade costs between the origin and the destination country, and on the fixed costs.[8]

The marginal costs in the exporting sector will be higher than the one in the FDI sector. Because y_1 and y_2 are produced with L, the marginal cost for domestic as well as export production is linear in τ,

$$mc_{ij} = a w_i \tau_{ij}$$

where when $i = j$ then $\tau_{ij} = 1$. The marginal cost for supplying the foreign market j via local sales of foreign affiliates is concave in τ,

$$mc_{M,ij} = a w_j^{1-\eta}\left(w_i \tau_{ij}\right)^{\eta}$$

This last marginal cost combines inputs from home and host country. More precisely, $w_j^{1-\eta}$ is the labor cost for input produced in country j and w_i^{η} is the labor cost for input imported in country j from the home country i.[9] Note that in this last marginal cost, trade costs matter, but only in relation to cost share, η, of the intermediate good y_1 used in the production of the final good. Using the mark up, $\sigma/(\sigma - 1)$, we can easily derive the price for each particular mode of supply decisions.

Mode of Supply Decisions The mode of supply decision choice involves the comparison of profit levels, taking into account the various fixed and variable trade costs. A firm can decide to: (1) not supply a market, (2) supply it via exports, or (3) supply it via local sales of foreign affiliates.[10]

The optimal mode of supply depends on a firm's productivity. As described previously, three cases are relevant:

Case (1). If the firm decides to not supply a market and exits, the operating profits are zero.

Case (2). If the firm in country i decides to supply market j via exports, the profits from exporting to market j are linearly decreasing in τ_{ij},

$$\pi_{ij} = \left[p_{ij}(a) - aw_i \tau_{ij} \right] q(a)_{ij} - w_j f_{ij}$$

where $q(a)_{ij}$ represents the quantity exported. Substituting the equilibrium price and quantity, we have

$$\pi_{ij} = \frac{1}{\sigma} \left(\frac{\sigma}{\sigma - 1} \right)^{(1-\sigma)} Y_j \left(w_i a \tau_{ij} \right)^{1-\sigma} / P_j^{1-\sigma} - w_j f_{ij} \tag{7.2}$$

where the fixed cost of exporting, f_{ij}, is evaluated at the foreign wage rate, w_j.[11]

Case (3). If the firm in country i decides to supply market j via FDI, the profits realized by a subsidiary located in the j country depend on τ_{ij},

$$\pi_{M,ij} = \left[p_M(a) - aw_j^{1-\eta} \left(w_i \tau_{ij} \right)^{\eta} \right] q(a)_{M,ij} - w_j f_{M,ij} \tag{7.3}$$

where $q(a)_{M,ij}$ represents the quantity supplied by the foreign affiliate. Substituting the equilibrium price and quantity, we have

$$\pi_{M,ij} = \frac{1}{\sigma} \left(\frac{\sigma}{\sigma - 1} \right)^{(1-\sigma)} Y_j \left(aw_j^{1-\eta} \left(w_i \tau_{ij} \right)^{\eta} \right)^{1-\sigma} / P_j^{1-\sigma} - w_j f_{M,ij}$$

where τ_{ij}^{η} is the trade costs associated with the intermediate good, y_1, imported from the home country. The foreign affiliate has to face both the fixed cost $f_{M,ij}$, evaluated at the foreign wage rate, and the trade costs that hit the imported intermediate.

To focus on the central case, we set parameters so that we get the same ranking as in Helpman, Melitz, and Yeaple (2004) when there are only two nations. Namely, only firms with sufficiently high productivity supply the foreign market at all, with the most productive supplying it via FDI rather than exports. Hence, the regularity condition we need is

$$\left(w_i \tau_{ij}\right)^{(\sigma-1)} w_j f_{ij} < \left(w_j^{1-\eta} \left(w_i \tau_{ij}\right)^{\eta}\right)^{\sigma-1} w_j f_{M,ij}$$

Rearranging terms, we get

$$f_{ij} < f_{M,ij} \frac{\left(w_j^{1-\eta} \left(w_i \tau_{ij}\right)^{\eta}\right)^{\sigma-1}}{\left(w_i \tau_{ij}\right)^{(\sigma-1)}} \tag{7.4}$$

That the price index depends on the probability distribution implies that in order to have explicit solutions for this model, we need to assume a particular functional form for $G(a)$. Following the empirical literature on firm size distribution (see Axtell 2001 and Chaney 2008), we assume that unit labor requirements are drawn from a Pareto distribution. The cumulative distribution function of a Pareto random variable a is:

$$G(a) = \left(\frac{a}{a_0}\right)^k \tag{7.5}$$

where k and a_0 are the shape and scale parameter, respectively. The shape parameter k represents the dispersion of cost draws. An increase in k would imply a reduction in the dispersion of firm productivity draws. Hence, the higher k is, the smaller the amount of heterogeneity.

The support of the distribution $[0, \ldots , a_0]$, is identical for every country, where a_0 represents the upper bound of this distribution. The productivity distribution of surviving firms will also be Pareto with shape k. More precisely, because a firm will start producing only if it has a productivity of at least $1/a_{ij}$, the probability distribution of supplying as an exporter, or as a foreign affiliate, is conditioned on the probability of successful entry in each market,

$$G(a / a_{ii}) = \left(\frac{a}{a_{ii}}\right)^k$$

The truncated cost distribution exploits the fractal nature of the Pareto. Here the support is $[0, \ldots , a_{ii}]$. Given the assumed parameterization, we can explicitly solve for the price index.

The total mass of potential entrants in country i is proportional to its labor income, $w_i L_i$. Hence, larger and wealthier countries have more entrants. The absence of free entry implies that firms generate net profits, which have to be redistributed. Following Chaney (2008), each worker owns w_i shares of the global fund. This fund collects profits from the firms and redistributes them to its shareholders.

Demand for Differentiated Goods   Total income in country j, Y_j, is the sum of workers' labor income in country j, $w_j L_j$, and of the dividends they get from their portfolio, $\pi w_j L_j$, where π is the dividend per share.

Given the optimal pricing of firms and the demand by consumers, we can find the export value from country i to country j by a firm with unit labor requirement a,

$$x_{ij}^X = p_{ij}^X q_{ij}^X = Y_j \left(p_{ij}^X\right)^{1-\sigma} / P_j^{1-\sigma}$$

where $p_{ij}^X = [\sigma/(\sigma-1)]aw_i\tau_{ij}$ and $q_{ij}^X = \left(p_{ij}^X\right)^{-\sigma}\beta Y_i / P_j^{1-\sigma}$. While affiliate sales by a firm located in j are

$$x_{ij}^M = p_{ij}^M q_{ij}^M = Y_j \left(p_{ij}^M\right)^{1-\sigma} / P_j^{1-\sigma}$$

where P_j represents the price index of good q in country j. The value of export and of total production in j's foreign affiliates are therefore similar to the one derived from homogeneous firms setup. They provide the basis for gravity equations of export and of affiliate sales.

Because only firms with $a \leq \bar{a}_{kj}$ can start producing, the ideal price index in country j is[12]

$$P_j^{1-\sigma} = \sum_{k=1}^N w_k L_k \left[\int_0^{a_{M,kj}} \left(w_j^{1-\eta}\left(w_k\tau_{kj}\right)^\eta\right)^{1-\sigma} a^{1-\sigma}dG(a) + \int_{a_{M,kj}}^{a_{kj}} \left(w_k\tau_{kj}\right)^{1-\sigma} a^{1-\sigma}dG(a) \right]$$

The dividends per share, π, are defined as

$$\pi = \frac{\sum_{k,l=1}^N w_k L_k \left[\int_0^{a_{M,kl}} \pi_{M,kl}dG(a) + \int_{a_{M,kl}}^{a_{kl}} \pi_{kl}dG(a) \right]}{\sum_{n=1}^N w_n L_n}$$

where in the square brackets we have the profits that a firm with a specific threshold level in country k earns from a specific mode of supply in country l.[13] A similar analysis can be extended to H sectors. In appendix 7B.3, we derive solutions for the profits.

7.4 Equilibrium with Heterogeneous Firms

To compute the equilibrium of the overall economy, we solve for the selection of firms into different modes of supply. We generate predictions for aggregate bilateral trade and FDI flows.

7.4.1 Productivity Threshold

From the profit a firm earns from exporting, we can derive the productivity threshold of the least productive firm in country i able to export to country j,

$$a_{ij}^{1-\sigma} = \lambda_1 \frac{w_j f_{ij}}{Y_j} \frac{P_j^{1-\sigma}}{\left(w_i \tau_{ij}\right)^{1-\sigma}} \tag{7.6}$$

where $\lambda_1 = \sigma \left(\dfrac{\sigma-1}{\sigma}\right)^{(1-\sigma)}$.[14] Although the productivity threshold of the least productive firm in country i able to open a foreign affiliate to country j is obtained by equating the operating profits from doing FDI equation (7.3), with the operating profit from doing export equation (7.2),

$$a_{M,ij}^{1-\sigma} = \lambda_1 \frac{w_j \left(f_{M,ij} - f_{ij}\right)}{Y_j} \frac{P_j^{1-\sigma}}{\left(w_j^{1-\eta}\left(w_i \tau_{ij}\right)^{\eta}\right)^{1-\sigma} - \left(w_i \tau_{ij}\right)^{1-\sigma}} \tag{7.7}$$

7.4.2 Equilibrium Price Indices

Because price index adjusts depending on country characteristics, it is possible to find tractable solutions for it. Thanks to the fact that the number of potential entrants, n_E, is exogenously given, the price index will depend only on country j's characteristics,

$$P_j^{1-\sigma} = (\sigma/(\sigma-1))^{1-\sigma} \times k/(k-\sigma+1) \times$$

$$\sum_{k=1}^{N} w_k L_k \left[a_{M,kj}^{k-\sigma+1} \left(w_j^{1-\eta}\left(w_k \tau_{kj}\right)^{\eta}\right)^{1-\sigma} + \left(a_{kj}^{k-\sigma+1} - a_{M,kj}^{k-\sigma+1}\right)\left(w_k \tau_{kj}\right)^{1-\sigma} \right]$$

Plugging the productivity thresholds from equations (7.6) and (7.7) we can solve for the price index in the destination country j as follows,

$$P_j = \lambda_2 Y_j^{\frac{b-1}{b(1-\sigma)}} \theta_j \left(\frac{Y}{1+\pi}\right)^{\frac{1}{b(1-\sigma)}} \tag{7.8}$$

where $b = k/(\sigma - 1)$, w_k is the wage paid to workers in country k for firms which are exporting the good, and w_j is the wage paid to the workers in country j that are producing the domestic varieties or the foreign affiliate varieties. In the previous expression, θ_j collects the following terms:

$$\theta_j^{b(1-\sigma)} = \sum_{k=1}^{\bar{N}} \frac{Y_K}{Y} \left[\left(w_j \left(f_{M,kj} - f_{kj} \right) \right)^{1-b} \left[\left(w_j^{1-\eta} \left(w_k \tau_{kj} \right)^{\eta} \right)^{1-\sigma} - \left(w_k \tau_{kj} \right)^{1-\sigma} \right]^b \right.$$
$$\left. + \left[w_j f_{kj} \right]^{1-b} \left(\left(w_k \tau_{kj} \right)^{1-\sigma} \right)^b \right]$$

where Y is the world output and λ_2 is a constant.[15] θ_j is an aggregate index of j's remoteness from the rest of the world. It can be thought as the "multilateral trade resistance" introduced by Anderson and van Wincoop (2003). It takes into consideration the role of the fixed cost as well as trade costs and intermediate input traded. Notice that because total income, Y, depends on the dividends received from the global fund, in equilibrium it turns out that dividend per share is a constant.

7.4.3   Equilibrium Variables

The mode of supply choice depends on each firm's productivity, the trade costs it has to face, aggregate demand, the amount of intermediates it needs, and the set of competitors. Using the general equilibrium price index from equation (7.23) into equations (7.6) and (7.7), we can solve for the productivity threshold:

$$\bar{a}_{ij}^{1-\sigma} = \lambda_4 \frac{w_j f_{ij}}{\left(w_i \tau_{ij} \right)^{1-\sigma}} \theta_j^{1-\sigma} \left(\frac{Y}{Y_j} \right)^{\frac{1}{b}} (1+\pi)^{-\frac{1}{b}} \tag{7.9}$$

$$\bar{a}_{M,ij}^{1-\sigma} = \lambda_4 \frac{w_j \left(f_{M,kj} - f_{ij} \right)}{\left(w_j^{1-\eta} \left(w_i \tau_{ij} \right)^{\eta} \right)^{1-\sigma} - \left(w_i \tau_{ij} \right)^{1-\sigma}} \theta_j^{1-\sigma} \left(\frac{Y}{Y_j} \right)^{\frac{1}{b}} (1+\pi)^{-\frac{1}{b}} \tag{7.10}$$

where λ_4 is a constant.[16] The productivity threshold in equation (7.9) is unambiguously positively affected by the wage rate in the origin country and trade costs. On the other side, the productivity threshold in equation (7.10) is ambiguously affected by the wage rate in i, η, and distance trade costs. A large w_j increases the productivity to be a MNF.

The share of imported intermediates plays an important role in determining the substitutability or the complementarity between trade and FDI strategies. A low amount of imported intermediates, η, makes the FDI strategy better off when distance increases; a high η fades out the source of ambiguity.[17] The lower the η is, the more destination countries a firm can reach via horizontal foreign direct investment (HFDI) when trade cost increases.

Then using the demand function, the equilibrium price as well as equation (7.23), we can find the firm-level exports and the firm-level affiliate sales, aggregate output, and dividends per share π:

$$x_{ij}^X = p_{ij}^X q_{ij}^X = \lambda_3 \times \theta_j^{\sigma-1} \times \left(\frac{Y_j}{Y}\right)^{\frac{1}{b}} \times (1+\pi)^{\frac{1}{b}} \times \left(w_i \tau_{ij}\right)^{1-\sigma} \times a^{1-\sigma} \tag{7.11}$$

$$x_{ij}^M = p_{ij}^M q_{ij}^M = \lambda_3 \times \theta_j^{\sigma-1} \times \left(\frac{Y_j}{Y}\right)^{\frac{1}{b}} \times (1+\pi)^{\frac{1}{b}} \times \left(w_j^{1-\eta}\left(w_i \tau_{ij}\right)^\eta\right)^{(1-\sigma)} \times a^{1-\sigma} \tag{7.12}$$

$$\pi = \lambda_5 \tag{7.13}$$

$$Y_j = (1+\pi)w_j L_j = (1+\lambda_5)w_j L_j \tag{7.14}$$

where λ_3 and λ_5 are constants.[18] The previous equations are functions of fundamentals only: the size, L_j; the wages; the trade barriers, τ_{ij}; the fixed costs, $f_{M,ij}$ and f_{ij}; the proportion of intermediate imported, η; and the measure of j's location with respect to the rest of the world, θ_j.

Similarly to Chaney (2008), exports by individual firms depend on the transportation cost τ_{ij} with an elasticity $1 - \sigma$. Here we also have the sales by a foreign affiliate, which depend on the share of intermediate produced in the foreign location, y_2, and imported from the home country, y_1. Firm-level FDI, equation (7.12), are unambiguously linked to trade costs: an increase in trade costs reduces the firm-level FDI.

Firm-level trade is the same as in Chaney 2008. Firm-level affiliate sales depend on the interaction between imported and locally produced inputs. The behavior of a single firm is similar to what a traditional model of trade and FDI with representative firms would predict for aggregate bilateral trade flows and affiliate sales.

Similarly to Chaney (2008) and Irarrazabal, Moxnes, and Opromolla (2013), we can derive gravity equations using equations (7.11) and (7.12). In the present model, aggregate bilateral trade and overseas affiliate sales will be different from traditional models.

Proposition 1 (aggregate trade). Using the firm-level exports, we can derive the total export (f.o.b.), X_{ij}^X, from country i to country j,

$$X_{ij}^X = \frac{Y_i Y_j}{Y} \theta_j^{b(\sigma-1)} \left(w_i \tau_{ij}\right)^{1-\sigma}$$
$$\times \left[\left(\frac{w_j f_{ij}}{\left(w_i \tau_{ij}\right)^{1-\sigma}}\right)^{1-b} - \left(\frac{w_j\left(f_{M,ij} - f_{ij}\right)}{\left(w_j^{1-\eta}\left(w_i \tau_{ij}\right)^\eta\right)^{1-\sigma} - \left(w_i \tau_{ij}\right)^{1-\sigma}}\right)^{1-b}\right] \tag{7.15}$$

Proof. See appendix 7B.1.∎

The gravity equation for export in equation (7.15) suggests that exports are a function of country sizes, Y_i and Y_j, wages, bilateral trade costs and fixed costs, and the measure of j's remoteness from the rest of the world.[19] In this equation, wages are endogenous and will thus respond to changes in trade policy. By neglecting this interaction and using partial equilibrium analysis, we conclude that aggregate export is negatively affected by trade costs and origin country wage rate.

To highlight the role of share of imported intermediates, η, consider the simplifying assumption of $w_i = w_j$. The cost of doing FDI is clearly proportional to the magnitude of η. Hence, the second element in the square bracket of equation (7.15) decreases with η, which implies that aggregate exports are increasing with the proportion of inputs being imported from the headquarters.

Remark 1. *Aggregate export sales decrease with distance, τ_{ij}. These exports decrease faster the larger are the elasticity of substitution, σ, and the wage rate in the origin country, w_i. These effects are slightly reduced if a large share of intermediate inputs is traded ($\eta \to 1$).*

To conclude, aggregate exports increase with η and w_j and decrease with w_i and τ_{ij}. In contrast with Chaney 2008, this aggregate trade equation takes into consideration the interaction between arm's-length and intrafirm trade.

Proposition 2 (aggregate affiliate sales). Using the firm-level affiliate sales, we can derive the total affiliate sales, X_{ij}^M, in country j,

$$X_{ij}^M = \frac{Y_i Y_j}{Y} \theta_j^{b(\sigma-1)} \left(w_j^{1-\eta} \left(w_i \tau_{ij} \right)^\eta \right)^{1-\sigma} \times \left(\frac{w_j \left(f_{Mij} - f_{ij} \right)}{\left(w_j^{1-\eta} \left(w_i \tau_{ij} \right)^\eta \right)^{1-\sigma} - \left(w_i \tau_{ij} \right)^{1-\sigma}} \right)^{1-b}$$

(7.16)

Proof. See appendix 7B.2.∎

The gravity equation for affiliate sales in equation (7.16) suggests that affiliate sales are a function of country sizes, Y_i and Y_j, wages, bilateral trade costs and fixed costs, intrafirm trade between affiliates, and the measure of j's remoteness from the Rest of the World (RoW).[20] The last term of equation (7.16) is responsible for ambiguous reactions of affiliate sales.

Increase in trade costs reduces both total trade and intrafirm trade, but the magnitude differs in relation to the amount of intermediate imported.[21] In general equilibrium, the increase in trade costs also affect wages. The final effect of trade policy on affiliate sales depends on how wages respond to τ_{ij}. Different wage responses generate different affiliate sales reactions.

Changes in trade barriers differently affect aggregate affiliate sales depending on how wages respond to trade liberalization. Increase in trade barriers might create an incentive to ship production to the foreign market to avoid a part of the trade costs.[22] This effect will increase the demand for labor in the destination country relative to the home country. When trade costs are sufficiently small and the difference between the wages is not too big, antiglobalization forces lead to an increase in aggregate local sales. This effect is boosted by a lower share of intrafirm trade.

Remark 2. *Aggregate affiliate sales are nonmonotonically related to distance. Different level of trade costs, τ_{ij}, elasticity of substitution, σ, and share of intermediate inputs traded, η, change the way distance affects* **equation (7.16)**. *Notice that the response of wages to trade policy will be crucial to determine the overall effect.*

It is straightforward to derive a similar expression for aggregate intrafirm trade, because in this model aggregate intrafirm trade is a fraction of affiliate sales. Thus, the gravity equation in equation (7.16) also includes aggregate intrafirm trade.

Proposition 3 (number of affiliates). The aggregate number of foreign affiliates is given by

$$
n_{M,ij} = w_i L_i \int_0^{\bar{a}_{M,ij}} dG(a)
$$

$$
= \frac{Y_i Y_j}{Y} \theta_j^{b(\sigma-1)} \lambda_4^{-b} \left(\frac{\left(w_j^{1-\eta} \left(w_i \tau_{ij} \right)^\eta \right)^{1-\sigma} - \left(w_i \tau_{ij} \right)^{1-\sigma}}{w_j \left(f_{M,ij} - f_{ij} \right)} \right)^b \tag{7.17}
$$

where we used the productivity threshold in equation (7.10).

If trade costs are sufficiently low, a change in distance initially increases the number of affiliates. Nevertheless, when distance becomes important, the number of firms decreases. This nonmonotonicity is lost if the trade cost and/or the elasticity of substitution are particularly high. On the contrary, low levels of σ and/or τ_{ij} generate a more persistent increase in the number of affiliates.

Remark 3. *The aggregate number of foreign affiliates has a nonmonotonic behavior with respect to distance. Low levels of η exacerbate this nonmonotonicity. The reverse is true for high σ and/or τ_{ij}.*

In this model, a decreasing number of firms continue to supply via FDI when τ_{ij} increases. More precisely, only the more productive firms continue to supply via FDI to the remote location. This result is in sharp contrast with the literature on proximity versus concentration, where the number of affiliates is increasing with distance. The introduction of this intrafirm linkage between headquarters and affiliate makes the FDI strategy sensitive to trade issues.

Proposition 4 (number of exporters). The aggregate number of exporters is

$$n_{X,ij} = w_i L \int_{\bar{a}_{M,ij}}^{\bar{a}_{ij}} dG(a) = w_i L_i \left(\bar{a}_{ij}^k - \bar{a}_{M,ij}^k \right)$$

$$n_{X,ij} = \frac{Y_i Y_j}{Y} \theta_j^{b(\sigma-1)} \lambda_4^{-b} \times \left[\left(\frac{(w_i \tau_{ij})^{1-\sigma}}{w_j f_{ij}} \right)^b - \left(\frac{\left(w_j^{1-\eta} (w_i \tau_{ij})^\eta \right)^{1-\sigma} - (w_i \tau_{ij})^{1-\sigma}}{w_j (f_M - f_{ij})} \right)^b \right]$$

(7.18)

where we used the productivity thresholds in equations (7.9) and (7.10). Interpreting the role of key variables in equation (7.18) is far from straightforward due to wage differentials, share of intrafirm trade, and elasticity of substitution.

Remark 4. *For high trade costs, τ_{ij}, and low levels of intrafirm trade, η, the aggregate number of exporting firms is unambiguously decreasing with trade costs.*

7.4.4   Relationship between Trade and FDI

The share of intermediate inputs traded within the boundary of the firm, η, characterizes the cost of doing FDI: it captures the interaction between FDI and trade. From equations (7.15) and (7.16), the following effects can be established. A reduction in η is responsible for an increase in affiliate sales and a decrease in trade. Nevertheless, a decrease in η does not unambiguously determine what will happen to intrafirm trade. A smaller η shifts production so that more host country national input, y_2, is used. Since the decrease in η increases affiliate sales, the use of home as well as host input increases. Let's consider the Hicksian factor demand for the intermediate good, y_1, imported from i to j. This Hicksian demand depends on the overall quantity produced in the foreign affiliate, $q_{Mij}(a)$, as well as on the share of intermediate good, η, used in the overseas affiliate final good production,

$$y_1^* = q_{Mij}(a) a \eta \left(\frac{w_j}{w_i \tau_{ij}} \right)^{1-\eta}$$

The overall effect of a decrease in η *on this* Hicksian factor demand and thus on intrafirm trade depends on which of these two effects dominate.

The larger the share of intermediate input traded (high η), the more similar the behavior of aggregate affiliate sales and arm's-length trade to changes in trade costs.[23] To stress the difference between this result and the proximity versus concentration result, we label this relationship this the *complementarity relationship*.

This complementarity relationship between arm's-length and affiliate sales is captured by gravity equation in equation (7.16).[24] The low level of intermediate input needed in the production of the overseas affiliate confirms the substitution between arm's-length and intrafirm trade. On the contrary, high levels trigger a complementarity between arm's-length and intrafirm trade: trade costs reduce both affiliate and export sales.

7.5   Empirical Evidence

In this section, we propose a description of the data and then connect the data to the main predictions of the model. The empirical exercise is made of two parts. First, using aggregate data over the period 1999–2004, we analyze how geographical barriers differently affect arm's length and intrafirm trade flows. Second, using disaggregated data at the North American Industry Classification System (NAICS) three-digit level, we give a role to sectoral differences and analyze how the role of distance might be linked to the specific sector considered.

For what concern the relationship between MNF's productivity and the proportion of intrafirm trade undertaken, which implicitly emerge from the model, lack of data availability prevent from possible tests. Nevertheless, exploiting empirical findings on exporters, it seems reasonable to expect that intrafirm trade is important and is concentrated across MNFs. In this scenario, a trade policy liberalization event might differently affect various groups of final good producers.

7.5.1   Data Description
Our analysis is based on two databases. The first set of data is collected by the BEA. These data contain U.S. exports of goods by U.S. parents

to majority-owned foreign affiliates by country and industry over the period 1999–2004.[25] Some BEA data can be suppressed to avoid disclosure of data of individual companies or are not available or are not defined. Moreover, these data on exports of goods by U.S. parents to majority-owned foreign affiliates also report zeros trade flows, which leaves us with 2,118 observation at the NAICS three-digit level.[26]

The second set of data are collected by the CID. These information concern U.S. export flows over the period 1990–2004. These trade data are then aggregated at the NAICS three-digit level. To make trade data comparable with BEA data, we reduce the sample to the same group of countries and sectors.[27] To obtain a more reliable measure of arm's-length trade, we subtract intrafirm trade from export values.

Our main explanatory variable is geographical distance, for which we use data from the Centre d'Etudes Prospectives et d'Informations Internationales (CEPII) database on bilateral distances. This measure will proxy the key variable in our theoretical model, τ_{ij}. More specifically, we use weighted distances, for which data on principal cities in each country are needed.[28] We complete our set of country variables with other controls. To control for trade openness, we include a dummy for regional trade agreement (RTA) and General Agreement on Tariffs and Trade (GATT)/World Trade Organization (WTO) membership of different partners of the United States. These measures of trade openness RTAs and GATT/WTO membership come from the CEPII dataset.[29]

7.5.2   Empirical Specification

In this section, we test the empirical validity of the main results of the chapter. We use a panel data approach to characterize the main determinants of intrafirm and arm's-length export flows. The model predicts that, ceteris paribus, intrafirm trade and related party trade are both decreasing with distance. The magnitude of the distance coefficient should be different between these two types of trade flows. According to Propositions 1 and 2, intrafirm trade is expected to be less sensitive than arm's-length trade to change in trade policy. Indeed, the internal linkages between the parent and the foreign affiliate should reduce the role played by geography as well as trade costs.

To examine how intrafirm trade and arm's-length export react to geographical barriers, we consider U.S. industry data. We follow the standard practice in assuming that the trade costs, τ_{ij}, is linear in log of geographic distance and a set of variables indicating trade link between origin and destination country, that is, language and legal system.

The baseline specification for the aggregate value of intrafirm trade from U.S. parent to the j destination country is

$$\ln VA_{ij}^{IF} = \beta_0 + \underbrace{\beta_1}_{=\eta(1-\sigma)} \ln(\tau_{ij}) + \beta_2 \ln Y_j + \beta_3 \ln(W_j) + \varepsilon_j \qquad (7.19)$$

where VA_{ij}^{IF} is overall intrafirm trade from the U.S. headquarters to the foreign subsidiary, Y_j is the GDP in the destination country, W_j is a vector of controls, and ε_j is an orthogonal error term. The model predicts that β_1 and β_3 should be negative and β_2 should be 1.

The baseline specification for the value of export from the United States to the j destination country is

$$\ln X_{ij} = \alpha_0 + \underbrace{\alpha_1}_{=(1-\sigma)} \ln(\tau_{ij}) + \alpha_2 \ln Y_j + \varepsilon_j \qquad (7.20)$$

where X_{ij} represents arm's-length trade from the United States to a particular destination country j, Y_j is the GDP in the destination country, W_j is the same vector of controls used for aggregate intrafirm trade, and ε_j is an orthogonal error term. Our theory predicts the α_1 coefficient to be bigger than β_1 in equation (7.19).

The elasticity of intrafirm trade with respect to the relative cost of FDI depends on firm heterogeneity. In more homogeneous sectors (high k), there is a smaller fraction of highly productive firms (MNFs). In this case, the aggregate intrafirm sales should be more sensitive to change in relative FDI costs. Hence when k is high the overall effect of trade costs is bigger; in more heterogeneous sectors (small k), the second element is smaller.

As a general strategy, we run ordinary least squares (OLS) regressions on aggregated and then on disaggregated NAICS 3 digits data. We will focus on overall as well as sectoral effects of distance on both type of trade flows. Due to the presence of zeros in intrafirm trade data, OLS estimates will be biased. To account for that, we perform a Heckman selection procedure in which we use as an excluded variable the quality of the legal system. This variable is proxied with the rule of law index from the Worldwide Governance Indicator (World Bank).[30] The Heckman selection model allows us to use information from zero intrasector trade flows to improve the estimates of the parameters in the regression model. This model provides consistent, asymptotically efficient estimates for all parameters in the model.

7.5.3 Results

Tables 7.1 and 7.2 report estimation results for the effect of geographical barriers on aggregate intrafirm and arm's-length data. Columns (1) to (3) show the results when adding controls to our main explanatory variable, distance. Coefficients have the expected sign. An increase in the level of trade barrier (geographical distance) is negatively associated with both types of trade flows. Nevertheless, the magnitude of the distance coefficient is not in line with our theoretical predictions: the effect of distance is stronger for arm's-length trade than for intrafirm trade. This result might be driven by the dominant role of a particular sector. To account for sector specific effects, a set of additional regressions are proposed in tables 7.3 to 7.5.

Tables 7.3 and 7.4 attempt to disentangle the importance of sectoral differences using the OLS procedure. Estimation results are obtained from disaggregated data at the NAICS three-digit level for both intrafirm and arm's-length trade. Columns (1) to (4) in both tables show

Table 7.1
Aggregate intrafirm trade

Dependent variables	Log intrafirm trade to country j in year t		
	(1)	(2)	(3)
GDP_{jt}	0.985***	0.944***	0.980***
	(0.051)	(0.055)	(0.054)
$Dist_{ij}$	−1.067***	−0.828***	−0.692***
	(0.216)	(0.245)	(0.239)
RTA		1.127**	1.067*
		(0.537)	(0.545)
$GATT/WTO$ member			2.548***
			(0.536)
$Constant$	4.108**	2.386	−1.604
	(1.638)	(1.833)	(1.913)
$Year fixed effects$	Yes	Yes	Yes
Observations	319	319	319
R^2	0.430	0.444	0.514

Notes: The regressions are OLS estimations of equation (7.16) for the period 1999–2004. The dependent variable is the logarithm of U.S. intrafirm trade to country j in year t. Fixed effects by year and a constant are included. GDP_{jt} is the natural log of the GDP of country j from the CEPII data. Heteroskedasticity-robust standard errors are reported in parentheses. ***, **, and * indicate significance at the 1%, 5%, and 10% levels, respectively.

Table 7.2
Aggregate arm's-length trade

Dependent variables	Log of arm's-length trade to country j in year t		
	(1)	(2)	(3)
GDP_{jt}	0.685***	0.618***	0.621***
	(0.032)	(0.027)	(0.027)
$Dist_{jt}$	−0.671***	−0.406***	−0.405***
	(0.129)	(0.101)	(0.102)
RTA		1.453***	1.468***
		(0.187)	(0.187)
GATT/WTO member			−0.349***
			(0.125)
Constant	20.009***	18.351***	18.636***
	(0.879)	(0.743)	(0.763)
Year fixed effects	Yes	Yes	Yes
Observations	329	329	329
R^2	0.568	0.627	0.630

Notes: The regressions are OLS estimations of equation (7.15) for the period 1999–2004. The dependent variable is the logarithm of U.S. arm's-length trade to country j in year t. The dependent variable excludes intrafirm trade. Fixed effects by year and a constant are included. GDP_{jt} is the natural log of the GDP of country j from the CEPII data. Heteroskedasticity-robust standard errors are reported in parentheses. ***, **, and * indicate significance at the 1%, 5%, and 10% levels, respectively.

the results when adding controls to the main explanatory variable. In particular, column (4) in table 7.3 shows the results when interacting distance with sector specific effect. Although the average effect of distance decreases intrafirm trade by 1.73, sector-distance interactions highlight that this effect differs across sectors. For example, in the transportation equipment sector, intrafirm trade flows decline by 1 percent, while in computer and electronic sector they decline by only 0.08 percent. Similarly, column (4) in table 7.4 shows that arm's-length trade declines on average by 0.72 percent and, again, sector-distance effects are quite heterogeneous. In the transportation equipment sector, arm's-length trade flows decline by 0.01 percent, while in computer and electronic sector they increase by 0.027 percent.

Controlling for sector disaggregation, we find that the magnitude of distance is smaller for intrafirm trade flows but only in the chemical sector. These results are only partially in line with the theoretical

Table 7.3
Intrafirm trade (NAICS 3)

Dependent variables	Log Intrafirm trade to country j in year t			
	(1)	(2)	(3)	(4)
GDP_{jt}	1.071***	0.998***	0.998***	0.998***
	(0.031)	(0.030)	(0.030)	(0.030)
$Dist_{jt}$	−1.225***	−0.927***	−0.931***	−1.726***
	(0.109)	(0.103)	(0.103)	(0.107)
RTA		1.644***	1.575***	1.575***
		(0.229)	(0.230)	(0.229)
GATT/WTO member			1.035***	1.035***
			(0.158)	(0.157)
dist_chem				1.398***
				(0.181)
dist_machn				1.093***
				(0.176)
dist_comput				1.646***
				(0.262)
dist_transp				0.635**
				(0.288)
Constant	−0.476	−2.360***	−3.273***	3.817***
	(0.781)	(0.742)	(0.762)	(0.898)
Year fixed effects	Yes	Yes	Yes	Yes
Sector fixed effects	Yes	Yes	Yes	Yes
Observations	2,118	2,118	2,118	2,118
R^2	0.453	0.472	0.482	0.498

Notes: The regressions are OLS estimations of equation (7.16) for the period 1999–2004. The dependent variable is the logarithm of U.S. intrafirm trade to country j in year t. Fixed effects by year, manufacturing sector three-digit NAICS and a constant are included. Manufacturing sectors available are: 311, 325, 333, 334, 335, 336. GDP_{jt} is the natural log of the GDP of country j from the CEPII data. Distance is interacted with three-digit NAICS. Heteroskedasticity-robust standard errors are reported in parentheses. ***, **, and * indicate significance at the 1%, 5%, and 10% levels, respectively.

Table 7.4
Arm's-length trade (NAICS 3)

Dependent variables	Log arm's-length trade to country j in year t			
	(1)	(2)	(3)	(4)
GDP_{jt}	0.721***	0.650***	0.653***	0.653***
	(0.016)	(0.014)	(0.014)	(0.013)
$Dist_{ij}$	−0.624***	−0.341***	−0.339***	−0.720***
	(0.058)	(0.047)	(0.048)	(0.068)
RTA		1.552***	1.572***	1.572***
		(0.089)	(0.089)	(0.089)
GATT/WTO member			−0.458***	−0.458***
			(0.079)	(0.075)
dist_chem				0.320***
				(0.092)
dist_machn				0.506***
				(0.092)
dist_comput				0.747***
				(0.126)
dist_transp				0.710***
				(0.118)
Constant	15.821***	14.050***	14.423***	17.814***
	(0.418)	(0.369)	(0.381)	(0.578)
Year fixed effects	Yes	Yes	Yes	Yes
Sector fixed effects	Yes	Yes	Yes	Yes
Observations	1,974	1,974	1,974	1,974
R^2	0.609	0.653	0.657	0.666

Notes: The regressions are OLS estimations of equation (7.15) for the period 1999–2004. The dependent variable is the logarithm of U.S. arm's length trade to country j in year t. The dependent variable excludes intrafirm trade. Fixed effects by year, sector three-digit NAICS and a constant are included. Manufacturing sectors considered are: 311, 325, 333, 334, 335, 336. GDP_{jt} is the natural log of the GDP of country j from the CEPII data. Distance is interacted with three-digit NAICS. Heteroskedasticity-robust standard errors are reported in parentheses. ***, **, and * indicate significance at the 1%, 5%, and 10% levels, respectively.

predictions. However, they confirm the importance of geographical distance in the organizational choices of the firm. It should be stressed that results presented in table 7.3 tend to be biased due to the presence of zeros in NAICS three-digit data.

To control for the presence of zeros in intrafirm data, table 7.5 presents robustness checks with a Heckman two-step procedure. The Heckman selection procedure proposed uses the quality of the legal system as the excluded variable. Column (4) shows that the average effect of distance is now reducing intrafirm trade flows by 1.6 percent. Accounting for sectoral differences generates results more strongly in line with the theoretical predictions. In the transportation equipment sector, intrafirm trade flows decline by 1.53 percent; they increase by 0.57 percent for the computer and electronic sector. For the transportation sector, the interacted distance coefficient is not significantly different from its average effect. To summarize, correcting for the presence of the zeros produces a distance coefficient that plays a smaller role for three out of four sectors: chemicals, computer and electronic, and machinery.

7.6   Conclusion

This chapter develops a model of trade that features heterogeneous firms, multinational firms, exporters, and intrafirm trade in a general equilibrium framework. Its main contribution is to explain the different impact of geographical distance on related-party versus arm's-length trade. It also provides empirical evidence to support the model's main predictions using BEA and CID data from different NAICS sectors over the period 1999–2004.

In this chapter, a trade policy intervention affects the trading activity of firms that occurs both within and outside the boundaries of the firm and across different sectors. Globalization should increase the volume of trade. However, two types of trade are affected by change in trade barriers: arm's-length and related-party trade. Measuring the response of arm's-length trade versus related-party trade to globalization pressures might be important to define specific policy intervention. As a consequence of a reduction in trade barriers, multinational activity increases proportionally with the percentage of intrafirm trade that MNFs are involved in; trade in final goods increases by a larger proportion than intrafirm trade.

Table 7.5
Intrafirm Trade: Heckman two-step procedure

Dependent variables	Log intrafirm trade to country j in year t			
	(1)	(2)	(3)	(4)
GDP_{jt}	1.234***	1.336***	1.381***	1.330***
	(0.141)	(0.143)	(0.144)	(0.135)
$Dist_{ij}$	−1.273***	−0.689***	−0.625***	−1.620***
	(0.110)	(0.130)	(0.134)	(0.233)
mills ratio	1.794***	1.994***	1.861***	1.261***
	(0.491)	(0.523)	(0.530)	(0.512)
RTA		2.127***	2.131***	2.020***
		(0.287)	(0.283)	(0.266)
GATT/WTO member			1.674***	1.584***
			(0.426)	(0.408)
dist_chem				1.387***
				(0.339)
dist_machn				1.433***
				(0.407)
dist_comput				2.196***
				(0.404)
dist_transp				0.094
				(0.412)
Constant	−2.038	−9.167***	−11.947***	−2.185***
	(2.144)	(2.577)	(2.958)	(2.247)
Year fixed effects	Yes	Yes	Yes	Yes
Sector fixed effects	Yes	Yes	Yes	Yes
Observations	2,118	2,118	2,118	2,118

Notes: The regressions are estimations of equation (7.16) for the period 1999–2004 using Heckman selection model with rule of law the excluded variable. In the first step, the dependent variable is the probability of intrafirm trade to country j in year t. In the second step, the dependent variable is the logarithm of U.S. intrafirm trade to country j in year t. Fixed effects by year, sector three-digits NAICS, and a constant are included. Manufacturing sectors available are: 311, 325, 333, 334, 335, 336. GDP_{jt} is the natural log of the GDP of country j from the CEPII data. Distance is interacted with three-digits NAICS. Standard errors are reported in parentheses. ***, **, and * indicate significance at the 1%, 5%, and 10% levels, respectively.

Appendix 7A provides data information; appendix 7B provides proofs of the propositions and equilibrium variables.

Appendix 7A   Information on Database

Table 7A.1
Data

Exports	CDI
Export from P to A	BEA database
GDP (current USD)	CEPII database
Distance	CEPII database
Data period	1999–2004

Table 7A.2
Table of countries

Argentina	Greece	Philippines
Australia	Guatemala	Poland
Austria	Hong Kong	Portugal
Bahamas	Honduras	Russian Federation
Barbados	Hungary	Saudi Arabia
Belgium	India	South Africa
Bermuda	Indonesia	Singapore
Brazil	Ireland	Spain
Canada	Israel	Sweden
Chile	Italy	Switzerland
China	Jamaica	Taiwan
Colombia	Japan	Thailand
Costa Rica	Korea, Republic of	Trinidad and Tobago
Czech Republic	Luxembourg	Turkey
Germany	Mexico	United Arab Emirates
Denmark	Malaysia	Venezuela
Dominican Republic	Nigeria	
Ecuador	Netherlands	
Egypt	Norway	
Finland	New Zealand	
France	Panama	
United Kingdom	Peru	

Table 7A.3
Table of sectors: NAICS 3 industry classification

311	Food manufacturing
325	Chemical manufacturing
333	Machinery manufacturing
334	Computer and electronic product manufacturing
335	Electrical equipment, appliance, and component manufacturing
336	Transportation equipment manufacturing

Appendix 7B   Proofs

In this appendix, we provide proofs of the propositions and equilibrium variables.

7B.1   Proposition 1
Proof. Total exports from i to j are given by

$$X_{ij}^X = w_i L_i \int_{\bar{a}_{M,ij}}^{\bar{a}_{ij}} x_{ij}^X dG(a)$$

a firm will be exporting if $a(v) \le \bar{a}_{ij}$. Using equations (7.9), (7.10), (7.11), (7.12), and the specific assumption about the distribution of the labor unit requirement, a, we obtain

$$X_{ij}^X = w_i L_i \int_{\bar{a}_{M,ij}}^{\bar{a}_{ij}} \lambda_3 \times \theta_j^{\sigma-1} \times \left(\frac{Y_j}{Y}\right)^{\frac{1}{b}} \times (1+\pi)^{\frac{1}{b}} \times (w_i \tau_{ij})^{1-\sigma} \times a^{1-\sigma} dG(a)$$

$$\text{with } \bar{a}_{ij}^{1-\sigma} = \lambda_4 \frac{w_j f_{ij}}{(w_i \tau_{ij})^{1-\sigma}} \theta_j^{1-\sigma} \left(\frac{Y}{Y_j}\right)^{\frac{1}{b}} (1+\pi)^{-\frac{1}{b}}$$

$$\text{and } \bar{a}_{M,ij}^{1-\sigma} = \lambda_4 \frac{w_j f_M - w_j f_{ij}}{\left(w_j^{1-\eta}(w_i \tau_{kj})^{\eta}\right)^{1-\sigma} - (w_i \tau_{ij})^{1-\sigma}} \theta_j^{1-\sigma} \left(\frac{Y}{Y_j}\right)^{\frac{1}{b}} (1+\pi)^{-\frac{1}{b}}$$

Using the assumption of the Pareto distribution and the productivity thresholds, we can then solve the integral and find equation (7.15).■

7B.2   Proposition 2
Proof. Total affiliate sales in country j are given by

$$X_{ij}^M = w_i L_i \int_0^{\bar{a}_{M,ij}} x_{ij}^M dG(a)$$

a firm will open a subsidiary in country j if $a(v) \le \bar{a}_{M,ij}$. Using equations (7.7) and (7.12) and the specific assumption about the distribution of the labor unit requirement, a, we obtain

$$X_{ij}^M = w_i L_i 0 \int\limits_{0}^{\bar{a}_{M,ij}} \lambda_3 \times \theta_j^{\sigma-1} \times \left(\frac{Y_j}{Y}\right)^{\frac{1}{b}} \times (1+\pi)^{\frac{1}{b}}$$

$$\times \left(w_j^{1-\eta}(w_i\tau_{ij})^\eta\right)^{(1-\sigma)} \times a^{1-\sigma} dG(a)$$

$$\text{with } \bar{a}_{M,ij}^{1-\sigma} = \lambda_4 \frac{w_j f_M - w_j f_{ij}}{\left(w_j^{1-\eta}(w_i\tau_{kj})^\eta\right)^{1-\sigma} - (w_i\tau_{ij})^{1-\sigma}} \theta_j^{1-\sigma} \left(\frac{Y}{Y_j}\right)^{\frac{1}{b}} (1+\pi)^{-\frac{1}{b}}$$

then solving the integral we get equation (7.16).∎

7B.3   Profits

In this appendix, we determine the dividend per share in the economy. In order to do this, we use the total profits from exporting from i to j (including trade within a country):

$$\Pi_{ij} = w_i L_i \left[\int\limits_{\bar{a}_{M,ij}}^{\bar{a}_{ij}} \frac{1}{\sigma} x_{ij} dG(a) - w_j f_{ij} dG(a) \right]$$

$$= \frac{X_{ij}}{\sigma} - w_j f_{ij} w_i L_i dG(a)$$

Note that when $i = j$, this expression represents domestic profit.[31] Because $n_{ij} = w_i L_i \int_{i a_{M,ij} i}^{a_{ij}} dG(a)$, the previous expression can be rewritten as

$$\Pi_{ij} = \frac{X_{ij}}{\sigma} - n_{ij} w_j f_{ij} \tag{7.21}$$

The total profits for country j's affiliates are

$$\Pi_{ij}^M = w_i L_i \int\limits_{0}^{\bar{a}_{M,ij}} \frac{1}{\sigma} x_{ij}^M dG(a) - w_j f_{Mj} dG(a)$$

$$= \frac{X_{ij}^M}{\sigma} - n_M w_j f_{Mj} \tag{7.22}$$

because $n_M = w_i L_i \int_0^{\bar{a}_{M,ij}} dG(a)$.

Total profits in this economy are

$$\Pi = \sum_i \sum_j \left(\Pi_{ij} + \Pi_{ij}^M\right)$$

$$= \sum_i \sum_j \left[\left(\frac{X_{ij}}{\sigma} + \frac{X_{ij}^M}{\sigma}\right) - \left(n_{ij} w_j f_{ij} + n_M w_j f_{Mj}\right) \right]$$

This expression is the sum of the overall profits produced by domestic, exporting, and FDI firms in every country. Remember that country j is receiving varieties from $N - 1$. More specifically, total sales in country j are determined by varieties sold by domestic firms, varieties exported to j, and varieties produced locally by foreign affiliates. Hence total import in country j are $\sum_i (X_{ij} + X_{ij}^M) = Y_j$, where we used the fact that trade is balanced. Substituting the equilibrium number of exporters and affiliates, we can rewrite the worldwide profits as

$$\Pi = \sum_j \left[\frac{Y_j}{\sigma} - c_4^{-b} Y_j \right] = Y \frac{1 - c_4^{-b}}{\sigma}$$

Hence dividends per share are

$$\pi = \frac{\Pi}{\sum_i w_i L_i} = \frac{\Pi}{Y}(1 + \pi) = \frac{1 - c_4^{-b}}{\sigma}(1 + \pi)$$

$$= \frac{\dfrac{1 - c_4^{-b}\sigma}{\sigma}}{\left(1 - \dfrac{1 - c_4^{-b}\sigma}{\sigma}\right)}$$

7B.4 Price Index
The price index is

$$P_j^{1-\sigma} = (\sigma / (\sigma - 1))^{1-\sigma} \times k / (k - \sigma + 1) \times$$

$$\sum_{k=1}^{N} w_k L_k \left[a_{M,kj}^{k-\sigma+1} \left[\left(w_j^{1-\eta} \left(w_k \tau_{kj} \right)^{\eta} \right)^{1-\sigma} - \left(w_k \tau_{kj} \right)^{1-\sigma} \right] + a_{kj}^{k-\sigma+1} \left(w_k \tau_{kj} \right)^{1-\sigma} \right]$$

Plugging in the productivity thresholds from equations (7.6) and (7.7), we can solve for the price index in the destination country j:

$$P_j^{1-\sigma} = (\sigma / (\sigma - 1))^{1-\sigma} \times k / (k - \sigma + 1) \times \sum_{k=1}^{N} w_k L_k \times$$

$$\left\{ \left[\lambda_1 \frac{w_j f_{M,kj} - w_j f_{kj}}{Y_j} \frac{P_j^{1-\sigma}}{\left(w_j^{1-\eta} \left(w_k \tau_{kj} \right)^{\eta} \right)^{1-\sigma} - \left(w_k \tau_{kj} \right)^{1-\sigma}} \right]^{1-b} \times \right.$$

$$\left[\left(w_j^{1-\eta} \left(w_k \tau_{kj} \right)^{\eta} \right)^{(1-\sigma)} - \left(w_k \tau_{kj} \right)^{1-\sigma} \right] +$$

$$\left[\lambda_1 \frac{w_j f_{kj}}{Y_j} \frac{P_j^{1-\sigma}}{\left(w_k \tau_{kj} \right)^{1-\sigma}} \right]^{1-b} \left(w_k \tau_{kj} \right)^{1-\sigma}$$

where $b = k/(\sigma - 1)$, w_k is the wage paid to workers in country k for firms that are exporting the good, and w_j is the wage paid to the workers in country j that are producing the domestic varieties or the foreign affiliate varieties. Then, solving for $P_j^{1-\sigma}$,

$$P_j^{b(1-\sigma)} = (\sigma/(\sigma-1))^{1-\sigma} \times k/(k-\sigma+1) \times \lambda_1^{1-b} \times (Y_j)^{b-1} \times$$

$$\sum_{k=1}^{N} w_k L_k \left[\left(w_j f_{M,kj} - w_j f_{kj}\right)^{1-b} \left[\left(w_j^{1-\eta}\right)^{1-\sigma} w_k^{\eta(1-\sigma)} \phi_{kj}^{\eta} - (w_k)^{1-\sigma} \phi_{kj} \right]^b +$$

$$\left[w_j f_{kj}\right]^{1-b} \left((w_k)^{1-\sigma} \phi_{kj} \right)^b \right]$$

where $\phi_{kj} = \tau_{kj}^{1-\sigma}$.

$$P_j = \left[(\sigma/(\sigma-1))^{1-\sigma} \times (k/(k-\sigma+1)) \times \lambda_1^{1-b} \right]^{\frac{1}{b(1-\sigma)}} \times (Y_j)^{\frac{b-1}{b(1-\sigma)}} \times$$

$$\left[\sum_{k=1}^{N} \frac{Y_K}{Y} \frac{Y}{1+\pi} \left[\left(w_j f_{M,kj} - w_j f_{kj}\right)^{1-b} \left[\left(w_j^{1-\eta}\right)^{1-\sigma} w_k^{\eta(1-\sigma)} \phi_{kj}^{\eta} - (w_k)^{1-\sigma} \phi_{kj} \right]^b +$$

$$\left[w_j f_{kj}\right]^{1-b} \left((w_k)^{1-\sigma} \phi_{kj} \right)^b \right]^{\frac{1}{b(1-\sigma)}}$$

which, after rearranging, becomes

$$P_j = \lambda_2 Y_j^{\frac{b-1}{b(1-\sigma)}} \theta_j \left(\frac{Y}{1+\pi} \right)^{\frac{1}{b(1-\sigma)}} \tag{7.23}$$

Notes

The author would like to thank participants at the CESifo Workshop, seminar participants at THEMA, and one anonymous referee for helpful comments and suggestions. The author gratefully acknowledges CESifo sponsorship for the workshop "Globalisation: Trade, FDI and the Multinational Firm," held in Venice July 18–19, 2011. The usual disclaimer applies.

1. In the literature, "intrafirm trade" refers to trade between U.S. companies and their foreign subsidiaries as well as trade between U.S. subsidiaries of foreign companies and their foreign affiliates. In this paper, the term "intrafirm trade" is sometimes used interchangeably with "related-party trade." Notice that, for exports, the term "related-party trade" is far less stringent than intrafirm: firms are considered related if either party owns, directly or indirectly, 10 percent or more of the other party.

2. Data are disaggregated at the NAICS three-digit level. Further details are provided in section 7.5.1.

3. Data on inward and outward direct investment, including data on direct investment positions and transactions and on the financial and operating characteristics of the multinational companies involved, are available at http://www.bea.gov/international/index.htm.

4. This finding also confirms the use of a model of firms' heterogeneity in which the number of firms depends on country size.

5. Bombarda (2007) proposes a model of intrafirm trade as well as distant dependent fixed cost. However, a model with only intrafirm trade is sufficient for the purpose of our study. In fact, the present model is isomorphic to a model with distant dependent fixed cost.

6. This model is related to Brainard 1993 and 1997.

7. In our model, when a firm chooses to serve foreign markets via FDI, it means local production of the intermediate good, y_2, only.

8. In this chapter, the trade costs, τ, is then proxied with geographical distance.

9. When $\eta = 0$, the model delivers the Helpman, Melitz, and Yeaple (2004) framework.

10. The export cutoff also includes the situation in which the local market is supplied by domestic firm sales.

11. Note that this model of supply collapses to domestic production when $i = j$, because $\tau_{ii} = 1$.

12. Because we are not conditioning, $G(a/a_{ij})$ as the number of firms will be the number of entrants and not the number of active firms. Moreover, we consider a_{ij} to be the unit labor requirement for exporting. Note that when $i = j$, $\tau_{ii} = 1$, so $a_{ij} = a_{ii}$, which corresponds to the cutoff of domestic firms.

13. Note that when $i = j$, $\tau_{ij} = 1$, so $\pi_{M,kl}(a_M) = \pi_{kl}(a_M)$. When $i = j$, we are considering the domestic firms.

14. We interpret $a^{1-\sigma}$ as a measure of productivity.

15. $\lambda_2^{b(\sigma-1)} = (\sigma/(\sigma-1))^{\sigma-1} \times (k-\sigma+1)/k \times \lambda_1^{b-1}$.

16. $\lambda_4 = \lambda_1/\lambda_2^{\sigma-1}$.

17. Low η makes FDI and Export act as substitutes. For certain parameter restrictions, the productivity threshold in equation (7.10) decreases in distance when η is low. For high η, the productivity threshold in equation (7.10) is increasing with distance. Therefore, FDI and export become complements for sufficiently high η: both strategies require a higher productivity level when distance increases.

18. $\lambda_3 = \lambda_2^{\sigma-1}(\sigma/(\sigma-1))^{1-\sigma}$, $\lambda_5 = ((1-\lambda_4^{-b}\sigma)/\sigma)/(1-(1-\lambda_4^{-b}\sigma)/\sigma)$.

19. Note that if both the intermediates are produced at home, $\eta = 1$, the FDI will be too costly, and every firm will end up being an exporter, because it is more profitable. The gravity in this case will be like in Chaney 2008:

$$X_{ij}^X = \beta \frac{Y_i Y_j}{Y} \theta_j^{b(\sigma-1)} f_{ij}^{1-b} \left(w_i \tau_{ij} \right)^{-k}.$$

When all the intermediates are produced in the foreign location, $\eta = 0$, we are back in the Helpman, Melitz, and Yeaple (2004) framework. Hence the gravity equation for export in the Helpman, Melitz, and Yeaple (2004) setup is:

$$X_{ij}^X = \beta \frac{Y_i Y_j}{Y} \theta_j^{b(\sigma-1)} \left(w_i \tau_{ij} \right)^{1-\sigma} \times \left[\left(\frac{f_{ij}}{\left(w_i \tau_{ij} \right)^{1-\sigma}} \right)^{1-b} - \left(\frac{f_{M,j} - f_{ij}}{w_j^{1-\sigma} - \left(w_i \tau_{ij} \right)^{1-\sigma}} \right)^{1-b} \right].$$

20. Note that if both the intermediates are produced at home, $\eta = 1$, the FDI will be too costly, because it will incur in trade costs plus greater fixed cost, $f_M > f_{ij}$. In this case, there will be no firm supplying via FDI because the cost will be prohibitive, that is, $\bar{a}_{M,ij} \to 0$, or $u^{1}_{M,ij} \to \infty$. Hence the gravity for FDI, X^M_{ij}, will be 0. When all the intermediates are produced in the foreign location, $\eta = 0$, we are back in the Helpman, Melitz, and Yeaple (2004) framework. Hence the gravity equation for FDI in the Helpman, Melitz, and Yeaple (2004) setup is:

$$X^M_{ij} = \beta \frac{Y_i Y_j}{Y} \theta_j^{b(\sigma-1)} w_j^{1-\sigma} \times \left(\frac{f_{M,j} - f_{ij}}{w_j^{1-\sigma} - \left(w_i \tau_{ij}\right)^{1-\sigma}} \right)^{1-b}.$$

In this setup, there is no role for complementarity between trade and FDI.

21. Higher levels of η make total trade and intrafirm trade look similar. In this circumstance, the existence of wage differential will be the key element.

22. Because intrafirm trade also incurs in trade costs, this incentive will be greater, the lower the amount of intrafirm trade is.

23. See equation (7.16).

24. The way in which the model is built is such that intrafirm trade is always a fraction of affiliate sales.

25. A majority-owned foreign affiliate is a foreign affiliate in which the combined direct and indirect ownership interest of all U.S. parents exceeds fifty percent. Majority-owned foreign affiliates are the predominant type of investment (UNCTAD 2009).

26. Information are available for sixty countries, six years, and six NAICS three-digit manufacturing sectors: Food, Chemical, Machinery, Computer and Electronic Product, Electrical Equipment, and Transportation Equipment. Notice that the presence of zeros in intrafirm flows and missing GDPs alter the number of observations in the dataset used.

27. See table 7A.3 for NAICS three-digit description.

28. The distance between the biggest cities of two countries is weighted by the share of the city in the overall country's population.

29. Additional information at http://www.cepii.fr/anglaisgraph/bdd/gravity.htm.

30. Rule of law captures perceptions of the extent to which agents have confidence in and abide by the rules of society, in particular the quality of contract enforcement.

31. If we are interested in the domestic profits from serving market I, we should compute: $\Pi_{ii} = w_i L_i \int_0^{\bar{a}_{ii}} \frac{1}{\sigma} x_{ii} dG(a) - \int_0^{\bar{a}_{ii}} f_{ii} dG(a)$. We should proceed in the same way for computing the number of firms entering a particular market i: $n_{ii} = w_i L_i \int_0^{\bar{a}_{ii}} dG(a)$. This expression delivers the overall number of firms existing in i.

References

Anderson, J., and E. van Wincoop. 2003. Gravity with gravitas: A solution to the border puzzle. *American Economic Review* 93:170–192.

Antràs, P. 2003. Firms, contracts, and trade structure. *Quarterly Journal of Economics* 118 (4): 1375–1418.

Antràs, P. 2005. Incomplete contracts and the product cycle. *American Economic Review* 95 (4): 1054–1073.

Antràs, P., and E. Helpman. 2004. Global sourcing. *Journal of Political Economy* 112 (3): 55280.

Axtell, Robert L. 2001. Zipf distribution of U.S. firm sizes. *Science* 293 (September): 1818–1820.

Bernard, A., J. B. Jensen, S. Redding, and P. Schott. 2007. Firms in international trade. *Journal of Economic Perspectives* 21 (3): 105–130.

Bernard, Andrew, J. Bradford Jensen, Stephen J. Redding, and Peter K. Schott. 2010. Intrafirm trade and product contractibility. *American Economic Review* 100:444–448.

Bombarda, P. 2007. The spatial pattern of FDI: Some testable hypotheses. HEI Working Papers, 24–2007.

Brainard, S. L. 1993. A simple theory of multinational corporations and trade with a trade-off between proximity and concentration. NBER Working Paper no. 4269.

Brainard, S. L. 1997. An empirical assessment of the proximity-concentration trade-off between multinational sales and trade. *American Economic Review* 87 (4): 520–544.

Chaney, T. 2008. Distorted gravity: The intensive and extensive margins of international trade. *American Economic Review* 98 (4): 1707–1721.

Corcos, Gregory, Irac Delphine, Giordano Mion, and Thierry Verdier. 2009. The determinants of intrafirm trade. Discussion Paper 7530, CEPR.

Dunning, John H. 1994. Multinational enterprises and the globalization of innovatory capacity. *Research Policy* 23 (1): 67–88.

Eaton, J., S. Kortum, and F. Kramarz. 2008. An anatomy of international trade: Evidence from French firms. NBER Working Paper no. 14610.

Ethier, W. 1986. The multinational firm. *Quarterly Journal of Economics* 101 (4): 805–833.

Grossman, G., and E. Helpman. 2002. Integration vs. outsourcing in industry equilibrium. *Quarterly Journal of Economics* 117 (1): 85–120.

Hanson, G. H., R. J. Mataloni, and M. J. Slaughter. 2001. Expansion strategies of U.S. multinational firms. NBER Working Paper no. 8433.

Helpman, E., M. J. Melitz, and S. R. Yeaple. 2004. Export versus FDI with heterogeneous firms. *American Economic Review* 94 (1): 300–316.

Irarrazabal, Alfonso, Andreas Moxnes, and Luca David Opromolla. 2013 The margins of multinational production and the eole of intra-firm trade. Forthcoming in *Journal of Political Economy*.

Keller, W., and S. R. Yeaple. 2008. Global production and trade in the knowledge economy. NBER Working Paper no. 14626.

Melitz, M. J. 2003. The impact of trade on intra-industry reallocations and aggregate industry productivity. *Econometrica* 71 (6): 1695–1725.

UNCTAD. 2001. *World Investment Report*. New York and Geneva: United Nations.

UNCTAD. 2009. *Training Manual on Statistics for FDI and the Operations of TNCs*. New York and Geneva: United Nations.

8 Make or Buy: On the Organizational Structure of Firms with Asymmetric Suppliers

Verena Nowak, Christian Schwarz, and Jens Suedekum

8.1 Introduction

Final goods producers differ widely in their sourcing strategies for intermediate inputs. For example, Nike mostly collaborates with external subcontractors, whereas Intel keeps the vast majority of components within the boundaries of the firm and thus relies heavily on vertically integrated suppliers that are directly owned and controlled by the mother company.[1] Most firms, however, actually pursue a hybrid sourcing strategy and choose different organizational modes for different suppliers.[2] In the production of the S40, for example, Volvo outsources such parts as the side mirror, the fuel tank, and the headlights, whereas other components (such as the main engine) are produced by vertically integrated subsidiaries.

This empirically pervasive phenomenon of hybrid sourcing is hard to understand with the seminal model of the multinational enterprise (MNE) that Antràs and Helpman (2004) have introduced into the international trade literature. In that framework, which assumes an environment with incomplete contracts, a producer provides headquarter services and interacts with one supplier that provides an essential manufacturing component for the final product. The producer chooses whether to outsource or vertically integrate that supplier, taking into account that this ownership decision ("make or buy") matters for the supplier's incentives to contribute to the relationship.[3] However, because there is just one single supplier, by construction the firm cannot be characterized by a coexistence of different organizational modes, even though this seems to be the most common organizational structure of MNEs in the data.

In this chapter, we provide an extension of the baseline model by Antràs and Helpman (2004) and consider a production process with headquarter services and two manufacturing components. These two components are imperfect substitutes and may be asymmetric in terms of their technological importance for the final good, in terms of their unit costs of production, and in terms of their inherent degree of sophistication. As in the baseline model, we assume an incomplete contracts environment that eventually leads to a bargaining over the surplus of the relationship. Yet, in contrast to Antràs and Helpman (2004) who assume a bilateral Nash bargaining between the producer and the single supplier, we encounter a more complex bargaining among three parties, the producer and the two asymmetric suppliers. Our solution approach relies on the Shapley value, similar as in Nowak, Schwarz, and Suedekum (2012) and in Schwarz and Suedekum (2011), which has proven to be a useful tool in the analysis of such multilateral bargaining scenarios (see Shapley 1953; Acemoglu, Antràs, and Helpman 2007). In this chapter, we illustrate in detail how asymmetries across components affect the bargaining powers of the two suppliers (i.e., their Shapley values), the revenue distribution within the firm, and ultimately, the producer's decision about the firm's organizational structure.

The main advantage of our model is the possible emergence of hybrid sourcing, that is, a firm structure in which one supplier is integrated and the other one is outsourced. We can thus analyze under which circumstances this realistic outcome of hybrid sourcing is likely to emerge, and if it emerges, which organizational mode is chosen for which component. Our model leads to a rich set of theoretical predictions about these issues, which we then contrast with insights from a recent empirical literature that has unraveled several new facts about the internal structure of MNEs. In particular, Alfaro and Charlton (2009) and Corcos et al. (2013) find that MNEs tend to keep high-skill inputs and components with a higher degree of asset specificity within their boundaries and to outsource simpler inputs from the early stages of the production process. It has been difficult so far to rationalize those empirical findings with the baseline model by Antràs and Helpman (2004), chiefly because that framework does not deal with multiple suppliers or inputs. Our extension with two suppliers/components is broadly consistent with these empirical patterns.

More specifically, our model suggests that hybrid sourcing occurs if the overall production process is neither too headquarter- nor too component-intensive. Given that the producer actually chooses hybrid sourcing, our model then predicts that the producer tends to keep the more "sophisticated" input, which requires more special expertise to be usable, within the boundaries of the firm. The simpler and more standard component is, in contrast, more likely to be outsourced. These theoretical results are in line with the empirical findings of Alfaro and Charlton (2009) and Corcos et al. (2013).

Recently, there have been notable developments in the theoretical literature on the organization of multinational firms based on the seminal approach by Antràs and Helpman (2004). More specifically, Antràs and Helpman (2008) have extended that framework to realistically allow for partial contractibility of the input investments. Antràs and Chor (2013) provide a framework to study the organization of global value chains in which intermediate inputs are refined by multiple vertically related suppliers until production eventually reaches its final stage. Our framework differs from that model because we consider two inputs on the same stage of the value chain that are both simultaneously combined with headquarter services to produce a final good. Other extensions are due to Du, Lu, and Tao (2009) and Van Biesebroeck and Zhang (2011). In the former model, the same input can be provided by two suppliers, and "bi-sourcing" (one supplier integrated and the other outsourced) can arise out of a strategic motive because it systematically improves the headquarters' outside option and thus the bargaining power. In our model, hybrid sourcing can emerge because of an entirely different motive. Van Biesebroeck and Zhang (2011) also study an incomplete contracts model with multiple suppliers. However, they do not focus on the organizational decision of outsourcing versus integration. Finally, in Nowak, Schwarz, and Suedekum (2012), we extend the present framework to allow for economies of scope and extra costs of outsourcing.[4]

The rest of this chapter is organized as follows. In section 8.2, we introduce our basic model framework. Section 8.3 analyzes the multilateral bargaining and introduces the solution concept of the Shapley value. In section 8.4, we illustrate how the producer's organizational decision affects the bargaining powers of the different agents and the revenue distribution inside the firm. Section 8.5 deals with the question of which organizational structure the producer ultimately chooses. Finally, section 8.6 provides a summary and a discussion of our main results.

8.2   The Model

8.2.1   Technology and Demand

We consider a firm that produces a final good y. Production of this final good requires headquarter services and two different manufacturing components. The headquarter services are denoted by h and are provided by the firm (the "producer") itself. The components are produced by suppliers. Specifically, we assume that there are two suppliers a and b who provide m_i ($i \in \{a,b\}$) units of their respective component.

The inputs are combined according to the following production function:

$$y = \theta \cdot \left(\frac{h}{\eta^H} \right)^{\eta^H} \cdot \left(\frac{M}{1-\eta^H} \right)^{1-\eta^H} \tag{8.1}$$

where

$$M = \left[\eta_a \cdot \left(\frac{m_a}{\eta_a} \right)^{\varepsilon} + \eta_b \cdot \left(\frac{m_b}{\eta_b} \right)^{\varepsilon} \right]^{\frac{1}{\varepsilon}} \tag{8.2}$$

The upper-tier production function, equation (8.1), is a standard Cobb-Douglas, where θ denotes the firm's overall productivity level, η^H is the headquarter intensity, and $\eta^M = 1 - \eta^H$ is the overall component intensity of the production process. The aggregate component input M is given by a constant elasticity of substitution (CES) function as in equation (8.2), where η_i denotes the input intensity of component i within the aggregate M (with $\eta_a + \eta_b = 1$). Finally, the parameter $\varepsilon \in (0,1)$ measures how well the two components can be substituted.

These parameters capture firms' technological differences within and across industries. To give an example, one may expect the headquarter intensity η^H to be high in pharmaceutical or software firms and low, say, in firms from the automotive industry. The parameter η_a (with $\eta_b = 1 - \eta_a$) captures the degree of asymmetry of the two components in terms of their technological importance. As an example, consider the production of perfume. This final good requires two component inputs: alcohol as the base material and the highly specific aroma compounds that differentiate the fragrances. Here, the substitutability across those components is low, and the aroma oil has a much higher input intensity than the alcohol. In sales agencies, on the other hand, inputs like technical support and customer services are more symmetric (η_a and η_b are more similar) and better substitutable (higher ε).

On the demand side, the firm faces an iso-elastic demand function for the final product

$$y = Y \cdot p^{-\frac{1}{1-\alpha}} \qquad (8.3)$$

where p is the price of the good, $Y > 1$ is a demand shifter, and $1/(1 - \alpha) > 1$ is the demand elasticity, with $\alpha \in (0,1)$. Combining equations (8.1) and (8.3) yields the firm's revenue level, which depends endogenously on the input provision levels h, m_a, and m_b:

$$R = \theta^{\alpha} \cdot Y^{1-\alpha} \cdot \left[\left(\frac{h}{\eta^H} \right)^{\eta^H} \cdot \left(\frac{\left(\eta_a \cdot \left(\frac{m_a}{\eta_a} \right)^{\varepsilon} + \eta_b \cdot \left(\frac{m_b}{\eta_b} \right)^{\varepsilon} \right)^{1/\varepsilon}}{1 - \eta^H} \right)^{1-\eta^H} \right]^{\alpha} \qquad (8.4)$$

8.2.2 The Firm's Organizational Choice

The producer's key decision in our model concerns the firm's organizational structure. For both components $i \in \{a,b\}$, the producer decides whether the respective supplier is an external ("outsourced") subcontractor or a subsidiary that is vertically integrated within the boundaries of the firm. This "make or buy" decision is made in an environment with incomplete contracts in which the provision levels of the relationship-specific inputs are not contractible, similar to Antràs and Helpman (2004) or Schwarz and Suedekum (2011). A hold-up problem thus arises and the producer and the two suppliers end up in a bargaining over the surplus value of the production; consequently, all parties tend to underinvest in their input provisions. The producer's ownership decisions matter for the bargaining powers of the three parties because an outsourced supplier maintains the full ownership and property rights over his input, whereas a vertically integrated supplier does not. The organizational structure thus ultimately affects both the total revenue level and its distribution.

We consider the following five-stage game that we solve by backward induction:

1. The producer chooses the firm's organizational structure. This decision is represented by a tuple $\Xi = \{\Xi_a, \Xi_b\}$, where $\Xi_i = O$ denotes outsourcing and $\Xi_i = V$ denotes vertical integration of the supplier of component $i \in \{a,b\}$. The tuple Ξ can thus take four possible realizations: $\{O,O\}$, $\{O,V\}$, $\{V,O\}$ or $\{V,V\}$.

2. Given the organizational decision, the firm offers contracts to potential suppliers. Contracts may include a participation fee τ_i (positive or negative) from supplier $i \in \{a,b\}$

3. There is a large number of potential suppliers for both components. Each potential supplier has an outside opportunity equal to w^M. Potential suppliers apply for the contract, and the producer chooses one supplier for each component $i \in \{a,b\}$.

4. The headquarter and the suppliers a and b decide independently on their noncontractible input provision levels (h and, respectively, m_a and m_b).

5. After the input investments are sunk, the three players bargain over the surplus value of the production of the final good. Output is produced and revenue is realized and distributed according to the outcome of the bargaining process.

Starting with stage 5, the surplus value over which the producer and the two suppliers bargain is the realized revenue level as given in equation (8.4). We denote the headquarters' revenue share by β^H and the suppliers' revenue shares by β_a and β_b. Revenue is distributed among the three players such that $\beta^H + \beta_a + \beta_b = 1$. For the modeling of the bargaining process, we use the Shapley value as the solution concept. This is a standard solution concept in multilateral bargaining contexts (see Shapley 1953; Acemoglu, Antràs, and Helpman 2007). The details of this bargaining game are analyzed in the next section.

In stage 4, both the producer and the suppliers choose their input provision levels, given the revenue shares that they anticipate to receive in the bargaining stage. The producer chooses h so as to maximize $\beta^H \cdot R - c^H \cdot h$, where c^H denotes the unit costs of headquarter services. Analogously, the supplier $i \in \{a,b\}$ maximizes $\beta_i \cdot R - c_i^M \cdot m_i$, where c_i^M denotes the unit cost level of the supplier who signed the contract. We show in the appendix to this chapter that the following input provision levels maximize the payoff of the producer and the suppliers, respectively:

$$h = \frac{\alpha \cdot \eta^H \cdot \beta^H}{c^H} \cdot R \tag{8.5}$$

and

$$m_i = \alpha \cdot (1 - \eta^H) \cdot \eta_i \cdot \frac{\left(\frac{\beta_i}{c_i^M}\right)^{\frac{1}{1-\varepsilon}}}{\eta_a \cdot \left(\frac{\beta_a}{c_a^M}\right)^{\frac{\varepsilon}{1-\varepsilon}} + \eta_b \cdot \left(\frac{\beta_b}{c_b^M}\right)^{\frac{\varepsilon}{1-\varepsilon}}} \cdot R$$

with

$$
R = \Theta \cdot \left[\left(\frac{\beta^H}{c^H} \right)^{\eta^H} \cdot \left(\eta_a \cdot \left(\frac{\beta_a}{c_a^M} \right)^{\frac{\varepsilon}{1-\varepsilon}} + \eta_b \cdot \left(\frac{\beta_b}{c_b^M} \right)^{\frac{\varepsilon}{1-\varepsilon}} \right)^{\left(\frac{1-\varepsilon}{\varepsilon}\right) \cdot (1-\eta^H)} \right]^{\frac{\alpha}{1-\alpha}}
$$

where

$$
\Theta \equiv Y \cdot (\alpha \cdot \theta)^{\frac{\alpha}{1-\alpha}}
$$

is an alternative measure of productivity. As can be seen from equation (8.5), both the revenue share and level affect the two parties' investment incentives: ceteris paribus, a higher revenue share β^H raises the headquarters' input provision h and, hence, the revenue level. However, a higher β^H lowers the remaining share $1 - \beta^H = \beta_a + \beta_b$ for the suppliers, and thereby their input provisions, which in turn reduces the revenue level. This relationship illustrates that the producer needs to properly incentivize the suppliers in order to tackle the underinvestment problem that is inherent in this game structure.

In stage 3, suppliers only apply for a contract when the overall payoff offered in stage 2 exceeds or at least equals the outside option w^M. A supplier's overall payoff is the anticipated revenue share and the participation fee, minus the costs of production. Thus, the participation constraint reads as

$$
\beta_i \cdot R - c_i^M \cdot m_i + \tau_i \geq w^M \tag{8.6}
$$

Because the producer can freely adjust the up-front payments in stage 2, those participation constraints will be satisfied with equality, that is,

$$
\beta_i \cdot R - c_i^M \cdot m_i + \tau_i = w^M \iff \tau_i = w^M - \beta_i \cdot R + c_i^M \cdot m_i \tag{8.7}
$$

Finally, in the first stage the producer chooses the firm's organizational structure in order to maximize her own payoff. Using equation (8.7), this behavior implies that the producer's problem is equivalent to maximizing the joint payoff of all players:

$$
\pi = R - c^H \cdot h - c_a^M \cdot m_a - c_b^M \cdot m_b - 2w^M \tag{8.8}
$$

which can be rewritten as follows by using the expressions from equation (8.5):

$$\lambda = O \begin{bmatrix} 1 & \alpha \end{bmatrix} \left[\eta^H \quad \beta^H \quad | \quad \eta^M \left(\frac{\eta_a \cdot \left(\frac{\beta_a}{c_a^M} \right)^{\frac{1}{1-\varepsilon}} + \eta_b \cdot \left(\frac{\beta_b}{c_b^M} \right)^{\frac{1}{1-\varepsilon}}}{\eta_a \cdot \left(\frac{\beta_a}{c_a^M} \right)^{\frac{\varepsilon}{1-\varepsilon}} + \eta_b \cdot \left(\frac{\beta_b}{c_b^M} \right)^{\frac{\varepsilon}{1-\varepsilon}}} \right) \right]$$

$$\left[\left(\frac{\beta^H}{c^H} \right)^{\eta^H} \cdot \left(\eta_a \cdot \left(\frac{\beta_a}{c_a^M} \right)^{\frac{\varepsilon}{1-\varepsilon}} + \eta_b \cdot \left(\frac{\beta_b}{c_b^M} \right)^{\frac{\varepsilon}{1-\varepsilon}} \right)^{\left(\frac{1-\varepsilon}{\varepsilon} \right) \cdot \left(1 - \eta^H \right)} \right]^{\frac{\alpha}{1-\alpha}} - 2 w^M$$

(8.9)

The producer cannot freely set the revenue shares subject to $\beta^H + \beta_a + \beta_b = 1$, but those shares are determined in the multilateral bargaining in the ultimate stage of the game. The revenue distribution thus hinges on the bargaining powers of the three agents, which are in turn crucially affected by two sets of factors: (1) technology parameters such as the input intensities η^H and η_i, unit costs c_i^M, and the degree of component substitutability ε, and (2) the organizational structure of the firm. Whereas the former set of factors is exogenous, the latter is endogenously chosen by the producer.

In other words, the producer maximizes equation (8.9) with respect to the tuple $\Xi = \{\Xi_a, \Xi_b\}$ subject to the technology parameters. This organizational decision pins down the bargaining powers and hence the revenue distribution, as it determines the ownership rights of the suppliers.

8.3 The Bargaining Process and the Shapley Value

We now turn to the formal description of the bargaining process and the solution concept of the Shapley value. Ultimately, our aim is to analyze which organizational structure the producer chooses, depending on the firm's technology. For this purpose, it is useful to proceed in three steps. The first step is to introduce some basics of the multilateral bargaining process and the Shapley value and to illustrate the impact of technological asymmetries across the two components on the revenue distribution within the firm. In this section, we still neglect the ownership dimension, however, and implicitly assume that both suppliers maintain the full property rights over their assets. Second, in section 8.4 we show how the Shapley values and the revenue distribution depend on the producer's organizational decision, and we discuss how this dependence interacts with the impacts of the exogenous technological factors. Finally, in section 8.5 we pull all pieces together and analyze the payoff-maximizing organizational choice.

8.3.1 Shapley Value: The Basics

The Shapley value (Shapley 1953) is the most widely used solution concept for multilateral bargaining contexts, satisfying the five fundamental conditions "individual fairness," "efficiency," "symmetry," "additivity," and the "null player." This bargaining furthermore assumes that potential outcomes are known by all agents. Recall, however, that it occurs after the investment decisions have been made, so the input productions (and thus the potential bargaining outcomes) are observable ex post to all participants.

According to Acemoglu, Antràs, and Helpman (2007, 923) a "player's Shapley value is the average of her contributions to all coalitions that consist of players ordered below her in all feasible permutations." Thus, to determine the Shapley values of the three players in our model, several steps are necessary:

1. Derivation of the set of feasible permutations
2. Calculation of the marginal contributions
3. Forming the average
4. Derivation of the Shapley value and the revenue distribution

Derivation of the Set of Feasible Permutations A coalition is a collaboration of players that comprises at least a non-empty subset of the players. With three players (the producer and the two suppliers) the coalition size can be theoretically one, two or three. It can be seen from (8.1) and (8.2) that the production of the final good requires headquarter services and at least one component. Hence, coalitions of size one earn zero revenue. The same applies for coalitions of two players that do not contain the producer. Such coalitions earn zero revenue as well.[5]

Within the coalitions, the players can be ordered in different ways and these different orderings are called *permutations*. In figure 8.1, we illustrate the set of all theoretically possible permutations and the relevant ("feasible") permutations that earn nonzero revenue. The position of a single player within a permutation indicates the entry sequence. For example, in the permutation {H,b,a}, supplier a was the last player to enter. When calculating marginal contributions, this entry sequence

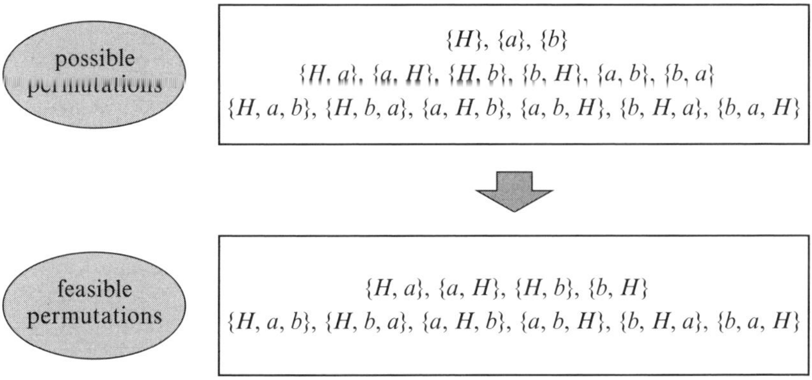

possible permutations

$$\{H\}, \{a\}, \{b\}$$
$$\{H, a\}, \{a, H\}, \{H, b\}, \{b, H\}, \{a, b\}, \{b, a\}$$
$$\{H, a, b\}, \{H, b, a\}, \{a, H, b\}, \{a, b, H\}, \{b, H, a\}, \{b, a, H\}$$

feasible permutations

$$\{H, a\}, \{a, H\}, \{H, b\}, \{b, H\}$$
$$\{H, a, b\}, \{H, b, a\}, \{a, H, b\}, \{a, b, H\}, \{b, H, a\}, \{b, a, H\}$$

Figure 8.1
Possible and feasible permutations.

is crucial as we consider the player in this last position to be the one who leaves an existing coalition.

Calculation of the Marginal Contributions The marginal contribution of a player is the difference between the revenue of the coalition when the respective player is part of it and the coalition's revenue when the respective player is not part of it. A player's marginal contribution to a coalition is determined only if the other players in this coalition "are ordered below her in all feasible permutations." In terms of figure 8.1, this means that we have to focus on those feasible permutations in which the respective player is in the last position. Consider, for example, supplier a: in a coalition with the producer, there are two possible permutations: $\{H,a\}$ and $\{a,H\}$. Supplier a is in the last position only with $\{H,a\}$, and we have to calculate only the marginal contribution for this permutation. For a coalition of size 3, there are two relevant permutations for the calculation of supplier a's marginal contribution, namely $\{H,b,a\}$ and $\{b,H,a\}$.

Let us first consider coalitions of size 2, that is, among the producer and one supplier i. When supplier i leaves this coalition, the producer becomes the sole player and the remaining total revenue is 0. Thus, the marginal contribution of the supplier in a coalition of size 2 (denoted by MC_i^2) equals the total revenue of this coalition:

$$MC_i^2 = \hat{H} \cdot m_i^{\alpha \cdot (1 - \eta^H)} \cdot \eta_i^{\frac{\alpha \cdot (1 - \varepsilon) \cdot (1 - \eta^H)}{\varepsilon}} \tag{8.10}$$

with $\hat{H} = \theta^\alpha \cdot Y^{1-\alpha} \cdot h^{\alpha \cdot \eta^H} \cdot (1 - \eta^H)^{-\alpha \cdot (1 - \eta^H)} \cdot (\eta^H)^{-\alpha \cdot \eta^H}$

The same reasoning applies to the producer, whose marginal contribution to a coalition of size 2 also equals the total revenue of this coalition:

$$MC_{Hi}^2 = \hat{H} \cdot m_i^{\alpha\left(1-\eta^H\right)} \cdot \eta_i^{\frac{\alpha\cdot(1-\varepsilon)\cdot(1-\eta^H)}{\varepsilon}} \tag{8.11}$$

where $i \in \{a,b\}$ indexes the supplier with whom the producer has formed the coalition.

Next, we consider coalitions of size 3. When supplier i leaves this coalition, the producer and the remaining supplier j can realize a revenue equal to $\hat{H} \cdot \left(m_j^\varepsilon \cdot \eta_j^{1-\varepsilon}\right)^{\alpha\left(1-\eta^H\right)/\varepsilon}$, so the marginal contribution of supplier i is

$$MC_i^3 = \hat{H} \cdot \left(\left(m_i^\varepsilon \cdot \eta_i^{1-\varepsilon} + m_j^\varepsilon \cdot \eta_j^{1-\varepsilon}\right)^{\frac{\alpha\left(1-\eta^H\right)}{\varepsilon}} - \left(m_j^\varepsilon \cdot \eta_j^{1-\varepsilon}\right)^{\frac{\alpha\left(1-\eta^H\right)}{\varepsilon}} \right) \text{ with } i \neq j \tag{8.12}$$

Yet if the headquarter leaves a coalition of three players, the revenue of the remaining two suppliers is again equal to 0. Hence, the marginal contribution of the producer is

$$MC_H^3 = \hat{H} \cdot \left(m_i^\varepsilon \cdot \eta_i^{1-\varepsilon} + m_j^\varepsilon \cdot \eta_j^{1-\varepsilon}\right)^{\frac{\alpha\left(1-\eta^H\right)}{\varepsilon}} \tag{8.13}$$

Forming the Average Starting from these marginal contributions, the Shapley value is calculated with the help of

$$SV_k = \sum_{S \subseteq N} \frac{(s-1)! \cdot (n-s)!}{n!} MC_k^s \tag{8.14}$$

with $k \in \{H,a,b\}$. Here, $n = 3$ is the number of all players, and s is the number of players in a coalition ($s \leq n$). The term $\dfrac{(s-1)! \cdot (n-s)!}{n!}$ captures the weights when forming the average across all feasible permutations, and it equals the probability that a specific player k is in the last position of such a feasible permutation.

In coalitions of two players ($s = 2$), this probability equals $\dfrac{(2-1)! \cdot (3-2)!}{3!} = 1/6$ for both suppliers a and b. As can be seen from figure 8.1, in total there are six theoretically possible coalitions of size 2, yet each supplier is in the last position only in one case. The producer, in turn, has a probability of $1/3$ of being in the last position in a feasible permutation of size two, namely $\{a,H\}$ and $\{b,H\}$, which both have an individual probability equal to $1/6$. For a coalition size of 3, the weight is $\dfrac{(3-1)!\,(3-3)!}{3!} = 1/3$ for all players, because there are six feasible permutations for this coalition size, and each player is in the last position twice.

Derivation of the Shapley Value and the Revenue Distribution   Using these probabilities and the marginal contributions calculated previously, we can now derive the Shapley values of the three players and the revenue shares that result in the multilateral bargaining. For supplier i, the Shapley value is given as follows:

$$SV_i = \frac{1}{6}\cdot MC_i^2 + \frac{1}{3}\cdot MC_i^3 \tag{8.15}$$

which is the weighted average of his marginal contribution to all feasible permutations where the other players are ordered below. Analogously, the Shapley value of the producer is

$$SV_H = \frac{1}{6}\cdot MC_{Hi}^2 + \frac{1}{6}\cdot MC_{Hj}^2 + \frac{2}{6}\cdot MC_H^3 \quad \text{with } i \neq j \tag{8.16}$$

Notice that because $MC_{Hi}^2 = MC_i^2$ and $MC_H^3 \geq MC_i^3$, the Shapley value of the producer exceeds that of a single supplier.

These Shapley values given in equations (8.15) and (8.16) form the basis for the determination of the revenue distribution. Namely, the revenue share of supplier $i \in \{a,b\}$ is given by the supplier's Shapley value divided by the firm's total revenue:

$$\beta_i = \frac{SV_i}{R} = \frac{m_i^{\alpha\left(1-\eta^H\right)}\cdot \eta_i^{\alpha(1-\varepsilon)(1-\eta^H)/\varepsilon} + 2\left(\left(m_i^\varepsilon\cdot \eta_i^{1-\varepsilon} + m_j^\varepsilon\cdot \eta_j^{1-\varepsilon}\right)^{\alpha\left(1-\eta^H\right)/\varepsilon} - \left(m_j^\varepsilon\cdot \eta_j^{1-\varepsilon}\right)^{\alpha\left(1-\eta^H\right)/\varepsilon}\right)}{6\cdot \left(m_a^\varepsilon\cdot \eta_a^{1-\varepsilon} + m_b^\varepsilon\cdot \eta_b^{1-\varepsilon}\right)^{\alpha\left(1-\eta^H\right)/\varepsilon}}. \tag{8.17}$$

These revenue shares are dependent on the input provision levels m_a and m_b, which in turn depend on the revenue shares. As a result, we cannot solve explicitly for the revenue shares of the suppliers. However, it is possible to display the underlying system of equations (see the appendix to this chapter) that we later on solve numerically.

For the determination of the producer's revenue share, one must take into account the efficiency, additivity, and null player axioms of the Shapley value approach. The sum of the marginal contributions must equal the total revenue. However, the allocation of the marginal contributions is not necessarily efficient, as the sum of the marginal contributions may deviate from the revenue of the coalition (see Hart 1990; Hart and Mas-Colell 1988). To assure that the total revenue is distributed among the three players, the revenue shares are thus only calculated for two players, namely the two suppliers. One player receives the residual revenue share, as in Hart and Moore (1990) and Acemoglu, Antràs, and Helpman (2007). We assume that the producer is this residual claimant because that is the only essential player (the "null player") in this bargaining game. Hence, the headquarter revenue share is given by $\beta^H = 1 - \beta_a - \beta_b$, where β_a and β_b follow from equation (8.17).

8.3.2   Illustration: The Revenue Distribution with Asymmetric Inputs

We now illustrate how the Shapley values and the revenue shares are affected by the exogenous technological factors. Specifically, we use numerical analysis to study the impact of variations in the following parameters:

1. The headquarter intensity of final goods production (η^H)
2. The input intensities of the suppliers (η_i)
3. The suppliers' unit costs (c_i^M)
4. The degree of component substitutability (ε)

Recall that throughout this section, we assume that both suppliers maintain full ownership of their assets. That is, in the multilateral bargaining they threaten to take away their entire input provision levels, respectively.

Headquarter Intensity η^H The headquarter intensity measures the technological importance of the producer's contribution to the final good. This is the key parameter to pin down the revenue distribution in the baseline model by Antràs and Helpman (2004), where η^H immediately implies the residual input intensity of the single manufacturing component. In Schwarz and Suedekum (2011), in which they consider multiple but symmetric components, η^H also pins down the input intensity of each of those single manufacturing inputs. In our model, there can be asymmetries across the two components that crucially

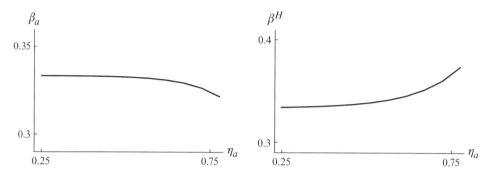

Figure 8.2
Variation of the headquarter intensity η^H ($\eta_a = \eta_b = 0.5$, $c_a^M = c_b^M = 1$, $c^H = 1$, $\varepsilon = 0.06$, and $\alpha = 0.92$).

affect the players' bargaining powers and the revenue distribution, as we will show shortly. However, to isolate the impact of η^H, it is useful to first consider the benchmark scenario in which the two components a and b are symmetric in terms of their input intensities ($\eta_a = \eta_b = 1/2$) and unit costs ($c_a^M = c_b^M = c^M$).

Figure 8.2 illustrates how the revenue distribution changes upon variation of η^H, keeping the other parameters fixed. The left panel refers to the revenue share (Shapley value over total revenue) of supplier a, which is identical to supplier b's revenue share because the two components are symmetric. The right panel depicts the residual share β^H as a function of η^H.

As can be seen, the higher is the headquarter intensity of final goods production, the lower is the revenue share of both suppliers and the higher is the producer's residual revenue share that follows from the multilateral bargaining process. The reason is simple: the higher η^H is, the lower the overall importance of the manufacturing components is for the production process. Both suppliers thus make lower marginal contributions to all relevant coalitions and thus have lower Shapley values as they threaten to take away fewer inputs. This lower bargaining power, in turn, implies a higher residual revenue share for the producer.

This outcome of the bargaining process is therefore qualitatively consistent with efficiency considerations from contract theory (Hart and Moore 1990). All parties underinvest into the relationship due to the presence of the hold-up problem. The higher (lower) η^H is, the slacker (fiercer) the suppliers' underinvestment problems are for the overall relationship. Hence, to ensure ex ante efficiency, it becomes less (more) important to incentivize the suppliers, and hence they should receive a smaller (larger) share of the surplus.

Technological Asymmetries across Components η_i We now study technological asymmetries across the two components. In the left panel of figure 8.3, we depict the revenue shares of suppliers a and b (β_a and β_b) as a function of η_a for given values of η^H, $c_a^M = c_b^M = c^M$, c^H, ε, and α. In the right panel, we illustrate the corresponding residual share for the producer.

The left graph shows that the supplier who provides the technologically more important input realizes the higher revenue share in the bargaining stage. In particular, the share β_a is increasing in η_a, whereas β_b is decreasing in η_a as $\eta_b = 1 - \eta_a$. Clearly, with $\eta_a > 1/2$ supplier a has a higher Shapley value than supplier b, because supplier a makes higher marginal contributions owing to the greater technological importance of his input. Put differently, supplier a has a higher bargaining power because he can threaten to take away the more important component.

Interestingly, the right panel of figure 8.3 shows that the producer's revenue share β^H is also affected by the degree of asymmetry of the two components, despite the fact that the headquarter intensity η^H is kept fixed in that figure. In particular, β^H is the lowest when the two components are symmetric (with $\eta_a = \eta_b = 1/2$), while β^H is increasing in the degree of asymmetry across components, that is, when η_a becomes larger or smaller than $1/2$.

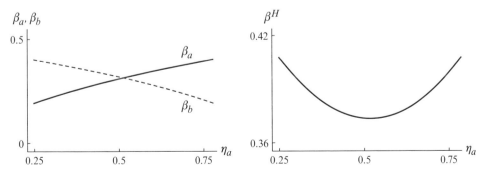

Figure 8.3
Technological asymmetry across components ($\eta^H = 0.8$, $c_a^M = c_b^M = 1$, $c^H = 1$, $\varepsilon = 0.06$, and $\alpha = 0.92$).

The intuition for this result can be grasped from the curvatures in the left panel of the figure. Consider a constellation in which component a has a low input intensity η_a. Hence, it follows from the bargaining setup that β_a is low and β_b is high. Now suppose that η_a increases in this scenario. This change leads to a more than proportional increase of β_a, while the reduction of β_b is small relative to the decrease of $\eta_b = 1 - \eta_a$. Overall, the increase of β_a is stronger than the decline of β_b, so that β^H must decrease. In contrast, increasing η_a in a constellation where η_a is already high leads to a relatively small increase of β_a and to a relatively strong reduction of β_b. Hence, β^H must increase. In other words, the β_a schedule is first concave and then convex in η_a, which in turn drives the U-shaped curve in the right panel of figure 8.3.

Economically, this means that unimportant suppliers have a higher marginal gain in bargaining power when becoming technologically more important, whereas the marginal gain in bargaining power is lower for important suppliers who already receive a large revenue share. It also means that the producer realizes the lowest bargaining power when the two suppliers are equally strong. Once the two suppliers become asymmetric in terms of the technological importance of their inputs, this also materializes in a higher bargaining strength of the producer.

Suppliers' Unit Costs c_i^M   Next, we consider the impact of asymmetries in the suppliers' unit costs. Figure 8.4 is analogous to figure 8.2 and depicts β_a (left panel) and β^H (right panel) as a function of the headquarter intensity η^H. The solid lines in both panels refer to the

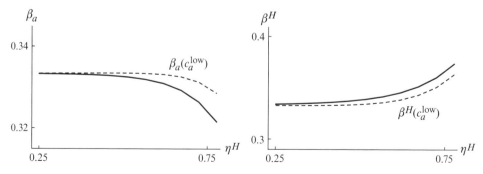

Figure 8.4
Asymmetries in suppliers' unit costs. Solid lines: $c_a^M = c_b^M = 1$; dashed lines: $c_a^M = 0.2$, $c_b^M = 1$ ($\eta_a = \eta_b = 0.5$, $c^H = 1$, $\varepsilon = 0.06$, and $\alpha = 0.92$).

benchmark case with symmetrical components (both in terms of input intensities and unit costs), whereas the dashed lines refer to the case in which input intensities are the same but unit costs c_a^M are lower than c_b^M.

As the left graph of figure 8.4 shows, the lower unit costs c_a^M raise supplier a's revenue share β_a. The intuition is that that lower unit costs lead to an increase in the input provision level of supplier a. Hence, supplier a's marginal contribution to all coalitions and his Shapley value go up.

The producer therefore ends up with a lower revenue share β^H for any given level of η^H, as can be seen in the right panel of figure 8.4, where the dashed line always runs below the solid one. That is, a unit cost reduction of one supplier (with constant unit costs of the other supplier) actually leads to a lower realized revenue share for the producer, because supplier a experiences a strong gain in his bargaining power. The total realized revenue for the producer need not go down, however, even if the revenue *share* may decrease, because the lower unit costs of supplier a also lead to a higher input provision and thus to a higher total revenue *level*. Still, it is interesting to note that the headquarter revenue share tends to be highest with a strong *technological* asymmetry across components (see figure 8.3), while a strong *cost* asymmetry across suppliers may actually lead to a lower headquarter revenue share.

In figure 8.5 we take η^H as given and couple the cost asymmetry with a technological asymmetry across components. The solid lines refer to benchmark without cost differences (see figure 8.3), whereas the dashed lines depict the case where supplier a is the low-cost supplier.

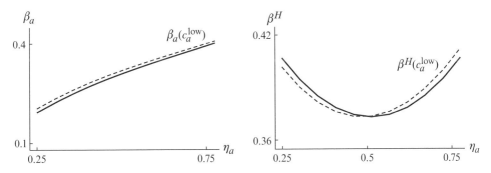

Figure 8.5
Asymmetries in suppliers' unit costs and input intensities. Solid lines: $c_a^M = c_b^M = 1$; dashed lines: $c_a^M = 0.2$, $c_b^M = 1$ ($\eta^H = 0.8$, $c^H = 1$, $\varepsilon = 0.06$, and $\alpha = 0.92$).

The left panel also shows that lower unit costs c_a^M lead to a higher revenue share β_a. Furthermore, the figure shows that this increase (the distance between the solid and the dashed curve) is stronger the lower η_a is. In other words, supplier a's marginal gain in bargaining power due to the lower unit cost is stronger if the input intensity of his component is low.[6] As a result of this, we see in the right panel of figure 8.5 that the headquarter revenue share goes down when η_a is low (because β_a rises substantially) whereas it goes up when η_a is high.

Degree of Component Substitutability ε Finally, another parameter that influences the Shapley values and the revenue distribution is the degree of component substitutability ε. In figure 8.6, we again display the revenue shares as a function of η^H assuming symmetric components, but we now consider different values of ε. In particular, the solid lines refer to the previous parameter constellation with $\varepsilon = 0.06$, whereas the dashed lines depict a case in which ε is higher ($\varepsilon = 0.09$). A higher degree of substitutability leads to lower revenue shares for the suppliers and to a higher headquarter revenue share. The intuition is that the better substitutability lowers the bargaining powers of the suppliers, because the total revenue decreases by less when one supplier leaves the coalition of size 3, as his contribution can be replaced more easily with the input of the other supplier.

As shown in the right panel of figure 8.7, the U-shape of the β^H curve with respect to η_a prevails when assuming a higher value of ε, yet this curve is shifted upward, that is, the residual share β^H is increasing in ε. Furthermore, the left panel shows that a higher value of ε leads to

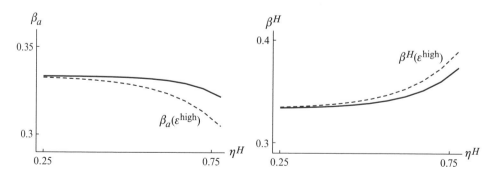

Figure 8.6
Component substitutability (I). Solid lines: $\varepsilon = 0.06$; dashed lines: $\varepsilon = 0.09$ ($\eta_a = \eta_b = 0.5$, $c_a^M = c_b^M = 1$, $c^H = 1$, and $\alpha = 0.92$).

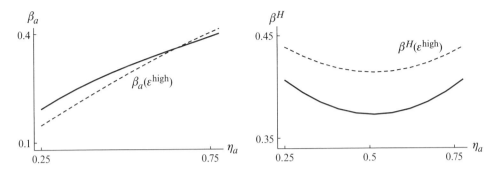

Figure 8.7
Component substitutability (II). Solid lines: $\varepsilon = 0.06$; dashed lines: $\varepsilon = 0.09$ ($\eta^H = 0.8$, $c_a^M = c_b^M = 1$, $c^H = 1$, and $\alpha = 0.92$).

a smaller revenue share β_a for low values of η_a but to a higher revenue share for high values of η_a. That is, for the unimportant component, higher substitutability clearly materializes in a lower bargaining power and the Shapley value goes down. Provided that one component is much more important than the other, however, better substitutability can even raise the bargaining power of the more important supplier. The reason is that the unimportant supplier experiences a substantial loss when ε goes up. This drop may, in turn, lead to a slight increase of both the producer's and the important supplier's revenue shares.

8.3.3   Shapley Value: A Brief Summary

We have introduced the Shapley value as the fundamental solution concept in the multilateral bargaining process in the ultimate stage of the game. Although our results rely on numerical simulations, we have derived some main insights that are worth summarizing:

1. With technological asymmetries across components, the supplier of the important component has a higher Shapley value and realizes a higher revenue share.

2. With cost asymmetries across components, the supplier of the low-cost component has a higher Shapley value and realizes a higher revenue share.

3. Higher headquarter intensity tends to raise the producer's realized revenue share. This share tends to be higher when components are asymmetric in terms of their technological importance.

4. Better component substitutability lowers the realized revenue shares of the suppliers and raises the producer's revenue share, provided that the inputs are not too asymmetric.

So far, our analysis has rested on the assumption that both suppliers maintain ownership and property rights over their inputs and thus threaten to withhold their entire input levels in the bargaining process. We now alter this assumption and thereby move to the analysis of the organizational decision of the producer.

8.4   Outsourcing versus Integration

In our game structure, the producer can decide whether to integrate supplier i within the boundaries of the firm or to keep the supplier as an external subcontractor. This ownership decision matters for the bargaining powers of the suppliers. Specifically, a vertically integrated supplier basically becomes an employee of the producer. The supplier therefore cannot threaten to take away the input during the bargaining, as the producer has the right to confiscate it. However, following the property rights approach to the firm (see Grossman and Hart 1986; Hart and Moore 1990; Antràs and Helpman 2004), we assume that the producer still cannot fully make use of that input if the vertically integrated supplier refuses to collaborate. In particular, the headquarter can effectively only use the fraction $(1 - \delta_i)$ of the input, which in turn gives vertically integrated suppliers some bargaining power.

The parameter δ_i is thus a natural measure for the "sophistication" of the respective input. If δ_i is low, the producer can use most of the leftovers of the input, even if the affiliated supplier has dropped out of the coalition. This will be the case if the respective input is easy to handle for the producer and does not require specific knowledge to be usable. In contrast, if δ_i is high, the threat of an integrated supplier to drop out of the coalition is much more severe. This will be the case with highly sophisticated components that require special expertise.

An outsourced supplier can still threaten to take away the entire input level in the bargaining process owing to his ownership rights, regardless of the degree of sophistication of his input.

8.4.1   Implications for Marginal Contributions and Shapley Values
This ownership decision affects the Shapley values, as it influences the suppliers' marginal contributions. Specifically, in coalitions of size 2,

the total revenue does not fall to 0 if the supplier i is in the last position of a feasible permutation and leaves the coalition. The producer can rather keep the part $(1 - \delta_i)$ of supplier i's input, and the remaining coalition of size one now earns $\hat{H} \cdot ((1-\delta_i) \cdot m_i)^{\alpha \cdot (1-\eta^H)} \cdot \eta_i^{\alpha \cdot (1-\varepsilon) \cdot (1-\eta^H)/\varepsilon}$. Therefore, the marginal contribution of a vertically integrated supplier to a coalition of size 2 is given by

$$MC_i^{2V} = \hat{H} \cdot \left(m_i^{\alpha\left(1-\eta^H\right)} \cdot \eta_i^{\frac{\alpha \cdot (1-\varepsilon) \cdot \left(1-\eta^H\right)}{\varepsilon}} - ((1-\delta_i) \cdot m_i)^{\alpha\left(1-\eta^H\right)} \cdot \eta_i^{\frac{\alpha \cdot (1-\varepsilon) \cdot \left(1-\eta^H\right)}{\varepsilon}} \right) \quad (8.18)$$

whereas the marginal contribution of an outsourced supplier and of the producer to such a coalition are given by equations (8.10) and (8.11), respectively, and correspond to the total revenue level.

Analogously, in a coalition of size 3, if the vertically integrated supplier i drops out, the remaining coalition of the producer and supplier j can still use the part $(1 - \delta_i)$ of supplier i's input. His marginal contribution thus becomes

$$MC_i^{3V} = \hat{H} \cdot \left(\begin{array}{c} \left(m_i^\varepsilon \cdot \eta_i^{1-\varepsilon} + m_j^\varepsilon \cdot \eta_j^{1-\varepsilon}\right)^{\frac{\alpha \cdot \left(1-\eta^H\right)}{\varepsilon}} \\ -\left(((1-\delta_i) \cdot m_i)^\varepsilon \cdot \eta_i^{1-\varepsilon} + m_j^\varepsilon \cdot \eta_j^{1-\varepsilon}\right)^{\frac{\alpha \cdot \left(1-\eta^H\right)}{\varepsilon}} \end{array} \right) \quad \text{with } i \neq j. \quad (8.19)$$

The marginal contributions of an outsourced supplier and of the producer to a coalition of size three are, respectively, given by equations (8.12) and (8.13). In the appendix to this chapter, we display the resulting system of equations to compute the Shapley values and the revenue shares for this generalized case where supplier can differ in terms of their organizational form.

8.4.2 Illustration: The Organizational Decision and the Revenue Distribution

We now illustrate the effects of the organizational decisions for the revenue distribution inside the firm. In figure 8.8, we depict the revenue share of supplier a as a function of the input intensity η_a for the four different organizational structures that the producer can choose in our model.[7] Several points are worth noting.

First, for any given level of η_a, the revenue share of supplier a is higher if he is outsourced than if he is vertically integrated. More specifically, the $\beta_a^{\{O,O\}}$ curve runs above the $\beta_a^{\{V,O\}}$ curve, and the $\beta_a^{\{O,V\}}$ curve

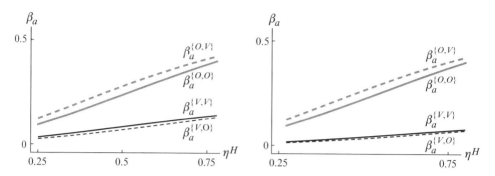

Figure 8.8
Outsourcing versus integration: the suppliers' revenue shares. Left panel: $\delta_a = \delta_b = 0.9$; right panel: $\delta_a = 0.7$, $\delta_b = 0.9$ ($\eta^H = 0.8$, $c_a^M = c_b^M = c^H = 1$, $\varepsilon = 0.2$, and $\alpha = 0.92$).

runs above the $\beta_a^{\{V,V\}}$ curve. The reason is that an outsourced supplier can threaten to withhold his entire input. Thus, an outsourced supplier makes higher marginal contributions to all feasible permutations (conditional on η_a) and thus has a higher Shapley value than an integrated supplier.

Second, notice that the revenue share of supplier a depends not only on his own organizational form but also on the organization of the other supplier. In particular, in both organizational forms supplier a receives a higher revenue share when supplier b is integrated than if supplier b is outsourced; that is, $\beta_a^{\{O,V\}} > \beta_a^{\{O,O\}}$ and $\beta_a^{\{V,V\}} > \beta_a^{\{V,O\}}$ for any given level of η_a. The intuition is that the producer can always rely on the fact that she would retain a part of input b when supplier b is vertically integrated. Because the two components are substitutes, the bargaining power of supplier a therefore decreases compared to the constellation where supplier b threatens to take away his entire input level.

Third, as in figure 8.3, supplier a's revenue share is increasing in the technological importance of his input regardless of the firm's organizational structure; that is, both outsourced and vertically integrated suppliers have a higher bargaining power if their respective input is technologically more important. Furthermore, the revenue shares $\beta_a^{\{O,V\}}$ and $\beta_a^{\{O,O\}}$ for outsourcing rise steeper in η_a than the curves $\beta_a^{\{V,V\}}$ and $\beta_a^{\{V,O\}}$. The reason is that the "threat potential" under vertical integration is a constant fraction of that under outsourcing. With rising technological importance, the marginal gain in bargaining power is thus stronger if the respective supplier a is outsourced.

Fourth, we can also conduct comparative statics with respect to the parameter δ_i. The right panel of figure 8.8 is analogous to the left part but assumes a lower value of δ_a while δ_b stays constant. In other words, we assume that input b is now "more sophisticated" because the producer can use a lower fraction $(1 - \delta_b)$ only if the respective supplier b is vertically integrated and then refuses to collaborate. As can be seen in figure 8.8, the curves $\beta_a^{\{O,O\}}$ and $\beta_a^{\{O,V\}}$ remain unchanged when δ_a is reduced, and the curves $\beta_a^{\{V,O\}}$ and $\beta_a^{\{V,V\}}$ are shifted downward and the distance between those curves becomes smaller. If supplier a is outsourced, the change in the "sophistication" of his input does not matter for his bargaining power because he maintains all ownership rights and threatens to withhold the entire input in the bargaining process. If he is vertically integrated, however, his bargaining power is now lower when his input becomes less sophisticated, because the producer is able to effectively use a higher fraction if supplier a refuses to collaborate. This difference in bargaining powers for supplier a also depends on the organizational structure of supplier b, as argued earlier.

Finally, figure 8.9 depicts the residual revenue shares for the producer assuming the same parameter constellations as in figure 8.8. Notice that the headquarter revenue share is the highest when both suppliers are integrated ($\beta_{\{V,V\}}^H$) and the lowest when both are outsourced ($\beta_{\{O,O\}}^H$). The intermediate cases with one integrated and one outsourced supplier range in between. The intuition is clear: because integrated suppliers have lower bargaining powers, the producer can retain a higher revenue share in the multilateral bargaining. A lower

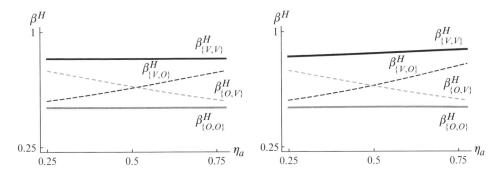

Figure 8.9
Outsourcing versus integration: the producer's revenue share. Left panel: $\delta_a = \delta_b = 0.9$; right panel: $\delta_a = 0.7$, $\delta_b = 0.9$ ($\eta^H = 0.8$, $c_a^M = c_b^M = c^H = 1$, $\varepsilon = 0.2$, and $\alpha = 0.92$).

value of δ_a as in the right panel of figure 8.9 leaves the $\beta^H_{\{O,O\}}$ unaffected but shifts up the other β^H–curves. The reason is the following: If supplier a is an integrated affiliate, his bargaining power declines when his input becomes easier to handle. The producer can thus retain an even larger revenue share for herself.

Figure 8.9 also shows that the shape of the β^H–curve with respect to η_a now depends on the organizational structure of the firm. If both suppliers are outsourced, we are back to the U-shaped curve that we have already seen in figure 8.3. Yet when supplier a is integrated and b is outsourced, the headquarters' revenue share is increasing in η_a, while it is decreasing in η_a when supplier a is outsourced and b is integrated. Economically, for these intermediate cases we can conclude that the producer's revenue share increases with a rising technological importance of the integrated supplier. If supplier a is integrated and provides a technologically more important input, his bargaining power increases, but by less than if he were an external subcontractor. The bargaining power of the outsourced supplier b goes down as η_a increases, and in sum β^H can go up because the increase of β_a was sufficiently small. On the other hand, if supplier a is outsourced and his input becomes more important, the rise in this bargaining power outweighs the declining bargaining power of the integrated supplier b, so that β^H goes down.

8.5   The Producer's Organizational Decision

Thus far, we have analyzed how variations in the technology parameters and in the firm's organizational form affect the players' Shapley values and their realized revenue shares. We can now move to the producer's final organizational decision in the first stage of the game. When making this decision, the producer of course anticipates the implications for the bargaining process and the resulting revenue distribution in the ultimate stage of the game. She effectively chooses the tuple $\{O,O\}$, $\{O,V\}$, $\{V,O\}$ or $\{V,V\}$ that maximizes the overall payoff of the relationship, as given in equation (8.9), taking into account the firm's technology parameters.

In this section, we illustrate this payoff-maximizing organizational choice and focus on the firm's organizational structure for different types and degrees of asymmetries across the two manufacturing components. In particular, we focus on the following three asymmetries:

1. Differences in the input intensities η_a and η_b

2. Differences in the unit costs c_a^M and c_b^M

3. Differences in the components' sophistication (the thread points) δ_a and δ_b

8.5.1 Differences in the Input Intensities

Suppose the two components differ in their technological importance for the production process but are symmetric in terms of unit costs and thread points. The left panel of figure 8.10 illustrates the producer's final organizational decision for this case. On the horizontal axis, we display the headquarter-intensity η^H, and on the vertical axis the degree of the technological asymmetry (with $\eta_a = 1/2$ being the benchmark with symmetric components). The different colors specify which organizational form is profit maximizing.

For sufficiently high headquarter-intensity, the producer chooses to vertically integrate *both* suppliers. What is the intuition for this result? When η^H is high, the components have low overall importance for the production process. The Shapley values of both suppliers would thus be quite low even as external subcontractors. By vertically integrating the suppliers, the producer further lowers their bargaining power and hence their incentives to contribute to the relationship. This exacerbation of the underinvestment problem for the suppliers is of lesser

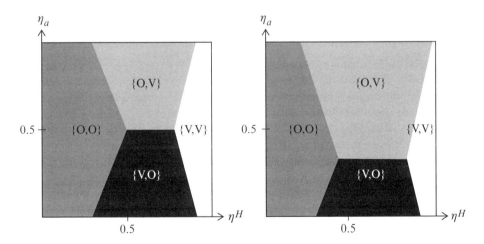

Figure 8.10
The organizational decision. Left panel: $c_a^M = c_b^M$ and $\delta_a = \delta_b$; right panel: $c_a^M < c_b^M$ and/or $\delta_a > \delta_b$.

importance for the total surplus, however. It is more important to leave a large revenue share to the producer in order to minimize her under-investment problem. Analogously, when η^H is sufficiently low, the producer chooses to outsource *both* suppliers. By leaving the ownership rights to the suppliers, their underinvestment problems are lowered because this decision endogenously leads to a higher Shapley value for them. In other words, the producer incentivizes the suppliers by effectively giving them more bargaining power.

The most interesting constellations occur for intermediate values of the headquarter intensity η^H. Here we find that the producer chooses to outsource one supplier while vertically integrating the other. Such a coexistence of two organizational forms within the same firm (hybrid sourcing) is an empirically highly relevant phenomenon (Tomiura 2007; Kohler and Smolka 2012). Quite naturally, such a firm structure cannot occur in the baseline model by Antràs and Helpman (2004) with just one single supplier/component, but it can occur in our framework with multiple (that is, at least two) suppliers.

When does hybrid sourcing occur, and which organizational mode is chosen for which component? The left panel of figure 8.10 suggests that a technological asymmetry across the two components makes the occurrence of hybrid sourcing overall more likely and that the producer tends to outsource the supplier with the technologically more important component. This effect can be seen by noting that the parameter range of η^H where hybrid sourcing is chosen expands the further away η_a is from the benchmark value of $1/2$. Furthermore, whenever input a is the more important one ($\eta_a > 1/2$), only the organizational form $\{O,V\}$ prevails—and never the form $\{V,O\}$. For $\eta_a < 1/2$ we observe the opposite: only the form $\{V,O\}$ but never the form $\{O,V\}$.

Intuitively, at intermediate values of η^H, both the headquarter services and the component inputs matter substantially for the production process. The uniform organizational structures $\{O,O\}$ and $\{V,V\}$ are thus not payoff maximizing, as they exacerbate the underinvestment problem for the producer or, respectively, for the suppliers to an undue extent. Hybrid sourcing leads to a better balance of these underinvestment problems, and it is then relatively more important to properly incentivize the supplier of the more important component by leaving him the property rights over his assets.

8.5.2   Differences in Unit Costs

Now assume that the suppliers differ not only in their input intensities but also in their unit costs. In particular, we assume that supplier a is the low-cost supplier such that $c_a^M < c_b^M$. As we have shown earlier, this increases the Shapley value of supplier a by raising his input provision level and thus his marginal contributions.

The qualitative consequences for the organizational decision are illustrated in the right panel of figure 8.10. Similar as before, the producer still chooses to outsource (integrate) both suppliers for sufficiently high (low) values of η^H. If headquarter services (components) are highly important for the production process, it is crucial to give enough bargaining power to the producer (the suppliers) in order to minimize their underinvestment problems.

The most interesting implication is visible in the intermediate range of η^H, where the producer chooses hybrid sourcing. As can be seen, the organizational form $\{O,V\}$ is now much more prevalent in the right panel (where a has lower unit costs than b) than in the left panel of figure 8.10 where unit costs are symmetric across suppliers. That is, if the producer chooses to outsource only one supplier, it is likely to be the one with the lower unit costs. The reason is that this low-cost supplier chooses a higher input provision level and thus becomes more valuable for the firm. It is therefore important to properly incentivize this supplier by granting him the ownership rights over his assets.

Notice, however, that there are also constellations where the other hybrid sourcing mode $\{V,O\}$ is chosen, namely if η_a is sufficiently low. In that case, supplier b's technological importance is so large that it becomes even more important to incentivize that supplier, despite the fact that he has higher unit costs.

8.5.3 Differences in the Components' Sophistication

Finally, we analyze the scenario in which components differ in their input intensities and their "sophistication" while again assuming that unit costs are symmetric. In particular, suppose that $\delta_a < \delta_b$ holds; that is, we may think of input b as being the more sophisticated component that requires more specific knowledge to be usable.

The implications are also illustrated in the right panel of figure 8.10, as they are qualitatively similar to the case with unit cost differences. Given that η^H is in the intermediate range so that hybrid sourcing is chosen, our main finding is that the producer would more easily outsource the *less* sophisticated input a. The more sophisticated input b is, in contrast, kept within the firm boundaries for a wider parameter range as long as η_a is not too low.

The low value of δ_a implies that supplier a would have a substantially lower Shapley value as an integrated subsidiary than as an external subcontractor. In other words, supplier a can hardly be incentivized within the firm boundaries because his input is so easy to handle that he hardly has any bargaining power vis-à-vis the producer. For supplier b, the difference in organizational forms matters less for his incentives. He has high bargaining power even as an affiliate of the firm, owning to the sophistication of his component.

This is the reason why why the producer would rather outsource the simpler component a, because the ownership rights are then an effective device to incentivize her supplier. This pattern changes only if component b is not only more sophisticated but also has a sufficiently higher input intensity. In that case, the standard incentive effect discussed in section 8.5.1 dominates, and we would observe the ownership structure $\{V,O\}$. If the input intensities are not too different, or if η_a even exceeds η_b, we have $\{O,V\}$ in the hybrid sourcing range.

8.6   Summary and Discussion

In this chapter, we have provided an extension of the seminal model by Antràs and Helpman (2004). They considered an incomplete contracts model in which a producer interacts with one single supplier and then decides on that supplier's organizational form ("make or buy"). In our extension, there are two asymmetric manufacturing components and hence three parties who bargain over the surplus of the relationship: the producer and the two respective suppliers. Our approach relies on the Shapley value, which is the standard solution concept for such multilateral bargaining situations.

Some of our main results are consistent with Antràs and Helpman 2004. For example, we also find that if the headquarter intensity of final goods production is very low, the firm will exclusively rely on outsourcing and that complete vertical integration is likely to prevail in highly headquarter-intensive firms. However, one key difference compared to Antràs and Helpman 2004 is that our model can quite naturally generate hybrid sourcing as the outcome of the producer's organizational choice. That is, our model may explain why firms choose different sourcing modes for different suppliers. Such a coexistence of organizational forms within the same firm is an empirically highly relevant phenomenon (Tomiura 2007; Kohler and Smolka 2012) and necessarily requires a model with multiple that is at least two) components.

Moreover, our model is well suited to analyze which sourcing mode is chosen for which supplier. We find that the producer tends to outsource the technologically more important components with a higher input intensity and components that are provided by suppliers with lower unit costs. Yet the producer tends to keep "sophisticated" inputs that require special expertise to be usable within the boundaries of the firm, while the producer chooses to outsource simpler and more standard components. These findings are consistent with the results by Nowak, Schwarz, and Suedekum (2012) and Schwarz and Suedekum (2011). In this chapter, we have explicitly highlighted the underlying theoretical foundations by discussing at length how these asymmetries across components affect the suppliers' bargaining powers (Shapley values) and their realized revenue shares in the negotiation with the producer.

Our results may provide a rationale for some recent empirical findings from the literature on multinational enterprises. In particular, Alfaro and Charlton (2009) and Corcos et al. (2013) report that MNEs tend to keep high-skill inputs, or components with a higher degree of asset specificity, within their boundaries. Although it is difficult to precisely formalize those notions of the "skill intensity" and the "asset specificity" of inputs, we believe that our theoretical results are consistent with those empirical findings. On one hand, our model predicts that outsourcing is more likely to occur for components with a higher input intensity, as this incentivizes the respective supplier. Yet inputs may also differ in terms of their inherent sophistication, which is not directly captured by their input intensities. Here, our theoretical results are in line with the empirical findings of Alfaro and Charlton (2009) and Corcos et al. (2013), as our model predicts that producers tend to keep more sophisticated manufacturing components in house.

Appendix 8A.1   Input Provision Levels

The headquarter and the suppliers choose the level of input provision that maximizes their profits $\beta^H \cdot R - c^H \cdot h$ or $\beta_i \cdot R - c_i^M \cdot m_i$, respectively. The first-order condition for the headquarter is

$$\pi_h^{H'} = \beta^H \cdot R_h' - c^H = \beta^H \cdot \frac{\eta^H \cdot R \cdot \alpha}{h} - c^H = 0 \Leftrightarrow h = \frac{\alpha \cdot \beta^H \cdot \eta^H \cdot R}{c^H} \tag{8.20}$$

Furthermore, the second-order condition is satisfied:

$$\pi_{hh}^{H''} = -\frac{\eta^H \cdot R \cdot \alpha \cdot (1 - \alpha \cdot \eta^H) \cdot \beta^H}{h^2} < 0 \tag{8.21}$$

Analogously, for supplier i the first-order condition is

$$\pi'_{i\,m_i} = \beta_i \cdot R'_{m_i} - c_i^M = \beta_i \cdot \frac{\left(\dfrac{m_i}{\eta_i}\right)^{-(1-\varepsilon)} \cdot \alpha \cdot (1 - \eta^H) \cdot R}{\left(\dfrac{m_a}{\eta_a}\right)^{\varepsilon} \cdot \eta_a + \left(\dfrac{m_b}{\eta_b}\right)^{\varepsilon} \cdot \eta_b} - c_i^M = 0 \tag{8.22}$$

The second-order condition is again satisfied:

$$\pi''_{i\,m_i m_i} = -\frac{\alpha \cdot \beta_i \cdot (1 - \eta^H) \cdot R \cdot \left(\dfrac{m_i}{\eta_i}\right)^{\varepsilon} \cdot \eta_i \cdot \left(\left(\dfrac{m_j}{\eta_j}\right)^{\varepsilon} \cdot \eta_j \cdot (1 - \varepsilon) + \left(\dfrac{m_i}{\eta_i}\right)^{\varepsilon} \cdot \eta_i \cdot (1 - \alpha \cdot (1 - \eta^H))\right)}{m_i^2 \cdot \left(\left(\dfrac{m_a}{\eta_a}\right)^{\varepsilon} \cdot \eta_a + \left(\dfrac{m_b}{\eta_b}\right)^{\varepsilon} \cdot \eta_b\right)^2} < 0 \tag{8.23}$$

This work shows that the input provision levels given in equation (8.5) are maximizing the individual payoffs of the producer and, respectively, the suppliers in the fourth stage of the game.

Appendix 8A.2   Shapley Values with Full Ownership Rights of Suppliers

Using equation (8.17), the system of equations to determine the Shapley values and the revenue shares of suppliers a and b is given by

$$\beta_a = \frac{1}{6} \cdot \left(\alpha \cdot (1 - \eta^H) \cdot \left(\frac{\alpha \cdot (1 - \eta^H)}{c_a^{M - \varepsilon/(1-\varepsilon)} \cdot \beta_a^{-\varepsilon/(1-\varepsilon)} \cdot \eta_a + c_b^{M - \varepsilon/(1-\varepsilon)} \cdot \beta_b^{-\varepsilon/(1-\varepsilon)} \cdot \eta_b} \right)^{-(1-\varepsilon)} \right)^{-\frac{\alpha \cdot (1-\eta^H)}{\varepsilon}}$$

$$\cdot \left(2 \cdot \left(\alpha \cdot (1 - \eta^H) \cdot \left(\frac{\alpha \cdot (1 - \eta^H)}{c_a^{M - \varepsilon/(1-\varepsilon)} \cdot \beta_a^{\varepsilon/(1-\varepsilon)} \cdot \eta_a + c_b^{M - \varepsilon/(1-\varepsilon)} \cdot \beta_b^{\varepsilon/(1-\varepsilon)} \cdot \eta_b} \right)^{-(1-\varepsilon)} \right)^{\frac{\alpha \cdot (1-\eta^H)}{\varepsilon}} \right.$$

$$-2 \cdot c_b^{M^{-\frac{\alpha \cdot (1-\eta^H)}{1-\varepsilon}}} \cdot \beta_b^{\frac{\alpha \cdot (1-\eta^H)}{1-\varepsilon}} \cdot \eta_b^{\frac{\alpha \cdot (1-\eta^H)}{1-\varepsilon}}$$

$$\cdot \left(\frac{\alpha \cdot (1-\eta^H)}{c_a^{M^{-\varepsilon/(1-\varepsilon)}} \cdot \beta_a^{\varepsilon/(1-\varepsilon)} \cdot \eta_a + c_b^{M^{-\varepsilon/(1-\varepsilon)}} \cdot \beta_b^{\varepsilon/(1-\varepsilon)} \cdot \eta_b} \right)^{\alpha \cdot (1-\eta^H)}$$

$$+ c_a^{M^{-\frac{\alpha \cdot (1-\eta^H)}{1-\varepsilon}}} \cdot \beta_a^{\frac{\alpha \cdot (1-\eta^H)}{1-\varepsilon}} \cdot \eta_a^{\frac{\alpha \cdot (1-\eta^H)}{1-\varepsilon}} \cdot \left(\frac{\alpha \cdot (1-\eta^H)}{\begin{array}{c} c_a^{M^{-\varepsilon/(1-\varepsilon)}} \cdot \beta_a^{\varepsilon/(1-\varepsilon)} \cdot \eta_a \\ + c_b^{M^{-\varepsilon/(1-\varepsilon)}} \cdot \beta_b^{\varepsilon/(1-\varepsilon)} \cdot \eta_b \end{array}} \right)^{\alpha \cdot (1-\eta^H)}$$

and

$$\beta_b = \frac{1}{6} \cdot \left(\alpha \cdot (1-\eta^H) \cdot \left(\frac{\alpha \cdot (1-\eta^H)}{\begin{array}{c} c_a^{M^{-\varepsilon/(1-\varepsilon)}} \cdot \beta_a^{\varepsilon/(1-\varepsilon)} \cdot \eta_a \\ + c_b^{M^{-\varepsilon/(1-\varepsilon)}} \cdot \beta_b^{\varepsilon/(1-\varepsilon)} \cdot \eta_b \end{array}} \right)^{-(1-\varepsilon)} \right)^{-\frac{\alpha \cdot (1-\eta^H)}{\varepsilon}}$$

$$\cdot \left(2 \cdot \left(\alpha \cdot (1-\eta^H) \cdot \left(\frac{\alpha \cdot (1-\eta^H)}{\begin{array}{c} c_a^{M^{-\varepsilon/(1-\varepsilon)}} \cdot \beta_a^{\varepsilon/(1-\varepsilon)} \cdot \eta_a \\ + c_b^{M^{-\varepsilon/(1-\varepsilon)}} \cdot \beta_b^{\varepsilon/(1-\varepsilon)} \cdot \eta_b \end{array}} \right)^{-(1-\varepsilon)} \right)^{\frac{\alpha \cdot (1-\eta^H)}{\varepsilon}} \right.$$

$$-2 \cdot c_a^{M^{-\frac{\alpha \cdot (1-\eta^H)}{1-\varepsilon}}} \cdot \beta_a^{\frac{\alpha \cdot (1-\eta^H)}{1-\varepsilon}} \cdot \eta_a^{\frac{\alpha \cdot (1-\eta^H)}{\varepsilon}} \cdot \left(\frac{\alpha \cdot (1-\eta^H)}{\begin{array}{c} c_a^{M^{-\varepsilon/(1-\varepsilon)}} \cdot \beta_a^{\varepsilon/(1-\varepsilon)} \cdot \eta_a \\ + c_b^{M^{-\varepsilon/(1-\varepsilon)}} \cdot \beta_b^{\varepsilon/(1-\varepsilon)} \cdot \eta_b \end{array}} \right)^{\alpha \cdot (1-\eta^H)}$$

$$+ c_b^{M^{-\frac{\alpha \cdot (1-\eta^H)}{1-\varepsilon}}} \cdot \beta_b^{\frac{\alpha \cdot (1-\eta^H)}{1-\varepsilon}} \cdot \eta_b^{\frac{\alpha \cdot (1-\eta^H)}{\varepsilon}} \cdot \left(\frac{\alpha \cdot (1-\eta^H)}{\begin{array}{c} c_a^{M^{-\varepsilon/(1-\varepsilon)}} \cdot \beta_a^{\varepsilon/(1-\varepsilon)} \cdot \eta_a \\ + c_b^{M^{-\varepsilon/(1-\varepsilon)}} \cdot \beta_b^{\varepsilon/(1-\varepsilon)} \cdot \eta_b \end{array}} \right)^{\alpha \cdot (1-\eta^H)}$$

We solve this system numerically for β_a and β_b by assuming specific values of the parameters.

Appendix 8A.3   Shapley Values for Different Organizational Structures

For different organizational structures, given by differences in the parameter δ, the system of equations to determine the Shapley values and the revenue shares of suppliers a and b is given by

$$\beta_a = \frac{1}{6} \cdot$$

$$\left(\alpha \cdot (1-\eta^H) \cdot \left(\frac{\alpha \cdot (1-\eta^H)}{c_a^{M-\varepsilon/(1-\varepsilon)} \cdot \beta_a^{\varepsilon/(1-\varepsilon)} \cdot \eta_a + c_b^{M-\varepsilon/(1-\varepsilon)} \cdot \beta_b^{\varepsilon/(1-\varepsilon)} \cdot \eta_b} \right)^{-(1-\varepsilon)} \right)^{-\frac{\alpha \cdot (1-\eta^H)}{\varepsilon}}$$

$$\left(\left(2 \cdot \left(\alpha \cdot (1-\eta^H) \cdot \frac{\alpha \cdot (1-\eta^H)}{\begin{array}{c} c_a^{M-\varepsilon/(1-\varepsilon)} \cdot \beta_a^{\varepsilon/(1-\varepsilon)} \cdot \eta_a \\ + c_b^{M-\varepsilon/(1-\varepsilon)} \cdot \beta_b^{\varepsilon/(1-\varepsilon)} \cdot \eta_b \end{array}} \right)^{-(1-\varepsilon)} \right)^{\frac{\alpha \cdot (1-\eta^H)}{\varepsilon}} \right.$$

$$-2 \cdot \left(c_b^{M-\frac{\varepsilon}{1-\varepsilon}} \cdot \beta_b^{\frac{\varepsilon}{1-\varepsilon}} \cdot \eta_b \cdot \left(\frac{\alpha \cdot (1-\eta^H)}{c_a^{M-\varepsilon/(1-\varepsilon)} \cdot \beta_a^{\varepsilon/(1-\varepsilon)} \cdot \eta_a + c_b^{M-\varepsilon/(1-\varepsilon)} \cdot \beta_b^{\varepsilon/(1-\varepsilon)} \cdot \eta_b} \right)^{\varepsilon} \right.$$

$$\left. + c_a^{M-\frac{\varepsilon}{1-\varepsilon}} \cdot \beta_a^{\frac{\varepsilon}{1-\varepsilon}} \cdot \eta_a \cdot \left(\frac{\alpha \cdot (1-\delta_a) \cdot (1-\eta^H)}{c_a^{M-\varepsilon/(1-\varepsilon)} \cdot \beta_a^{\varepsilon/(1-\varepsilon)} \cdot \eta_a + c_b^{M-\varepsilon/(1-\varepsilon)} \cdot \beta_b^{\varepsilon/(1-\varepsilon)} \cdot \eta_b} \right)^{\varepsilon} \right)^{\frac{\alpha \cdot (1-\eta^H)}{\varepsilon}}$$

$$+ c_a^{M-\frac{\alpha \cdot (1-\eta^H)}{1-\varepsilon}} \cdot \beta_a^{\frac{\alpha \cdot (1-\eta^H)}{1-\varepsilon}} \cdot \eta_a^{\frac{\alpha \cdot (1-\eta^H)}{\varepsilon}} \cdot \left(\left(\frac{\alpha \cdot (1-\eta^H)}{\begin{array}{c} c_a^{M-\varepsilon/(1-\varepsilon)} \cdot \beta_a^{\varepsilon/(1-\varepsilon)} \cdot \eta_a \\ + c_b^{M-\varepsilon/(1-\varepsilon)} \cdot \beta_b^{\varepsilon/(1-\varepsilon)} \cdot \eta_b \end{array}} \right)^{\alpha \cdot (1-\eta^H)} \right.$$

$$\left. \left. \left. - \left(\frac{\alpha \cdot (1-\delta_a) \cdot (1-\eta^H)}{c_a^{M-\varepsilon/(1-\varepsilon)} \cdot \beta_a^{\varepsilon/(1-\varepsilon)} \cdot \eta_a + c_b^{M-\varepsilon/(1-\varepsilon)} \cdot \beta_b^{\varepsilon/(1-\varepsilon)} \cdot \eta_b} \right)^{\alpha \cdot (1-\eta^H)} \right) \right) \right)$$

and

$$\beta_b = \frac{1}{6} \cdot \left(\alpha \cdot (1-\eta^H) \cdot \left(\frac{\alpha \cdot (1-\eta^H)}{\begin{array}{c} c_a^{M-\varepsilon/(1-\varepsilon)} \cdot \beta_a^{\varepsilon/(1-\varepsilon)} \cdot \eta_a \\ + c_b^{M-\varepsilon/(1-\varepsilon)} \cdot \beta_b^{\varepsilon/(1-\varepsilon)} \cdot \eta_b \end{array}} \right)^{-(1-\varepsilon)} \right)^{-\frac{\alpha(1-\eta^H)}{\varepsilon}}$$

$$\left(\left(2\cdot\left(\alpha\cdot(1-\eta^H)\cdot\left(\frac{\alpha\cdot(1-\eta^H)}{c_a^{M^{-\varepsilon/(1-\varepsilon)}}\cdot\beta_a^{\varepsilon/(1-\varepsilon)}\cdot\eta_a+c_b^{M^{-\varepsilon/(1-\varepsilon)}}\cdot\beta_b^{\varepsilon/(1-\varepsilon)}\cdot\eta_b}\right)^{-(1-\varepsilon)}\right)^{\frac{\alpha\cdot(1-\eta^H)}{\varepsilon}}\right.\right.$$

$$-2\cdot\left(c_a^{M^{\frac{\varepsilon}{1-\varepsilon}}}\cdot\beta_a^{\frac{\varepsilon}{1-\varepsilon}}\cdot\eta_a\cdot\left(\frac{\alpha\cdot(1-\eta^H)}{c_a^{M^{-\varepsilon/(1-\varepsilon)}}\cdot\beta_a^{\varepsilon/(1-\varepsilon)}\cdot\eta_a+c_b^{M^{-\varepsilon/(1-\varepsilon)}}\cdot\beta_b^{\varepsilon/(1-\varepsilon)}\cdot\eta_b}\right)^{\varepsilon}\right.$$

$$\left.+c_b^{M^{-\frac{\varepsilon}{1-\varepsilon}}}\cdot\beta_b^{\frac{\varepsilon}{1-\varepsilon}}\cdot\eta_b\cdot\left(\frac{\alpha\cdot(1-\delta_b)\cdot(1-\eta^H)}{c_a^{M^{-\varepsilon/(1-\varepsilon)}}\cdot\beta_a^{\varepsilon/(1-\varepsilon)}\cdot\eta_a+c_b^{M^{-\varepsilon/(1-\varepsilon)}}\cdot\beta_b^{\varepsilon/(1-\varepsilon)}\cdot\eta_b}\right)^{\varepsilon}\right)^{\frac{\alpha\cdot(1-\eta^H)}{\varepsilon}}$$

$$+c_b^{M^{-\frac{\alpha\cdot(1-\eta^H)}{1-\varepsilon}}}\cdot\beta_b^{\frac{\alpha\cdot(1-\eta^H)}{1-\varepsilon}}\cdot\eta_b^{\frac{\alpha\cdot(1-\eta^H)}{1-\varepsilon}}\cdot\left(\left(\frac{\alpha\cdot(1-\eta^H)}{c_a^{M^{-\varepsilon/(1-\varepsilon)}}\cdot\beta_a^{\varepsilon/(1-\varepsilon)}\cdot\eta_a+c_b^{M^{-\varepsilon/(1-\varepsilon)}}\cdot\beta_b^{\varepsilon/(1-\varepsilon)}\cdot\eta_b}\right)^{\alpha\cdot(1-\eta^H)}\right.$$

$$\left.\left.\left.-\left(\frac{\alpha\cdot(1-\delta_b)\cdot(1-\eta^H)}{c_a^{M^{-\varepsilon/(1-\varepsilon)}}\cdot\beta_a^{\varepsilon/(1-\varepsilon)}\cdot\eta_a+c_b^{M^{-\varepsilon/(1-\varepsilon)}}\cdot\beta_b^{\varepsilon/(1-\varepsilon)}\cdot\eta_b}\right)^{\alpha\cdot(1-\eta^H)}\right)\right)\right).$$

Similar to appendix 8A.2, we solve this system numerically for β_a and β_b by assuming specific values of the parameters.

Notes

This chapter was prepared for the CESifo volume "Firms in the International Economy: Closing the Gap between International Economics and International Business." We thank seminar participants at the CESifo summer institute 2011 in Venice and an anonymous referee for helpful suggestions. All errors and shortcomings are our responsibility.

1. See Antràs and Rossi-Hansberg 2009 for a detailed discussion of several examples of MNEs.

2. See Tomiura 2007; Jabbour 2012; Kohler and Smolka 2012; and Jabbour and Kneller 2010 for systematic evidence on the importance of hybrid sourcing strategies in multinational firms.

3. As will become clearer later in this chapter, this model structure with incomplete contracts is characterized by hold-up and underinvestment problems, because inputs are relationship specific and investment costs are sunk. An outsourced supplier then tends to have higher bargaining power vis-à-vis the producer, as he can threaten to withhold his entire input level. A vertically integrated supplier is basically an employee of the producer and hence has no ownership rights over his inputs. However, following the property rights approach to the firm (see Grossman and Hart 1986; Hart and Moore 1990),

we assume that the producer cannot fully make use of that input if the vertically integrated supplier refuses to collaborate, which in turn gives some bargaining power to those subsidiaries.

4. For a recent review of the literature, see Antràs 2013.

5. A key difference of our model compared to Antràs and Helpman (2004) is that not all inputs are essential in our framework. Namely, a coalition of the producer with one supplier earns positive revenue as long as $\varepsilon > 0$ in the CES function (equation [8.2]). Antràs and Helpman (2004) consider a setup with a producer and one manufacturing component, in which the two inputs are combined in a Cobb-Douglas fashion. They assume a bilateral Nash bargaining.

6. This is consistent with the argument of the concave/convex shape of the β_a schedule in figure 8.3.

7. We assume fixed values for the headquarter intensity η^H and the substitutability ε in this section, and we assume that the two suppliers have identical unit costs. Changes in those parameters would have qualitatively similar effects as illustrated in section 8.3.

References

Acemoglu, D., P. Antràs, and E. Helpman. 2007. Contracts and technology adoption. *American Economic Review* 97 (3): 916–943.

Alfaro, L., and A. Charlton. 2009. Intra-industry foreign direct investment. *American Economic Review* 99 (5): 2096–2119.

Antràs, P. 2013. Grossman-Hart (1986) goes global: Incomplete contracts, property rights, and the international organization of production. Forthcoming in *Journal of Law, Economics and Organization*.

Antràs, P., and D. Chor. 2013. Organizing the global value chain. Forthcoming in *Econometrica*.

Antràs, P., and E. Rossi-Hansberg. 2009. Organizations and trade. *Annual Review of Economics* 1:43–64.

Antràs, P., and E. Helpman. 2008. Contractual frictions and global sourcing. In *The Organization of Firms in a Global Economy*, ed. E. Helpman, D. Marin, and T. Verdier, 9–54. Cambridge, MA: Harvard University Press.

Antràs, P., and E. Helpman. 2004. Global sourcing. *Journal of Political Economy* 112 (3): 552–580.

Corcos, G., D. M. Irac, G. Mion, and T. Verdier. 2013. The determinants of intra-firm trade. Forthcoming in *Review of Economics and Statistics*.

Du, J., Y. Lu, and Z. Tao. 2009. Bi-sourcing in the global economy. *Journal of International Economics* 77 (2): 215–222.

Grossman, S. J., and O. D. Hart. 1986. The costs and benefits of ownership: A theory of vertical and lateral integration. *Journal of Political Economy* 94 (4): 691–719.

Hart, S. 1990. Advances in value theory. In *Game Theory and Applications, Location*, ed. T. Ichiishi, A. Neyman, and Y. Tauman, 166–175. New York: Academic Press.

Hart, S., and A. Mas-Colell. 1988. The potential of the Shapley value. In *The Shapley Value: Essays in Honor of Lloyd S. Shapley*, ed. A. E. Roth, 127–137. Cambridge: Cambridge University Press.

Hart, O., and J. Moore. 1990. Property rights and the nature of the firm. *Journal of Political Economy* 98 (6): 1119–1158.

Jabbour, L. 2012. Slicing the value chain internationally: Empirical evidence on the offshoring strategy by French firms. *The World Economy* 35 (11): 1417–1447.

Jabbour, L., and R. Kneller. 2010. Multiple offshoring: evidence for French firms, unpublished manuscript. University of Nottingham.

Kohler, W., and M. Smolka. 2012. Global Sourcing: Evidence from Spanish Firm-level Data. In*Quantitative Analysis of Newly Evolving Patterns of International Trade: Fragmentation, Offshoring of Activities, and Vertical Intra-Industry Trade*, ed. Robert M. Stern, 139–193. Singapore: World Scientific Publishing.

Nowak, V., C. Schwarz, and J. Suedekum. 2012. On the organizational structure of multinational firms—Which sourcing mode for which input? IZA Discussion Paper 6564, Bonn.

Schwarz, C., and J. Suedekum. 2011. Global sourcing of complex production processes. CESifo Working Paper Series no. 3559.

Shapley, L. 1953. A value for n-person games. In *Classics in Game Theory*, ed. H. W. Kuhn, 69–79. Princeton: Princeton University Press.

Tomiura, E. 2007. Foreign outsourcing, exporting, and FDI: A productivity comparison at the firm level. *Journal of International Economics* 72 (1): 113–127.

Van Biesebroeck, J., and L. Zhang. 2011. Global sourcing of a complex good. CEPR Discussion Paper No. 8614.

9 Global Value Chains during the Great Trade Collapse: A Bullwhip Effect?

Carlo Altomonte, Filippo Di Mauro, Gianmarco Ottaviano, Armando Rungi, and Vincent Vicard

9.1 Introduction

The Great Trade Collapse is one of the most striking features of the recent global financial crisis, with the ongoing recovery still driving a wedge between output and trade. Apart from its magnitude, the fall in trade during the crisis has also been quite homogeneous across all countries: more than 90 percent of Organisation for Economic Co-operation and Development (OECD) countries have exhibited simultaneously a decline in exports and imports exceeding 10 percent. The fall has also been very fast, with trade virtually grinding to a halt in the last quarter of 2008. All these findings have led to qualifying the drop in trade during the crisis as "severe, sudden and synchronized" (Baldwin and Evenett 2009, 1). A number of transmission mechanisms (Baldwin 2009) have been proposed that could account for such peculiarities, making the latest generalized trade drop quite unique among the many episodes of trade decline after a financial crisis (Abiad, Mishra, and Topalova 2010). Among those mechanisms, a particular role has been attributed to the emergence of global supply chains over the last decade and to the different compositional effects of the demand shock on trade and GDP. A role has also been acknowledged for the credit crunch suffered by internationalized firms (Bricongne et al. 2012).

Considering the transmission mechanism of global value chains, a first argument is that the magnitude of the trade drop is due to a problem of multiple accounting. In a world increasingly characterized by vertical specialization—that is, with goods produced sequentially in stages across different countries—the same component of a final good is exchanged (and thus recorded at gross value as trade) several times before the final product reaches the consumer. As a result, for a given reduction in income, trade should decline "not only by the value of the finished product, but also by the value of all the intermediate trade flows that went into creating it" (Yi 2009; but also previously Bergoeing et al. 2004).

A second channel that relates the magnitude and the synchronization of the latest trade drop to the emergence of global value chains is the inherent adjustment in inventories after a demand shock that the existence of interfirm linkages implies. The wider fluctuations in terms of trade elasticities are in this case an overreaction due to adjustments in the stocks of intermediate inputs by firms involved in complex supply chains (Stadtler 2008; Escaith, Lindenberg, and Miroudot 2010; Freund 2009). According to this argument, known as the "bullwhip effect" (Forrester 1961), each participant to a supply chain had a greater observed variation in demand during the crisis and the initial negative shock propagated up the value chain. The logic is as follows. When final demand is subject to volatility, businesses typically face forecast errors against which they try to shelter by building safety stocks of inventories. Upstream participants to a supply chain face greater demand volatility than downstream ones, so the need for such stocks rises moving up the value chain. The result is that variations in final demand are amplified as one moves away from the final customer. When applied to the current context, the foregoing logic implies that with falling demand, orders decreased more than proportionally because firms were able to draw on inventories after expectations of lower future demand. Firms involved in value chains reduced their stocks more than proportionally while the shock propagated up the value chain. Alessandria, Kaboski, and Midrigan (2011) successfully tested this argument for the United States.

Exploiting transaction-level French trade data matched with ownership data for the period 2007–2009, we first find evidence of an overreaction of trade in intermediates in line with that suggested by Alessandria, Kaboski, and Midrigan (2011), then we notice different dynamics of value chains according to their organizational mode: trade of intermediates among related parties reacted with a faster drop at the outburst of the crisis and a faster recovery thereafter. In other words, verticalized multinational groups were able to adjust faster to the negative demand shock. Although a role for the financing capabilities internal to the group cannot be excluded in softening the financial constraints in times of recovery, our hypothesis is that hierarchies of firms belonging to the same multinational groups are better able to optimize inventories management and do not suffer from the informative asymmetries of buyer/supplier contracts when compared with value chains consisting of independent parties. From this perspective, the different (better) management of inventories by internalized firms can be considered a firm-specific advantage (FSA) that prevails on country- and industry-level characteristics. And indeed, the bullwhip effect is a notion studied and developed in the fields of business and management that allows us to shed more light on the costs and benefits of an enlarged firm (better, group) boundary. For a detailed discussion of the notion of FSAs as opposed to country and industry contexts, see also chapter 1.

For example, to better manage orders along the supply chain, Wal-Mart stores frequently transmit sales data to the headquarters, which then use this information to fine-tune the shipments from suppliers to stores through the distribution center. Clearly, the successful implementation of this sort of demand-driven strategies requires a degree of trustful collaboration and information sharing that is much easier to attain among related than independent parties.

The chapter is organized as follows. In section 9.2, we introduce our newly assembled dataset that allows us to capture interfirm proprietary linkages and we provide some descriptive statistics of the peculiarities of value chains organized by multinational business groups. In section 9.3, we exploit our dataset to draw some stylized facts that relate the trade collapse to the organizational modes of value chains. In section 9.4, we discuss the results of our empirical investigation. In section 9.5, we present some concluding remarks.

9.2   The Dataset: Trade and Interfirm Linkages

Our transaction-level dataset has been built exploiting three different available sources: French customs' monthly data for exports and imports by firms; Orbis by Bureau van Dijk for annual balance sheet data; and the Ownership Database by Bureau van Dijk for data on intragroup linkages. In particular, the first source allowed us to collect over 62 million monthly transactions of products classified according to the Harmonized Commodity Description and Coding System (HS) six-digit classification with their countries of origin and destination for the period 2007M1 to 2009M12; we therefore cover the whole period of the trade collapse and the following recovery. The second source reports the core and secondary economic activities of firms involved or not in international trade, as well as annual data on firms' size and financial accounts. The third source, which is based on information provided by companies themselves or by national official bodies when in charge, allows us to track the proprietary network of affiliates belonging to the same headquarters and located worldwide.

The final outcome is a sample with different levels of interlocking economic disaggregation, from consolidated multinational groups to single affiliates, from industries to products, which are traded by single firms organized as multinational groups or as independent firms. Moreover, space disaggregation and a time disaggregation are present in the sample. The former enables us to consider both the geographical dispersion of trade flows and the locations of the property networks of hierarchies composed by a French or a foreign headquarters and their own affiliates worldwide. The disaggregation by month, on the other hand, allows us to properly split the period of analysis following the timing of the financial crisis and hence its fast transmission to firm trading activities.

We end up with over 62 million transactions by 167,833 exporting and/or importing firms located in France in the period 2007–2009 from all sector of economic activities, including manufacturing, services, and primary industries. Out of the total number of recorded firms, only 6,760 are owned by a foreign multinational group (defined as a group with at least one affiliate and the headquarters abroad) and 9,482 are part of a French multinational group (with the headquarters in France and at least one affiliate abroad). The number of headquarters—that is, the number of multinational groups to which the affiliates belong—is 5,754 (either foreign or French), whereas the total figure for the world-wide affiliates to which French firms can be linked (either as headquarters or as domestic affiliates of French multinational groups) is about 690,500.

Thanks to the information provided by the Ownership Database, we are able to track the complete control chains of these groups, from the bottom of the network up to the final ultimate owner, considering also cross-participations and taking the majority of 50.01 percent as the threshold to identify corporate control. This last threshold is already adopted as an international standard to define MNEs' activities (OECD 2011), and by international accounting standards when attributing control on profits and hence tax liabilities across national borders.[1]

We then define a "trading firm" as a firm that exports and/or imports at least one product in a month in the period of analysis, with two thresholds provided by French Customs, according to which it is mandatory to report trading activity only when exports to a non-EU country exceed 1,000 euro for each transaction and when exports to all EU-countries exceed 150,000 euro on a yearly basis. On the other hand, the only limitation of firm level sources is the selectivity of the mandatory presentation of a yearly balance sheet, which leaves out some 2,000 firms registered as trading from the French Customs. These firms, however, account for only 1.20 percent of the total number of trading firms and 0.55 percent of trade volumes.[2]

To better exploit the information at the product level, we have employed the correspondence tables provided by the United Nations (UN) Statistics Division and EUROSTAT, to convert the transactions of HS six-digit products into Classification of Products by Activity (CPA) categories. These are easily grouped in four-digit European Classification of Economic Activities (NACE) revision 2, which is the industrial classification we employ for firm-level analysis, and in Broad Economic Categories (BEC) reclassified according to System of National Accounts (SNA), which distinguishes between capital, consumption, and intermediate goods, according to the main end use of traded products. A further classification capturing the distinction between durable and nondurable goods has also been adopted: the Main Industrial Grouping (MIG) by EUROSTAT has allowed us to reclassify trade flows in order to account for the different demand shocks that those two categories of goods have suffered during the crisis.[3]

The sample covers all industries in manufacturing, services and primary sectors, as shown in table 9.1, where a matching of ownership and firm-level trade data provides a picture of the sectoral degree of internationalization. Firms pertaining to multinational groups, whether French or foreign, have the lion's share of trade: 65 percent of export and 62 percent of import flows (figure 9.1). In the sample, there is a prevalence of service firms, among which those involved in distribution activities (whether wholesale or retail) account for about 56 percent of the total service industry (43 percent of the whole sample).[4] Firms involved in the distribution industry are recognized to have an important role as intermediaries in trade (see, e.g., Bernard, Grazzi, and Tomasi 2010, Ahn, Khandelwal, and Wei 2011), establishing so-called indirect modes of exporting and importing. In our sample, wholesalers are prevalently both importers and exporters and retailers are prevalently importers. Whereas the vast majority (89 percent) of firms in the sample do not belong to any group, group affiliation (whether French or foreign) increases with firm size (figure 9.2).

Table 9.1
Sample coverage by macro sectors and ownership status, number of firms

	Ownership status (no. firms)				Trading status (no. firms)			
	Affiliates to French groups	Affiliates to foreign groups	Independent firms	Total	Exporters and importers	Only exporters	Only importers	Total
Primary sectors	185	51	2,454	2,690	437	1,693	560	2,690
	6.88%	1.90%	91.23%	100.00%	16.25%	62.94%	20.82%	100.00%
Manufacturing	2.869	2.065	31.847	36.781	18.113	10.997	7.671	36.781
%	7.80%	5,61%	86.59%	100.00%	49.25%	29.90%	20.86%	100.00%
Services	6.426	4.639	117.242	128,307	35.046	42.429	50.832	128.307
%	5.01%	3.62%	91.38%	100.00	27.31%	33.07%	39.62%	100.00%
of which Wholesale trade	1.948	2.310	45.412	49,670	20.164	12.618	16.888	49,670
%	3.92%	4.65%	91.43%	100.00%	40.60%	25.40%	34.00%	100.00%
Retail trade	547	224	21.579	22,350	4.191	6.185	11.974	22,350
%	2.45%	1.00%	96.55%	100.00%	18.75%	27.67%	53.57%	100.00%

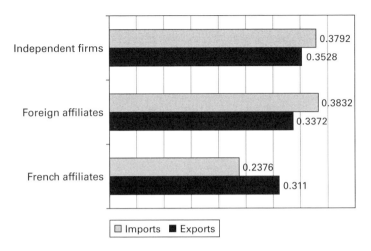

Figure 9.1
Trade volumes by ownership status.
Source: Author's elaboration from Bureau van Djik and French customs data.

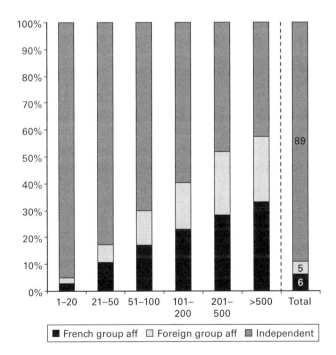

Figure 9.2
Ownership status by firm size (employment).
Source: Authors' elaboration on Bureau van Djik data.

In figure 9.3, we group affiliates by headquarters and plot their distribution in terms of size, where size is measured by number of affiliates. In this case, thanks to the coverage of our dataset, we are able to consider all foreign affiliates worldwide of foreign groups operating in France, as well as the total number of affiliates of French groups, thus drawing a more complete picture of the network of firms developed within multinational business groups. Recalling the definition provided earlier, a French group is included in our dataset if it has at least one affiliate abroad and its headquarters in France, whereas a foreign group (with foreign headquarters) owns at least one affiliate in France. In the graph and the table provided in figure 9.3, we report some descriptive statistics of the group size distribution by affiliates and locations of headquarters.

Group size is heterogeneous in terms of number of affiliates, resembling a Pareto distribution with a shape parameter of 6.61 for all groups and even higher for French groups. As illustrated in graph (a) in figure 9.3, multinational business groups operating in France are very dispersed, with a long right tail where a top 1 percent of headquarters control more than 1,000 affiliates and a median size of 10, while almost 40 percent of these groups are very simple organizations with one headquarter and only one affiliate. Groups with a French headquarters and a trading activity in France are on average smaller than foreign-owned trading groups, with a median size of four affiliates. In table (b) of figure 9.3, providing a geographical coverage of home economies, we observe that 4,637 headquarters are actually located in European Union (EU) members (2,964 in France), with a significant share in the United States and the rest in Europe and Japan. Considering the whole network to which affiliates in France can be connected through proprietary linkages, we have a total of 690,501 coaffiliates worldwide. In the fourth column of table (b) in figure 9.3, we collect them by home economy of the headquarters and calculate average and median size for some countries/regions. Here we note how, on average, groups originated in the rest of Asia (mainly Japan, Korea, and Taiwan) are usually very much concentrated in affiliates, followed at a distance by few African groups involved in extractive activities and U.S. groups. Brazil, Russia, India, and China (BRIC) altogether report only thirty-one multinational business groups with trading activity in France, and almost two-thirds of them (nineteen) are based in India.

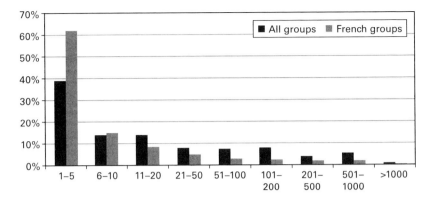

(a) Group size distribution by no. affiliates (worldwide)

Home economy	No. headquarters	(%) on total headquarters	No. affiliates	Avg. affiliates per headquarters	Median no. affiliates
EU-27	4,637	80.59%	429,760	93	2
Of which France	*(2,964)*	*(51.51%)*	*(144,050)*	*(49)*	*(4)*
Rest of Europe	350	6.08%	46.239	132	13
NAFTA	638	11.09%	140,521	220	14
Of which United States	*(599)*	*(10.41%)*	*(135,881)*	*226*	*(15)*
BRIC	31	0.54%	5,880	190	10
ASEAN	9	0.16%	5,122	569	39
Rest of Asia	154	2.68%	49,244	319	13
Of which Japan	*(138)*	*(2.40%)*	*(40,690)*	*(295)*	*(13)*
Africa	10	0.17%	2,446	245	19
Middle East	44	0.76%	7,149	162	9
South America	8	0.14%	1,305	163	8
Oceania	23	0.40%	4,611	200	16
Total	5,754		690,501	120	10
Pareto k-parameter	6.61				
For French groups	*(9.36)*				

(b) Group home economies, average size and dispersion.

Figure 9.3
Group affiliation and worldwide networks, all groups vs. French groups.

9.3   Global Value Chains, Organizational Modes, and Trade Collapse

9.3.1   The Great Trade Collapse in France

By now it has been acknowledged that the origin of the great trade collapse mostly lies in a huge demand shock (Baldwin and Taglioni 2009). Commodity prices tumbled when the price bubble burst in mid 2008 and continued to follow world demand in its downward spiral. The price movements and diminished demand sent the value and volume of commodities trade diving. The production and exports of manufacturing collapsed as the Lehman Brothers–induced shock-and-awe caused consumers and firms to wait and see. Private demand for all sorts of "postponeables" crashed. The large observed drop in trade-to-GDP ratio can be ascribed to the ensuing compositional effect as postponeable products represent a larger share in trade than in GDP and global supply chains may have played a role in synchronizing the demand shock to GDP and the demand shock to trade.

According to the finding by Alessandria, Kaboski, and Midrigan (2011), supply chains shaped the response to demand shock through an adjustment in inventories by single firms involved in complex buyer-supplier relationships. The shape would show a "bullwhip effect" (a V-shape, first dropping and then rebounding after a negative shock), explained by the reduction of stocks in times of crisis in order to adjust for new expectations about future demand. Forward and backward linkages within a supply chain and uncertainty about the real dimension of the demand shock would allow for its amplified transmission up the chain because each participant firm has a greater observed variation in demand for its production of (intermediate) goods. The bullwhip effect after a negative demand shock is depicted in figure 9.4, in which a simple value chain, composed of one retailer and two manufacturers, adjusts its orders exploiting previously stocked inventories as a buffer.

In our transaction-level data, we have a first confirmation of the postponement story (figures 9.5 and 9.6), as we plot growth rates calculated on a year-on-year basis from January 2007 to December 2009, with trends reported as moving averages of two lagged periods. A generalized drop of total trade flows is observed from September 2008, and an overall reversal begins from June 2009.

In an effort to capture compositional effects, we first show in figure 9.5 an aggregation by three broad categories of products (consumption

Orders (flows)

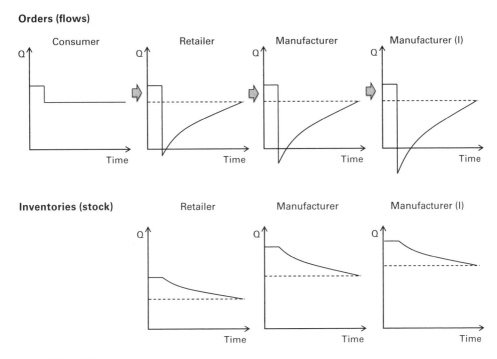

Figure 9.4
A bullwhip effect after a negative demand shock.

goods, intermediates, and capital goods) and then, in figure 9.6, we decompose consumption goods in durable and nondurable components, always for exports and imports in the bottom and top panels respectively.[5]

Assuming that trade in intermediate goods and capital goods is entirely driven by firm-to-firm relationships, whereas consumption goods are directed to final consumers (possibly through the mediation of firms involved in distribution activities), we observe that the first two categories react much more than the latter both along the export and the import dimensions. Indeed, although export and import growth rates of consumption register respectively an average of –6 percent and –4 percent in the middle of the crisis, the same averages for intermediates are –30 percent and –32 percent. On the other hand, capital goods show a different dynamics, sinking later and having yet to invert the ensuing downward trend in December 2009, while on the consumption side, the durable component hit exports harder, with negative rates reaching a peak of –23 percent in July 2009, when total export volumes were already recovering.

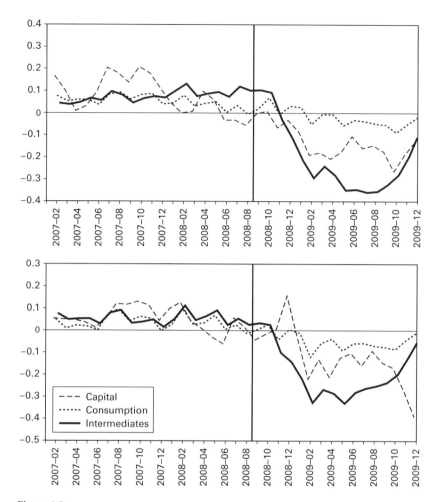

Figure 9.5
French trade in 2007–2009 by end-user (BEC-SNA) categories, year-on-year monthly flows. Imports in top panel. Exports in bottom panel.

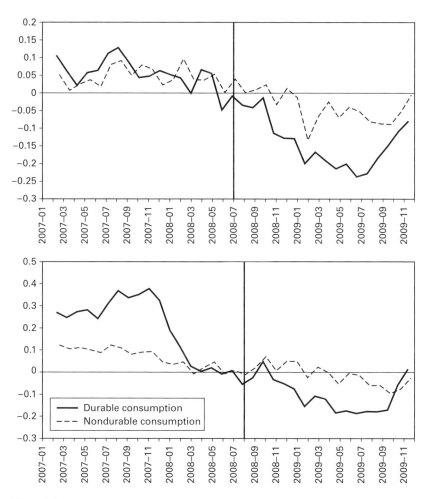

Figure 9.6
French trade in 2007–2009, durable vs. nondurable consumption, year-on-year monthly
flows. Imports in top panel. Exports in bottom panel.

The final outcome on the overall change in total trade volumes is then the result of a compositional effect, with trade in intermediates being more important (about 58 percent of both import and export volumes) than trade in consumption goods (nowadays only 25 percent of total French trade). Hence the magnitude of the drop is clearly due to the exceptionally negative growth rates of both intermediates and capital goods, which are originated by the emergence of global value chains and have a higher weight on the overall export and import performance. Firms facing declining profits and uncertain demand have reduced their investment in capital goods and their acquisition of inputs; that is, they have reduced production capacity, waiting for better future prospects. Indeed, at this stage of the analysis we could already dismiss the hypothesis of a multiple accounting effect as proposed by Yi (2009), because if the magnitude of the drop would be due to the same intermediate component crossing national borders several times, also growth rates of all final goods should reflect this effect, without regard to the durability of consumption, once the intermediate component is transferred to their gross value.

In the following analysis, we assess the role of the different organizational modes of a value chain during the crisis.

9.3.2 The Role of Global Value Chains

The emerging importance of global value chains is recognized by the increasing trade in intermediate inputs that nowadays represents a share between 56 percent and 73 percent of overall trade flows in goods and services for developed economies (Miroudot, Lanz, and Ragoussis 2009). Indeed, trade in intermediate inputs is itself an indication that firms across national borders are engaged in backward and forward linkages, hence establishing global value chains where final goods or services undergo separate processing processes across different national borders before reaching the final consumer. From the point of view of a single firm, the decision is to relocate part of the production abroad with the establishment of affiliates or to license an unaffiliated supplier outside its own boundary of economic activity. Several theoretical models explain the choice between these two organizational modes (see, e.g., Antràs 2005; Grossman and Helpman 2005; Feenstra and Spencer 2005; Helpman 2006) that originate intrafirm (better, intragroup) trade in the first case and arm's-length trade in the second case.

In the end, the internalization of production processes leads to the emergence of multinational business groups that collect affiliates under the coordinated direction of headquarters, that is, hierarchies of firms linked by complex control chains that organize their activities under a unique control rather than through market relationships. Although the analysis of the determinants of the internalization of production processes is beyond the scope of this chapter, the interested reader can refer to chapters 7 and 8. Moreover, chapter 1 provides a comparison of the economics and business literatures on the topic, highlighting that scholars in both fields can find a common ground derived from the seminal works by Coase (1937) on the one side and Penrose (1959) on the other.

As we have seen in the data presented in the previous section, in the case of France for the period 2006–2009, affiliates operating in France that are part of a multinational business group account for the majority of trade volumes, as they are responsible for about 65 percent of exports and 62 percent of imports even if they represent only 7 percent of the total number of firms. As we have seen, this concentration of trading activity among multinational business groups is paired with a relevant degree of heterogeneity in terms of size. Unfortunately, from our data we are still not able to directly measure intragroup trade via related parties, because exports and imports by affiliates located in France can include both a component of trade with related parties abroad (intragroup trade) and a complementary component of trade with nonrelated parties (arm's-length trade). On the contrary, in the case of trading activity by French nonaffiliates, we can be sure that international trade is exclusively at arm's length.

To solve this problem, we are able to proxy intragroup trade by building on the findings of Bas and Carluccio (2011), showing that 88 percent of trade by affiliates in France in a certain destination/origin is made either following a "pure outsourcing" (arm's-length, in our words) strategy or a "pure offshoring" (intragroup) strategy, with a mere 12 percent of cases following a mixed (outsourcing and offshoring) strategy.[6]

Henceforth, we assume that trade occurs within the boundary of the business group when transactions undertaken by French affiliates in a given partner country find in the same country a corresponding subsidiary that belongs to the same multinational business group. Although it allows us to bypass the lack of related-party data, such a proxying assumption could still bias our measure of intragroup trade because it might include a nonobserved share of arm's-length trade due to the mixed strategy of outsourcing and offshoring. This issue can be considered an acceptable bias if one is willing to believe, as we do, that the latter is not correlated with any specific characteristic of the sample firms. On the other hand, we have no doubt that if transactions are undertaken by independent firms, or if they are not directed toward a country in which there are coaffiliates, those transactions are exclusively at arm's length because by construction they fall outside the boundaries of the multinational business group. Following our approximation, we can then estimate a total of 48 percent of exports and 46 percent of imports in 2007 being undertaken as intragroup trade.

To validate our measure, we can rely on a number of references against which to compare our proxy of French trade among related parties. In 1999, the "Enquête sur les échanges intra-groupe," a survey on firms representing 55 percent of French imports and 61 percent of French exports, estimated that 32 percent of transactions (not trade volumes) were among related parties. Among these 93 percent were transactions by firms located in developed countries (mainly the European Union and the United States). Given the spectacular increase of outsourcing/offshoring decisions over the last decade, our estimate of 48 percent does not seem inconsistent with these numbers. More interestingly, a partial direct validation is possible considering bilateral trade between France and the United States. Indeed, according to the Related Party Database by the U.S. Census Bureau (as reported by Lanz and Miroudot 2011), 55.9 percent of imports from France in 2009 are originated by intragroup trade, a figure not very distant from the 61.9 percent we find in our dataset in the same year (exports from France to the United States); in this case, the overestimation would be 10.7 percent, slightly less than what reported by Bas and Carluccio (2011) as a mixed strategy. Furthermore, using Census Bureau data as a cross-country reference, the amount of intragroup trade in the United States (46.8 percent of exports) is very similar to our estimation for France (48 percent).

In figure 9.7, we therefore report monthly growth rates of trade volumes distinguishing between end user categories (consumption goods, capital goods, and intermediates) as in figure 9.5, but now taking into account whether transactions are intragroup or arm's length, as proxied by our methodology. Consistent with our prior work, in both graphs of figure 9.7, trade originated by vertical integration—that is, intragroup, graph (a) in the case of intermediates and graph (d) in the case of total trade—drops faster at the outburst of the crisis but rebounds also faster once the recovery begins, when rates have become

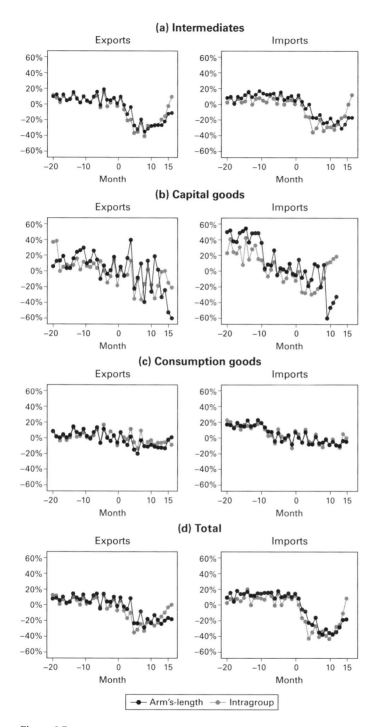

Figure 9.7
Organizational modes and trade collapse in 2007–2009, monthly growth rates, year-on-year basis.

positive again at the end of 2009, with values well above 10 percent; on the contrary, in the same period, arm's-length growth rates show still a consistent decline: 11 percent for export of intermediates and –17 percent for import of intermediates. The organizational modes of global value chains thus seem to show a different dynamic that was concealed when looking at more aggregate data. Total trade flows for both imports and exports are clearly driven by the trend in intermediates, as in graph (a) of figure 9.7, thus confirming the compositional effect of the trade collapse induced by the creation of complex supply chains and the fact that intermediates account for about 60 percent of total volumes. Also, the faster drop and faster rebound of intragroup trade is determined by the sole trade in intermediates, because in the case of consumption and capital goods such a different trend is not observed.

In the econometric analysis of section 9.4, we test whether the different behavior of multinational groups is confirmed by looking at disaggregated data and controlling for several compositional effects.

9.3.3   The Geography of the Trade Collapse

In the remainder of this section, we verify whether geography matters for the dynamics of trade flows during the crisis. In table 9.2, we provide a geographical dimension of the organizational modes before and after September 2008, showing the heterogeneity of intragroup and arm's-length growth by key partner countries/areas. In figures 9.8 and 9.9, we draw two maps, identifying only the performance after the beginning of the drop. The indicator we adopt here is an integration index that considers both imports and exports originated by, respectively, arm's-length and intrafirm trade averaging them from 2007M9 to 2009M12.[7]

In contrast with the finding of other authors (Kaplinsky and Farooki 2010; Cattaneo, Gereffi and Staritz 2010), we do not observe in our case that trade originated by value chains shifted substantially after the crisis toward emerging economies. Rather, quite the opposite, the integration of the BRIC nations seems to take place well before the crisis and to stop afterward, with negative growth rates. A notable exception is China, where we observe that even during the crisis, arm's-length trade was not disrupted (+0.1 percent) and intragroup trade fell considerably less than in the case of other French emerging partners (with the exception of some African countries that instead have registered positive growth rates for the whole period).

Table 9.2
Organizational modes and trade collapse, monthly growth rates, year-on-year basis, 2007–2009

	Arm's length		Intrafirm	
	Pre-crisis	Post-crisis	Pre-crisis	Post-crisis
OECD	4.08	−16.54	5.73	−16.16
Emerging economies	7.78	−11.77	9.57	−13.34
EU-27	6.05	−18.29	7.25	−15.15
EU-15	6.19	−16.61	2.68	−16.99
New EU members	5.9	−20.25	12.98	−12.83
NAFTA	2.8	−13.17	5.46	−13.20
United States	0.12	−7.00	−1.37	−11.98
Canada	6.53	−20.06	6.78	−0.83
BRIC	15.11	−12.20	17.4	−24.65
China	13.34	0.09	11.31	−5.67
Brazil	16.23	−17.94	14.53	−25.25
India	14.49	−13.58	23.5	−26.50
Russia	16.35	−17.38	20.26	−41.17
ASEAN	0.33	−11.34	27.9	−8.70
Africa	8.81	−2.83	10.85	−6.64
Middle East	9.53	−6.58	2.03	−3.41
South America	2.88	−4.07	3.89	−15.21

Vertical integration (intragroup) has on average fallen from September 2008 to December 2009 for both OECD High Income Countries and Emerging Economies, with a slightly different dynamic at the beginning of 2009, when recovery begun a quarter earlier for intermediates exported in emerging economies, until the end of the same year, when growth rates became positive again. In absolute terms, trade is more substantial in OECD countries (74.8% of export values and 74.6% of import values in 2007).[8] Among developed partners, French-based value chains with the European Union were severely hit, both in the case of historical EU-15 and in the case of new EU members, whereas intragroup trade with Canada was more resilient. With the United States, the negative trend began well before the crisis.

Summing up, in line with the worldwide synchronized nature of the demand shock, it seems that we can rule out a specific role of geography in affecting the dynamics of the trade flows differently across organizational modes. In any case, we also control for the latter possible compositional effect in our econometric specification, to which we now turn.

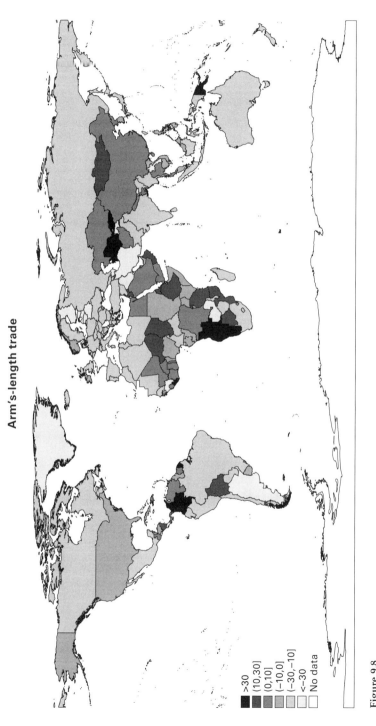

Figure 9.8
Arm's-length trade and trade collapse, average growth rates, year-on-year basis.

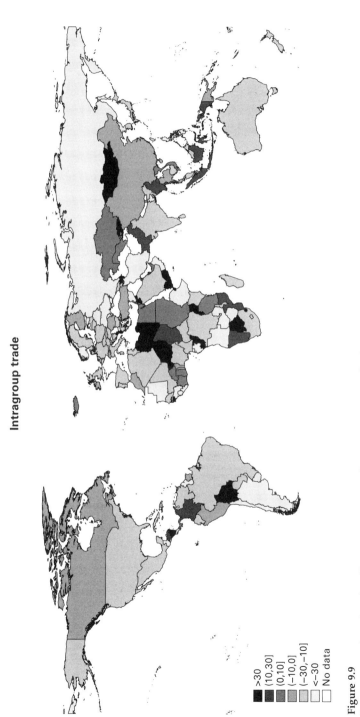

Intragroup trade

>30
(10,30]
(0,10]
(−10,0]
(−30,−10]
<−30
No data

Figure 9.9
Intragroup trade and trade collapse, average growth rates, year-on-year basis.

9.4 Empirical Strategy and Results

In this section, we test whether trade performance due to participation to value chains has been responsible for the magnitude of the drop, and whether the two alternative modes of organization of interfirm linkages have shown a different resilience during the crisis for both imports and exports.

Our estimation strategy takes as dependent variable (g_{isct}), the midpoint growth rate of trade flows, specific for product s traded by firm i in country c of origin/destination and month t. The midpoint growth rate, already employed by Bricongne et al. (2012) for the French case during the crisis, correctly approximates the observed aggregate growth rates of exports but, unlike other methods, it controls for composition effects avoiding an attrition bias caused by the entry and exit of sample observations and for monthly seasonality.[9]

The latter is regressed against a number of relevant controls via the following specification:

$$g_{isct} = \beta_0 + \beta_1\Lambda + \beta_2\Lambda * recovery + \gamma_j + \varepsilon_{isct}$$

where

$$\Lambda = \alpha_1 interm_{isct} + \alpha_2 intragroup_{isct} + \alpha_3(interm * intragroup)_{isct} + OECD_{isct}$$

Among the set of regressors in Λ, the term $interm_{isct}$ stands for a binary variable that equals 1 if the traded product is an intermediate good and 0 otherwise, and $intragroup_{isct}$ is another binary variable that equals 1 if the flow is traded intragroup and 0 otherwise, following our approximation of intragroup versus arm's-length trade introduced in the previous section. The interaction between the intermediate and the intragroup dummies $(interm * intragroup)_{isct}$ is to be interpreted as the subset of trade flows that involve the exchange of intermediate goods between affiliates belonging to the same headquarter, that is, a global value chain represented by a verticalized multinational group with backward and/or forward linkages. The binary variable $OECD_{isct}$ allows us to control for a geographic compositional effect induced by possibly different demand shocks registered in OECD countries after the financial crisis.

Taking into account the period from 2008M09 to 2009M12—that is, from the beginning of the trade collapse until the last available month of our data—we differentiate the impact of our set of regressors Λ in two subperiods through the dummy *recovery*, that is, before and after

2009M06. This is the month when overall trade flows began their recovery in France after a negative peak. Moreover, this is the month in which conventionally the world economy starts to experience a generalized resumption of world trade. Finally, compositional effects potentially induced by a change in the sectoral pattern of trade flows are captured by a set of NACE four-digit industry fixed effects (γ_j).

In tables 9.3 and 9.4, we report the results for French exports and imports growth rates, respectively. In the first column of both tables 9.3 and 9.4, we confirm that once considering only the end use of products and controlling for sector compositional effects, the magnitude of the drop is due to trade in intermediates (inputs)—namely, to products that are exchanged by firms that establish backward and forward linkages either by proprietary or by buyer/supplier relationships, as observed in figure 9.5. In particular, although we have an average negative growth rate for the whole period of, respectively, –8.8 percent and –6.1 percent for exports and imports (the coefficient of the constant term), a further negative and significant effect is to be added for trade in intermediates. A bullwhip shape due to trade in intermediates is however detected from the estimation in the second column: at a negative premium for intermediates at the outburst of the crisis corresponds a positive premium once the recovery begins. Both the magnitude of the drop and the pattern of recovery are to be attributed to trade in intermediate goods that constitute already almost 60 percent of flows as we already know from aggregated data.

In the third column, we begin to control for the organizational mode of the value chain, that is, if products are exchanged by firms on the basis of proprietary or buyer/supplier relationships, regardless of their end use. In this case, on average over the entire period, intragroup trade shows no significant difference with respect to arm's-length trade in the case of exports, and a better performance in the case of imports. This finding shows that at least on the import side, trade flows within multinational groups (regardless of their end use) during the considered period have in general been more resilient than those undertaken by independent firms.

In the fourth column, we start controlling for the interaction between the organizational mode of the value chain and the end use of traded products. For exports flows, the positive and significant coefficient on the interaction implies that intragroup trade on the average of the entire period has grown more in intermediates than in other end use

Table 9.3
Exports and global value chains

Dependent variable: Midpoint growth rates	OLS (i)	OLS (ii)	OLS (iii)	OLS (iv)	OLS (v)	CLS (vi)
Intermediates	-0.009***	-0.013***	-0.009***	-0.012***	-0.012***	-0.012***
	(0.001)	(0.002)	(0.001)	(0.001)	(0.002)	(0.002)
Intragroup			-0.001	-0.007***	0.010***	0.012***
			(0.001)	(0.001)	(0.002)	(0.002)
Intermediates × intragroup				0.013***	-0.008**	-0.008**
				(0.002)	(0.003)	(0.003)
OECD						-0.022***
						(0.002)
Recovery		-0.002			0.006***	0.008***
		(0.001)			(0.002)	(0.002)
Intermediates × recovery		0.010***			-0.000	-0.000
		(0.002)			(0.002)	(0.002)
Intragroup × recovery					-0.038***	-0.038***
					(0.003)	(0.003)
Intermediates × intragroup * recovery					0.048***	0.049***
					(0.005)	(0.005)
OECD × recovery						-0.003
						(0.002)
Constant	-0.088***	-0.088***	-0.088***	-0.087***	-0.089***	-0.073***
	(0.001)	(0.001)	(0.001)	(0.001)	(0.001)	(0.002)
Industry fixed effects	Yes	Yes	Yes	Yes	Yes	Yes
Observations	11,985,900	11,985,900	11,985,900	11,985,900	11,985,900	11,985,900
Adjusted R²	0.0010	0.0010	0.0010	0.0010	0.0010	0.0010

Note: *, **, *** stand respectively for significance at 90%, 95%, and 99%. Robust standard errors in parentheses.

Table 9.4
Imports and global value chains

Dependent variable: Midpoint growth rates	OLS (i)	OLS (ii)	OLS (iii)	OLS (iv)	OLS (v)	OLS (vi)
Intermediates	-0.006***	-0.013***	-0.008***	-0.001	-0.006***	0.004**
	(0.001)	(0.001)	(0.001)	(0.001)	(0.002)	(0.001)
Intragroup			0.026***	0.046***	0.064***	0.074***
			(0.001)	(0.002)	(0.002)	(0.002)
Intermediates * intragroup				-0.032***	-0.045**	-0.051**
				(0.002)	(0.003)	(0.003)
OECD						-0.083***
						(0.002)
Recovery		-0.007***			-0.001	-0.023***
		(0.003)			(0.001)	(0.002)
Intermediates × recovery		0.015***			0.012***	0.007***
		(0.002)			(0.002)	(0.002)
Intragroup × recovery					-0.043***	-0.047***
					(0.004)	(0.003)
Intermediates × intragroup × recovery					0.029***	0.032***
					(0.005)	(0.005)
OECD × recovery						0.031***
						(0.002)
Constant	-0.061***	-0.058***	-0.066***	-0.069***	-0.069***	-0.010***
	(0.001)	(0.001)	(0.001)	(0.001)	(0.001)	(0.001)
Industry fixed effects	Yes	Yes	Yes	Yes	Yes	Yes
Observations	15,432,528	15,432,528	15,432,528	15,432,528	15,432,528	15,432,528
Adjusted R^2	0.0009	0.0009	0.0009	0.0009	0.0010	0.0012

Note: *, **, *** stand respectively for significance at 90%, 95%, and 99%. Robust standard errors in parentheses.

categories. In the case of imports, the opposite effect holds. However, as observed in figure 9.7, these effects are the outcome of two very different dynamics over time, with trade in intermediates first dropping and then recovering. Hence it could well be the case that in the case of exports, intragroup trade in intermediates has recovered more than it originally dropped during the crisis, while such a recovery has not yet fully occurred in the case of imports. Our prior is instead more general, as it postulates only that intragroup trade in intermediates recovered more quickly (or fell faster) than all the other forms of trade (by end use or organizational form).

To test for the latter hypothesis, in the fifth column of both tables 9.3 and 9.4 we then split the effect between the crisis and the recovery period to test whether there is such a difference in dynamics. The sign of the dummy identifying the recovery period shows that exports indeed performed better after the through of the crisis, independently on end uses or organizational modes. Moreover, the positive and significant coefficient on the triple interaction term implies that during the recovery, exports of intermediates have performed better when taking place within multinational groups than at arm's length, thus confirming our hypothesis. Along the same lines, on average imports do not show any differential performance during the recovery across end uses or organizational modes, again consistent with the idea that the *overall* growth of intragroup trade in intermediates has been insufficient to absorb the effect of the collapse. However, once again, the positive and significant coefficient on the triple interaction term implies that during the recovery imports of intermediates have in any case performed *relatively* better when taking place within multinational groups than at arm's length, in line with our assumption.

In the sixth column, we finally check whether results are robust to a geographic compositional effect induced by the different (stronger) demand shocks coming from OECD countries. In general, we observe a negative premium for transactions that involve a developed partner at the beginning of the crisis. However, in the second period of our analysis there seems to be no difference in trends of exports between developed and developing partners, while imports from OECD countries recovered strongly. This result is in contrast with what suggested by Kaplinsky and Farooki (2010) and Cattaneo, Gereffi, and Staritz (2010), according to whom the trade drop entailed also a substantial shift of value chains toward emerging economies. More important for our goals, our previous results on the triple interaction term are confirmed.

To sum up, for both exports and imports of intermediates, we find that trade flows have grown more when undertaken intragroup versus at arm's length, as soon as total trade begun its recovery. This result is consistent with the findings by Alessandria, Kaboski, and Midrigan (2011) for the United States, attributing in general the faster drop and rebound of intermediates to adjustment in inventories. More specifically, we show that the overreaction at the beginning of the period, then compensated by a faster recovery in the aftermath, is particularly pronounced for verticalized multinational groups versus arm's-length trade. This finding shows a different and faster response of value chains organized by multinational groups. Our explanatory hypothesis is that the internalization of activities within the boundary of a group allows for a better management of information flows coming from the bottom of the value chain so that production and inventories can be more swiftly adjusted to demand shocks.

9.5 Conclusions

In this chapter, we analyzed the trade performance of global value chains during the Great Trade Collapse. Exploiting a unique transaction-level dataset matching French monthly trade data with ownership information for the period 2007–2009, we have been able to distinguish the trade performance of two alternative organizational modes of the value chain: internalization of activities by multinational business groups, entailing trade among related parties, and the establishment of buyer/supplier contracts, entailing arm's-length trade.

We first provided some stylized facts on multinational business groups: affiliation to a headquarters is a concentrated phenomenon because affiliates in France account for about 65 percent of exports and 62 percent of imports even if they represent less than 10 percent of the total number of trading firms. Moreover, the distribution of multinational business groups by size, measured by number of affiliates worldwide, is very dispersed, resembling a Pareto distribution.

Second, in order to assess the role of global value chains at the outburst of the crisis, we have econometrically tested the differential performance of trade in intermediates. This factor has been shown to be the main determinant of the magnitude of the collapse. We have also found that intragroup trade in intermediates exhibited specific dynamics, with a faster drop followed by a faster rebound than trade in other end categories. In other words, trade that originated within hierarchies of firms reacted faster to the negative demand shock but also recovered faster in the following months than did arm's-length trade. Among the alternative channels of transmission of the demand shock to trade performance proposed in previous studies, the adjustment in inventories seems the most consistent with these findings. As in the case of the United States, studied by Alessandria, Kaboski, and Midrigan (2011) for the general case of intermediates, amplified fluctuations of trade with respect to GDP could be associated to the so-called bullwhip effect (Forrester 1961; Stadtler 2008), that is, a magnification of the initial demand shock along the supply chain due to an adjustment of production and stocks to new expectations. In this case, the finding of a better performance of intragroup trade could also be explained by better handling of inventories, thanks to the ability to react faster and optimize management of stocks within the boundaries of the group.

At this stage of the analysis, we cannot exclude a role for trade credit constraints, as hierarchies of firms may have relied on an internal capital market that softened the crunch of external sources of financing. This result would, however, explain a faster recovery but not a faster drop. Hence although an interaction of both determinants (optimization of inventories management and softer financial constraints) may have been relevant as suggested by Escaith, Lindenberg, and Miroudot (2010), among others, softer financial constraints alone would not be able to account for the observed patterns of the data.

Appendix: End-User Categories of Trade Flows

BEC is a reclassification of traded goods according to their main end use. It was developed by the UN Statistics Division to be matched with the System of National Accounts. Our data, originally registered as HS six-digit flows, were converted first by BEC categories and then grouped by basic classes of the SNA following table 9A.1.

An alternative classification by end-use is MIG, proposed by Eurostat, which is based primarily on NACE rev. 2 industrial sectors and allows us to distinguish between durables and nondurables. Starting with HS product flows, we first converted them in NACE economic activities and then reclassified following table 9A.2.

Table 9A.1
Correspondence table, from BEC to the SNA

Basic classes SNA	Broad economic categories (BEC)
Capital goods	41. Capital goods (exc. transport)
	521. Transport equipment, other, industrial
Consumption goods	112. Food and beverages, primary, mainly for household consumption
	122. Food and beverages, processed, mainly for household consumption
	51. Transport equipment, passenger motor cars
	522. Transport equipment, other, nonindustrial
	61. Consumer goods, durable
	62. Consumer goods, semi-durable
	63. Consumer goods, nondurable
Primary (intermediates)	111. Food and beverages, primary, mainly for industry
	21. Industrial supplies, primary
	31. Fuels and lubricants, primary
Parts and components (intermediates)	42. Capital goods, parts and accessories
	53. Transport equipment, parts and accessories
Semifinished goods (intermediates)	121. Food and beverages, processed, mainly for industry
	22. Industrial supplies, processed
	322. Fuels and lubricants, processed, other

Source: United Nations

Table 9A.2
Correspondence table, from NACE rev. 2 to MIG

Main industrial groupings (MIG)	Nomenclature statistique des activités économiques dans la Communauté européenne (NACE), revision 2
Capital goods	251. – 252. – 253. – 254. – 262. – 263. – 265. – 266. – 28. – 29. – 301. – 302. – 303. – 304. – 325. – 33.
Consumer durable goods	264. – 267. – 275. – 309. – 31. – 321. – 322.
Consumer nondurable goods	101. – 102. – 103. – 104. – 105. – 107. – 108. – 11. – 12. – 139. – 14. – 15. – 18. – 204. – 21. – 323. – 324. – 329.
Intermediate goods	07. – 08. – 09. – 106. – 109. – 131. – 132. – 133. –16. – 17. – 201. – 202. – 203. – 205. – 206. – 22. – 23. – 24. – 255. – 256. – 257. – 259. – 261. – 268. – 271. – 272. – 273. – 274. – 279.
Energy	05. – 06. – 19. – 35. – 36.

Source: Eurostat

Notes

1. An advantage of this criterion is also to partition affiliates among groups while avoiding double counting by different headquarters. For a more complete reference on methodologies to track group control chains from affiliates to ultimate headquarters, see Altomonte and Rungi 2012.

2. The original source of Bureau van Djik's database for French firms are the Tribunaux de Commerce, which are responsible for collecting balance sheet data according to national legislation, according to which some smaller "sociétés de personne" and "sociétés cooperatives" are exempted from the obligation of a complete balance sheet.

3. MIG end-use categories are based on the NACE rev. 2 classification and are defined by the European Commission regulation (EC) no. 656/2007 of June 14, 2007.

4. According to NACE rev. 2, two-digit industry codes, firms involved in wholesale trade are classified as NACE code 46 and firms involved in retail trade are classified as NACE code 47.

5. Capital goods, consumption goods, and intermediates are main end user categories from BEC classification of traded products reclassified according to the System of National Accounts; see table 9A.1 in the appendix to this chapter for details. MIG allows for a reclassification of consumption goods among durables and nondurables on the basis of the end use of final consumer. For details, see table 9A.2 in the appendix to this chapter.

6. In the international trade and business studies literatures, the term "offshoring" is sometimes used indifferently to define either a general relocation of activities abroad (including both intragroup and arm's-length trade) or, more specifically, activities that are internalized by the firm (only intragroup). Bas and Carluccio (2011) prefer to use the term "(pure) offshoring" for trade originated by vertical integration only, hence "intragroup trade."

7. Our vertical integration indices are given by ($exports_{ijkt}$ + $imports_{ijkt}$) / ($exports_{ijt}$ + $imports_{ijt}$), where i is the home country, j is the partner country, k is either arm's-length trade or intrafirm trade to/from the partner country, and t is time. As the denominator, we have the sum of total imports and exports between home i and partner j in the same period. This indicator measures the degree of participation to value chains and can virtually range from [0,1], from economies that are completely closed to offshoring/outsourcing activities to economies that rely exclusively on value chains.

8. According to an OECD definition, its members can be distinguished between High-Income countries and Middle-Income countries. This latter category includes only Turkey, Chile, and Mexico, and we exclude it from our variable. The definition of emerging economies is more controversial. Here we have adopted the one provided by Dow Jones that lists 35 countries.

9. Applying the mid-point growth rate to our specific case, we have: $g_{isct} = (X_{isct} - X_{isc(t-12)})$ / ($0.5 \times (X_{isct} + X_{isc(t-12)})$). The rate is bounded in the range [−2, +2] with the extremes of the interval indicating the emergence (+2) or the disappearance (−2) of flows in month t with respect of the same month of the previous year ($t - 12$). For other applications of this methodology, see also Davis and Haltiwanger 1992 and Buono, Fadinger, and Berger 2008.

References

Abiad, A., P. Mishra, and P. Topalova. 2011. How does trade evolve in the aftermath of financial crises? IMF Working Paper WP113.

Ahn, J., A. K. Khandelwal, and S.-J. Wei. 2011. The role of intermediaries in facilitating trade. *Journal of International Economics* 84 (1): 73–85.

Alessandria, G., J. P. Kaboski, and V. Midrigan. 2011. US trade and inventory dynamics. *American Economic Review* 101 (3): 303–307.

Altomonte, C., and A. Rungi. 2012. Business groups as hierarchies of firms: Determinants of vertical integrations and performance. European Central Bank Working Paper 1554.

Antràs, P. 2005. Property rights and the international organization of production. *American Economic Review* 95 (2): 25–32.

Baldwin, R. 2009. Introduction: The great trade collapse: what caused it and what does it mean? In *The Great Trade Collapse: Causes, Consequences and Prospects*, ed. R. Baldwin. VoxEU.org e-book. http://www.voxeu.org/article/great-trade-collapse-what-caused-it -and-what-does-it-mean.London: CEPR.

Baldwin, R., and S. Evenett, eds. 2009. Introduction and recommendations for the G20. In *The Collapse of Global Trade, Murky Protectionism, and the Crisis: Recommendations for the G20*. ed. Richard Baldwin and Simon Evenett, 1–12. London: CEPR.

Baldwin, R., and D. Taglioni. 2009. The great trade collapse and trade imbalances. In *The Great Trade Collapse: Causes, Consequences and Prospects*, ed. R. Baldwin. VoxEU.org e-book, http://www.voxeu.org/article/great-trade-collapse-and-trade-imbalances. London: CEPR.

Bas, M., and J. Carluccio. 2011. Wage bargaining and the boundaries of the multinational firm. CEPR DP 7867.

Bergoeing, R., T. J. Kehoe, V. Strauss-Kahn, and K. M. Yi. 2004. Why is manufacturing trade rising even as manufacturing output is falling? *American Economic Review* 94 (2): 134–138.

Bernard, B. A., M. Grazzi, and C. Tomasi. 2010. Intermediaries in international trade: direct versus indirect modes of export. Mimeo.

Bricongne, J. C., L. Fontagne, G. Gaulier, D. Taglioni, and V. Vicard. 2012. Firms and the global crisis: French exports in the turmoil. *Journal of International Economics*. 87 (1): 134–146.

Buono, I., H. Fadinger, and S. Berger. 2008. *The Micro Dynamics of Exporting: Evidence from French Firms, MPRA Paper 12940*. Munich: University Library of Munich.

Cattaneo, O., G. Gereffi, and C. Staritz. 2010. *Global Value Chains in a Postcrisis World*. Ed. IBRD. Washington, DC: World Bank: Washington.

Coase, R. H. 1937. The nature of the firm. *Economica* NS4:386–405.

Davis, S. J., and J. C. Haltiwanger. 1992. Gross job creation, gross job destruction, and employment reallocation. *Quarterly Journal of Economics* 107 (3): 819–863.

Escaith, H., N. Lindenberg, and S. Miroudot. 2010. International supply chains and trade elasticity in times of global crisis. World Trade Organization (Economic Research and Statistics Division) Staff. Working Paper ERSD-2010-08.

Feenstra, R. C., and B. Spencer. 2005. Contractual versus generic outsourcing: the role of proximity. NBER Working Paper no. 11885.

Forrester, J. 1961. *Industrial Dynamics*. Waltham, MA: Pegasus Communications.

Freund, C. 2009. The trade response to global downturns. historical evidence. World Bank Working Papers 5015.

Grossman, G. M., and E. Helpman. 2005. Outsourcing in a global economy. *Review of Economic Studies* 72 (1): 135–159.

Helpman, E. 2006. Trade, FDI, and the organization of firms. *Journal of Economic Literature* 44 (4): 580–630.

Kaplinsky, R., and M. Farooki. 2010. What are the implications for global value chains when the market shifts from the North to the South? Policy Research Working Paper 5205, World Bank.

Lanz, R., and S. Miroudot. (2011). Intra-firm trade: patterns, determinants and policy implications. OECD Trade Policy Working Papers No. 114.

Miroudot, S., R. Lanz, and A. Ragoussis. 2009. Trade in intermediate goods and services. OECD Trade Policy Working Paper 93, OECD Publishing.

OECD. 2011. *OECD guidelines for multinational enterprises*. Paris: OECD Publishing.

Penrose, E. 1959. *The theory of the growth of the firm*. New York: Wiley.

Stadtler, H. 2008. Supply chain management—An overview. In *Supply Chain Management and Advanced Planning*, 4th ed., ed. H. Stadtler and C. Kigler, 9–36. Berlin-Heidelberg: Springer-Verlag.

Yi, K. M. 2009. The collapse of global trade: the role of vertical specialization. In *The Collapse of Global Trade, Murky Protectionism, and the Crisis: Recommendations for the G20*. ed. R. Baldwin and S. Evenett, 45–48. London: CEPR.

IV Innovation and Technology Transfer

10 Multinationals' Technology Transfers and Firms' Performance

María García-Vega and Elena Huergo

10.1 Introduction

Foreign direct investment (FDI) has dramatically increased in the last few years all over the world. Many studies show that FDI can provide positive externalities to local economies (Markusen 1995; van Pottelsberghe and Lichtenberg 2001, among others). One possible reason is that multinational enterprises (MNEs) transfer technology to their foreign subsidiaries that can be partly appropriated by local firms.[1] Although the impact of FDI to local firms has been extensively analyzed (e.g., Findlay 1978; Fosfuri, Motta, and Rønde 2001; Girma and Wakelin 2001; Haskel, Pereira, and Slaughter 2007; Glass and Saggi 1999, 2002; Keller and Yeaple 2009), the transfer of knowledge from foreign MNEs to their subsidiaries has been difficult to study empirically.[2] In this chapter, we empirically analyze the impact of technology flows from foreign MNEs to their subsidiaries on innovation and labor productivity.

The empirical evidence is provided using data on approximately 8,800 innovative Spanish companies for the years 2004 to 2006. The dataset that we use comes from a survey of innovating Spanish firms conducted by the Spanish Statistical Office. This survey provides detailed information on acquisitions of research and development (R&D) services within the business group, which is our measure of technology transfers. We show that subsidiaries from foreign MNEs are both more likely to obtain technology transfers and are more labor-productive than local companies. This result is consistent with several studies that highlight the productivity advantage of MNEs (for a survey, see, e.g., Syverson 2011). Like Cassiman and Mendi (2008) and Stiebale and Reize (2011), we find that an average subsidiary of a foreign MNE is not more innovative than other companies. In contrast, we show that subsidiaries from foreign MNEs that obtain technology transfers within their business group are more innovative than the average firm and also than subsidiaries from national groups. Finally, we compare the impact of product, process, and organizational innovations on labor productivity for three types of companies: subsidiaries from foreign MNEs with technology transfers, subsidiaries from foreign MNEs without technology transfers, and the rest of the companies that belong to a business group. We find that the impact of product, process, and organizational innovations on labor productivity is much higher for subsidiaries from foreign MNEs than for other companies. Specifically, we show that the effect of organizational innovations on labor productivity, which is related to changes designed to enhance a firm's capacity to transfer knowledge and to integrate different teams and departments within the company, is the main advantage of subsidiaries from foreign MNEs. We also show that the impact of product, process, and organizational innovations is similar for subsidiaries of foreign MNEs with acquisitions of technological services from the group and for those subsidiaries without these purchases. Subsidiaries from foreign MNEs without R&D from the group seem to achieve the same productivity levels than subsidiaries with R&D from the group using other sources of external R&D. These results suggest that subsidiaries' productivity advantage is related not only to a direct transfer of technology, as accounted for by the acquisitions of technological services within the group, but also to other nonpecuniary technological flows such as organizational innovations. These findings suggest that multinationals transfer not only traditional R&D inputs but also a business strategy based on an efficient organization of work.

Our results are related to Sadowski and Sadowski-Rasters (2006), who find that Dutch foreign subsidiaries are more innovative than domestic firms mostly because they obtain external knowledge. Our findings are also consistent with Guadalupe, Kuzmina, and Thomas (2010), who show that organizational innovations are particularly important for Spanish firms acquired by foreign MNEs. Our main contribution is that we measure the extent to which technology transfers influence a subsidiary's innovation and labor productivity. Similar to Bloom, Sadun, and Van Reenen (2012), we find that the organizational form of foreign MNEs influences their productivity. In our case, we analyze the influence of organizational innovations on labor productivity.

A number of papers develop ideas that differ from but complement ours. García-Vega and Huergo (2011) show that technology transfers within MNEs depend on the level of trust between the country of origin of the MNE and the country where the subsidiary operates. One difference between this study and ours is that we focus on the consequences of technology transfers. Smeets and Abramovsky (chapter 11, this volume) show the importance of foreign subsidiaries to generate knowledge and to what extend foreign inventions can substitute innovations created in the headquarters. This chapter, however, does not address questions related to technology transfers and firms' performance. Finally, our chapter is also related to García-Vega, Hoffmann, and Kneller (2012), who examine how R&D structures are influenced by technology transfers from technological leading and nonleading countries to newly acquired affiliates operating in Spain. This work contrasts with our study, which analyzes the relationship between technology transfers and innovation.

The rest of the chapter is organized as follows. Section 10.2 describes the data and empirically motivates the article. Section 10.3 presents the empirical results, and section 10.4 concludes.

10.2   Empirical Motivation

10.2.1   The Data
The dataset we use comes from a survey of innovating Spanish firms (Panel de Innovación Tecnológica, PITEC). It is a panel database constructed from two ongoing statistics: the Technological Innovation survey and the statistics about R&D activities, carried out both of them by the Spanish National Institute of Statistics.[3] Although 2003 is the first year of the panel, in this chapter we use only the years 2004 to 2006 for reasons of comparability.[4] In order to avoid simultaneity problems, some variables specified in the following sections are included with a one-period lag. Given the short period of the panel and that many variables are simultaneously determined, our findings do not necessarily imply causal relationships but correlations. The empirical analysis is conducted for the years 2004 and 2006, for which we have information from 8,795 innovating firms (27,475 observations), that is, firms that perform R&D internally and/or buy R&D services from other companies or institutions.

10.2.2   The Main Variables
In the survey, the company reports whether it belongs to a private business group and also whether it is the headquarters, a subsidiary, a

joint venture, or an associated company.[5] If the firm has at least 50 percent of foreign capital participation, we consider the company to be a *foreign MNE*. If in addition, it is a subsidiary, we call this type of company a *subsidiary of a foreign MNE*.

Our measure of technology transfers is acquisitions of R&D services from the group. These purchases include: "contracts, informal agreements, etc. Funds to finance other companies, research associations, etc., that do not directly imply purchases of R&D services are excluded" (PITEC database, n.d.). Note that this variable also excludes the acquisition of software, royalties, and investments in foreign R&D capacity.

Our main variables are labor productivity, which is constructed as the firm's sales over the number of employees and different measures of innovation. In particular, we construct three variables that measure innovation: (1) the dummy variable "product innovations," which takes the value 1 if the enterprise reports having introduced new or significantly improved products in the current or previous two years; (2) the dummy variable "process innovations," which takes the value 1 if the enterprise reports having introduced new or significantly improved production processes in the current or previous two years; and (3) the dummy variable "organizational innovations," which takes the value 1 if the enterprise answers yes to the following question: "During the three years XXXX to XXXX, the firm has introduced new or significantly modified management methods or structures in the company in order to improve the use of the firm's knowledge, the quality of the services, or the efficiency of the labor force."

The definition and construction of the other variables are specified in the following sections and in appendix 10A.

10.2.3 Descriptive Analysis

To motivate our focus in the chapter, we first present some salient patterns from the database. Figure 10.1 shows that the proportion of subsidiaries from foreign MNEs that buy R&D services within their business group is 3.3 percentage points higher than in the case of national subsidiaries. Table 10.1 reports some descriptive statistics, and table 10.2 shows a probit model with firms' characteristics that affect the probability of buying technology within the business group.[6] Column (1) in table 10.2 shows, for the sample of companies that belong to a business group, that subsidiaries are 2.7 percentage points more likely to buy technology within the group than other types of companies that belong to a business group. This percentage doubles

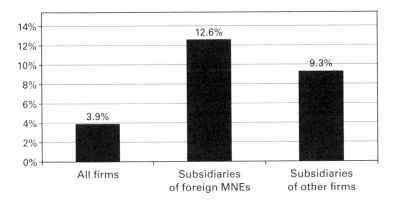

Figure 10.1
Percentage of firms with purchases of R&D services within the group.

for subsidiaries that are part of a foreign MNE, as shown in column (2), suggesting that an important part of the technology transfer goes from a firm's headquarters toward the subsidiaries. This observation is in line with the results of Fors (1997), who shows for Swedish firms that R&D is transferred from home to foreign plants.

In both columns of table 10.2, we observe that companies with technology transfers invest more resources in internal R&D than firms without technology transfers and that a large proportion of their sales come from new products. In addition, as expected, companies tend to buy less technology within the group the lower the importance is that they attribute to internal sources of information. Overall, the patterns in table 10.2 suggest that there is a transfer of technology from foreign headquarters toward subsidiaries. It also shows that companies that buy technology seem to be more market- or customer-focused than other types of firms, as suggested by the relevance of the "sales coming from new products" variable in the estimations.

10.3   Empirical Framework and Econometric Results

Our main goal is to analyze the influence of technology transfers on innovation and labor productivity. In order to do that, we follow a two-step approach. First, we evaluate whether subsidiaries from foreign MNEs are more innovative than other types of firms. Specifically, we distinguish between subsidiaries from foreign MNEs with technology transfers and those without transfers. Second, we study the effect of different types of innovations on labor productivity, differentiating

Table 10.1
Descriptive statistics

	All firms	Firms belonging to a business group	Subsidiaries of foreign MNE
Belonging to a group (d)	0.392	1.000	1.000
Cooperation (d)	0.289	0.342	0.322
Exporter (d)	0.313	0.364	0.474
External R&D intensity (in logs.)	2.031	2.513	2.412
Formal protection (d)	0.285	0.288	0.246
Innovations			
Product innovation (d)	0.519	0.513	0.517
Process innovation (d)	0.528	0.556	0.554
Organizational innovation (d)	0.490	0.519	0.501
Internal R&D intensity (in logs.)	6.893	6.515	6.217
Labor productivity (in logs.)	11.644	12.021	12.300
Non-subsidiary and belonging to a group (d)	0.129	0.330	0.000
Obstacles to innovation			
Lack of finance	1.537	1.339	1.200
Lack of information	1.080	0.984	0.855
Lack of personnel	1.195	1.080	0.951
No need of innovation	0.786	0.793	0.797
Patent (d)	0.127	0.137	0.130
Physical investment intensity (in logs.)	6.247	6.815	7.013
Purchases of R&D services from the group (in logs.)	0.472	1.204	1.570
Sales from new product (%)	20.451	18.658	17.296
Size (in logs.)	4.359	5.283	5.618
Sources of information			
Internal	2.154	2.079	2.089
Clients	1.226	1.147	1.105
Competitors	1.849	1.816	1.785
Suppliers	1.874	1.802	1.827
Subsidiary of foreign MNE (d)	0.097	0.248	1.000
Subsidiary of national group (d)	0.165	0.421	0.000
Number of observations	27,475	10,762	2,671

Note: The symbol (d) means dummy variable. For organizational innovations, the number of available observations in each sample is, respectively, 16,050, 6,579, and 2,671.

Table 10.2
Probability of buying R&D services within the same business group

	Firms belonging to a business group (1)			MNEs (2)		
	dy/dx		Std. E.	dy/dx		Std. E.
Subsidiary of foreign MNE (d)	0.031	***	0.008	0.066	***	0.066
Internal R&D expenditures$_{t-1}$	0.004	***	0.001	0.004	***	0.004
Cooperation$_{t-1}$ (d)	0.057	***	0.008	0.062	***	0.062
Patents$_{t-1}$ (d)	0.018	**	0.009	0.015		0.015
Size	0.008	***	0.002	0.005		0.005
Sales from new products$_{t-1}$	0.0004	***	0.0001	0.0007	***	0.002
Internal sources of information	0.013	***	0.004	0.026	***	0.026
Pseudo R2	0.10			0.12		
Log likelihood	−2,217.8			−669.5		
Number of observations	7,590			2,042		

Note: The symbol (d) means dummy variable. Std. E.: Estimated standard error. All regressions include a constant, and geographical and high-tech and medium high-tech industry dummies. We report marginal effects (dy/dx) at sample means from a probit model. * = significant at 10%, ** = significant at 5%, *** = significant at 1%.

between subsidiaries from foreign MNEs with technology transfers and those without transfers.

10.3.1   Technology Transfers and Innovations

We first want to quantify the impact of technology transfers obtained by subsidiaries from foreign MNEs on the generation of new knowledge, controlling for some economic variables. As a baseline equation, let new knowledge, which we denote by k_i, take the following form:

$$k_i = s_i \alpha + r_i \, \gamma + x_i' \delta + u_i \qquad (10.1)$$

where s_i is a dummy variable that takes the value one if the ith company is a subsidiary of a foreign multinational operating in Spain. We call this variable "subsidiary of foreign MNE." The variable r_i is the firm's innovation effort, and the vector x_i captures further economic variables that influence a firm's production of knowledge variable, which we explain shortly.

We consider innovative effort to be a public good within the firm, so it can be used to produce several innovative outputs without depletion.

Therefore, we model k_i as a vector of innovative outputs. We use three proxies for this variable: product, process, and organizational innovations, which are measured as dummy variables indicating whether the firm has introduced product, process, or organizational innovations, respectively.

We measure the firms' innovative effort r_i by three variables: we consider the lagged value of internal R&D expenditures per employee (in logarithms) and its square to control for potential nonlinearities, and we also include the ratio of external R&D over total employment.

The vector x_i contains some economic variables that influence a firm's innovations. We believe that being part of a business group can increase innovativeness due to economies of scale to generate new knowledge. For this reason, we include a dummy variable that takes the value 1 if the company is a subsidiary of a national group, and a dummy variable that takes the value 1 if the firm is a nonsubsidiary of a business group. Therefore, our reference groups are companies that do not belong to business groups. This approach allows us to compare the effect of being part of a foreign group or of being part of a national group on innovation. We include the variable "physical investment per employee" in order to allow for complementarities between process innovation and investment in capital that embodies new process technologies.

In the survey, the firms report the factors that hamper their innovations. We construct four variables that measure whether the firm finds lack of finance, lack of personnel, lack of information, or no need for innovation as important obstacles to innovation. We also include a measure of formal protection of intellectual property as an indicator of the appropriability conditions faced by the firm. As is well known in the literature (see, e.g., Spence 1984), the capacity to capture innovation returns increases firms' incentives to innovate. Consequently, we expect firms to be more successful in product and process innovation activities if they find the information coming from customers, suppliers, or competitors to be important. In the case of organizational innovations, we believe that information from internal sources within the enterprise or the enterprise group also favors the success of this type of innovation.

Finally, we include a variable that accounts for size, measured as the number of employees in logarithms, and a set of geographical and high-tech and medium high-tech industry dummies. The reason for including geographical dummies in the specification is to capture the impact of agglomeration effects on the generation of spillovers. The explanation with the detailed construction of control variables and the list of high-tech and medium high-tech activities can be found in appendixes 10A and 10B respectively.

In table 10.3, we report the estimation of the knowledge production equation (10.1) as three separate probit equations for the process, product, and organizational innovation indicators. We estimate by maximum likelihood. We show the estimation of product innovation in column (1), process innovation in column (2), the number of types of innovation in columns (3) and (4),[7] and organizational innovations in column (5). Our results show that in all cases, the "subsidiary of a foreign MNE" dummy is not significantly different from zero. In contrast, nonsubsidiaries of a business group are on average more innovative than the rest of the companies.

The "R&D expenditures" and "formal protection" variables influence product, process, and organizational innovations positively. With respect to sources of information, suppliers are important for product innovation, and clients are important for process innovation. Consistent with Crespi et al. 2008, our results suggest that companies get valuable information from competitors.

Table 10.4 reports the influence of technology transfers on innovation, distinguishing between companies with technology transfers (measured as R&D acquisitions from the group) and companies with other external R&D expenditures. We also differentiate between subsidiary of foreign MNEs, subsidiary of a national group, and nonsubsidiary. In these estimations, the reference group is companies that do not belong to a business group and do not engage in external R&D. The results show that subsidiaries of foreign MNEs with transfers within the group are more likely to have product and process innovations than other types of firms. However, they have organizational innovations similar to those in other firms. Other external R&D also increases the probability of innovating, but there are no significant differences across firms. To summarize, the findings suggest that an average subsidiary of a foreign MNE is not more innovative than other type of firms, with the exception of subsidiaries of foreign MNEs with technology transfers from their group.

10.3.2 Innovation, Technology Transfers, and Labor Productivity

We now turn to the productivity analysis. We analyze the impact on labor productivity of the different types of innovations for firms with technology transfers and without technology transfers from the group.

Table 10.3
Innovation equations: baseline specification

	(1) Product innovation		(2) Process innovation		Number of types of innovations (3) From 0 to 1		(4) From 1 to 2		(5) Organizational innovation	
	dy/dx	Std. E.	dy/dx	Std. E.	dy/dx	Std. E.	dy/dx	Std. E.	dy/dx	Std. E.
Belonging to a group (d)										
Subsidiary of foreign MNE	0.017	0.013	−0.004	0.013	0.0002	0.0002	0.007	0.009	0.008	0.015
Subsidiary of national group	−0.013	0.011	−0.015	0.010	−0.0007	0.0006	−0.011	0.007	−0.008	0.012
Nonsubsidiary	0.011	0.011	0.022 *	0.011	0.0004 **	0.0001	0.015 *	0.008	0.052 ***	0.013
Size	0.010 ***	0.003	0.037 ***	0.003	0.0010 ***	0.0002	0.021 ***	0.002	0.038 ***	0.004
Physical investment	0.007 ***	0.001	0.016 ***	0.001	0.0005 ***	0.0001	0.010 ***	0.001	0.008 ***	0.001
Internal R&D$_{t-1}$	0.046 ***	0.004	0.058 ***	0.004	0.0024 ***	0.0005	0.050 ***	0.002	0.020 ***	0.004
Internal R&D squared$_{t-1}$	−0.001 ***	0.000	−0.003 ***	0.000	−0.0001 ***	0.0000	−0.002 ***	0.000	−0.000 ***	0.000
External R&D$_{t-1}$	0.007 ***	0.001	0.007 ***	0.001	0.0003 ***	0.0001	0.007 ***	0.001	0.005 ***	0.001
Formal protection (d)	0.188 ***	0.008	0.065 ***	0.008	−0.0063 ***	0.0014	0.119 ***	0.006	0.131 ***	0.010
Sources of information										
Internal	0.152 ***	0.004	0.176 ***	0.004	0.0074 ***	0.0015	0.153 ***	0.003	0.115 ***	0.005
Suppliers	0.055 ***	0.004	−0.018 ***	0.004	0.0009 ***	0.0002	0.018 ***	0.003	−0.017 ***	0.005

Table 10.3
(continued)

| | Number of types of innovations | | | | | | | | | |
| | (1) Product innovation | | (2) Process innovation | | (3) From 0 to 1 | | (4) From 1 to 2 | | (5) Organizational innovation | |
	dy/dx	Std. E.	dy/dx	Std. E.	dy/dx	Std. E.	dy/dx	Std. E.	dy/dx	Std. E.
Clients	−0.022 ***	0.004	0.048 ***	0.004	0.0006 ***	0.0002	0.013 ***	0.003	−0.001	0.005
Competitors	0.024 ***	0.005	0.071 ***	0.004	0.0022 ***	0.0005	0.045 ***	0.003	0.006	0.006
Obstacles to innovation										
Lack of finance	0.012 ***	0.005	0.012 ***	0.004	0.0006 ***	0.0002	0.011 ***	0.003	0.026 ***	0.005
Lack of personnel	0.016 ***	0.005	0.027 ***	0.005	0.0009 ***	0.0003	0.019 ***	0.004	0.021 ***	0.006
Lack of information	0.033 ***	0.006	0.024 ***	0.006	0.0013 ***	0.0003	0.027 ***	0.004	0.033 ***	0.008
Not needed	−0.056 ***	0.005	−0.022 ***	0.005	−0.0017 ***	0.0004	−0.036 ***	0.003	−0.025 ***	0.006
Log pseudo-likelihood	−12,671.7		−13,588.2		−21,140.2				−9,639.1	
Pseudo R²	0.33		0.29		0.30				0.13	
Number of observations	27,475		27,475		27,475				16,050	

Note: The reference group is companies that do not belong to a business group. All regressions include geographical and high-tech and medium high-tech industry dummies. The "Number of types of innovation" variable is a variable that takes three values: 0 (default), 1 if the company has only product or only process innovation, and 2 if the company has both product and process innovation. The symbol (d) means dummy variable. *Std. E.*: Estimated standard error. In columns (1), (2), and (5), we report marginal effects (dy/dx) at sample means from probit models. In columns (3) and (4), the marginal effects are computed from an ordered probit model. * = significant at 10%, ** = significant at 5%, *** = significant at 1%.

Table 10.4
Innovation equations accounting for technology transfers

	(1) Product innovation		(2) Process innovation		Number of types of innovations (3) From 0 to 1		(4) From 1 to 2		(5) Organizational innovation	
	dy/dx	Std. E.	dy/dx	Std. E.	dy/dx	Std. E.	dy/dx	Std. E.	dy/dx	Std. E.
Belonging to a group (d)										
Subsidiary of foreign MNE	0.004	0.014	-0.018	0.014	-0.0004 *	0.0006	-0.006	0.009	0.007	0.016
Subsidiary of national group	-0.020	0.011	-0.015	0.011	-0.0010	0.0007	-0.014 *	0.007	0.001	0.013
Non-subsidiary	-0.002	0.012	0.023 *	0.012	0.0003 *	0.0002	0.011	0.008	0.056 ***	0.014
Firms with R&D from the group (d)										
Subsidiary of foreign MNE	0.033 ***	0.008	0.025 ***	0.008	0.0013 ***	0.0004	0.027 ***	0.005	0.012	0.009
Subsidiary of national group	0.024	0.016	0.006	0.012	0.0006	0.0004	0.013	0.007	0.020	0.019
Non-subsidiary	0.029	0.019	0.002	0.022	0.0006	0.0007	0.012	0.015	0.000	0.024
Firms with other external R&D (d)										
Subsidiary of foreign MNE	0.014 **	0.005	0.019 ***	0.004	0.0007 ***	0.0002	0.015 ***	0.003	0.015 ***	0.006
Subsidiary of national group	0.011 ***	0.003	0.007 **	0.002	0.0004 ***	0.0001	0.008 ***	0.002	0.002	0.003
Non-subsidiary	0.015 ***	0.003	0.007 **	0.003	0.0004 ***	0.0001	0.009 ***	0.002	0.007 **	0.004
Non-belonging to a group	0.006 ***	0.002	0.006 ***	0.002	0.0003 ***	0.0001	0.006 ***	0.001	0.012 ***	0.002
Size	0.009 ***	0.003	0.037 ***	0.003	0.0010 ***	0.0002	0.020 ***	0.002	0.037 ***	0.004
Physical investment	0.006 ***	0.001	0.016 ***	0.001	0.0005 ***	0.0001	0.010 ***	0.001	0.008 ***	0.001
Internal R&D$_{t-1}$	0.046 ***	0.004	0.057 ***	0.004	0.0024 ***	0.0005	0.050 ***	0.002	0.020 ***	0.004

Table 10.4
(continued)

| | Number of types of innovations | | | | | | | | | |
| | (1) Product innovation | | (2) Process innovation | | (3) From 0 to 1 | | (4) From 1 to 2 | | (5) Organizational innovation | |
	dy/dx	Std. E.	dy/dx	Std. E.	dy/dx	Std. E.	dy/dx	Std. E.	dy/dx	Std. E.
Internal R&D squared$_{t-1}$	-0.001 ***	0.000	-0.003 ***	0.000	-0.0001 ***	0.0000	-0.002 ***	0.000	0.000	0.000
Formal protection (d)	0.188 ***	0.008	0.065 ***	0.008	-0.0064 ***	0.0014	0.119 ***	0.006	0.130 ***	0.010
Sources of information:										
Internal	0.152 ***	0.004	0.176 ***	0.004	0.0072 ***	0.0015	0.153 ***	0.003	0.114 ***	0.005
Suppliers	0.055 ***	0.004	-0.018 ***	0.004	0.0008 ***	0.0002	0.017 ***	0.003	-0.018 ***	0.005
Clients	-0.022 ***	0.004	0.048 ***	0.004	0.0006 ***	0.0002	0.014 ***	0.003	0.000	0.005
Competitors	0.025 ***	0.005	0.071 ***	0.004	0.0021 ***	0.0005	0.045 ***	0.003	0.007	0.006
Obstacles to innovation:										
Lack of finance	0.012 **	0.005	0.012 **	0.004	0.0005 **	0.0002	0.011 ***	0.003	0.025 ***	0.005
Lack of personnel	0.016 ***	0.005	0.027 ***	0.005	0.0009 ***	0.0003	0.020 ***	0.004	0.020 ***	0.006
Lack of information	0.033 ***	0.006	0.024 ***	0.006	0.0013 ***	0.0003	0.027 ***	0.004	0.034 ***	0.008
Not needed	-0.055 ***	0.005	-0.022 ***	0.005	-0.0017 ***	0.0004	-0.035 ***	0.003	-0.024 ***	0.006
Log pseudo-likelihood	-12,653.7		-13,593.7		-21,131.2				-9,627.5	
Pseudo R^2	0.34		0.29		0.30				0.13	
Number of observations	27,475		27,475		27,475				16,050	

Note: The reference group is companies that do not belong to a business group and without external R&D. See also the note in table 10.3.

In this case, we focus our analysis on the sample of 4,658 companies (10,762 observations) that belong to a business group, as only these firms can perform intragroup purchases of R&D services. We assume that firms produce output using a Cobb-Douglas technology function with labor, capital, and knowledge inputs. We express the ratio of output over labor in the following equation:

$$y_i = \beta_1 z_i + k_i'\beta_2 + \beta_3 w_i \tag{10.2}$$

where y_i is sales per employee. This is our measure of labor productivity. The variable z_i refers to classical inputs, measured as investments in physical capital; k_i is the vector of new knowledge described in the previous section and measured as product, process, and organizational innovations; and w_i accounts for additional controls, which we describe shortly.

In order to get a first approximation of the determinants of labor productivity, in table 10.5 we estimate the model without the variables that measure new knowledge and include the subsidiary of a foreign MNE dummy. We include the physical investment per employee variable. As a control variable, we add an indicator of whether the firm

Table 10.5
Labor productivity equation: baseline specification, sample of companies that belong to a business group

	(1)			(2)		
	Coefficient		Std. E.	Coefficient		Std. E.
Subsidiary of foreign MNE (d)	0.272	***	0.022			
Subsidiary of foreign MNE with R&D from the group (d)				0.169	***	0.045
Exporter$_{t-1}$ (d)	0.332	***	0.025	0.358	***	0.025
Physical investment intensity	0.051	***	0.003	0.050	***	0.003
Size	0.113	***	0.041	0.138	***	0.042
Size squared	−0.016	***	0.004	−0.017	***	0.004
R²	0.15			0.15		
W_high-tech	0.0000			0.0000		
Number of observations	10,762			10,762		

Note: The symbol (d) means dummy variable. *Std. E.*: Estimated standard error. Coefficients reported from OLS regression. All regressions include regional dummies and dummies for high and mid-high technology sectors. Corresponding coefficients are not shown, but W_high-tech reports the *p*-value of a test of the joint significance of the defined variables. * = significant at 10%, ** = significant at 5%, *** = significant at 1%.

exported in previous year, because it has been shown that exporters are more productive than other firms (see, e.g., Bernard and Jensen 1999). We include this variable with a one-period lag in order to avoid simultaneity problems. We also add the size of the firm and its square to control for economies of scale. Finally, we include a set of geographical and industry dummies.

These technology transfers increase a foreign subsidiary's labor productivity by approximately 17 percentage points. Comparing columns (1) and (2), subsidiaries from MNEs with R&D from the group seem less labor-productive than those without R&D transfers from the group. A possible explanation is that MNEs without R&D from the group obtain other external technology or other type of nonpecuniary knowledge that enhance their productivity. We explore this issue in the following regressions measuring the efficiency of different types of innovation on labor productivity.

In table 10.6, we report the impact of product, process, and organizational innovation on labor productivity. In order to avoid potential endogeneity problems, we follow the approach of Griffith et al. (2006). For the firm's innovative outputs, k_i, we take the predicted values from the estimated probit model reported in table 10.4. All types of innovation have a significant and positive effect on labor productivity, although organizational innovations seem to influence labor productivity to a lower extent. In these estimates, as labor productivity is measured in logarithms, for each coefficient β, $\exp(\beta) - 1$ gives approximately the proportional difference between innovators and noninnovators. Regardless the type of innovation, the difference is above 20 percent in favor of innovators, being the highest at 26.2 percent for product innovations.

The previous estimations have the limitation that we cannot account for the differential impact of innovation on the labor productivity of subsidiaries of foreign MNEs and other types of firms or whether there are unobserved factors associated with purchases of R&D services for subsidiaries of foreign MNEs. We address this issue by comparing the impact of product, process, and organizational innovations on labor productivity for three types of companies: foreign subsidiaries with acquisitions of technological services from companies of the same group, foreign subsidiaries without these purchases, and the rest of the companies.[8]

We present the results in table 10.7. First, we find that the impact of product and process innovations on labor productivity is approximately

Table 10.6
Innovation and labor productivity: sample of companies that belong to a business group

	(1)		(2)		(3)	
	Coefficient	Std. E.	Coefficient	Std. E	Coefficient	Std. E.
Product innovation (p)	0.233 ***	0.042				
Process innovation (p)			0.211 ***	0.039		
Organizational innovation (p)					0.184 ***	0.058
Exporter$_{t-1}$ (d)	0.343 ***	0.025	0.350 ***	0.025	0.354 ***	0.025
Physical investment intensity	0.045 ***	0.004	0.044 ***	0.004	0.047 ***	0.004
Size	0.153 ***	0.042	0.142 ***	0.042	0.142 ***	0.042
Size squared	−0.018 ***	0.004	−0.018 ***	0.004	−0.018 ***	0.004
R²	0.14		0.14		0.14	
W_high-tech	0.0000		0.0000		0.0000	
Number of observations	10,762		10,762		10,762	

Note: The symbol (p) means predicted value. Predicted values come from the estimated probit model reported in table 10.4. The symbol (d) means dummy variable. *Std. E.*: Estimated standard error. All regressions include geographical dummies, a constant and dummies for high and mid-high technology sectors. Corresponding coefficients are not shown, but W_high-tech reports the *p*-value of a test of the joint significance of the defined variables. * = significant at 10%, ** = significant at 5%, *** = significant at 1%.

Table 10.7
Innovation and labor productivity equation accounting for technology transfers: sample of companies that belong to a business group

	(1)			(2)			(3)		
	Coefficient		Std. E.	Coefficient		Std. E.	Coefficient		Std. E.
Product innovation (p):									
Subsidiary of foreign MNE with R&D from the group	0.442	***	0.071						
Subsidiary of foreign MNE without R&D from group	0.472	***	0.049						
Nonsubsidiary of foreign MNE	0.171	***	0.042						
Process innovation (p):									
Subsidiary of foreign MNE with R&D from the group				0.442	***	0.068			
Subsidiary of foreign MNE without R&D from the group				0.431	***	0.047			
Non-subsidiary of foreign MNE				0.152	***	0.040			
Organizational innovation (p):									
Subsidiary of foreign MNE with R&D from the group							0.509	***	0.090
Subsidiary of foreign MNE without R&D from the group							0.538	***	0.067
Nonsubsidiary of foreign MNE							0.136	**	0.058
Exporter$_{t\text{-}1}$ (d)	0.046	***	0.004	0.334	***	0.025	0.046	***	0.004
Physical investment intensity	0.330	***	0.025	0.044	***	0.004	0.332	***	0.025
Size	0.135	***	0.042	0.129	***	0.042	0.123	***	0.042
Size squared	-0.017	***	0.004	-0.017	***	0.004	-0.017	***	0.004
R^2	0.16			0.15			0.15		
W_high-tech	0.0000			0.0000			0.0000		
Number of observations	10,762			10,762			10,762		

Note: The symbol (p) means predicted value. Predicted values come from the estimated probit model reported in table 10.4. The symbol (d) means dummy variable. *Std. E.*: Estimated standard error. All regressions include geographical dummies, a constant, and dummies for high and mid-high technology sectors. Corresponding coefficients are not shown, but W_high-tech reports the *p*-value of a test of the joint significance of the defined variables. * = significant at 10%, ** = significant at 5%, *** = significant at 1%.

three times higher for subsidiaries of foreign MNEs than for other companies. The difference is even greater in the case of organizational innovations, showing the significant influence that transferring knowl edge and integrating different teams and departments within the company have on labor productivity for subsidiaries of foreign MNEs. Second, we show that the effect of any type of innovations on productivity is quite similar between subsidiaries with acquisitions of technological services and foreign subsidiaries without these technology transfers, suggesting that the latter achieve similar productivity levels using other sources of external R&D.

As compared to table 10.6, in table 10.7 the magnitude of the premium for innovators affiliated to foreign MNEs more than doubles. However, for nonsubsidiaries, the size of the impact of any type of innovation on productivity is 5 percentage points smaller.

Finally, as robustness checks, we have performed separate estimates for different subsamples obtained by splitting the sample in table 10.7 according to firms' size (large firms vs. SMEs), activity sector (manufacturing vs. services), and technological intensity (companies in high-tech industries vs. low-tech industries). The results (not reported here to economize on space)[9] suggest that the patterns depicted before remain very similar for large firms, services companies and firms in low-tech sectors. In these cases, innovations generated by subsidiaries of foreign MNEs keep on having a greater effect on productivity than innovations of nonsubsidiaries. However, affiliates of foreign MNEs without R&D purchases from the group now appear to be the most productive subsidiaries. Other remarkable outcome is that for services firms belonging to business groups, the impacts of any type of innovation are substantially higher than for manufacturing subsidiaries, pointing out that new knowledge is also a key channel to achieve productivity improvements in services industries.

10.4   Summary and Concluding Remarks

In this chapter, we analyze the impact of technology transferred by foreign MNEs to their subsidiaries, using data on innovative Spanish firms for the years 2004 to 2006. Our results show that subsidiaries of foreign MNEs are on average more productive but not more innovative than other types of firms, with the exception of subsidiaries of foreign MNEs that obtain technology transfers. We argue that part of the observed productivity advantage is related to these technology transfers. Moreover, another part of the productivity advantage is due to other nonpecuniary technological flows. We show that the effect of organizational innovations on labor productivity is the main difference between subsidiaries of foreign MNEs and other types of firms. These findings suggest that multinationals transfer not only traditional innovations but also a business strategy based on a productive organization of work. A rigorous test of this other channel as well as other effects of technology transfers such as its impact on employment is left for future research.

Appendix 10A: Definitions of Variables

Cooperation: Dummy variable that takes the value 1 if the enterprise had some cooperative arrangements on innovation in the current or previous two years.

Exporter: Dummy variable that takes the value 1 if the enterprise exported in the current year.

External R&D expenditures: In the database, the companies are asked about the expenditures in the current year corresponding to "acquisitions of R&D services outside the firm through contracts, informal agreements." This variable is included in the logarithms.

Formal protection: Dummy variable that takes the value 1 if the enterprise used design pattern, trademarks, or copyright to protect inventions or innovations in the current or previous two years.

High-tech and medium high-tech sectors: Set of industry dummies according to the firm's main business activity in the case of high and mid-high technology sectors (NACE2 codes 24, 29, 30, 31, 32, 33, 34, 35, 64, 72, 73). See table 10B.1.

Innovations:

Product innovation: Dummy variable that takes the value 1 if the enterprise reports having introduced new or significantly improved products in the current or previous two years.

Process innovation: Dummy variable that takes the value 1 if the enterprise reports having introduced new or significantly improved production processes in the current or previous two years.

Organizational innovation: Dummy variable that takes the value 1 if the enterprise reports having introduced "new or significantly modified management methods, or structures in the company in order to improve the use of the firm knowledge, the quality of the services, or the efficiency of the labor force" in the current or previous two years

Internal R&D expenditures: In the database, the companies are asked about the expenditures in the current year corresponding to "creative work performed in a systematic way inside the firm, with the goal of increasing the volume of knowledge to devise new applications, as new products (goods or services) or new or significantly improved processes."

Labor productivity: Sales per employee in the current year. This variable is included in the logarithms.

Obstacles to innovation:

Lack of finance: Average of scores of importance of cost obstacles for innovation by the firm. Cost obstacles include no suitable internal or external financing available and high costs of innovation. The scores are numbers that vary from 0 (unimportant) to 3 (crucial).

Lack of personnel: Score of importance of lack of qualified personnel for innovation as an obstacle to innovation by the firm. The scores are numbers that vary from 0 (unimportant) to 3 (crucial).

Lack of information: Average of scores of importance of lack of information for innovation as an obstacle to innovation by the firm. Lack of information includes lack of information on technology and lack of market information. The scores are numbers that vary from 0 (unimportant) to 3 (crucial).

No need for innovation: Average of scores of importance of no need for innovation as an obstacle to innovation by the firm. No need for innovation includes little interest for innovations by customers and no need for innovation because of earlier innovations. The scores are numbers that vary from 0 (unimportant) to 3 (crucial).

Patent: Dummy variable that takes the value 1 if the firm applied for patents in the current or previous two years.

Purchases of R&D services from the group: External R&D expenditure of companies that belong to the same business group.

Physical investment intensity: Gross investments in tangible goods in the current year per employee. This variable is included in the logarithms.

Regional dummies (geographical spillover effects):

Basque Country: Dummy variable that takes the value 1 if the firm is located in the Basque Country.
Catalonia: Dummy variable that takes the value 1 if the firm is located in Catalonia.
Madrid: Dummy variable that takes the value 1 if the firm is located in Madrid.

Sales from new products: Share of turnover in the current year due to new or significantly improved products introduced in the current or previous two years.

Services: Dummy variable that takes the value 1 if the firm belongs to the services sectors (NACE2 codes 50–93).

Size: Number of employees in the current year. This variable is included in the logarithms.

Sources of information: In the database, the companies are asked: "In the current and previous two years, what was the importance of each of the following sources of information in order to innovate?" For each of the sources, the company can answer that the importance of the source was high, intermediate, or low, or that the source was not relevant. We assign a number that varies from 1 (not relevant) to 4 (high importance) for each answer.

Internal: This variable refers to the following source: information from internal sources within the enterprise or the enterprise group in the current or previous two years.
Competitors: This variable refers to the information from competitors and other enterprises from the same industry in the current or previous two years.
Clients: This variable refers to the information from customers or clients in the current or previous two years.
Suppliers: This variable refers to the information from suppliers in the current or previous two years.

Subsidiary of foreign multinational: Dummy variable that takes the value 1 if the enterprise is a subsidiary of a private firm with at least 50 percent foreign capital participation.

Appendix 10B: Classification of Sectors

Table 10B.1
Classification of high-tech and medium high-tech sectors

NACE-Rev.1	Sectors
	High and medium high-tech manufacturing sectors
24	Chemicals and chemical products
29	Machinery and equipment n.e.c.
30	Office machinery and computers
31	Electrical machinery and apparatus n.e.c.
32	Radio, television and communication equipment
33	Medical, precision and optical instruments
34	Motor vehicles, trailers and semi-trailers
35	Other transport equipment
	High-tech services
64	Post and telecommunications
72	Computer and related activities
73	Research and development

Notes

We would like to thank two anonymous referees and conference and seminar participants at the 10th ETSG (Warsaw) CESifo Conference on "Globalisation, Trade, FDI and the Multinational Firm"; and the Universidad Complutense of Madrid. This research has been partially funded by the CICYT projects SEJ2007–65520/ECON and ECO2010–18947/ECON.

1. For a summary on the relationship between headquarters and subsidiaries as a part of a multinational network, see chapter 1 of this volume.

2. An exception is the work of Girma, Kneller, and Pisu (2007), who analyze productivity gains through acquisition FDI.

3. The database is constructed on the basis of the annual Spanish responses to the Community Innovation Survey (CIS). This survey is specifically designed to analyze R&D and other innovating activities following the recommendations of the OSLO Manual on performing innovation surveys (see OECD 2005). The survey is targeted to industrial companies whose main economic activity corresponds to sections C, D, and E of NACE 93, except nonindustrial companies because of the imprecision of methodological marking in the international context by other branches of activity. The questions we quote in this chapter are the English versions from the CIS questionnaire. These questions are the exact equivalent of the Spanish questionnaire.

4. Initially, the panel was assembled with two samples of firms surveyed on the basis of a census: firms with 200 or more employees and firms with internal R&D expenditures in 2003. In 2004, the panel was enlarged with two new sets of firms employing fewer

than 200 employees: firms with external R&D expenditure but without internal R&D expenditure, and noninnovative firms.

5. A group consists of two or more legally defined enterprises under common ownership.

6. We use a specification similar to Cassiman and Veugelers's (2006) to explain R&D acquisitions. The main control variables account for economies of scale and scope as well as firms' absorptive capacities. The definitions of the control variables are reported in appendix 10A.

7. The "number of types of innovation" variable is a variable that takes three values: 0 (default), 1 if the country has only product or only process innovation, and 2 if the company has both product and process innovation. In this way, we account for companies that have product and process innovations simultaneously.

8. As in the previous estimations, in order to avoid endogeneity problems, for the innovation variables, we take the predicted values from the estimated probit model reported in table 10.4.

9. The estimates are available from the authors upon request.

References

Bernard, A., and J. Jensen. 1999. Exceptional exporter performance: cause, effect, or both? *Journal of International Economics* 47 (1): 1–25.

Bloom, N., R. Sadun, and J. Van Reenen. 2012. Americans do I.T. better: US multinationals and the productivity miracle. *American Economic Review* 102 (1): 167–201.

Cassiman, B., and P. Mendi. 2008. Innovation strategies among multinational firms: Empirical evidence from Spain. Mimeo.

Cassiman, B., and R. Veugelers. 2006. In search of complementarity in innovation strategy: internal R&D and external knowledge acquisition. *Management Science* 52 (1): 68–82.

Crespi, G., C. Criscuolo, J. Haskel, and M. Slaughter. 2008. Productivity growth, knowledge flows, and spillovers. NBER Working Paper No. 13959.

Findlay, R. 1978. Relative backwardness, direct foreign investment, and the transfer of technology: a simple dynamic model. *Quarterly Journal of Economics* 92 (1): 1–16.

Fors, G. 1997. Utilization of R&D results in the home and foreign plants of multinationals. *Journal of Industrial Economics* 45 (2): 341–358.

Fosfuri, A., M. Motta, and T. Rønde. 2001. Foreign direct investment and spillovers through workers' mobility. *Journal of International Economics* 53 (1): 205–222.

García-Vega, M., P. Hoffmann, and R. Kneller. 2012. The internationalisation of R&D and the knowledge production function. CESifo Working Paper Series no. 3751.

García-Vega, M., and E. Huergo. 2011. Trust and technology transfers. http://www.etsg.org/ETSG2010/papers/GarciaVega.pdf.

Girma, S., R. Kneller, and M. Pisu. 2007. Do exporters have anything to learn from foreign multinationals? *European Economic Review* 51 (4): 981–998.

Girma, S., and K. Wakelin. 2001. Regional underdevelopment: is FDI the solution? A semiparametric analysis. CEPR Discussion Paper no. 2995.

Glass, A., and K. Saggi. 1999. Foreign direct investment and the nature of R&D. *Canadian Journal of Economics.* 32 (1): 92–117.

Glass, A., and K. Saggi. 2002. Multinational firms and technology transfer. *Scandinavian Journal of Economics* 104 (4): 495–513.

Griffith, R., E. Huergo, J. Mairesse, and B. Peters. 2006. Innovation and productivity across four European countries. *Oxford Review of Economic Policy* 22 (4): 483–498.

Guadalupe, M., O. Kuzmina, and C. Thomas. 2010. Innovation and foreign ownership. NBER Working Paper no. 16573.

Haskel, J., S. Pereira, and M. Slaughter. 2007. Does inward foreign direct investment boost the productivity of domestic firms? *Review of Economics and Statistics* 89 (3): 482–496.

Keller, W., and S. Yeaple. 2009. Multinational enterprises, international trade, and productivity growth: Firm-level evidence from the United States. *Review of Economics and Statistics* 91 (4): 821–831.

van Pottelsberghe, B., and F. Lichtenberg. 2001. Does foreign direct investment transfer technology across borders? *Review of Economics and Statistics* 83 (3): 490–497.

Markusen, J. 1995. The boundaries of multinational enterprises and the theory of international trade. *Journal of Economic Perspectives* 9 (2): 169–189.

PITEC database. N.d. http://icono.fecyt.es/PITEC/Paginas/descarga_bbdd.aspx.

OECD. 2005. *Oslo Manual Guidelines for Collecting and Interpreting Innovation Data*, 3rd ed. Paris: OECD.

Sadowski, B., and G. Sadowski-Rasters. 2006. On the innovativeness of foreign affiliates: Evidence from companies in The Netherlands. *Research Policy* 35 (3): 447–462.

Spence, M. 1984. Cost reduction, competition, and industry performance. *Econometrica* 52 (1): 101–121.

Stiebale, J., and F. Reize. 2011. The impact of FDI through mergers and acquisitions on innovation in target firms. *International Journal of Industrial Organization* 29 (2): 155–167.

Syverson, C. 2011. What determines productivity. *Journal of Economic Literature* 49 (2): 326–365.

11 Innovation Offshoring and Inventor Substitution

Roger Smeets and Laura Abramovsky

11.1 Introduction

Since the 1980s, there has been substantial growth in the share of activities that multinational firms (MNEs) locate or relocate outside their home country. Initially, mainly so-called blue-collar production activities were being offshored to low-wage locations (Hummels, Ishii, and Yi 2001), followed by white-collar service jobs (Amiti and Wei 2009). More recently, MNEs have also appeared to be increasingly offshoring high-skill intensive innovation activities. UNCTAD (2005) reports an increase in foreign affiliate R&D expenditures (as a share of total business R&D) from 10 percent in 1993 to 16 percent in 2002. Linking patents from the European Patent Office (EPO) to European multinationals, Abramovsky and colleagues (2008) document general increases in offshore inventor employment during the period 1990–2004. Data from the U.S. Bureau of Economic Analysis (BEA) further show that the foreign affiliate research and development (R&D) expenditure shares of U.S. MNEs have increased from 9.5 percent in 1999 to 14.5 percent in 2008.

Driven by the fear of job losses, national governments generally worry about and take measures against MNE offshoring (Mankiw and Swagel 2006). Such sentiments are likely to be even stronger in the case of innovation offshoring, as innovation is usually associated with high-skill employment. Nonetheless, academic research has been ambiguous in its conclusions regarding the impact of (production) offshoring on domestic employment. Some studies indeed find substitution between foreign and domestic workers (Braconier and Ekholm 2000; Muendler and Becker 2010); others find additional evidence of complementarities (Brainard and Riker 1997; Desai, Foley, and Hines 2009; Harrison and McMillan 2011). Moreover, to our knowledge, so far no study has investigated the employment effects of innovation offshoring.

In this chapter, we aim to fill this gap. In particular, we study to what extent inventors employed by European MNEs at home and abroad are substitutes or complements to each other. To do so, we use a linked dataset of European patents and European MNEs (see Abramovsky et al. 2008). This dataset enables us to make two additional contributions. First, unlike previous studies on production offshoring, which focus on just one home country (usually the United States), we study MNEs from multiple home countries. In particular, we consider the innovation offshoring decisions of MNEs from eight European home countries to fourteen European host countries, as well as the United States. This broader scope is important, as previous studies suggest that the extent of innovation offshoring is likely to vary considerably among MNEs from different home countries (Cantwell 1995; Ambos 2005). Moreover, this broader scope allows us to generalize the findings of our study beyond the context of one particular home country.

Second, we account for substitution (or complementarity) patterns along two different margins: the extensive margin (i.e., the decision whether to employ foreign inventors) and the intensive margin (i.e., how many foreign inventors to employ). Our approach is very similar to that of Muendler and Becker (2010), who also distinguish between these two margins. Important, though, we specify an unconditional second-stage (intensive margin) model that allows us to retain all observations when estimating the system of inventor demand equations. We argue that this is a more natural approach of accounting for differential extensive margin selection mechanisms across different locations.

Our results can be summarized as follows: first, we find evidence of substitution between MNEs' home and foreign inventors. Foreign inventor employment appears more sensitive to home-country wage changes than home inventor employment to foreign wage changes. In particular, we find that a 1 percent increase in home wages induces an increase in foreign inventor demand of 0.6 to 0.7 percent along the extensive margin, but not along the intensive margin. Foreign wage changes do not significantly affect home country inventor demand along any of the two margins. Second, we find that foreign inventor demand is quite elastic regarding own wage changes, but again, only along the extensive margin. Finally, there is also evidence of extensive margin cross-location inventor substitution among foreign locations, with elasticities around 1. Virtually none of these substitution patterns are apparent when not distinguishing between these two margins, indicating the importance of separating them. Our results imply that cross-location inventor substitution indeed occurs, but only when deciding on whether to employ inventors in a particular foreign location. Once this decision has been made, and inventors are employed in different locations, there is no evidence of further (intensive margin) substitution.

The rest of this chapter is structured as follows: the next section briefly discusses the literature on innovation offshoring and its determinants. Section 11.3 lays out the empirical strategy, with a particular emphasis on how to account for second-stage selection bias. Section 11.4 discusses the data and presents some descriptive features of our sample of MNEs. Section 11.5 presents the empirical results. Finally, section 11.6 concludes.

11.2 Innovation Offshoring

Studies investigating the consequences of innovation offshoring are still fairly limited. For a long time, the dominant view in international economics (IE) and international business (IB) has been that MNEs keep their R&D and innovation close to home as part of their headquarters operations (Vernon 1966). However, various studies have demonstrated that MNEs are increasingly internationalizing their innovation by taking parts of it offshore. For example, in a sample of large U.S. and European MNEs, Cantwell (1995) documents that their share of U.S. patents originating abroad almost doubled (on average) from 7.9 percent in 1920–1939 to 14.5 percent in 1969–1990. However, he also shows that these averages veil important heterogeneity among different home countries. For example, whereas U.S. MNEs' foreign patent share remained stable at 6.8 percent, that of German MNEs increased from 4 percent to 13.7 percent, whereas Belgian MNEs actually saw their shares decrease from 95 percent to 60.6 percent. Using a variety of different sources, UNCTAD (2005) documents similar increases, as well as similar home-country heterogeneity, in the share of foreign affiliate-based R&D shares of MNEs from different home countries.

From a theoretical point of view, a paradigm that has taken a strong foothold in the IB literature is that MNEs offshore part of their innovation in order to tap into local pockets of technology. In this respect, Kuemmerle (1999) talks about a home base augmenting investment motive. It implies that MNEs operate abroad to access assets and capabilities that they do not yet possess but that are present abroad (e.g., in foreign technology clusters). Relatedly, Le Bas and Sierra (2002) talk about a technology sourcing or seeking investment motive, which is aimed at obtaining substitute technologies abroad (rather than complementary technologies, as under home base augmenting motives). Cantwell and Mudambi (2005) develop a slightly different perspective in which the foreign subsidiary is not just a passive absorber of external knowledge but also combines or recombines this knowledge and creates new capabilities in the process, which they call a competence creating investment motive.

These developments have led many scholars to wonder about the empirical drivers of innovation offshoring. In this respect, studies have highlighted both push factors, which push MNEs' innovation away from home, as well as pull factors, which pull MNEs' innovation toward foreign countries. As an example of the former, Lewin, Massini, and Peeters (2009) find that a relative shortage of home country scientists and engineers is an important driver of innovation offshoring. Opportunities for labor cost arbitrage seem of less importance. On the other hand, Demirbag and Glaister (2010) find that differences in R&D wages determine the R&D offshoring pattern. At the firm level, they find that R&D offshoring experience in general, and in a specific host country in particular, are also significant drivers of the innovation offshoring decision. On the "pull" end, Jensen and Pedersen (2011) demonstrate that innovative activities of Danish firms are mainly offshored to (Western) European countries and the United States, where the match between the high-skill intensive activities and the local environment is optimal.

Surprisingly few studies have explicitly investigated the consequences of innovation offshoring. Nonetheless, studies have been carried out on MNE host country (reverse) knowledge diffusion (see chapter 4) as well as intrafirm parent-affiliate knowledge diffusion (e.g., Branstetter, Fisman, and Foley 2006; Garcia-Vega and Huergo 2013), hence indirectly capturing at least part of innovation offshoring. However, to our knowledge there are no studies that investigate the consequences of innovation offshoring for the employment of (knowledge) workers in the different countries involved. This finding is in contrast to the increasing number of studies that investigate such consequences for production offshoring (Brainard and Riker 1997; Braconier and Ekholm 2000; Desai, Foley, and Hines 2009; Muendler and Becker 2010; Harrison and McMillan 2011). We now turn to this issue.

11.3 Empirical Strategy

Consider a firm i that produces an output to be sold worldwide and innovations to augment the production of this product. We assume that inventors are the only inputs used in producing innovations.[1] Inventors in turn are employed both at home and in foreign locations. For simplicity, we assume that knowledge production is separable from the production of the final product (see Fifarek and Veloso 2010).

In period t, a firm i produces knowledge employing inventors in different locations ($l = 1, \ldots, L$) including home, under exogenous variable-input prices that vary over locations $(w_t^1, \ldots, w_t^L)$. The output of such knowledge production is a count of patents P_{it}.[2] Our departing point is the specification of a translog cost function for a firm's production of knowledge, which is a flexible functional form that approximates many well-behaved cost functions (Berndt and Wood 1975):

$$\ln C_{it} = \varphi + \alpha \ln P_{it} + \sum_{l=1}^{L} \beta_l \ln w_t^l + 0.5 \sum_{l=1}^{L} \sum_{k=1}^{L} \gamma_{lk} \ln w_t^l \ln w_t^k + \sum_{l=1}^{L} \psi_l \ln P_{it} \quad (11.1)$$

From cost minimization, linear homogeneity in factor prices implies that $\sum_{l=1}^{L} \beta_l = 1$ and $\sum_{l=1}^{L} \gamma_{lk} = \sum_{l=1}^{L} \gamma_{kl} = \sum_{l=1}^{L} \psi_l = 0$. Moreover, there are $L(L-1)/2$ symmetry restrictions $\gamma_{lk} = \gamma_{kl}$. Noting that, by Shephard's lemma, inventor demand in location l is given by $I_{it}^l = \partial C_{it} / \partial w_t^l$, taking derivatives of (1) with respect to w_t^l yields wage bill shares S_{it}^l in location l:

$$\frac{\partial \ln C_{it}}{\partial \ln w_t^l} = I_{it}^l \frac{w_t^l}{C_{it}} = S_{it}^l = \beta_l + \sum_{k=1}^{L} \gamma_{lk} \ln w_t^k + \psi_l \ln P_{it} + v_{it}^l \quad (11.2)$$

where we have added an error term v_{it}^l. Equation (1.2) is the main estimating equation. It is usually estimated as a system for all locations l simultaneously using, for example, seemingly unrelated regression (SUR) techniques (Harrison and McMillan 2011; Muendler and Becker 2010). The estimated γ_{lk} values can be used to compute own and cross-wage and substitution elasticities (more on this shortly).[3]

As we mentioned in the introduction to this chapter, our sample is characterized by many firms with zero inventor demand in one or more locations and hence zero wage bill shares S_{it}^l. An MNE's inventor demand decision might be decomposed into two margins: an extensive margin decision (whether to employ inventors) and an intensive margin decision (how many inventors to employ). As argued by Muendler and

Becker (2010), not accounting for (first-stage) extensive margin selection in (second-stage) intensive margin demand is problematic from both an econometric as well as an economic point of view. If (unobserved) factors affect both margins simultaneously, from an econometric point of view the stage-two error term will not be mean zero if first-stage selection is not accounted for (Heckman 1979). Economically, MNEs might respond to intercountry wage differentials by substituting inventors at the extensive margin yet complementing them along the intensive margin (or vice versa).

To illustrate this latter point, consider a MNE that is faced with relatively high home country wages, perhaps because home country inventor supply in its particular area of innovation is relatively scarce. Such a MNE might consider to relocate (part of) its innovation activities abroad, thus replacing (part of) its home country inventors. This behavior implies inventor substitution at the extensive margin. However, once innovating abroad, new discoveries or inventions might increase demand for home country inventors and their particular skills. This effect constitutes inventor complementarity along the intensive margin. When not accounting for these two distinct effects, MNEs paying relatively high home country wages are overrepresented in the group of firms with positive foreign inventor demand, suggesting substitution between home and foreign inventors.[4]

Muendler and Becker (2010) tackle this issue by specifying a two-stage estimation procedure that—after imposing some simplifying assumptions—reduces to a standard two-stage Heckman selection model (Heckman 1979). In particular, they first estimate location-specific selection equations for each location l. They use these estimates to compute an inverse Mill's ratio, which is then included as an explanatory variable in the relevant second-stage inventor demand equation to capture selection bias.[5] However, a problem that arises using this approach in this particular context is that the selection mechanism is not uniform across locations within firms. That is, a firm that chooses location l to employ foreign inventors might not choose location k ($l \neq k$), implying that the size of the conditional sample of MNEs in the second stage differs across locations, which is problematic when estimating a *system* of inventor demand equations.

Muendler and Becker (2010) "stack" their data when estimating the second-stage inventor demand, which means that they include all firms (regardless of their extensive margin decision) but set wages (and other explanatory variables) in locations of absence to zero.[6] Here we take a slightly different approach that we derive from the literature on censored systems of consumer demand (Shonkwiler and Yen 1999; Su and Yen 2000; Yen 2005). To fix ideas, suppose that the first-stage selection equation by MNE i at time t regarding location l is given by

$$d_{it}^l = 1(h(\mathbf{x}_{it-1}^l \beta) + \varepsilon_{it}^l > 0) \tag{11.3}$$

where $1(.)$ is the indicator function and $\mathbf{x}_{it-1}^l$ is a vector of lagged (firm- and location-specific) explanatory variables. Hence, second-stage inventor shares $S_{it}^l > 0$ iff $d_{it}^l = 1$ and $S_{it}^l = 0$ otherwise. If we assume that ε_{it}^l and v_{it}^l—from equation (11.2)—are bivariately normally distributed, we know that the conditional expectation of v_{it}^l is given by (e.g., Heckman 1979)

$$E(v_{it}^l \mid \varepsilon_{it}^l > -\mathbf{x}_{it-1}^l \beta) = \delta \frac{\phi(h(\mathbf{x}_{it-1}^l \beta))}{\Phi(h(\mathbf{x}_{it-1}^l \beta))} \tag{11.4}$$

where $\phi(.)$ denotes the normal probability density function, $\Phi(.)$ the cumulative normal distribution function, and δ the covariance between v_{it}^l and ε_{it}^l. The ratio on the right-hand side of (4) is the inverse Mill's ratio. In a usual Heckman selection model, we are interested in the *conditional* mean of the second stage outcome—that is, conditional on a positive first-stage decision—which yields

$$E(S_{it}^l \mid \mathbf{z}_{it}^l, \mathbf{x}_{it-1}^l, d_{it}^l = 1) = \mathbf{z}_{it}^l \gamma + \delta \frac{\phi(h(\mathbf{x}_{it-1}^l \beta))}{\Phi(h(\mathbf{x}_{it-1}^l \beta))} \tag{11.5}$$

where we have replaced the right-hand side of equation (11.2) by $\mathbf{z}_{it}^l \gamma$ for ease of notation. However, as mentioned previously, in this particular application in which we estimate a *system* of inventor demand equations in the second stage, we are interested in estimating the *unconditional* expectation so that we can retain all observations (zero and positive) in the second stage. Hence, from the model in equation (11.5) we can immediately derive the unconditional expectation as[7]

$$E(S_{it}^l \mid \mathbf{z}_{it}^l, \mathbf{x}_{it}^l) = \Phi(h(\mathbf{x}_{it-1}^l \beta)) \mathbf{z}_{it}^l \gamma + \delta \phi(h(\mathbf{x}_{it-1}^l \beta)) \tag{11.6}$$

which is similar to the unconditional expectation of the Tobit model, except that the conditioning sets $\mathbf{z}$ and $\mathbf{x}$ are allowed to differ (Amemiya 1984). Hence, instead of estimating equation (11.6) in one step, we first estimate the selection models in equation (11.3), compute $\hat{\Phi}(.)$ and $\hat{\phi}(.)$ and then estimate equation (11.6) in the second step. This approach allows us to derive separate estimates of wage coefficients

on the extensive and intensive margins of substitution, allowing them
to differ in sign as well.

The estimation strategy is as follows: first, we estimate $I - 1$ (univariate) probit models in equation (11.3), omitting the home country, as we
consider only MNEs that have positive home country inventor demand
in our sample period. From these estimates, we then compute $\hat{\Phi}(.)$ and
$\hat{\phi}(.)$, which we use to estimate the system of equations in equation (11.6)
by means of SUR techniques (again, we omit the home country from
this step because otherwise the matrix of second-stage error terms
becomes singular). In this second step, we impose the homogeneity and
symmetry restrictions on the γs outlined earlier. The standard errors
obtained in the second step are biased in two ways: first, the use of $\hat{\Phi}(.)$
and $\hat{\phi}(.)$—instead of $\Phi(.)$ and $\phi(.)$—biases the standard errors downward. Second, Shonkwiler and Yen (1999) show that the error term in
(6) is heteroskedastic, causing estimation to be inefficient. Therefore,
we report bootstrapped standard errors when reporting estimation
results on the second stage later in this chapter.

Our approach places similar restrictions on cross-equation error correlations as that in Muendler and Becker (2010). That is, we do not
allow for any first-stage cross-equation correlations except the cross-
equation information captured by the vector of conditioning variables
x. As demonstrated in Muendler and Becker (2010), this approach
amounts to assuming that the covariances between ε_{it}^l and ε_{it}^k for $k \neq l$
are constant. Moreover, our approach assumes that the potential cor-
relation between ε_{it}^l and v_{it}^k for $k \neq l$ is fully captured by $\hat{\Phi}_k(.)$ and $\hat{\phi}_k(.)$.
Muendler and Becker (2010) motivate this assumption by arguing that
any such correlation will be induced by a firm-specific disturbance,
which is both part of ε_{it}^k and ε_{it}^l so that correction for selection into location k is sufficient to correct for this correlation.[8]

The estimated γ values from the labor cost-share equations in equation (2) themselves do not have a straightforward economic interpretation. However, they can be used to compute wage elasticities and
elasticities of substitution. In particular, own and cross wage elasticities
can be computed as

$$\varepsilon_{ll} = \frac{\partial S_{it}^l}{\partial w_t^l}\frac{w^l}{S^l} + S^l - 1; \quad \varepsilon_{lk} = \frac{\partial S_{it}^l}{\partial w_t^k}\frac{w^k}{S^l} + S^k \text{ for } k \neq l \tag{11.7}$$

In the "simple" (uncorrected) system of inventor demand equations,
the first ratio in ε_{ll} (ε_{lk}) simplifies to $\gamma_{ll}/w_t^l (\gamma_{lk}/w_t^k)$. However, when cor-

recting for first-stage selection, the expressions become slightly more complex:

$$\frac{\partial S^l_{it}}{\partial w^k_t} = \underbrace{\frac{\gamma_{lk}}{w^k_t}\,\hat{\Phi}(.)}_{\text{intensive}} + \underbrace{\hat{\phi}(.)\frac{\partial h}{\partial w^k_t}S^l - \delta\hat{\phi}(.)\hat{h}(.)\frac{\partial h}{\partial w^k_t}}_{\text{extensive}} \quad \forall k,l \tag{11.8}$$

Substituting equation (11.8) into equation (11.7) yields the selection-corrected own and cross-wage elasticities.

We can further use these wage elasticities to derive elasticities of substitution. A common measure for the ease of substitution between two inputs is the Allen elasticity (Allen 1938), which in the context of a translog cost equation is given by Binswanger (1974):

$$\sigma^A_{ll} = \frac{\varepsilon_{ll}}{S^l}\,;\,\sigma^A_{lk} = \frac{\varepsilon_{lk}}{S^k} \tag{11.9}$$

This elasticity measures the change in inventor demand in location l relative to k, given a wage change in k relative to l. Although it is fairly widely used, it has been criticized on the grounds that it does not measure the curvature of input isoquants and that its symmetric properties are undesirable (Blackorby and Russell 1989).[9] Because of these drawbacks, Blackorby and Russell (1989) propose an alternative substitution elasticity called the Morishima elasticity, which is given by

$$\sigma^M_{lk} = \varepsilon_{kl} - \varepsilon_{ll}$$
$$= \frac{d\ln I_k}{d\ln w^l_t} - \frac{d\ln I_l}{d\ln w^l_t} = \frac{d\ln I_k - d\ln I_l}{d\ln w^l_t} \tag{11.10}$$

Hence, the Morishima elasticity measures the change in inventor demand in location k relative to l, given a wage change in l (while keeping w^k_t constant).[10] Later in this chapter, we report both wage and Morishima substitution elasticities. Standard errors for these elasticities are computed by simultaneously bootstrapping both the selection, from equation (11.3), and the inventor demand, from equation (11.6).

11.4   Data

Our dataset links patent data from the EPO to European MNEs from eighteen European countries and the United States.[11] The patent data are derived from the EPO Worldwide Patent Statistical Database (PATSTAT) and the MNE (parent and subsidary) data from Bureau van

Dijk's Amadeus (Europe) and Icarus (U.S.) databases. The initial match was undertaken using company names and executed at different levels, such as exact matches and stem name matches. For more details regarding the matching procedure, see Abramovsky et al. 2008. The final dataset links patents to firms—either domestic firms, parents, or affiliates—and (foreign) affiliates to parent firms.

Each patent contains a host of information. We are especially interested in the inventors that are responsible for the patent and their country of residence. By comparing the home country of the different inventors on an MNE's patents with the home country of the MNE (parent) itself, we are able to determine whether the inventor is a home country inventor or a foreign inventor.[12] Individual inventors are identified through so-called person IDs, which are numeric codes belonging to individual inventors. However, in many cases the same inventor receives multiple codes for instance due to the differential use of small and capital letters, the addition of a professional title, a middle name, or other factors (see Lissoni, Sanditov, and Tarasconi 2006).

When counting inventors, we take two different routes: first, instead of counting *unique* inventors, we count inventors × patents. That is, if firm i takes out three patents in year t that each list five inventors, we count a total of fifteen inventors, regardless of whether a single inventor appears on more than one patent. Hence we potentially double-count unique inventors, essentially assuming that an inventor gets re-employed every time he or she is listed on a patent. The disadvantage of this approach is that we are inflating inventor counts; the advantage is that we do not have to worry about unique inventors receiving multiple inventor IDs.[13] Moreover, one could argue that an inventor that appears on multiple patents is more productive and that counting an inventor multiple times is warranted from an efficiency unit perspective. In our second approach, we use a relatively simple standardization of inventor names: first, we lowercase all full names. We then parse the lowercased full names into different components and create a new inventor ID for (1) inventors with similar first and surnames, (2) as under (1) and similar middle names, (3) as under (2) and a similar professional title. Results reported in this chapter use the first counting method but are highly similar when using the second.[14]

Our main explanatory variable—both in the selection equation as well as the inventor cost share equation—concerns wages w_t^l. We simultaneously require exogenous variation in these wages (as they are location specific) as well as sufficient cross-MNE variation because we

estimate the first-stage selection equations in (3) univariately (i.e., location by location, so that cross-location variation in wages only is insufficient). Moreover, given that we consider a very particular type of labor
(inventors), we would also like to have a more precise measure of wages
than a simple average (or median) wage rate. With these considerations
in mind, we use the EU KLEMS high-skilled hourly wage data, which
vary both across countries as well as within a country across broad
industry groups (O'Mahoney and Timmer 2009). Even though the definition of "high-skilled" differs slightly across countries, generally
speaking it captures wages paid to persons with university degrees (see
table 5.3 in Timmer et al. 2007). Wages are all computed in constant
(1995) euros, using the GDP deflators provided in EU KLEMS.

The inventor demand model, from equation (11.2), is in terms of
inventor cost shares, which means that for each location l we have to
compute the costs of employing inventors there relative to total MNE
costs. Inventor costs in location l at time t are computed by multiplying
inventor demand with the prevailing wage rate $\left(I_{it}^l \times w_t^l\right)$ and total
MNE-wide costs is the sum of these costs over all the locations in which
it is active (i.e., $\sum_{l=1}^{\hat{L}} I_{it}^l \times w_t^l$ with $\hat{L}$ as the total number of locations in
which MNE i is active in period t).

We largely follow Muendler and Becker 2010 as well as the literature
on the drivers of offshoring (see section 11.2) in specifying the first-stage
selection equation, arguing that location selection in period t is based
on information in period $t - 1$. In order to compute extensive margin
substitution or complementarity, in the selection equation for location
l we include both (period $t - 1$) wages in location l and in locations $k \neq l$.
Moreover, as argued in Muendler and Becker 2010, sunk investment
costs might be a particularly important factor determining whether to
employ inventors in a particular location. Following an established
literature in international economics (e.g., Roberts and Tybout 1997) we
capture the relevance of sunk costs through a past-presence indicator
that takes a value of 1 if the MNE employed inventors in location l in
period $t - 1$ and 0 otherwise.[15] Alternatively, following Demirbag and
Glaister 2010, this variable can be thought of as capturing past location-
specific innovation offshoring experience. We also include past presence indicators for location $k \neq l$ to capture interdependencies between
different location decisions, as well as innovation offshoring experience
in general (Demirbag and Glaister 2010). Additionally, earlier studies
have shown that the quality and quantity of the host location knowledge
stock is an important aspect of MNEs' innovation location/relocation

decisions (Griffith, Harrison, and van Reenen 2006; Jensen and Peder-sen 2011). Therefore, we also include a control variable measuring the amount of academic publications produced in a particular location and year, as this can be assumed to be relatively exogenous to MNE activity.[16] Finally, we include a number of MNE-level controls (Demirbag and Glaister 2010): the firm's age, the number of foreign affiliates, its operating revenue, and the capital-to-labor ratio.[17]

The second-stage equation includes (period t) wages as direct explanatory variables, as well as MNE-level total patent counts P_{it} so that we can compute constant-output wage and substitution elastici-ties. The impact of location and firm-specific variables included in the first-stage selection equation are captured by the inclusion of $\hat{\phi}(.)$ and $\hat{\Phi}(.)$ in equation (6).

Estimating equations (3) and (6) in a system of eighteen countries imposes heavy requirements on sample size, as the matrix of wage-coefficients contains $(18 \times 17)/2$ estimates (recall that we omit the home country from estimation). To reduce the dimensionality in the wage coefficient matrix, we follow the existing literature in this field and group the different countries together into four aggregate groups: HOME (which is the home country of each MNE), WEU (Western Europe, including Germany, France, the Netherlands, Sweden, Finland, the United Kingdom, and Belgium), the United States, and CSEU (Central and Southern Europe, including Poland, Czech Republic, Spain, Portugal, Italy, and Greece).[18] Furthermore, year-by-year inven-tor counts generate a substantial number of zero counts, even in a MNE's home country. The reason is that many of our sample firms do not take out patents in each year. In order to reduce the number of zero inventor counts, we aggregate individual years into three different three-year time periods, using the priority year as stated on each patent:[19] 1997–1999 (period 1), 2000–2002 (period 2), and 2003–2005 (period 3). In sum, $L = 4$ and $t = 3$ in our final sample.

In creating our sample of MNEs, we want to make sure that the firms in our sample employ at least some foreign inventors at some point during the sample period and that their innovation activities are struc-tural rather than incidental. To ensure that these conditions are met, we first construct the overall firm-level patent distribution per country and select only those firms that are in the top 5 percent of the distribu-tion in terms of their total patent count. Second, we select only firms that have at least one foreign inventor in at least one time period. We also impose that a MNE should have a positive home country inventor count in each time period (recall that we do not consider HOME as an *optional* location). This method results in a sample of 462 MNEs based in eight different home countries.[20] Table 11.1 presents the distribution of MNEs across the different home countries, as well as the country-specific patent cutoffs. For example, we have 153 UK MNEs in our sample, which make up 33 percent of our sample and have at least 9 patents in their portfolio.

The average (median) number of inventors employed at home by the MNEs in our sample is 99 (24). For the number of foreign inventors, these numbers are 184 (16). These figures show that the distribution of inventors is rather skewed in our sample, especially for foreign inventors. Table 11.2 presents the (average and median) number of home and

Table 11.1
MNE distribution across home countries

Home country	No. of MNEs	Percent of total sample	5 percent patent cutoff
United Kingdom	153	33.1	9
France	87	18.8	15
Italy	58	12.6	9
Sweden	47	10.2	13
Denmark	41	8.9	15
Netherlands	32	6.9	14
Finland	25	5.4	15
Belgium	19	4.1	18

Table 11.2
MNE inventor distribution

Home country	Home inventors			Foreign inventors		
	Mean	St. dev.	Median	Mean	St. dev.	Median
United Kingdom	59.0	161.4	17	164.1	766	16
France	183.8	370.4	29	303.7	916.3	20
Italy	61.4	140.5	15	27.9	52.9	6
Sweden	111.3	328.2	23	240.9	906.6	27
Denmark	71.2	169.2	25	88.5	303.2	12
Netherlands	112.1	245.1	25.5	243.5	559.1	19
Finland	182.0	692.5	30.5	178.2	711.4	10
Belgium	47.9	56.2	32.5	236.6	613.1	33

foreign inventors employed by our sample of MNEs (and its standard deviation), split up by home country of the MNEs. The skewed distribution of inventor counts is mirrored for the individual home countries. In most countries, the average foreign inventor count exceeds the average home inventor count, but this pattern is largely reversed when looking at median counts (with Sweden as a notable exception). These numbers are consistent with the notion that mainly large MNEs are offshoring (parts of) their innovative activities.

As discussed in section 11.3, the dependent variable in equation (2) is the inventor cost share in each location l. Table 11.3 presents the different (average and median) inventor cost shares for MNEs from the different home countries for all four locations. The inventor cost shares are largest in HOME, followed by WEU, USA, and CSEU. This ordering is identical for MNEs from all the individual home countries, with the exception of Finland, where the United States–based inventors are responsible for a slightly larger cost share (on average) than WEU-based inventors. These results are not surprising, given that we consider MNEs based in only eight (Western) European countries. Looking at the median labor cost shares in the United States, and even more so in CSEU, also demonstrates the problem of "zeros" in our empirical setup. Overall, the percentage of zeros in each of the three foreign (i.e., non-HOME) locations is 37.2 percent (WEU), 54.7 percent (USA), and 77.5 percent (CSEU).

Table 11.4 presents a transition matrix, showing the percentage of MNEs in our sample that drops or adds one or more locations in period

Table 11.3
MNE inventor cost share distribution

	HOME		WEU		USA		CSEU	
Home country	Mean	Median	Mean	Median	Mean	Median	Mean	Median
United Kingdom	0.718	0.819	0.137	0.029	0.137	0.003	0.008	0.000
France	0.786	0.883	0.128	0.046	0.078	0.003	0.008	0.000
Italy	0.743	0.850	0.166	0.010	0.074	0.000	0.018	0.000
Sweden	0.719	0.836	0.228	0.122	0.048	0.000	0.005	0.000
Denmark	0.789	0.889	0.138	0.054	0.071	0.000	0.003	0.000
Netherlands	0.730	0.846	0.187	0.073	0.077	0.000	0.006	0.000
Finland	0.770	0.869	0.110	0.037	0.120	0.016	0.001	0.000
Belgium	0.647	0.719	0.273	0.191	0.070	0.000	0.009	0.000

Table 11.4
Location transitions between $t = 2$ and $t = 3$ (%)

		L in $t = 3$				
		1	2	3	4	
L in $t = 2$	1	7.6	14.5	2.4	0.0	24.5
	2	10.8	17.7	7.8	0.4	36.8
	3	2.4	6.3	10.8	5.0	24.5
	4	0.2	1.1	4.1	8.9	14.3
		21.0	39.6	25.1	14.3	100.0

3 relative to period 2.[21] As can be seen, there is quite a bit of persistence in location patterns. The majority of MNEs that serve either two, three, or four locations in period 2 also do so in period 3. A clear exception is the share of MNEs serving just one location: in period 3 the share of MNEs employing inventors in two locations increases by approximately 3 percentage points, which is more than compensated for by a decrease in the share of MNEs serving one market in period 3. The share of MNEs employing inventors in three locations also increases by approximately 0.5 percentage points. Hence overall we observe an increase (over time) in the number of locations in which the MNEs in our sample employ inventors.

Figure 11.1 shows the development of high-skill wages in the three different locations during our sample period. Wages have slightly increased during the sample period in WEU and CSEU. For the United States, the picture looks quite different. There is a strong increase between the first and second period (approximately €11) and a substantial drop between the second and third period (approximately €7). It should be noted that these results to some extent are an artifact of the introduction of the euro in 2001 and the strong development of the euro-dollar exchange rate during the period following this introduction. Also, the comparison between WEU and CSEU on one hand and USA on the other is somewhat blurred by the fact that the wages in WEU and CSEU are averages of multiple countries.

To further illustrate this latter point, consider figure 11.2, which plots the development of hourly high-skill wages in the eight individual MNE home countries (all of which, except Italy, are part of the WEU country group). This figure illustrates that there is substantial cross-country variation in both the *levels* of wages, as well as the *development* of wages over time. In terms of levels, Belgium and the United Kingdom

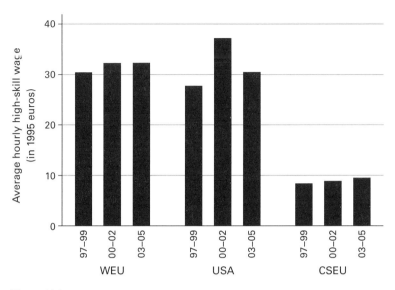

Figure 11.1
Hourly high-skill wages in constant (1995) euros.

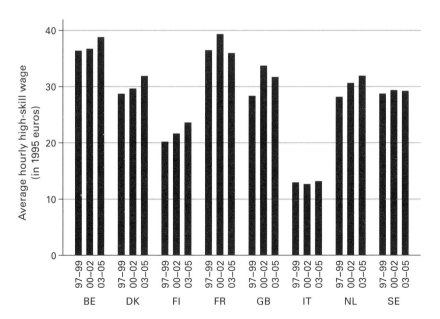

Figure 11.2
Hourly high-skill wages in constant (1995) euros.

are at the upper end of the distribution and Italy is clearly at the lower end. In terms of wage developments, most countries have experienced a general increase in (average) high-skill wage rates, although France and the United Kingdom are two clear exceptions, with trends similar to those of the United States in figure 11.1.

Finally, table 11.5 presents some descriptive statistics and cross-correlations for the different dependent and independent variables included in the model(s). The correlations between the three different wage variables are rather high, especially between WEU wages and CSEU wages. Given that these wages are incorporated simultaneously in estimating equations (3) and (6), a multicollinearity problem might arise. As to our knowledge there are no other, more disaggregated wage data available, we have to accept this high degree of correlation and be cautious of it when interpreting the results.

11.5   Empirical Results

In order to determine the extent of inventor substitution or complementarity, as well as the importance of correcting for extensive margin location decisions, we proceed in two steps. First, we estimate the inventor cost share equations in equation (11.2) by means of SUR techniques without correcting for first-stage selection. After having derived the relevant wage and substitution elasticities, we then estimate the model in two stages: first the univariate location-specific selection equations in equation (11.3), and second the corrected system of stage-two inventor demand equations in equation (11.6).

Columns (1) through (3) in table 11.6 present the uncorrected SUR estimation results. The WEU wage coefficient is negative and significant in the WEU model and positive and significant in the USA model. For the USA wage coefficient, these results are exactly reversed. We also find a positive effect of the MNE-level patent count on inventor cost shares in WEU and USA. In the CSEU model, none of the coefficients are significant. Moreover, the explanatory power of all three models is rather low.

As mentioned earlier, the wage coefficients in table 11.6 are uninformative. Therefore, table 11.7 computes the wage and (Morishima) substitution elasticities as given by equations (11.7) and (11.10). First consider the wage elasticities: all own-wage elasticities are negative, as expected, except for the CSEU own wage elasticity, although this is not significant. In fact, only HOME's own wage elasticity is

Table 11.5
Sample descriptives and correlation matrix

		Mean	St. Dev.	1.	2.	3.	4.	5.	6.	7.	8.	9.	10.	11.	12.	13.	14.	15.	16.
1.	WEU presence	0.63	0.48	1															
2.	USA presence	0.45	0.50	0.22	1														
3.	CSEU presence	0.23	0.42	0.21	0.25	1													
4.	WEU costshare	0.16	0.22	0.58	-0.04	0.04	1												
5.	USA costshare	0.10	0.19	0.02	0.60	0.06	-0.11	1											
6.	CSEU costshare	0.01	0.04	-0.08	-0.03	0.37	-0.03	-0.03	1										
7.	WEU wage[a]	3.51	0.30	-0.07	0.00	-0.10	0.01	0.09	0.04	1									
8.	USA wage[a]	3.69	0.38	-0.10	0.01	-0.10	-0.03	0.12	0.00	0.84	1								
9.	CSEU wage[a]	2.40	0.38	-0.06	-0.02	-0.09	0.04	0.07	0.06	0.95	0.76	1							
10.	Firm age[b]	25.4	32.7	0.23	0.20	0.18	0.13	0.15	0.03	0.01	-0.03	0.01	1						
11.	No. of subsidiaries[b]	16.2	47.5	0.16	0.11	0.17	0.06	0.00	0.01	-0.09	-0.09	-0.08	0.25	1					
12.	Operating revenue[a,b]	11.6	3.17	0.22	0.21	0.21	0.15	0.14	0.03	0.15	0.04	0.16	0.38	0.28	1				
13.	Capital–labour ratio[a,b]	4.73	1.71	0.12	0.06	0.13	0.06	-0.03	0.00	-0.11	-0.14	-0.07	0.08	0.12	0.05	1			
14.	WEU academic articles[b]	2,303	535	0.12	0.00	0.06	0.08	-0.11	-0.03	-0.19	-0.28	-0.14	-0.03	0.00	0.00	0.24	1		
15.	USA academic articles[b]	24,641	5,579	0.09	0.02	0.11	0.02	-0.10	-0.04	-0.44	-0.51	-0.40	-0.02	0.07	-0.04	0.26	0.83	1	
16.	CSEU academic articles[b]	1,139	277	0.01	0.09	0.06	-0.03	0.00	-0.03	0.09	-0.16	0.04	0.04	0.00	0.07	0.09	0.66	0.66	1
17.	Total (firm-level) patents[a]	1.91	1.48	0.50	0.47	0.54	0.20	0.15	0.02	-0.09	-0.12	-0.08	0.42	0.31	0.46	0.24	0.16	0.17	0.09

Table 11.6
SUR estimation results (corrected and uncorrected)

	Uncorrected			Corrected		
	(1)	(2)	(3)	(4)	(5)	(6)
	WEU	USA	CSEU	WEU	USA	CSEU
HOME	−0.026	−0.010	−0.006	−0.078*	−0.124***	−0.083**
wages	(0.019)	(0.015)	(0.004)	(0.040)	(0.047)	(0.042)
WEU wages	0.087**	−0.065**	0.004	0.054	−0.039	0.063
	(0.039)	(0.026)	(0.017)	(0.179)	(0.263)	(0.19)
USA wages	−0.065**	0.085***	−0.010	−0.039	0.188***	−0.025
	(0.026)	(0.025)	(0.007)	(0.065)	(0.075)	(0.036)
CSEU wages	0.004	−0.010	0.012	0.063	−0.025	0.044
	(0.017)	(0.007)	(0.012)	(0.119)	(0.171)	(0.15)
Total patents	0.023***	0.016***	0.001	−0.076*	−0.176***	−0.007
	(0.005)	(0.004)	(0.001)	(0.044)	(0.045)	(0.017)
Normal PDF				−0.005	−0.024**	−0.005
				(0.008)	(0.011)	(0.004)
Constant/	0.104***	0.023	0.019	0.372	0.335	0.114
NormalCDF	(0.025)	(0.017)	(0.014)	(0.265)	(0.435)	(0.258)
R-squared	0.029	0.024	0.009	0.400	0.338	0.075
Observations	924	924	924	924	924	924
All firms	462	462	462	462	462	462

Notes: Dependent variables are inventor cost shares in WEU, USA, and CSEU. Robust standard errors within parentheses. Total patents measured in logs. * = $p < 0.1$; ** = $p < 0.05$; *** = $p < 0.01$.

significant, implying that a 1 percent increase in HOME wages reduces HOME inventor employment by 0.2 percent. The HOME-WEU and HOME-USA cross-wage elasticities are also significant, and positive in both directions, implying substitution. Note that the "column" elasticities are substantially smaller than the "row" elasticities, implying that HOME inventor demand is substantially less responsive to WEU and USA wage changes than WEU and USA inventor demand to HOME wage changes. The estimated elasticities fall largely within the range [0.15, 0.75] as reported in Hamermesh (1993), who provides a survey of different studies up until 1990.

The bottom of table 11.7 reports Morishima substitution elasticities. These numbers clearly show the consequence of the asymmetric wage elasticities on the cross-country substitution elasticities.[22] In particular, the HOME-WEU and HOME-USA substitution elasticities have lost their significance in the first column but remain significant in the row.

Table 11.7
Uncorrected wage and substitution elasticities

		Inventor demand change in l			
	Wage elasticities	HOME	WEU	USA	CSEU
Wage	HOME	−0.202***	0.575***	0.638***	−0.02
change in k		(0.045)	(0.179)	(0.225)	(0.534)
	WEU	0.121***	−0.286	−0.531	0.697
		(0.038)	(0.773)	(1.513)	(2.579)
	USA	0.082***	−0.324	−0.011	−1.149
		(0.029)	(0.261)	(0.392)	(0.911)
	CSEU	0	0.035	−0.095	0.472
		(0.006)	(0.522)	(0.922)	(2.306)

		Inventor demand change in l relative to k			
	Morishima elasticities	HOME	WEU	USA	CSEU
	HOME	−0.202***	0.777***	0.840***	0.182
		(0.045)	(0.213)	(0.25)	(0.545)
	WEU	0.407	−0.286	−0.245	0.983
		(0.782)	(0.773)	(1.722)	(2.698)
	USA	0.093	−0.313	−0.011	−1.137
		(0.396)	(0.485)	(0.392)	(1.001)
	CSEU	−0.472	−0.437	−0.567	0.472
		(2.308)	(2.397)	(2.452)	(2.306)

Notes: Bootstrapped standard errors within parentheses (500 draws). * = $p < 0.1$; ** = $p < 0.05$; *** = $p < 0.01$.

That is, a 1 percent increase in HOME wages increases WEU inventor demand by 0.86 percent relative to HOME inventor demand, yet the reverse effect is absent, and the HOME-USA inventor substitution yields similar results. These results are a natural consequence of the wage elasticities reported in the top panel of table 11.7. An increase in HOME wages significantly reduces HOME inventor demand while simultaneously increasing WEU and USA inventor demand. Hence the change in the *ratio* of the two following a HOME wage increase is unambiguously positive. However, due to the absence of significant own-wage effects in WEU and USA, reverse substitution is (statistically) absent, because the rise in HOME inventor demand following WEU or USA wage increases is not reinforced by simultaneous falls in WEU or USA inventor demand.

We now turn to the two-stage estimation of equations (11.3) and (11.6) in order to investigate whether the MNEs also substitute or complement inventors along the extensive margin and whether this behavior biases the uncorrected estimates. Table 11.8 presents the estimation results of the three univariate probit models. In terms of wage coefficients, we observe only a positive significant effect of HOME wages on CSEU location selection (but recall the high degree of correlation between the different wages in section 11.4). Furthermore, we see a strong and positive effect of past presence on current location decisions, confirming the persistence of location patterns that we already observed in table 11.4. However, there also seems to be cross-location correlation as witnessed by the significance of the "off-diagonal" elements of the lagged presence indicators. Overall, MNEs that employ inventors in any of the foreign locations are also more likely to employ inventors in the remaining ones, which signals the importance of general experience in innovation offshoring (except for MNEs with WEU presence deciding whether to employ inventors in CSEU). The control variables also add some explanatory power: firm age is positive and significant in the WEU and USA models, operating revenue exerts a positive effect on location decisions in all models, and the capital-labor ratio has a weakly positive effect in the CSEU model. Finally, the host location knowledge base—as captured by the number of academic articles—is marginally significant and positive only in the WEU model.

From the estimates in table 11.8 we compute the marginal and cumulative distribution functions—$\hat{\phi}(.)$ and $\hat{\Phi}(.)$—and use these to estimate equation (11.6). Columns (4) through (6) in table 11.6 report the corrected SUR estimation results. The estimates are quite different from those in columns (1) through (3): HOME wages have a negative and significant effect on inventor cost shares in WEU and USA. Moreover, the USA wage has a strong and positive effect on the USA inventor cost share. The normal probability density function enters only the WEU model significantly and negatively. The explanatory power of the CSEU model increases slightly, and that of the WEU and USA models increases substantially.

Table 11.9 presents the corrected wage and substitution elasticities, derived using the formulation in equation (11.8). The elasticities have changed substantially relative to the uncorrected ones in table 11.7. First consider the wage elasticities in the top panel: all the elasticities in the first column have lost their significance, as have the elasticities in the first row, except for the HOME-WEU elasticity, which has decreased

Table 11.8
Probit estimates

	(1)	(2)	(3)
	WEU	USA	CSEU
HOME wage	0.006	0.006	0.014**
	(0.006)	(0.006)	(0.006)
WEU wage	−0.011	0.014	−0.032
	(0.021)	(0.019)	(0.024)
USA wage	−0.006	−0.001	−0.000
	(0.004)	(0.004)	(0.005)
CSEU wage	0.013	−0.034	0.022
	(0.035)	(0.032)	(0.042)
WEU presence	0.753***	0.169*	0.089
	(0.105)	(0.096)	(0.110)
USA presence	0.175*	1.031***	0.354***
	(0.097)	(0.100)	(0.104)
CSEU presence	0.366***	0.518***	1.150***
	(0.135)	(0.121)	(0.125)
Firm age	0.006***	0.003**	0.002
	(0.002)	(0.002)	(0.002)
No. of subsidiaries	0.003	0.000	0.001
	(0.004)	(0.001)	(0.001)
(Log) Operating revenue	0.030*	0.028*	0.037**
	(0.018)	(0.015)	(0.019)
(Log) Capital-labour ratio	0.014	0.004	0.048*
	(0.033)	(0.027)	(0.027)
(Log) Academic articles	0.000*	−0.000	0.000
	(0.000)	(0.000)	(0.000)
Constant	−0.930***	−1.391***	−1.775***
	(0.354)	(0.360)	(0.338)
Observations	924	924	924
Firms	462	462	462
Pseudo R2	0.168	0.195	0.227
Obs. Prob.	0.628	0.453	0.225
Pred. Prob.	0.663	0.453	0.185

Notes: Robust standard errors within parentheses. Coefficients are marginal effects, evaluated at the mean. All variables are one-period lagged values. * = $p < 0.1$; ** = $p < 0.05$; *** = $p < 0.01$.

Table 11.9
Corrected wage and substitution elasticities

		Inventor demand change in l			
Wage change in k	Wage elasticities	HOME	WEU	USA	CSEU
	HOME	0.126 (0.102)	0.493** (0.218)	0.191 (0.244)	−1.606 (1.183)
	WEU	0.05 (0.064)	−0.742 (0.693)	0.091 (0.345)	1.913 (3.578)
	USA	−0.073 (0.066)	−0.159 (0.275)	−0.019 (0.364)	−0.609 (0.959)
	CSEU	−0.104 (0.064)	0.323 (0.506)	−0.207 (0.192)	0.327 (2.967)
		Inventor demand change in l relative to k			
	Morishima elasticities	HOME	WEU	USA	CSEU
	HOME	0.126 (0.102)	0.368 (0.279)	0.066 (0.309)	−1.732 (1.235)
	WEU	0.792 (0.716)	−0.742 (0.693)	0.833 (0.913)	2.654 (4.168)
	USA	−0.053 (0.406)	−0.14 (0.58)	−0.019 (0.364)	−0.589 (1.038)
	CSEU	−0.43 (2.994)	−0.004 (3.391)	−0.534 (2.933)	0.327 (2.967)

Notes: Bootstrapped standard errors within parentheses (500 draws). * = $p < 0.1$; ** = $p < 0.05$; *** = $p < 0.01$.

somewhat in value but only marginally so. Not correcting for selection induces a substitution bias in the WEU-HOME, USA-HOME, and HOME-USA wage elasticities (compare Muendler and Becker 2010); that is, they are biased upward. Once we account for the selection bias, we no longer find any substitution between HOME and USA. Although the other corrected wage elasticities are not significant, there are some notable changes in their magnitudes. For instance, the HOME-CSEU elasticity increases from small and negative in table 11.7 to big and negative in table 11.9, again suggesting substitution bias in the uncorrected results.[23] The opposite happens to the WEU-CSEU elasticity, which changes from small and positive before correction to large and positive after correction. This result suggests a complementarity bias when not correcting for the extensive margin. Moreover, the own wage elasticities of all three foreign locations are also substantially affected. In particular, the USA and CSEU own wage elasticities flip signs, from negative to positive and vice versa, respectively

These wage elasticity adjustments following selection corrections naturally carry over to the substitution elasticities reported in the lower panel of table 11.9. In particular, the HOME-WEU and the HOME-USA elasticities are no longer significant. Note that the changes in WEU and USA inventor employment relative to HOME employment following a change in HOME wages are no longer reinforced by a (significant) change in HOME inventor demand. For the HOME-WEU substitution elasticity, the increase in WEU inventor employment following an increase in HOME wage apparently is not strong enough to yield a significant substitution elasticity.

Taken together, these results clearly suggest that location selection introduces bias when not accounted for. In order to analyze this finding more explicitly, table 11.10 decomposes the extensive and intensive margin inventor employment adjustments.[24] The first column in both panels reproduces the numbers from the first columns in table 11.9 because HOME is not an optional location, and hence its inventor employment effects cannot be decomposed into an extensive and intensive margin.

First, again consider the wage elasticities reported in the top panel of the table. The first noteworthy result is that the impact of HOME wages on foreign inventor employment goes through the extensive margin for each foreign location and that the effects are quite substantial. In particular, a 1 percent increase in HOME wages increases WEU, USA, and CSEU inventor employment through location/relocation by approximately 0.75 to 0.8 percent. Only for the WEU is there an additional and significant impact on intensive margin inventor employment. Closer inspection of the different margins also sheds light on the differences in elasticities between tables 11.9 and 11.7: for instance, the large drop and insignificance of the HOME-USA wage elasticity appears to be caused mainly by an intensive margin elasticity that is close to 0. Conversely, the substantial decrease in the HOME-CSEU wage elasticity is almost solely driven by the strongly negative (yet insignificant) intensive margin elasticity.

A second notable result is that all extensive margin own-wage elasticities are negative and significant. In addition, they are remarkably similar in magnitude, implying that a 1 percent increase in a (foreign) location's own wage induces a 0.9 percent decrease in inventor employment along the extensive margin (which is remarkably more sensitive

Table 11.10
Corrected wage and substitution elasticities—Extensive and intensive margins

Wage change in k	Wage elasticities	Inventor demand change in l						
		HOME	WEU		USA		CSEU	
		Overall	Ext	Int	Ext	Int	Ext	Int
HOME		0.126	0.809***	0.426**	0.787***	0.145	0.762***	-1.627
		(0.102)	(0.075)	(0.195)	(0.049)	(0.234)	(0.251)	(1.094)
WEU		0.05	-0.961***	-0.625	0.279*	-0.033	0.101	1.967
		(0.064)	(0.236)	(0.619)	(0.164)	(0.298)	(0.728)	(3.132)
USA		-0.073	-0.001	-0.064	-0.921***	-0.003	0.095	-0.608
		(0.066)	(0.08)	(0.251)	(0.064)	(0.348)	(0.125)	(0.948)
CSEU		-0.104	0.068	0.263	-0.09	-0.11	-0.933***	0.268
		(0.064)	(0.165)	(0.442)	(0.099)	(0.164)	(0.118)	(2.946)

	Morishima elasticities	Inventor demand change in l relative to k						
		HOME	WEU		USA		CSEU	
		Overall	Ext	Int	Ext	Int	Ext	Int
	HOME	0.126	0.683***	0.3	0.662***	0.02	0.637***	-1.753
		(0.102)	(0.125)	(0.263)	(0.115)	(0.301)	(0.269)	(1.152)
	WEU	0.792	-0.961***	-0.625	1.24***	0.928	1.062	2.928
		(0.716)	(0.236)	(0.619)	(0.284)	(0.826)	(0.774)	(3.685)
	USA	-0.053	0.921***	0.858	-0.921***	-0.003	1.016***	0.313
		(0.406)	(0.098)	(0.551)	(0.064)	(0.348)	(0.141)	(1.019)
	CSEU	-0.43	1.001***	1.197	0.844***	0.824	-0.933***	0.268
		(2.994)	(0.195)	(3.332)	(0.145)	(2.906)	(0.118)	(2.946)

Notes: Bootstrapped standard errors within parentheses (500 draws). $* = p < 0.1$; $** = p < 0.05$; $*** = p < 0.01$.

than HOME's insignificant overall own-wage elasticity). At the same time, none of the intensive margin own-wage elasticities are significant. Again, the separate margin effects illuminate some of the differences between tables 11.9 and 11.7. For example, for WEU the corrected elasticity drops substantially in magnitude. The reason is that both margins' elasticities are negative and relatively large in absolute magnitude.

Finally, consider the substitution elasticities in the bottom panel of table 11.10. The HOME extensive margin cross-elasticities in the top row are all significant and indicate substitution, whereas the intensive margin cross-elasticities in the top row are all insignificant. These results are driven by both the relatively big extensive margin cross-wage elasticities in the top panel and the fact that both the foreign extensive and intensive cross-wage elasticities are evaluated relative to HOME's own *overall* wage elasticity, which is insignificant. Additionally, the relatively high own-wage elasticities reported in the top panel of the table induce generally significant substitution between foreign locations along the extensive margin as well. With values around 1, these elasticities are rather large. Finally, many of the cross-location extensive margin substitution elasticities for the foreign regions are also positive, significant, and relatively large. This finding indicates that at least at the extensive margin, inventors within MNEs in different foreign locations also function as substitutes to each other.

11.6   Conclusion

We study the extent to which the offshoring of innovation by large (European) MNEs induces substitution or complementarity between inventors in different locations. Our results can be summarized as follows: first, we find evidence of substitution between MNEs' home and foreign inventors. However, this substitution appears to be a one-way street: only foreign employment changes in response to home country wage changes, not the other way around. Moreover, the substitution of foreign inventors for home country inventors occurs only along the extensive margin. Second, once accounting for the extensive and intensive margins, we find that inventors in most foreign locations are substitutes to each other, yet again only along the extensive margin. Finally, foreign inventor employment is also rather own-wage elastic along the extensive margin.

The low responsiveness of home country inventor demand to foreign wage changes, as well as the complete absence of any consequent substitution patterns, suggests that worries about the increase of foreign cheap high-skilled labor might be exaggerated. Our estimates suggest that we should not expect substantial high-skilled home country job displacement following these developments. On the contrary, domestic wage developments appear to be a more acute threat to the amount of high-skill activity performed at home. Our results demonstrate that excessive home country premia over foreign wages induce substitution away from home inventors and toward foreign inventors, yet only through location/relocation decisions. Once an MNE is actually employing inventors abroad, further changes in this employment do not significantly affect home country inventors. Even though we do not find evidence of actual complementarity along the intensive margin, substitution does not seem to take place, either.

Similar conclusions hold for the substitution of inventors across foreign locations. MNEs appear to engage relatively strongly in this type of substitution. However, in these cases, the effects also largely take place through location/relocation decisions, not through (marginal) intensive margin employment decisions. Taken together, our results imply that when MNEs start innovation activities abroad from scratch, this move might substantially affect inventors in all their existing locations (both domestic and foreign). Yet changes in inventor employment in existing operations leave the demand for inventors elsewhere relatively unaffected.

Our study also suffers from a number of shortcomings that open up avenues for future research. Our sample of countries only includes (mostly) developed European countries and the United States. Some important newly developing and high-growth countries—notably Brazil, Russia, India, and China (BRIC)—are missing from the sample, even though many of the current political discussions center around these exact countries. Even though our patent data indicate that only a minority of inventors employed by the MNEs in our sample are located in these countries, extending the analyses to these countries should still be of interest. This work also requires the availability of reasonably disaggregated and accurate wage data.[25]

Second, in our analyses we have aggregated together all firms and patents, ignoring potential differences between industries. Yet several studies have demonstrated that the extent and patterns of innovation offshoring differ substantially across industries or even individual patent technology classes, making it likely that the relevance of such distinctionsalso hold for employment consequences (e.g., Pavitt 1984; Cantwell 1995; Ambos 2005; Fifarek and Veloso 2010). Due to the limited number of MNEs in our sample, as well as the rather substantial estimation demands, we have not been able to tackle this issue. Our results should consequently be interpreted as broad averages over decision-making processes in heterogeneous environments. Investigating the differential substitution and complementarity patterns for different industries would be a fruitful avenue for future research.

Third, our estimation procedure puts quite severe restrictions on the correlations between the different error terms, both within the first-stage selection equation and between the first-stage and second-stage equations. Allowing for more flexible correlation structures—as in Yen 2005, for example—should improve upon the accuracy of the estimated effects, as well as the efficiency of estimation. Alternatively, other first-stage selection models (such as multinomial logit models) might be considered instead.

Finally, our study does not say anything about the implied welfare effects of any of the substitution or complementarity patterns considered here. A natural question that arises is whether in the aggregate the displacement of home country inventors is welfare improving. The answer to this question depends not only on the productivity changes experienced by the (home country) operations of the MNEs but also on the efficiency and effectiveness to which the freed labor is reallocated toward different activities.

Notes

The first author was a visiting scholar at the IFS during the initial stages of this project. He would like to thank the IFS for its hospitality, as well as the CPB Netherlands Bureau for Economic Policy Research for providing funding. We would further like to thank Richard Blundell, Rachel Griffith, Helen Miller, Lars Nesheim, and the participants at the CESifo 2011 Summer Institute for useful discussions and suggestions. Any remaining errors are our own.

1. This assumption is not as restrictive as it may seem at first sight, because most R&D expenditure usually goes to R&D staff in wages and salaries. For example, in the United States in 2006, around half of total business R&D expenditure was in salaries and wages (compare table 6 in NSF 2011). Nevertheless, if one is concerned about not including other important inputs, then we need to know how this could bias our results. In this case, we measure the substitution along an isoinventor curve, instead of an isoquant, so what we estimate is an upper bound of the elasticity of substitution between inventors in different locations, given that we are not allowing for substitution with other inputs (compare Hamermesh 1993, 67–68). Also, because the firm's market share in the market for technologies is assumed constant by holding the number of patents constant, we do not attempt to consider scale effects that can affect the employment of inventors worldwide and can have an impact in the reallocation of activity within an industry across firms. Presumably, for these types of firms market share is endogenous, so we will have to take this into account when interpreting our results; not allowing for scale effects when

they exist usually makes the estimates an upper bound (compare Hamermesh 1993, 24–25; 73–74).

2. In our sample, all patents are assigned to applicants (i.e., the parent or one of its subsidiaries) so that patents can potentially be assigned to locations l. This setup would call for a multiproduct (i.e., multilocation) cost function approach as in Muendler and Becker 2010. However, inputs and outputs (patents) of the innovative process are easily separable, and MNEs often strategically decide where to hold their intellectual property (Griffith, Miller, and O'Connell 2011). Therefore, we consider knowledge output at the MNE level rather than in each specific location.

3. Our research methodology assumes that all inputs are supplied elastically to the firm in a competitive labor market. If not, the quantity of the factor cannot be adjusted (and demand elasticities are reduced). Labor markets might not be competitive for multinational firms and highly skilled workers, such as inventors, and hence the cost function will not be first-degree homogeneous in paid wages. However, the cost function can still be first-degree homogenous in reservation wages as measured by outside average wages in each location, and these are exogenous to the firm (Muendler and Becker 2010).

4. Of course, the opposite can also occur, such as when MNEs that employ foreign inventors can make a credible relocation threat, hence commanding relatively low home wages. Because we have no a priori expectation of which situation is more likely to occur, we cannot be sure about the estimation bias without accounting for selection.

5. Estimating separate first-stage (probit) selection models assumes that there is no correlation between first-stage location selection decisions other than that included in the set of conditioning variables. Moreover, correcting location l inventor demand by location l selection only does not allow for cross-location selection and demand correlation other than through firm-specific shocks. See Muendler and Becker 2010 for a detailed explanation.

6. More specifically, explanatory variables are interacted with presence dummies, taking a value of 1 when a MNE is present in a particular location and 0 otherwise. Stacking the data in this way appears problematic, as it induces endogeneity of the modified explanatory variables with respect to inventor demand. Moreover, Shonkwiler and Yen (1999) and Chen and Yen (2005) demonstrate that correcting the second-stage demand system by location-specific inverse Mill's ratios does not repair the selection bias. Specifically, the unconditional expectation reduces to the uncorrected second-stage equation in the limit—that is, when the latent variable approaches $-\infty$, in which case it *should* reduce to 0. The resulting estimates can be shown to be biased.

7. This equation is derived from the fact that—when estimating the first stage by means of probit—$\Pr(d_{it}^l = 1) = \Phi(h(\mathbf{x}_{it-1}^l \beta))$ and that $E(S_{it}^l \mid z_{it}^l, x_{it-1}^l, d_{it}^l = 0) = 0$.

8. Yen (2005) derives a maximum likelihood estimator that allows for a full set of nonzero and nonconstant error covariances (both within and between first- and second-stage equations). However, this estimation procedure is computationally intensive, as it requires evaluation of multiple probability integrals (compare Chen and Yen 2005).

9. The symmetry of the Allen elasticity of substitution follows from the (imposed) symmetry in the translog cost function, that is, $\gamma_{lk} = \gamma_{kl}$. However, note that this property no longer holds when correcting for first-stage selection, as should be clear from equation (11.8): $(\partial S_{it}^l / \partial w_t^k \neq \partial S_{it}^k / \partial w_t^l)$.

10. Note that because of this definition, there is no natural own substitution elasticity definition.

11. The countries are Belgium, Czech Republic, Denmark, Finland, France, Germany, Greece, Italy, Ireland, Luxembourg, Netherlands, Norway, Poland, Portugal, Spain, Sweden, Switzerland, United Kingdom, and United States.

12. Note that we cannot rule out that, for example, a UK inventor on the patent of a UK MNE is employed in France, as we have information on only the country of residence of the inventor.

13. As discussed in Lissoni, Sanditov, and Tarasconi 2006, this is a nontrivial issue that requires quite a substantial standardization routine.

14. In fact, comparing the number of unique inventor IDs we created under the second approach with the inventor IDs in the PATSTAT database shows that lowercasing names induces a big drop in inventor counts. The subsequent parsing and combination or recombination of different name parts reduces the inventor count only minimally.

15. Muendler and Becker (2010) also demonstrate that in a model of entry with sunk costs, the selection equation can be rewritten completely in terms of past presence indicators.

16. Data for national academic publications in different academic fields are taken from the NSF (2010). We follow the approach in Abramovsky and Simpson 2011 and use a survey by Cohen and colleagues (2002) to link academic publications to the industries based on the importance of public research by academic discipline for different industries (see table 3 in Cohen et al. 2002). For service industries (not covered in Cohen et al. 2002), we use an arithmetic average of publications in all academic fields as the publication count.

17. We tend to lose quite a number of observations due to missing data on some of these MNE-level controls. In order to retain a sufficiently large sample, we impute missing data with home country (four-digit) industry-specific averages. For the remaining missing data, we then use home country (two-digit) industry-specific averages as imputations.

18. Note that we have excluded Ireland, Luxembourg, Norway, and Switzerland from the analysis. The first two countries have a very small patent count in general, and almost no foreign firms employ any inventors there. For Norway and Switzerland, EU KLEMS does not provide (wage) data. We have also experimented with different partitioning of the country sample—in particular, adding Sweden, Finland, and Denmark together under SCAN, as well as Poland and the Czech Republic under CEU. However, this approach resulted in very small inventor counts in both groups, heavily biasing the computed wage and substitution elasticities.

19. We use the priority year, as this is the year that is closest to the actual date of innovation (e.g., Ernst 2001). Because there might be a lag between the actual inventive activity and the priority year, this approach could induce a bias in our estimates. The fact that we aggregate individual years into three-year time periods partly alleviates this issue. For example, if the inventive activity of a patent with priority year 1999 was actually conducted in 1998 or 1997, we still capture it in period 1. Because we do not know the patent or even firm-specific time lags between innovation and patent application, it is impossible to correct for this bias in our estimates.

20. These eight home countries are the United Kingdom, Italy, France, the Netherlands, Sweden, Finland, Denmark, and Belgium. In the other countries, at least one of our three aggregate foreign locations was absent in the foreign employment decisions of the relevant MNEs. Because we want to establish inventor substitution (complementarity)

between all four locations, we decided not to consider these countries as home locations. The exception is Germany: even though German MNEs employ inventors in all locations, their share of home country employment is close to 90 percent, which strongly deviates from the average in our sample. Including Germany strongly affects the wage and substitution elasticities because its home country inventor costs share in equation (11.7) is very high (and similarly, the foreign inventor cost shares are very low). As suggested in Farrell 2005, this result might be due to the rather inflexible labor market in Germany, making it difficult for German firms (MNEs) to lay off domestic workers in response to offshoring opportunities.

21. Note that because the selection model in equation (11.3) uses lagged regressors, we estimate the inventor demand model in equation (11.6) for only the periods 2 and 3.

22. We report the own-wage elasticities on the diagonal of the Morishima substitution elasticity matrix, but note (as before) that this elasticity has no natural "own" elasticity interpretation.

23. Note that the negative elasticities imply complementarity. Hence the change from a small negative elasticity before correction to a big negative elasticity after correction implies that the uncorrected results were biased toward substitution.

24. Note that although this decomposition is additive in equation (11.8), it is not after substituting equation (11.8) into equation (11.7). We follow the approach in Muendler and Becker (2010) and put one of the two margins in equation (11.8) to 0 in order to compute the impact of a wage change on the other margin.

25. In this respect, it is noteworthy to point out ongoing efforts to collect similar statistics for these (and other) countries as those provided by EU KLEMS. See http://www .worldklems.net for more information.

References

Abramovsky, L., R. Griffith, G. MacCartney, and H. Miller. 2008. The location of innovation activity in Europe. IFS Working Paper 08-10.

Abramovsky, L., and H. Simpson. 2011. Geographic proximity and firm-university innovation linkages: Evidence from Great Britain. *Journal of Economic Geography* 11 (6): 949–977.

Allen, R. G. 1938. *Mathematical Analysis for Economists*. London: Macmillan.

Ambos, B. 2005. Foreign direct investment in industrial research and development: A study of German MNEs. *Research Policy* 34 (4): 395–410.

Amemiya, T. 1984. Tobit models: a survey. *Journal of Economic Literature* 24 (1–2): 3–61.

Amiti, M., and S.-J. Wei. 2009. Service offshoring and productivity: Evidence from the US. *World Economy* 32 (2): 203–220.

Berndt, E. R., and D. O. Wood. 1975. Technology, prices, and the derived demand for energy. *Review of Economics and Statistics* 57 (3): 259–268.

Binswanger, H. P. 1974. A cost function approach to the measurement of elasticities of factor demand and elasticities of substitution. *American Journal of Agricultural Economics* 56 (2): 377–386.

Blackorby, C., and R. R. Russell. 1989. Will the real elasticity of substitution please stand up? (A comparison of the Allen/Uzawa and Morishima elasticities.) *American Economic Review* 79 (4): 882–888.

Braconier, H., and K. Ekholm. 2000. Swedish multinationals and competition from high and low-wage locations. *Review of International Economics* 8 (3): 448–461.

Brainard, S. L., and D. A. Riker. 1997. Are US multinationals exporting us jobs? NBER Working Paper 5958.

Branstetter, L., R. Fisman, and C. F. Foley. 2006. Do stronger intellectual property rights increase international technology transfer? *Quarterly Journal of Economics* 121 (1): 321–349.

Cantwell, J. 1995. The globalisation of technology: What remains of the product cycle model? *Cambridge Journal of Economics* 19 (1): 155–174.

Cantwell, J., and R. Mudambi. 2005. MNE competence-creating subsidiary mandates. *Strategic Management Journal* 26 (12): 1109–1128.

Chen, Z., and S. Yen. 2005. On bias correction in the multivariate sample-selection model. *Applied Economics* 37 (21): 2459–2468.

Cohen, W. M., R. R. Nelson, and J. P. Walsh. 2002. Links and impacts: The influence of public research on industrial R&D. *Management Science* 48 (1): 1–23.

Demirbag, M., and K. W. Glaister. 2010. Factors determining offshore location choice for R&D projects: A comparative study of developed and emerging regions. *Journal of Management Studies* 47 (8): 1534–1560.

Desai, M. A., C. F. Foley, and J. R. Hines. 2009. Domestic effects of the foreign activities of US multinationals. *American Economic Journal: Economic Policy* 1 (1): 181–203.

Ernst, H. 2001. Patent applications and subsequent changes of performance: Evidence from time-series cross-section analyses on the firm level. *Research Policy* 30 (1): 143–157.

Farrell, D. 2005. Offshoring: Value creation through economic change. *Journal of Management Studies* 42 (3): 675–683.

Fifarek, B., and F. Veloso. 2010. Offshoring and the global geography of innovation. *Journal of Economic Geography* 10 (4): 559–578.

Garcia-Vega, M., and E. Huergo. 2013. Multinationals' technology transfers and firms' performance. In *Firms in the International Economy: Closing the Gap between International Economics and Business*, 287–316. Cambridge, MA: MIT Press.

Griffith, R., R. Harrison, and J. van Reenen. 2006. How special is the special relationship? Using the impact of US spillovers on UK firms as a test of technology sourcing. *American Economic Review* 96 (5): 857–875.

Griffith, R., H. Miller, and M. O'Connell. 2011. Corporate taxes and the location of intellectual property. CEPR Discussion Paper 8424.

Hamermesh, D. 1993. *Labor Demand*. Princeton: Princeton University Press.

Harrison, A., and M. McMillan. 2011. Offshoring jobs? Multinationals and US manufacturing employment. *Review of Economics and Statistics* 93 (3): 857–875.

Heckman, J. 1979. Sample selection bias as a specification bias. *Econometrica* 47 (1): 153–161.

Hummels, D., J. Ishii, and K.-M. Yi. 2001. The nature and growth of vertical specialization in world trade. *Journal of International Economics* 54 (1): 75–96.

Jensen, P. D. O., and T. Pedersen. 2011. The economic geography of offshoring: The fit between activities and local context. *Journal of Management Studies* 48 (2): 352–372.

Kuemmerle, W. 1999. Foreign direct investment in industrial research in the pharmaceutical and electronics industries—Results from a survey of multinational firms. *Research Policy* 28 (2–3): 179–193.

Le Bas, C., and C. Sierra. 2002. Location versus home country advantages in R&D activities: Some further results on multinationals' location strategies. *Research Policy* 31 (4): 589–609.

Lewin, A. Y., S. Massini, and C. Peeters. 2009. Why are companies offshoring innovation? The emerging global race for talent. *Journal of International Business Studies* 40 (6): 901–925.

Lissoni, F., B. Sanditov, and G. Tarasconi. 2006. The KEINS database and academic inventors: methodology and contents. CESPRI Working Paper 181.

Mankiw, N. G., and P. L. Swagel. 2006. The politics and economics of offshore outsourcing. *Journal of Monetary Economics* 53 (3): 1027–1056.

Muendler, M.-A., and S. O. Becker. 2010. Margins of multinational labor substitution. *American Economic Review* 100 (5): 1999–2030.

NSF. 2010. *Science and Engineering Indicators 2010*. Arlington, VA: National Science Foundation.

NSF. 2011. *Research and Development in Industry: 2006–07*. Arlington, VA: National Science Foundation.

O'Mahoney, M., and M. Timmer. 2009. Output, input, and productivity measures at the industry level: The EU KLEMS database. *Economic Journal* 119 (538): F374–F402.

Pavitt, K. 1984. Sectoral patterns of technical change: towards a taxonomy and a theory. *Research Policy* 13 (6): 343–373.

Roberts, M., and J. Tybout. 1997. The decision to export in Colombia: an empirical model of entry with sunk costs. *American Economic Review* 87 (4): 545–564.

Shonkwiler, J. S., and S. T. Yen. 1999. Two-step estimation of a censored system of equations. *American Journal of Agricultural Economics* 81 (4): 972–982.

Su, S.-J. B., and S. T. Yen. 2000. A censored system of cigarette and alcohol consumption. *Applied Economics* 32 (6): 972–982.

Timmer, M., T. van Moergastel, E. Stuivewold, and G. Ypma. (2007). EU KLEMS growth and productivity accounts, version 1.0, part I, methodology. http://euklems.net.

UNCTAD. 2005. World Investment Report 2005. TNCs and the internationalization of R&D. United Nations Conference on Trade and Development, New York and Geneva.

Vernon, R. 1966. International investment and international trade in the product cycle. *Quarterly Journal of Economics* 80 (2): 190–207.

Yen, S. T. 2005. A multivariate sample-selection model: estimating cigarette and alcohol demands with zero observations. *American Journal of Agricultural Economics* 87 (2): 453–466.

12 Heterogeneous Firms, Trade, and Economic Policy: Insights from a Simple Two-Sector Model

Michael Pflüger and Stephan Russek

12.1 Introduction

The robust empirical finding that exporting firms are not only rare but also systematically different from firms that merely serve domestic consumers has challenged both the old Ricardian and neoclassical trade theories as well as the new trade theories along the lines of Krugman, Brander, and Spencer. To account for the empirical fact that exporting firms are typically larger and more productive than nonexporters, a new generation of trade models was developed that takes the heterogeneity of firms in terms of their productivity into account.[1] Seminal models have been developed by Melitz (2003), Bernard et al. (2003), and Yeaple (2005).[2]

A very recent strand of research has started to explore the economic policy implications of these theories of heterogeneous firms and trade. This policy research has looked at a wide spectrum of issues ranging from the gains of trade to the effects of trade liberalization and the role of country asymmetries; it has also dealt with issues such as subsidies to market entry, the research infrastructure, and the role of business conditions that are amenable to government interventions. The aim of this chapter is to synthesize key lessons of this policy research in a unifying analytical framework.

We use a tractable model from which we can generate the results and conclusions from the existing policy literature with utmost simplicity. Our framework builds on Demidova's (2008) two-sector version of the Melitz (2003) model with a competitive sector that produces a "traditional good" in addition to the monopolistically competitive sector with heterogeneous firms ("modern sector"). The shipment of the traditional good is costless, whereas trade costs must be incurred to ship the output of the modern sector. We follow Demidova (2008) in using a CES-Dixit-Stiglitz (1977) utility representation for the varieties produced in the modern sector. However, in contrast to Demidova, we assume a simple standard specification of the research and development process and work with a quasi-linear upper-tier utility function as in Pflüger and Suedekum 2013. These two changes allow us to gain the tractability that is needed to generate the policy implications as closed-form results.[3]

It is worthwhile to reflect on the simplifying assumptions that underpin our framework. Note that quasi-linear preferences eliminate income effects from the modern sector and that the introduction of a traditional good that is produced under constant returns to scale implies that the real wage in terms of this good is fixed and the terms of trade are tied down. Hence two channels that are often highlighted in general equilibrium trade theory are ruled out. Yet the two assumptions that we impose are very often used in trade and economic geography, for a number of reasons. First, the "traditional sector" is purposefully introduced in order to analyze the workings of the modern sector without interference from conventional terms of trade effects (Helpman and Krugman 1985, 1989). Moreover, even though the real wage is then fixed in terms of the traditional good, it remains variable in terms of the modern good. For example, the real wage is raised in terms of modern goods if productivity improves or trade cost fall for the varieties that are produced by that sector. Second, combining the assumption of the existence of an outside sector with a quasi-linear utility function—even though it gives the model a partial equilibrium flavor because income effects are eliminated—does not remove the interaction between product and labor markets, such that we still have a full-fledged model of trade (Tabuchi and Thisse 2006). Third, quasi-linear preferences have been shown to "behave reasonably well in general equilibrium settings" (Dinopoulos, Fujiwara, and Shimomura 2011; Combes, Mayer, and Thisse 2008). Finally, quasi-linear utility functions have extensively been used to study normative issues in trade and geography (e.g., Ottaviano and Thisse 2002). The reason is that the utilitarian concept of welfare is a valid and reasonable concept under this individual preference specification, as the marginal utility is then constant and income redistributions do not affect aggregate welfare. These considerations and the simplicity implied by these assumptions explains why the recent literature on trade and geography is full with examples that use these twin assumptions (e.g., Ottaviano, Tabuchi, and Thisse 2002; Antràs and Helpman 2004; Melitz and Ottaviano 2008), which also explains why we resort to a model of this type.

Our strategy is to first lay out and solve the model with an extensive list of country characteristics and business conditions under autarky and international trade.[4] Thereafter, we consider tailored versions of the model to trace out key normative results and policy implications that have been derived in the recent policy literature. We preview the main issues in the rest of this section.

Policy analysis was initiated by Melitz (2003), who showed that due to a selection effect, countries reap welfare gains by opening up to trade (i.e., there are gains from trade) and who also showed that reciprocal trade liberalization is welfare enhancing for all parties, again as a result of firm selection. His analysis was confined to a setting where countries are identical in all respects, though. Yet countries do differ along many dimensions, such as size, technologies, and a variety of other business conditions, in practice. Economic policy is a significant determinant of these conditions in a variety of ways. Governments have an impact on the time it takes to set up business and the costs of market entry more generally. The policy environment has a strong influence on a country's level of corruption, on the costs to enforce contracts, and on the costs to provide protection against crime, product piracy, and product imitation. Technology policies shape a country's technology potential. These considerations raise the question of whether Melitz's results still hold when such a diversity of country asymmetries is taken into account.

Recent theoretical research has shown the gains from trade to be robust even when countries are strongly asymmetric in many dimensions (Demidova 2008; Pflüger and Russek 2013a). However, recent work also shows that matters may be different when countries already engage in trade. Technological improvements in one country's modern sector then unambiguously hurt the trading partner (Demidova 2008). When business conditions in a broad sense are superior in one country, trade liberalization brings a welfare benefit to the superior country, whereas the inferior country may experience a welfare loss (Pflüger and Russek 2013a). Moreover, it has also been shown that the liberalization path matters, that is, whether liberalization is unilateral or reciprocal (Melitz and Ottaviano 2008; Pflüger and Russek 2013a). Of course, it is known from traditional trade theory that a country experiences welfare losses when its terms of trade deteriorate. The mechanism of why welfare losses may occur in the new theories of trade with heterogeneous firms is altogether different, however. It is due to a relative improvement of the competitive position of firms in the superior country.[5] The assumption of a traditional sector that rules out terms of trade changes proves useful to clarify the new source of welfare losses.

Further important policy questions have been addressed in recent work. One strand of research recognizes that governments are heavily engaged in the regulation of entry by requiring licenses, permits, and other legal barriers. On the other hand, they also provide various types of support for the foundation of new firms, such as subsidies to market entry and research and development (R&D) activities. Interestingly, in contrast to classical trade policy instruments (such as import tariffs or export subsidies), these policies are perceived as largely domestic issues and are therefore not put under scrutiny by bodies such as the World Trade Organization (WTO). It is nonetheless important to ask whether these policies have international repercussions and how they play out (Pflüger and Suedekum 2013).

The process of market exit is yet another issue that has received attention recently. Melitz (2003) focused on a stationary equilibrium in which firms die with a constant probability irrespectively of their productivity and are replaced by new entrants. However, there is overwhelming empirical evidence showing that highly productive firms are much less prone to firm death than unproductive ones. Incorporating this fact into our theoretical framework delivers insights for the average death rates of mature firms and their determinants. For example, the switch from autarky to trade implies not only an increase in the average productivity of firms but also a reduction in the risk of business exit (Pflüger and Russek 2013b).

The structure of the article is as follows. Section 12.2 covers the model under autarky. Section 12.3 sets up and solves a two-country version. Section 12.4 contains our policy analysis. We successively cover the issues that we previously raised. Section 12.5 provides a brief conclusion.

12.2   The Model

12.2.1   General Setup
A traditional industry n produces a homogeneous numéraire good under constant returns to scale and perfect competition, and a modern monopolistic competitive industry c produces a continuum of differentiated varieties under increasing returns. Each variety is produced by a single firm. Firms' productivities are heterogeneous. Labor is the only

factor of production in the economy. There are L workers who supply one unit of labor each. We first look at a single country in autarky.

12.2.2 Preferences
Household h's preferences over the homogenous good n^h and the set of modern varieties, Ω, are defined by a logarithmic quasi-linear utility function with CES subutility c^h,[6]

$$u^h = \beta \ln c^h + n^h \quad \text{with } c^h = \left[\int_{z \in \Omega} q^h(z)^\rho \, dz \right]^{1/\rho} \tag{12.1}$$

where $0 < \rho < 1$ and $\beta > 0$ are constant parameters and $q^h(z)$ expresses h's consumption of variety z. The elasticity of substitution between any two varieties is given by $\sigma \equiv 1/(1 - \rho) > 1$.

The budget constraint reads $Pc^h + n^h = w$ where w is h's (wage) income and

$$P = \left[\int_{z \in \Omega} p(z)^{1-\sigma} \, dz \right]^{\frac{1}{1-\sigma}} \tag{12.2}$$

is the perfect price index of the CES aggregate. Utility maximization implies demand functions $c^h = \beta/P$ for the modern good and $n^h = w - \beta$ for the traditional good, respectively. Household h's indirect utility is $v^h = w - \beta \ln P + \beta(\ln \beta - 1)$. Because households are identical, we drop the index h from now on. We assume $\beta < w$ to ensure non-negative demand for the homogeneous good. Aggregation over households implies that the overall expenditure on the modern industry, PcL, equals βL. Aggregate demand for variety z is $q(z) = p(z)^{-\sigma} P^{\sigma-1} \beta L$ and total revenue for that variety is $r(z) = p(z)q(z) = [P/p(z)]^{\sigma-1} \beta L$.

12.2.3 Technology and Pricing
The numéraire sector transforms a units of labor into one unit of output. The wage is then pinned down at $w = 1/a$. Technologies in the modern sector are such that $l = f + q/\phi$ units of labor are needed to produce q units of output. The fixed overhead labor f is the same for all firms; the variable labor requirement $(1/\phi)$ differs across firms. Firms have zero mass. Each firm then perceives a demand curve with constant price elasticity $-\sigma$. Profit maximization implies that a firm with marginal cost (w/ϕ) charges the price

$$p(\phi) = \frac{w}{\rho\phi} \tag{12.3}$$

where, using our previous definition, $\rho = (\sigma - 1)/\sigma$. Revenue and profits of this firm are then given by $r(\phi) = \beta L(\rho\phi P/w)^{\sigma-1}$ and $\pi = r(\phi)/\sigma - wf$, respectively. A firm with higher productivity level ϕ charges a lower price, sells a larger quantity, and has higher revenue and profits. Because all firm-specific variables differ only with respect to ϕ, the CES price index in equation (12.2) can be rewritten as

$$P = M^{1/(1-\sigma)} p(\tilde{\phi}) = M^{1/(1-\sigma)} \frac{w}{\rho\tilde{\phi}} \text{ where } \tilde{\phi} \equiv \left[\int_0^\infty \varphi^{\sigma-1} \cdot \mu(\varphi) d\varphi \right]^{1/(\sigma-1)} \tag{12.4}$$

and where M denotes the mass of manufacturing firms (and varieties) in the market, $\mu(\phi)$ is the productivity distribution across these active firms with positive support over a subset of $(0,\infty)$ and $\tilde{\phi}$ is an average productivity level as introduced by Melitz (2003).

12.2.4   Entry and Exit

There exists a mass of potential entrepreneurs who can enter the modern sector, once they incur an up-front investment of f_e units of labor. At each point in time, a mass of M^E entrepreneurs decides to enter. Upon entry, these entrepreneurs learn about their productivity ϕ, which is drawn from a common and known distribution function $G(\phi)$ with support $(0,\infty)$ and density $g(\phi)$. This effect is termed the "productivity lottery." After the productivity is revealed, an entrant decides whether to exit immediately or to remain active in the market, in which case the firm earns constant per-period profits $\pi(\phi)$. It will exit immediately if $\pi(\phi) < 0$, that is, $r(\phi) < \sigma wf$. Hence, only firms whose productivity draw exceeds the cutoff $\phi^* > 0$ at which profits are zero, $\pi(\phi^*) = 0$, remain active. Once in the market, every firm may be hit each period with constant probability δ by a negative shock that forces it to shut down and exit. We focus on a stationary equilibrium without time discounting such that in each period, the mass of market entrants equals the mass of firms that are forced to shut down. Analytically, $prob_i M^E = \delta M$, where $prob_i \equiv 1 - G(\phi^*)$ is the probability to draw a productivity no smaller than the cutoff ϕ^*. The endogenous productivity distribution among surviving firms, $\mu(\phi)$, is thus the conditional (left-truncated) exante distribution $g(\phi^*)$ on the domain $[\phi^*,\infty)$.

12.2.5 Equilibrium and Parameterization

The equilibrium in the modern sector is characterized by a free entry condition (FEC) and a zero cutoff profit condition (ZCPC) as in Melitz 2003. Assuming risk neutrality, potential entrepreneurs enter the market (i.e., participate in the productivity lottery) until the value of entry $v^E = E\left[\sum_{t=0}^{\infty}(1-\delta)^t\,\pi(\phi)\right] - w\,f_e$ is driven to zero (FEC). Intuitively, this condition expresses that the expected stream of profits that can be reaped in the market in the infinite lifetime is at least as high as the upfront investment wf_e. The ZCPC commands that the cutoff firm makes zero profits, $\pi(\phi^*) = 0$. Intuitively, because the upfront investment is sunk, firms engage in production if profits are non-negative. The equilibrium cutoff productivity ϕ^* simultaneously satisfies the FEC and the ZCPC (see appendix 12A at the end of this chapter). Melitz (2003) shows that such an equilibrium cutoff exists for a general class of productivity distributions. However, a closed-form solution of the model is not obtained unless an adequate specification is chosen for the productivity distribution. We follow much of the literature in assuming Pareto-distributed productivities, $G(\phi) = 1 - (\phi_{min}/\phi)^k$ and $g(\phi) = G'(\phi) = k\phi_{min}^k\phi^{-k-1}$, where $\phi_{min} > 0$ is the lower bound for productivity draws and $k > 1$ is the shape parameter.[7] Apart from allowing a closed-form solution for the cutoff, this specification has the merit to be backed by the empirics (e.g., Del Gatto, Mion, and Ottaviano 2006, Ikeda and Suoma 2009). The ex post probability of productivities is then given by $\mu(\phi) = g(\phi)/[1 - G(\phi^*)] = k\phi^{*k}\phi^{-(k+1)}$ if $\phi > \phi^*$ and $\mu(\phi) = 0$ otherwise. It follows that $\tilde{\phi} = [k/(k-(\sigma-1))]^{1/(\sigma-1)}\,\phi^*$, where we strengthen our previous assumption to $k > \sigma - 1$. Using these expressions in FEC and ZCPC yields the autarky equilibrium cutoff

$$\phi_{aut}^* = \left[\frac{(\sigma-1)}{(k-\sigma+1)}\,\frac{f}{f_e}\,\frac{\phi_{min}^k}{\delta}\right]^{\frac{1}{k}} \tag{12.5}$$

Throughout this chapter, we assume the condition $([(\sigma-1)\cdot f]/[(k-\sigma+1)\cdot f_e\cdot\delta])^{1/k} > 1$ to ensure that $\phi_{aut}^* > \phi_{min}$. The equilibrium cutoff is independent of the number of workers L, positively related to the elasticity of substitution σ, the fixed labor f to serve the market, and the lower bound ϕ_{min}, and negatively related to the fixed investment of labor at the entry stage f_e, the death rate δ, as well as the Pareto-shape parameter k.[8] Moreover, the autarky cutoff ϕ_{aut}^* is unaffected by the labor coefficient in the competitive sector a because this coefficient affects the wage and hence the fixed costs to enter and serve the market equiproportionately. Once ϕ^*_{aut} is determined, all other endogenous variables are easily derived (appendix 12B). The autarky price level is $P_{aut} - (\beta L / \sigma f)^{1/(1-\sigma)} w^{\sigma/(\sigma-1)} (1 / \rho \phi^*_{aut})$ and a household's indirect utility is then

$$
v_{aut} = w - \beta \ln \left[\left(\frac{\beta L}{\sigma f} \right)^{\frac{1}{1-\sigma}} w^{\frac{\sigma}{\sigma-1}} \left(\frac{1}{\rho \phi^*_{aut}} \right) \right] + \beta (\ln \beta - 1) \tag{12.6}
$$

12.3   The Open Economy

12.3.1   Country Asymmetries
We now turn to an open economy with two countries , where H = home and F = foreign. These countries may differ with respect to country size, the labor coefficient in the traditional sector a_i, technologies in the modern sector as expressed by the lower bounds ϕ_{mini} of the Pareto-distribution, exit rates δ_i, the fixed up-front investment for entry in the modern sector $f_{e,i}$ and the fixed labor input f_i to serve domestic markets.

12.3.2   Trade Costs
If (after learning its productivity ϕ_i) a firm from country i decides to export to country j, it faces an additional country-specific fixed cost f_{xi} on top of the domestic per-period fixed costs f_i that accrue regardless of export status. We assume that $f_{xi} > f_i$ to ensure that only a section of the domestic firms is active in trade. We also assume $f_{xi} > f_j$ so that the fixed labor input that has to be incurred to serve the export market exceeds the fixed labor that foreign competitors must incur in their home market. Moreover, there are variable iceberg costs to serve foreign consumers: for one unit to arrive in j, a firm from country i must ship $\tau_{ij} > 1$ units. We shall allow for the possibility that $\tau_{ij} \neq \tau_{ji}$, for instance, due to different trade policies or trade infrastructures. Trade in the traditional good is costless. As long as both countries produce this good—an assumption that we shall maintain throughout the chapter—the law of one price dictates that the foreign wage is tied to the domestic wage, $W \equiv w_F/w_H = a_H/a_F$, where W denotes the relative foreign wage. Note that $w_i = 1/a_i$ by our choice of the numéraire. Hence we do not impose factor prize equalization.

12.3.3   Domestic and Export Cutoffs
The domestic cutoff productivities ϕ^*_H and ϕ^*_F are derived by making use of the conditions of free entry and zero cutoff profits that become inter-

dependent in the open economy. If a firm from country i exports to country j, its export profits are given by $\pi_{xi}(\phi) = r_{xi}(\phi)/\sigma - w_i f_{xi}$, where $r_{xi}(\phi) = (\tau_{ij} w_i / \rho\phi)^{1-\sigma} P_j^{\sigma-1} \beta L_j$ is the export revenue. There is a critical productivity threshold ϕ_{xi}^* where such a firm breaks even on the export market, that is, $\pi_{xi}(\phi_{xi}^*) = 0$. We call this the *export ZCPC*. Furthermore, a firm from country i that serves its home market i derives profits $\pi_i(\phi) = r_i(\phi)/\sigma - w_i f_i$, where $r_i(\phi) = (w_i / \rho\phi)^{1-\sigma} P_i^{\sigma-1} \beta L_i$ is the associated revenue. The ϕ_i^* where this firm breaks even is defined by $\pi_i(\phi_i^*) = 0$. We call this the *domestic ZCPC*. The revenue equations imply a link between export cutoffs and domestic cutoffs, $\phi_{xH}^* = W^{-\sigma/(\sigma-1)} t_H \phi_F^*$ and $\phi_{xF}^* = W^{\sigma/(\sigma-1)} t_F \phi_H^*$, where $t_i \equiv \tau_{ij}(f_{xi}/f_j)^{1/(\sigma-1)}$ (see appendix 12C). The FEC for country i commands that firms enter the market until the value of entry is zero, $prob_i\, \mathrm{E}\left[\pi_i(\phi)/\delta_i \middle| \phi > \phi_i^*\right] + prob_{xi}\, \mathrm{E}\left[\pi_{xi}(\phi)/\delta_i \middle| \phi > \phi_{xi}^*\right] = w_i\, f_{ei}$. The first term on the left-hand side (LHS) formalizes the expected profits on the domestic market and the second term expresses expected profits on the export market where $prob_{xi} \equiv 1 - G_i(\phi_{xi}^*)$ denotes the probability for a productivity draw high enough to enter the export market. The right-hand side (RHS) expresses the entry costs.

The resulting equilibrium cutoff productivities are derived as follows (see appendix 12D):

$$\phi_H^* = \left[\frac{(\sigma-1)}{(k-\sigma+1)}\frac{f_H}{f_{eH}}\frac{\phi_{\min H}^k}{\delta_H}\cdot\left[\frac{1-\Phi_F\Phi_H}{1-\Delta^{\delta,f_e,\phi_{\min},w}\cdot\Phi_H}\right]\right]^{\frac{1}{k}}$$

$$= \phi_{H,aut}^*\cdot\left[\frac{1-\Phi_F\Phi_H}{1-\Delta^{\delta,f_e,\phi_{\min},w}\cdot\Phi_H}\right]^{\frac{1}{k}}$$

$$\phi_F^* = \left[\frac{(\sigma-1)}{(k-\sigma+1)}\frac{f_F}{f_{eF}}\frac{\phi_{\min F}^k}{\delta_F}\cdot\left[\frac{1-\Phi_F\Phi_H}{1-\Phi_F/\Delta^{\delta,f_e,\phi_{\min},w}}\right]\right]^{\frac{1}{k}}$$

(12.7)

$$= \phi_{F,aut}^*\cdot\left[\frac{1-\Phi_F\Phi_H}{1-\Phi_F/\Delta^{\delta,f_e,\phi_{\min},w}}\right]^{\frac{1}{k}}$$

where $\Phi_i \equiv \tau_{ij}^{-k}\left(f_j/f_{xi}\right)^{(k-\sigma+1)/(\sigma-1)}$ are measures of trade openness that rise as variable trade costs τ_{ij} and/or the fixed cost ratio f_{xi}/f_j fall. Notice that $f_{xi} > f_j$ entails $0 \le \Phi_i < 1$. The parameter $\Delta^{\delta,f_e,\phi_{\min},w} \equiv DF_e T^k W^{\sigma k/(\sigma-1)}$ captures international differences (ratios) concerning exit rates $D \equiv \delta_F/\delta_H$, entry investments $F_e \equiv f_{eF}/f_{eH}$, technologies in the manufacturing sector as proxied by the lower productivity bounds of the Pareto-distribution $T \equiv \phi_{\min H}/\phi_{\min F}$ and wage differentials $W \equiv w_F/w_H = a_H/a_F$ caused by productivity differences in the competitive sector. Note that $\Delta^{\delta,f_e,\phi_{\min},w}$ rises when home business conditions turn in favor of domestic firms.

12.3.4 Parameter Restrictions

We impose three parameter conditions on the open economy. First, we want to ensure that both sectors are active in both countries, $M_i > 0$ (nonspecialization in production), both before and after trade, which occurs whenever $\Phi_F \cdot (\lambda + 1)/(\lambda + \Phi_H \Phi_F) < \Delta^{\delta, f_e, \phi_{\min}, w} < (1 + \lambda \Phi_H \Phi_F)/[\Phi_H \cdot (1 + \lambda)]$, where $\lambda \equiv L_H / L_F$ denotes the labor endowment ratio across countries (see appendix 12F). Second, in equilibrium the export cutoffs have to exceed the domestic cutoffs, $\phi_{xi}^* > \phi_i^*$ so that, in line with the empirics, only domestically active firms can export. This behavior is guaranteed by the assumption $(1 + f_F / f_{xF}) \cdot \Phi_F / [1 + \Phi_H \Phi_F \cdot (f_F / f_{xF})] < \Delta^{\delta, f_e, \phi_{\min}, w} < [1 + \Phi_H \Phi_F \cdot (f_H / f_{xH})]/[\Phi_H \cdot (1 + f_H / f_{xH})]$. And third, it must hold true that $\phi_i^* > \phi_{\min, i}$. It can be verified that the third condition is implied by the first and the second condition. Intuitively, the parameter restrictions imply that in an *overall* sense business conditions in the two countries must not be too different.

12.3.5 Trade Balance and Open Economy Equilibrium

To complete the characterization of the open economy equilibrium, we must impose balanced trade. This step allows us to derive the masses of firms and the CES price indices $P_i = (\beta L_i / \sigma f_i)^{1/(1-\sigma)} w_i^{\sigma/(\sigma-1)} (\rho \phi_i^*)^{-1}$ (see appendix 12E). The indirect utility then follows as

$$v_i = w_i - \beta \ln \left[\left(\frac{\beta L_i}{\sigma f_i} \right)^{\frac{1}{1-\sigma}} w_i^{\frac{\sigma}{\sigma-1}} \left(\frac{1}{\rho \phi_i^*} \right) \right] + \beta (\ln \beta - 1) \tag{12.8}$$

12.4 Policy Analysis

12.4.1 Gains from Trade and Trade Liberalization with Identical Countries

We start our policy analysis by replicating Melitz's (2003) central results within our framework, which is easily achieved by assuming identical countries.[9] Abstracting from all country differences (such that $\Delta^{\delta, f_e, \phi_{\min}, w} = 1$ and $\Phi_H = \Phi_F = \Phi$) and normalizing the labor productivity in the traditional sector to be $a_i = a_j = 1$, we have $w_i = w_j = 1$. The cutoffs under trade, from equation (12.9), then become $\phi_i^* = \phi_{i, aut}^* (1 + \Phi)^{1/k}$ both for H and for F. Because $\Phi > 0$, it is immediately clear that the cutoff under trade exceeds the cutoff under autarky, $\phi_i^* > \phi_{i, aut}^*$, which entails that the switch from autarky to trade implies a welfare benefit—the gains from trade! Moreover, a liberalization of trade costs (i.e., increasing the trade freeness Φ) yields an increase in the cutoff, $d\phi_i^* / d\Phi > 0$ that implies that (reciprocal) trade liberalization yields welfare benefits.

Underlying these positive welfare effects is the aggregate productivity effect identified by Melitz (2003). Both the switch from autarky to trade and the liberalization of trade lead to market entry of firms, which reduces the demand for each producer and thereby drives the least productive firms out of business. This selection process raises the cutoff productivity, the aggregate productivity, and the consumer's welfare.[10]

12.4.2 The Technology Potential

Productivity differences are a classic topic in international economics ever since Ricardo's (1821) *On the Principles of Political Economy and Taxation*. Altogether new and different insights arise when technological asymmetries across countries are allowed for in models with heterogeneous firms. The seminal contribution by Demidova (2008) highlights differences in the technology potential in the sense that the productivity lottery in one country stochastically dominates another country's lottery or, to put it more prosaically, that firms, upon making an upfront entry investment, have access to a better pool of technologies in some than in other countries. Following Melitz (2003), Demidova (2008) departs from a general distribution of the productivity lottery, but the essence of her analysis can also be conveyed by working with the Pareto specification of the productivity lottery. A straightforward way to give one country—say, H—a better technology potential in the heterogeneous sector is then to assume that the minimal productivity draw in H exceeds the minimal productivity draw in country F, that is, $\phi_{minH} > \phi_{minF}$.[11]

Assuming $\phi_{minH} > \phi_{minF}$ and abstracting from all other country asymmetries, Demidova's main policy insights are easily derived within our framework. Equation (12.5) shows that the productivity cutoff under autarky is higher in country H compared to country F and hence so is country H's welfare level. For the open economy, we now have $\Delta^{\delta, f_e, \phi_{min}, w} = T^k = (\phi_{minH} / \phi_{minF})^k$ and $\Phi_H = \Phi_F = \Phi$. The cutoffs, equation (12.7), are then given by $\phi_H^* = \phi_{H,aut}^* \cdot [(1-\Phi^2)/(1-T^k \cdot \Phi)]^{1/k}$ and $\phi_F^* = \phi_{F,aut}^* \cdot [(1-\Phi^2)/(1-\Phi / T^k)]^{1/k}$, respectively. A comparison with equation (12.5) reveals that despite differences in technology potentials, both the laggard country (F) and the leading country (H) achieve gains from trade.[12]

An intriguing new insight emerges when a unilateral improvement in the technology potential in one country (H), as a result of technology policy or improvements in the research infrastructure, for example, takes place. This result immediately entails $d\phi_H^* / dT > 0$ and $d\phi_F^* / dT < 0$. Intuitively, a unilateral improvement in the technology potential of country i raises the profitability of the domestic market and gives local firms a competitive edge over their foreign competitors. This change stimulates entry in country i and reduces the incentive to enter the modern industry in country j. The induced selection effect then leads to higher cutoffs and welfare in i and lower cutoffs and welfare in j. Productivity improvements are thus unambiguously a boon for the country where these improvements take place but a bane for the other country.[13]

A further issue concerns the welfare effect of symmetric trade integration if the two countries differ with respect to their technology potential (but are identical in all other respects).[14] Is immiserization of one country then possible? Exploring the effect of $d\Phi_H = d\Phi_F = d\Phi$ on the two countries' cutoffs and indirect utilities entails the conclusion that immiserization in the technologically inferior country *would* occur iff $\Delta^{\delta, f_e, \phi_{\min}, w} < (2\Phi) / (1 + \Phi^2)$ or $\Delta^{\delta, f_e, \phi_{\min}, w} > (1 + \Phi^2) / (2\Phi)$. However, we have ruled out such parameter constellations in section 12.3 in order to obtain a consistent analysis. More precisely, the parameter conditions for immiserization are also the conditions under which the laggard country becomes fully specialized in the traditional good sector. Hence we conclude that symmetric trade liberalization must improve welfare in both countries.[15] We show in section 12.4.5., however, that immiserization is possible if the two countries differ in further business conditions.

12.4.3 Entry Subsidies and International Policy Competition

An entrepreneur who is about to start business is faced with sunk costs related to research and development and legal entry barriers such as licenses and permits. Governments also provide numerous programs of support for the foundation of new firms, however. Such subsidies to market entry and R&D are very widely used. Unlike classical trade policy instruments (import tariffs or export subsidies), these policies are perceived as largely domestic issues and therefore not scrutinized by bodies such as the WTO. Pflüger and Suedekum (2013) explore the implications of entry subsidies from the backdrop of these observations within the framework laid out in sections 12.2 and 12.3.[16] Governments unconditionally provide entry subsidies s that reduce the entry costs for (potential) firms from their *raw* level f_e to the *effective* level $\tilde{f}_e \equiv f_e - s$.

These subsidies are assumed to be financed by a lump-sum tax t levied on households. The budget constraint of the government is then given by $t \cdot L = s \cdot M^E$. If governments are benevolent, they choose the subsidy such that the indirect utility of households $v(\cdot)$ is maximized subject to the budget constraint. We assume in the following discussion that countries are identical, with the exception of possible differences in entry subsidies.[17]

Starting with autarky, the welfare-maximizing entry subsidy can be derived as $s^*_{aut} = f_e / \sigma$ and is therefore positively related to raw entry costs f_e and negatively to the elasticity of substitution σ.[18] To intuitively understand this result, it should be noted that the two-sector economy exhibits one market distortion: the monopoly power of firms in the modern sector relative to the traditional sector.[19] Output is too low in the modern sector because prices are too high, as indicated by σ, which determines the markup on marginal costs (see equation [12.3]). This distortion explains why s^*_{aut} is negatively related to σ. The larger the distortion, the stronger the incentive to subsidize, because the entry subsidy induces firm entry, tougher competition, and a higher cutoff—that is, a selection effect, which implies that the firms that remain in the market are more productive. The optimal entry subsidy s^*_{aut} is a second-best policy, however. Clearly, a direct way to target the distortion is to subsidize consumption (or, alternatively, production) of the differentiated varieties at the markup rate $1/\sigma$ (as is shown analytically in Pflüger and Suedekum 2013). The positive relationship between s^*_{aut} and f_e is intuitive because a reduction in the raw entry costs tightens the welfare-enhancing selection of firms, so s^*_{aut} is smaller.

Policies that target the entry of firms are highly pervasive, in practice. Hence it is important to understand their implications for the international economy. Suppose we have two identical countries (such that $\Delta^{\delta, f_e, \phi_{\min}, w} = 1$ and $\Phi_H = \Phi_F = \Phi$ in our model) whose governments competitively choose their entry subsidies. Note that by equation (12.7), a decrease of the entry costs in one country (H) raises the cutoff productivity in that country and lowers the cutoff in F. Intuitively, the increased competition and selection induced by the entry subsidies is transmitted to the other country. Export market entry becomes more difficult for foreign enterprises, as domestic firms are now more productive and competitive. Hence the foreign country experiences a negative selection effect and a welfare-reducing fall in its productivity cutoff. The Nash equilibrium subsidy is calculated to be $s^* = [f_e(1 - \Phi)(1 + \Phi(\sigma - 1))]/[\sigma + \Phi(\sigma - 2)]$, so a bell-shaped relationship emerges between s^* and trade freeness Φ.[20] Starting at prohibitive trade costs, $\Phi = 0$, the Nash subsidy is $s^* = f_e/\sigma$. It then rises in Φ, reaches a peak and falls continuously thereafter, reaching $s^* = f_e/\sigma$ at $\Phi = (\sigma - 2)/\sigma$ and it approaches $s^* = 0$ when trade is completely costless, $\Phi = 1$. It is instructive to compare this Nash equilibrium with the optimal cooperative entry subsidy that maximizes the sum of indirect utilities of both regions jointly. This optimal cooperative subsidy can be shown to coincide with the optimal entry subsidy under autarky, f_e/σ (Pflüger and Suedekum 2013). A comparison reveals that the subsidies coincide at $\Phi = 0$ and at $\Phi = (\sigma - 2)/\sigma$ and that the Nash equilibrium oversubsidizes in the range $0 < \Phi < (\sigma - 2)/\sigma$ and undersubsidizes in the range $(\sigma - 2)/\sigma < \Phi < 1$.

The optimal cooperative subsidy is the same as under autarky—intuitively so, as the motive to grant this subsidy remains the same, albeit for two countries now. What is the reason for the nonmonotonic effect of trade liberalization on the Nash equilibrium subsidies and hence the difference between Nash subsidies and the cooperative solution, though? Any difference must be due to externalities that are internalized by the cooperative solution but not internalized in the competitive policy equilibrium. In fact, two international externalities are associated with entry subsidization in the open economy. There is a negative (inverse) selection effect that drives down the cutoff in the other economy, as already mentioned. However, there is also a positive fiscal externality in that the foreign budget is relaxed as the number of foreign firms trying to enter falls. Netting out these externalities leads to the result that the net externality is negative for low levels of trade freeness and high for high levels of trade freeness, which rationalizes the results of over-and undersubsidization, respectively.

These considerations imply that there are gains from policy cooperation by which the net externality is internalized. Importantly, it depends crucially on the level of trade freeness whether the switch to policy cooperation involves a decrease or increase of the subsidies. Moreover, a complete (joint) removal of all entry subsidies would lead to a welfare loss.

12.4.4   Research Infrastructure and Policy Competition
Governments in developed economies support R&D in various ways, such as through public research projects, subsidies to private R&D, or innovation funds and support for higher education. Looking at per capita R&D spending in constant U.S. dollars for twenty-one OECD

countries in the years 2000 and 2007/08, Bohnstedt, Schwarz, and Suedekum (2012) find that the United States ($381) and the Nordic countries (Norway $356, Sweden $353, Finland $334) are the leaders in 2007–2008 and that these countries have experienced strong increases from 2000 on. However, the weighted average has also substantially risen from $233 to $287.[21]

Bohnstedt, Schwarz, and Suedekum (2012) provide a theoretical analysis of the effects of international trade on the choice of public research and development expenses in terms of the model laid out in sections 12.2 and 12.3. They assume that governments levy a lump-sum tax to finance basic research that is assumed to raise a country's technological potential as expressed by the minimum productivity draw $\phi_{\min i}$ of the Pareto distribution.[22] They identify two motives for public research policies. The benevolent motive is to tighten firm selection, which raises a country's average productivity, reduces the average consumer price, and increases welfare. This motive exists in autarky already, as an inspection of equation (12.5) reveals: the domestic cutoff rises in $\phi_{\min i}$. There is a further motive in open economies. If one government chooses a higher level of expenditures on R&D than the other, the relative technology potential $T \equiv \phi_{\min H}/\phi_{\min F}$ changes in favor of that country and its firms obtain a competitive advantage over their foreign competitors. Firms in the laggard country then face tougher import competition and have greater difficulties to export their products. It follows from equation (12.7) that a change in $T \equiv \phi_{\min H}/\phi_{\min F}$ raises the cutoff in the leading country and lowers the one in the laggard country. If countries decide noncooperatively, they overinvest in R&D, as they do not take into account the negative cross-country externality that they exert on each other. Hence welfare gains can be reaped by supranational policy cooperation.

Bohnstedt, Schwarz, and Suedekum (2012) then go on by allowing the possibility of positive cross-country R&D spillovers. Investments into basic research in one country thus increase not only the domestic but also the foreign technology potential. In terms of our model, such spillovers can be formalized by $\phi_{\min i} = f(\phi_{\min j})$, where $f(\cdot)$ is an increasing function in its argument. This positive cross-country externality (partially) offsets the negative competition externality such that the overinvestment problem is mitigated. If these R&D spillovers are sufficiently strong, the overinvestment problem might even turn into an underinvestment problem. In the light of recent research that shows that spillovers are highly localized (see, e.g., Keller 2004), the latter outcome is questionable, though.

12.4.5   Business Conditions

Business conditions are shaped by a multitude of factors. We have highlighted some of these conditions in sections 12.4.1–12.4.4. Government policy is a significant determinant of all these factors. This observation is the starting point of the analysis by Pflüger and Russek (2013a). They consider the comprehensive set of factors that we integrated into our analytical framework and focus on the impact of trade and industrial policies on national productivities and welfare.

With respect to the shift from autarky to international trade, it becomes immediately apparent from an inspection of the cutoffs in equation (12.7) that both countries achieve gains from trade even if they are asymmetric with respect to a variety of national business conditions. Moreover, even in the case in which business conditions are so disparate that the shift from autarky to trade drives the laggard country into full specialization in the traditional sector, and all manufactures are produced in the leading country, there are gains from trade for both countries.[23]

Concerning the impact of bilateral trade integration, it can be shown that a symmetric reduction in trade costs (i.e., $d\Phi_H = d\Phi_F > 0$) leads to welfare gains in both countries iff aggregate business conditions, measured by $\Delta^{\delta, f_e, \phi_{\min}, w}$, are similar, that is, for the parameter range $(\Phi_H + \Phi_F)/(1 + \Phi_H^2) < \Delta^{\delta, f_e, \phi_{\min}, w} < (1 + \Phi_F^2)/(\Phi_H + \Phi_F)$. Otherwise, the laggard country in terms of these aggregated business conditions experiences welfare losses, whereas the leader gains. Hence although we have shown that differences in technology potentials do not suffice to obtain immiserization of the laggard country (section 12.4.2), such immiserization becomes a distinct possibility once we account for asymmetric business conditions in a much more comprehensive sense. This finding becomes evident by noting that $\Delta^{\delta, f_e, \phi_{\min}, w} \equiv DF_e T^k W^{\sigma k/(\sigma-1)}$ can deviate from unity even if $T \equiv \phi_{\min H}/\phi_{\min F} = 1$, which expresses that technology potentials are identical.[24] Furthermore, note that with differences in country size and market accessibility the parameter range of nonimmiserization no longer coincides with the condition of nonspecialization. Hence in contrast to section 12.4.2., immiserization of the laggard is a possible outcome (appendix 12F provides a numerical example).

The effect of bilateral trade integration can be decomposed into two unilateral trade integration measures. Unilateral trade integration is understood as an opening of a country's border for products from its trading partner without an equivalent measure on behalf of its trading partner (e.g., $d\Phi_H > 0$ whereas $d\Phi_F = 0$). A unilateral border opening facilitates export activities of foreign firms, which tightens competition abroad and increases the cutoff and the level of welfare of the trading partner. The liberalizing country, instead, faces tougher import competition so that the domestic cutoff and the domestic level welfare of decrease.[25]

Concerning the effects of industrial policies, Pflüger and Russek (2013) show that it is not only productivity improvements (as highlighted by Demidova 2008) but improvements in business conditions in a much broader sense that impinge negatively on welfare of a country's trading partner. It follows immediately from the cutoffs in equation (12.7) and the indirect utility in equation (12.8) that this statement holds true with respect to comparative advantages due to lower wages, a lower exit risk, and an easier market entry.[26] Importantly, asymmetric effects on productivities and on welfare obtain in the two countries even if countries have identical technology potentials. Furthermore, policies are sensitive to the level of trade integration. The smaller are trade costs, the greater is the impact on productivities and, hence, welfare. This result mimics what has previously been obtained in models of the new trade theory and the new economic geography with homogeneous firms (compare Helpman and Krugman 1985; Venables 1987; Baldwin et al. 2003) and the underlying mechanism is the same in both settings (see also Ossa 2011).

12.4.6 Government Policies and National Exit Risk

Following Melitz (2003), we have so far assumed that the exit risk of *mature* firms (i.e., firms that successfully entered the market after drawing their productivity) is given by the constant exogenous probability of firm death δ and therefore independent of the productivity of the firm. The merits of this simplification are twofold. First, the assumption facilitates the establishment of a stationary equilibrium in which the productivity range, and hence the average productivity, of surviving firms is endogenously determined (Melitz 2003, 1701). Second, if we take the group of firms whose entry is not successful into account, the model accords with the empirical finding that new entrants have, on average, lower productivity and higher exit probability than incumbents (Melitz 2003, 1701) or, to view it from a different angle, that exiting firms have a lower productivity, on average, than surviving firms (Redding 2011, 6).

In spite of these merits, the assumption that mature firms face a constant exogenous death probability is strong (Redding 2011, 6). Empirical research with *firm-level* data consistently finds for many countries and across the spectrum of firms that less productive firms are much more likely to exit markets than more productive ones. This finding directly contradicts the assumption of a constant δ.[27] Moreover, looking at the perceived risk of firm exit in European countries as documented by CreditReform (2007, 2009), a private research institute and consultancy, and contrasting these numbers with the labor productivity (as measured by the average gross value added per hour) in these countries shows that the two are negatively correlated (Pflüger and Russek 2013b).[28] Such a negative correlation at the *country level* is clearly at odds with Melitz (2003) and the framework we laid out in sections 12.2 and 12.3 because the exit risk of mature firms is constant by assumption and the exit rate of young entrants is positively correlated with the productivity cutoff—and so is an economy's overall exit risk, by implication.

Pflüger and Russek (2013b) develop a simple modification of this model to bring it in line with the mentioned facts. The key assumption is that the firm-level exit risk of mature firms is inversely related to their respective productivity ϕ, as expressed by $\delta = \delta(\phi)$, where $\delta'(\phi) < 0$. This black-box specification expresses the notion that the organizational capital in the form of the general and financial management skills of entrepreneurs and managers helps firms to adapt to their environment and to become more productive, thus contributing to their survival.

Using $\delta = \delta(\phi)$ in the framework of sections 12.2 and 12.3, a stationary equilibrium can be endogenously derived, and it can be shown that the risk of firm exit for mature firms, young entrants, and the overall economy are fully determined by the productivity cutoff ϕ^* (Pflüger and Russek 2013b). This analysis holds for general specifications of the productivity lottery $g(\phi)$ and of the relationship $\delta(\phi)$. For ease of exposition, we assume a Pareto distribution of firm productivities and we work with the simple specification, $\delta(\phi) = 1/\phi$, in the following. The average death rate of mature firms is then given by $[(k-1)/k]\cdot\phi^{*-1}$, the average death rate of startups (entrants) follows as $[(k-1)/k]\cdot[\phi^{*k-1}/\phi_{\min}^k - \phi^{*-1}]$ and the overall average death rate is $[(k-1)/k]\cdot[\phi^{*k-1}/\phi_{\min}^k]$. These results reveal that the average death rate of entrants and the overall average death rate are positively linked to ϕ^* and the average death rate of mature firms is negatively correlated with ϕ^*. If we take the perceived insolvency exit risk across countries as a proxy for the exit risk that mature firms face, our model is thus able to provide an explanation for the negative correlation between the exit risk and labor productivity at the country level.

The model can then also be used to analyze how trade and industrial policies pursued by governments impact national exit risks. The key link is the impact that government policies exert on the productivity cutoff, because each type of exit risk is fully determined by ϕ^*. Pflüger and Russek (2013b) show that the qualitative impact of government policies on the cutoff productivities in the international equilibrium is the same whether δ is exogenous or depends on a firm's productivity. Hence we can draw on the results of the previous sections to obtain implications for the exit risk of mature firms on which we focus here. For example, the expected risk of business exit falls when a country moves from autarky to trade. Intuitively, trade opening induces a competition effect that drives up the productivity threshold to survive and hence also the average productivity of firms. The country-specific exit risk falls as firms become more productive on average. To take another example, because improvements in various business conditions positively affect the productivity cutoff, they imply a fall in national exit risks.

A cursory look at data involving the perceived insolvency risk and various business conditions reveals that these predictions are consistent with the observations (Pflüger and Russek 2013b). Clearly, solid econometric work is necessary to go beyond simple correlations. The causality issue needs to be addressed, in particular. Moreover, further and better data involving a much broader sample of countries are desirable. The simple model specification discussed in this section appears to be an adequate starting point for deeper empirical investigations, however.

12.5   Conclusion

Using a simple two-sector model of monopolistic competition in the spirit of the new trade theory as a unifying framework, this chapter has synthesized recent research that started to explore economic policy implications of the theories of heterogeneous firms and trade. Key lessons of this research are as follows: first, there are gains from trade even if the countries under consideration differ in the conditions of doing business. Second, differences in technology potentials have strong asymmetric effects for trading partners in the sense that the leading countries win and lagging countries lose in welfare terms. Third, seemingly domestic policies such as subsidies to entry or subsidies to R&D have strong international repercussions. Noncooperatively chosen policies typically deviate from optimal cooperative policies in nontrivial ways, so there is scope for

388   Michael Pflüger and Stephan Russek

welfare-improving policy coordination. Fourth, symmetric trade liberalization may lead to immiserization in the country with inferior business conditions. Fifth, a reexamination of the exit process of firms which takes into account that more productive mature firms are less likely to die delivers new insights for the average rate of firm death at the country level.

The analytical ease with which the model can be employed to address country asymmetries should make it an attractive tool to study other policy issues, such as policy competition in further instruments, multicountry extensions to address preferential trade agreements, and political economy applications in future work.

Appendix 12A: The FEC and ZCPC Condition

Using $\pi(\phi) = r(\phi)/\sigma - wf$ and $r(\phi) = (\phi/\tilde{\phi})^{\sigma-1} r(\tilde{\phi})$, where $\tilde{\phi} \equiv E[\phi^{\sigma-1} | \phi > \phi^*]^{1/(\sigma-1)}$ is a measure of average productivity, and imposing $v^E = 0$, the FEC can be derived as $\pi(\tilde{\phi}) = \delta w f_e / [1 - G(\phi^*)]$. Using $\pi(\tilde{\phi}) = [r(\tilde{\phi})/\sigma] - wf$ and $r(\phi^*) = (\phi^*/\tilde{\phi})^{\sigma-1} r(\tilde{\phi})$, the ZCPC condition can be expressed as a function of the average productivity level $\tilde{\phi}$: $\pi(\tilde{\phi}) = \left[(\tilde{\phi}/\phi^*)^{\sigma-1} - 1 \right] w f$.

Appendix 12B: Firm Masses, the Price Level, and Indirect Utility under Autarky

In equilibrium, the aggregate expenditure on manufacturing must be equal to the aggregate revenue of manufacturing firms, $\beta L = M r(\tilde{\phi})$. Using $r(\tilde{\phi}) = (\tilde{\phi}/\phi^*)^{\sigma-1} \sigma w f$, $\tilde{\phi} = [k/(k-(\sigma-1))]^{1/(\sigma-1)} \phi^*$, and the equilibrium cutoff in equation (12.5), the number of active firms can be derived, $M_{aut} = \dfrac{\beta L[k-(\sigma-1)]}{\sigma k w f}$. The condition of stationarity then implies the number of entrants, $M_{aut}^E = \dfrac{(\sigma-1)\beta L}{\sigma k w f_e}$. Using M_{aut} and $\tilde{\phi} = [k/(k-(\sigma-1))]^{1/(\sigma-1)} \phi^*$ in equation (12.4) yields the price level, $P_{aut} = (\beta L / \sigma f)^{1/(1-\sigma)} w^{\sigma/(\sigma-1)} (1/\rho \tilde{\phi}_{aut}^*)$ and the indirect utility is then as in equation (12.6).

Appendix 12C: The Link between the Productivity Cutoffs in the Open Economy

From the ZCPC conditions it follows that $r_i(\phi_i^*) = (\rho \phi_i^* P_i)^{\sigma-1} \beta L_i = \sigma w_i f_i$ and $r_{xi}(\phi_{xi}^*) = (\tau_{ij} w_i / \rho \phi_{xi}^*)^{1-\sigma} P_j^{\sigma-1} \beta L_j = \sigma w_i f_{xi}$. Hence, we have

$$\frac{r_H(\phi_H^*)}{r_F(\phi_F^*)} = \frac{w_H f_H}{w_F f_F} \Rightarrow \frac{\phi_H^*}{\phi_F^*} = W^{-\sigma/(\sigma-1)} \frac{P_F}{P_H} \left(\frac{f_H L_F}{f_F L_H}\right)^{1/(\sigma-1)} \qquad (12C.1)$$

$$\frac{r_{xH}(\phi_{xH}^*)}{r_{xF}(\phi_{xF}^*)} = \frac{w_H f_{xH}}{w_F f_{xF}} \Rightarrow \frac{\phi_{xH}^*}{\phi_{xF}^*} = W^{-\sigma/(\sigma-1)} \frac{\tau_{HF}}{\tau_{FH}} \frac{P_H}{P_F} \left(\frac{f_{xH} L_H}{f_{xF} L_F}\right)^{1/(\sigma-1)} \qquad (12C.2)$$

$$\frac{r_{xi}(\phi_{xi}^*)}{r_i(\phi_i^*)} = \frac{f_{xi}}{f_i} \Rightarrow \frac{\phi_{xi}^*}{\phi_i^*} = \tau_{ij} \left(\frac{f_{xi}}{f_i}\right) \frac{P_i}{P_j} \left(\frac{L_i}{L_j}\right)^{1/(\sigma-1)} \qquad (12C.3)$$

Combining equations (12C.1) and (12C.3) leads to $\phi_{xH}^* = W^{-\sigma/(\sigma-1)} t_H \phi_F^*$ and $\phi_{xF}^* = W^{\sigma/(\sigma-1)} t_F \phi_H^*$, where $t_i \equiv \tau_{ij}(f_{xi}/f_i)/(\sigma-1)$.

Appendix 12D: Determination of Equilibrium Cutoffs in the Open Economy

The FEC for country i is given by

$$\left(1 - G_i(\phi_i^*)\right) \cdot E\left[\pi_i(\phi)|\phi > \phi_i^*\right] + \left(1 - G_i(\phi_{xi}^*)\right) \cdot E\left[\pi_{xi}(\phi)|\phi > \phi_{xi}^*\right] = w_i \cdot f_{ei} \cdot \delta_i$$
$$(12D.1)$$

As $\pi_i(\phi) = r_i(\phi)/\sigma - w_i f_i$, we can write the expected domestic profits as

$$E\left[\pi_i(\phi)|\phi > \phi_i^*\right] = \frac{1}{\sigma} E\left[r_i(\phi)|\phi > \phi_i^*\right] - w_i f_i$$

Using $r_i(\phi) = (\rho\phi/w_i)^{\sigma-1} P_i^{\sigma-1} \beta L_i$ and the Pareto specification, we obtain

$$E\left[\pi_i(\phi)|\phi > \phi_i^*\right] = \left(\frac{r_i(\phi_i^*)}{\sigma} \frac{k}{k-\sigma+1} - w_i f_i\right)$$

On substituting $r_i(\phi_i^*) = \sigma w_i f_i$ which is implied by the domestic ZCPC, $\pi_i(\phi_i^*) = 0$, we have

$$E\left[\pi_i(\phi)|\phi > \phi_i^*\right] = \frac{\sigma-1}{k-\sigma+1} w_i f_i \qquad (12D.2)$$

The expected export profits are determined in the same manner. Now we use export profits, export revenue, and the previous parameterizations as well as the export ZCPC to obtain

$$E\left[\pi_{xi}(\phi)|\phi > \phi_{xi}^*\right] = \frac{\sigma-1}{k-\sigma+1} w_i f_{xi} \qquad (12D.3)$$

Substituting equations (12D.2) and (12D.3) into equation (12D.1) and using $G_i(\phi) = 1 - (\phi_{\text{min}i}/\phi_i)^k$ implies $\frac{\sigma-1}{k-\sigma+1} \phi_{\text{min}i}^k f_i \left(\phi_i^*\right)^{-k} + \frac{\sigma-1}{k-\sigma+1} \phi_{\text{min}i}^k f_{xi} \left(\phi_{xi}^*\right)^{-k}$

$= f_{ei} \cdot \delta_i$. Writing this equation out for $i = H, F$ and using the relationships between export cutoffs and domestic cutoffs, $\phi_{xH}^* = W^{-\sigma/(\sigma-1)} t_H \phi_F^*$ and $\phi_{xF}^* = W^{\sigma/(\sigma-1)} t_F \phi_H^*$ as derived in appendix 12C yields two equations that can be solved for the cutoffs ϕ_H^* and ϕ_F^* as stated in equation (12.7).

Appendix 12E: Firm Masses, the Price Level, and Indirect Utility under Trade

To derive the firm masses in the open economy equilibrium, we must impose balanced trade. From the perspective of the domestic economy, this condition is given by

$$cprob_{xH} M_H r_{xH} \left(\tilde{\phi}_{xH} \right) = cprob_{xF} M_F r_{xF} \left(\tilde{\phi}_{xF} \right) + (w_H - \beta) L_H - (1 - \gamma_H) L_H / a_H$$

where $cprob_{xi} \equiv prob_{xi} / prob_i = \left(\phi_i^* / \phi_{xi}^* \right)^k$ is the conditional probability to become an exporter in country i and γ_H denotes the share of labor employed in the modern sector in country H. The LHS of equation (12.8) gives the value of country H's manufacturing exports and the first term on the RHS gives the value of manufacturing imports. The second and third terms on the RHS are the values of domestic consumption and production of the traditional good, respectively. Any imbalance in trade in manufacturing must be matched by a trade surplus or deficit in this numéraire. Now use this balanced trade condition and substitute $M_i = \gamma_i L_i w_i / \bar{r}_i$, where $\bar{r}_i \equiv r_i \left(\tilde{\phi}_i \right) + cprob_{xi} r_{xi} \left(\tilde{\phi}_{xi} \right)$, $w_H = 1/a_H$ and $\beta(L_H + L_F) = \gamma_H L_H w_H + \gamma_F L_F W_F$. Solving for the γ_i then gives

$$\gamma_H = \frac{\beta}{w_H} \frac{\bar{r}_H}{r_H(\tilde{\phi}_H)} \frac{1 - \Phi_F / \Delta^{L,\phi^*}}{1 - \Phi_H \Phi_F} \quad \text{and} \quad \gamma_F = \frac{\beta}{w_F} \frac{\bar{r}_F}{r_F(\tilde{\phi}_F)} \frac{1 - \Phi_H \cdot \Delta^{L,\phi^*}}{1 - \Phi_H \Phi_F} \quad \text{where}$$

$$\Delta^{L,\phi^*} \equiv \frac{f_F}{f_H} \frac{L_H}{L_F} W^{\frac{k\sigma}{\sigma-1}} \left(\frac{\phi_F^*}{\phi_H^*} \right)^k = \frac{L_H}{L_F} \frac{\Delta^{\delta, f_e, \phi \min, w} - \Phi_F}{1 - \Delta^{\delta, f_e, \phi \min, w} \Phi_H} \text{ is an increasing measure}$$

of relative conditions favoring business in H (against F). Using γ_i, the masses of firms are immediately implied by $M_i \bar{r}_i = \gamma_i L_i w_i$ where $r_i \left(\tilde{\phi}_i \right)$ follows from the domestic ZCPC and is given by $r_i \left(\tilde{\phi}_i \right) = \sigma k f_i w_i / [k - (\sigma - 1)]$. Hence, we have

$$M_H = \frac{[k - (\sigma - 1)] \beta L_H}{\sigma k f_H w_H} \cdot \left(\frac{1 - \Phi_F / \Delta^{L,\phi^*}}{1 - \Phi_H \Phi_F} \right) = M_{H,aut} \cdot \left(\frac{1 - \Phi_F / \Delta^{L,\phi^*}}{1 - \Phi_H \Phi_F} \right) \quad (12E.1)$$

$$M_F = \frac{[k - (\sigma - 1)] \beta L_F}{\sigma k f_F w_F} \cdot \left(\frac{1 - \Phi_H \Delta^{L,\phi^*}}{1 - \Phi_H \Phi_F} \right) = M_{F,aut} \cdot \left(\frac{1 - \Phi_H \Delta^{L,\phi^*}}{1 - \Phi_H \Phi_F} \right)$$

The number of exporting firms is implied by $M_{xi} = cprob_{xi} M_i$ and the mass of entrants follows according to $M_i^E = \phi_{\min i}^{-k}\phi_i^{*k}\delta_i M_i$. The consumption variety available in country i is $M_{ti} = M_i + M_{xj}$.

With the price setting rule defined by equation (12.3), the price level can be rewritten as $P_i = M_{ti}^{\frac{1}{1-\sigma}}\cdot p_i\left(\tilde{\phi}_{ti}\right)$. The variable $\tilde{\phi}_{ti} = \left\{(1/M_{ti})\right.$ $\left[M_i\tilde{\phi}_i^{\sigma-1} + M_{xj}\left(w_j/w_i\right)^{1-\sigma}\tau_{ji}^{1-\sigma}\tilde{\phi}_{xj}^{\sigma-1}\right]\right\}^{\frac{1}{\sigma-1}}$ is an average productivity of all firms (domestic and foreign) that serve consumers in country i. Consumers in country i spend $M_{ti}\, r_i\left(\tilde{\phi}_{ti}\right) = \beta L_i$ on manufacturing varieties and the average firm revenue is related to the revenue of the cutoff firm according to $r_i\left(\tilde{\phi}_{ti}\right) = \left(\tilde{\phi}_{ti}/\phi_i^*\right)^{\sigma-1} r_i\left(\phi_i^*\right)$. With $r_i\left(\phi_i^*\right) = \sigma w_i f_i$, it follows that $M_{ti} = \beta L_i\left(\tilde{\phi}_{ti}/\phi_i^*\right)^{1-\sigma}/\sigma w_i f_i$. On substitution, this yields for the price level $P_i = \left(\beta L_i/\sigma f_i\right)^{1/(1-\sigma)} w_i^{\sigma/(\sigma-1)}\left(\rho\phi_i^*\right)^{-1}$. Notice that the derivation of the price level is independent from the derivation of the productivity thresholds and observe that it is completely general (it does not depend on the Pareto parameterization).

Appendix 12F: Parameter Restrictions

Nonspecialization

Using equation (12E.1) and imposing $M_i \geq 0$, both countries have manufacturing producers if $\Phi_F < \Delta^{L,\phi^*} < 1/\Phi_H$. By substituting $\Delta^{L,\phi^*} \equiv \lambda\cdot\left(\Delta^{\delta,f_e,\phi_{\min},w} - \Phi_F\right)/\left(1 - \Delta^{\delta,f_e,\phi_{\min},w}\cdot\Phi_H\right)$, where $\lambda \equiv L_H/L_F$ is the ratio of labor endowment in H relative to F, and solving for $\Delta^{\delta,f_e,\phi_{\min},w}$, this condition for nonspecialization in both countries can be rewritten as

$$\Phi_F\frac{\lambda+1}{\lambda+\Phi_H\Phi_F} < \Delta^{\delta,f_e,\phi_{\min},w} < \frac{1}{\Phi_H}\frac{1+\lambda\Phi_H\Phi_F}{1+\lambda}$$

Meaningful Export Cutoffs

We assume that only firms that serve the domestic market can export, that is, $\phi_{xi}^* > \phi_i^*$. From equation (12C.3), it follows that this holds true whenever $\tau_{ij}(f_{xi}/f_i)^{1/(\sigma-1)}(P_j/P_i)(L_i/L_j)^{1/(\sigma-1)} > 1$. Substituting $P_i = \left(\beta L_i/\sigma f_i\right)^{1/(1-\sigma)} w_i^{\sigma/(\sigma-1)}\left(\rho\phi_i^*\right)^{-1}$ and rearranging yields $f_{xi}/f_j > \tau_{ij}^{1-\sigma}$ $\left(w_j/w_i\right)^{\sigma}\left(\phi_i^*/\phi_j^*\right)^{\sigma-1}$. Using the equilibrium cutoffs reported in equation (12.7) and solving the inequality for $\Delta^{\delta,f_e,\phi_{\min},w}$, we have meaningful export cutoffs, whenever

$$\frac{1+f_F/f_{xF}}{1+\Phi_H\Phi_F\cdot\left(f_F/f_{xF}\right)}\cdot\Phi_F < \Delta^{\delta,f_e,\phi_{\min},w} < \frac{1+\Phi_H\Phi_F\cdot\left(f_H/f_{xH}\right)}{1+f_H/f_{xH}}\cdot\frac{1}{\Phi_H}$$

Note that in Demidova 2008 the condition $\phi_{xi}^* > \phi_i^*$ implies $\phi_{xi}^* > \phi_j^*$ (i.e., that a domestic firm finds it easier to break even in its domestic market than a foreign exporter does) because her model assumes $W = 1$. However, in the presence of a possibly large wage differential, it is quite conceivable that an exporting firm might find it easier to break even than a local firm does. Hence the implication will not carry over to our model, in general.

Linking the Restrictions
To ensure that there is a range of parameters that simultaneously fulfills both inequalities, we have to make sure that the lower bound of each parameter restriction is smaller than the upper bound of the other. This approach boils down to the necessary parameter restriction

$$\frac{f_H}{f_{xH}} \cdot \Phi_H \Phi_F < \lambda < \left(\frac{f_F}{f_{xF}} \cdot \Phi_H \Phi_F \right)^{-1}$$

Numerical Examples
For the reader's convenience we provide two numerical examples to illustrate that there is a broad parameter space despite the parameter restrictions made in this chapter.

Assume $\lambda = 0.9, f_H/f_{xH} = 0.8, f_F/f_{xF} = 0.7$. (A). If $\Phi_H = 0.5$ and $\Phi_F = 0.35$, the nonspecialization condition reads $0.62 < \Delta^{\delta, fe, \phi\min, w} < 1.21$, the condition for meaningful export cutoff is $0.53 < \Delta^{\delta, fe, \phi\min, w} < 1.26$ and the linking condition $0.14 < \lambda < 8.16$, which is fulfilled by $\lambda = 0.9$. The interval for mutual gains from symmetric trade liberalization is given by $0.68 < \Delta^{\delta, fe, \phi\min, w} < 1.21$. For $0.62 < \Delta^{\delta, fe, \phi\min, w} < 0.68$, country H loses, and country F wins. (B) If $\Phi_H = 0.4$ and $\Phi_F = 0.65$, the nonspecialization condition is $1.07 < \Delta^{\delta, fe, \phi\min, w} < 1.62$, the condition for meaningful export cutoff is $0.94 < \Delta^{\delta, fe, \phi\min, w} < 1.67$ and the linking condition is $0.21 < \lambda < 5.49$. If $1.07 < \Delta^{\delta, fe, \phi\min, w} < 1.35$ both countries win by symmetric trade integration. For $1.35 < \Delta^{\delta, fe, \phi\min, w} < 1.62$ country F loses, whereas country H gains.

Notes

1. The introduction to this book puts this in broader perspective.

2. Bernard et al. (2007, 2011) and Mayer and Ottaviano (2007) summarize the empirical work. Helpman (2006) and Redding (2011) survey the theories of heterogeneous firms and trade.

3. Melitz and Ottaviano (2008) provide an alternative two-sector model of monopolistic competition with heterogeneous firms. They employ the linear demand system with

horizontal product differentiation along the lines of Ottaviano, Tabuchi, and Thisse (2002), which allows them to capture a pro-competitive effect that is absent in the Dixit-Stiglitz specification. However, as many of the recent works have used the latter specification as in Melitz 2003, we use it to facilitate their exposition and discussion.

4. Sala and Yalcin (2012) bring in managerial characteristics, as well.

5. Compare chapter 1 of this volume for a broad perspective on the competitive position of firms.

6. Demidova 2008, from which our analysis departs, assumes Cobb-Douglas preferences. We follow Pflüger and Suedekum 2013.

7. See, for example, Bernard et al. 2003, Helpman, Melitz, and Yeaple 2004, Baldwin 2005, and Melitz and Ottaviano 2008.

8. Due to the pro-competitive effect, the markups on marginal costs are lower and the cutoff productivities therefore higher under autarky (and also under international trade), the greater the domestic market size/labor force is in the Melitz and Ottaviano (2008) model, by contrast.

9. Our model deviates from that of Melitz (2003) in three aspects. First, he used a one-sector increasing returns economy, whereas we consider a two-sector model. Second, we consider an extensive list of country asymmetries. Third, Melitz leaves the productivity lottery unspecified; we assume a Pareto distribution. Of course, the Melitz (2003) model is easily reformulated with the Pareto specification (Baldwin 2005).

10. This process is similar to the "competition effect" known in the New Economic Geography (e.g., Baldwin et al. 2003) as the reduction of demand associated with the market entry of firms works through a fall in the price level—see equation (12.2); the price level P, which falls, when the mass of firms rises and remember that $q(z) = p(z)^{-\sigma}P^{\sigma-1}\beta L$. In the original Melitz (2003) model in which the wage is normalized to 1 and no traditional sector exists, this fall in the price level amounts to an increase in the real wage $1/P$, which is why this process can also be thought of as working through the domestic factor market. Notice, that this effect is *distinct from the pro-competitive effect* that arises in models where the markup over marginal costs is nonconstant and is reduced when more firms enter the market (see Ottaviano, Tabuchi, and Thisse 2002 and Melitz and Ottaviano 2008).

11. This special case has also been analyzed by Falvey, Greenaway, and Yu (2011) and by Melitz and Ottaviano (2008).

12. Note that the parameter restrictions from section 12.3 still hold. Hence the multiplicative terms of the international cutoffs are greater than 1 and the national cutoff productivities under trade greater than under autarky.

13. This qualitative finding was also obtained in Melitz and Ottaviano 2008. Note that this finding contrasts with the effects of technological progress in traditional trade models, which are ambiguous as a result of terms of trade effects induced by technological progress.

14. Felbermayr, Jung, and Larch (2012) provide an analysis of trade policy competition in a one-sector Melitz framework.

15. This qualitative finding is also obtained by Melitz and Ottaviano (2008). Demidova (2008) obtains a different result. She shows that with a Cobb-Douglas upper-tier utility and a general distribution of firm productivities, an immiserization might possibly occur in the laggard country in the absence of specialization.

16. Chor (2009) studies FDI subsidies.

17. Introducing further asymmetries does not alter the basic insight (see Pflüger and Suedekum 2013).

18. The result is obtained by maximizing equation (12.6) subject to $t \cdot L = s \cdot M^E$, taking the equilibrium responses of the economy as described in appendix 12E into account.

19. Note that a one-sector version of the model of monopolistic competition does not exhibit this distortion; see, for example, Demidova and Rodríguez-Clare 2009.

20. We focus on $\sigma > 2$ because it appears to be the relevant case empirically (see Pflüger and Südekum 2013).

21. Expenditures have fallen only in Japan and the Netherlands (Bohnstedt, Schwarz, and Suedekum 2012).

22. On a more technical level, they assume a simple concave specification between a country's tax income and its level of basic research on one hand and another simple specification between the level of basic research and the minimum productivity draw $\phi_{\text{min}i}$ on the other. Their analysis proceeds similarly to Pflüger and Suedekum (2013).

23. The specialization model is laid out in Pflüger and Russek 2013a.

24. Note that differences in country size are inconsequential here. This result was already obtained by Baldwin and Forslid (2006) and Baldwin (2005). However, these authors concluded that symmetric trade integration *must* raise welfare in both countries. The difference to our findings can be explained by noting that the authors did *not* account for differences in technology potentials *or* the comprehensive set of business conditions that we highlight.

25. This result was already obtained by Melitz and Ottaviano (2008).

26. Differences in f_i have an additional effect on productivities, as they change the relative access of foreign firms to the domestic market (as $\Phi_i \equiv \tau_{ij}^{-k} \left(f_j / f_{xi} \right)^{(k-\sigma+1)/(\sigma-1)}$). See Pflüger and Russek 2013 for details.

27. See Pflüger and Russek 2013b for a list of country studies.

28. Data on perceived national exit risks are used because comparable cross-country data on firm exits are not available. Although great efforts have been made to develop comparable statistics on firm dynamics in many countries in recent years (see Bartelsman, Haltiwanger, and Scarpetta 2009), these efforts have largely been independent, however. Hence the data reflect strong country idiosyncrasies. For example, in contrast to Germany, countries such as Spain, Italy, and Greece do not embrace small enterprises in their statistics. Moreover, in these Mediterranean countries firms often choose less formal and juridical ways to deal with bankruptcy that are also not included in the data (e.g., a settlement or a moratorium; see CreditReform 2007, 2009). Hence their insolvency rates are strongly biased downward.

References

Antràs, P., and E. Helpman. 2004. Global sourcing. *Journal of Political Economy* 112:552–580.

Baldwin, R. 2005. Heterogeneous firms and trade: testable and untestable properties of the Melitz model. NBER Working Paper no. 11471.

Baldwin, R., and R. Forslid. 2006. Trade liberalization with heterogeneous firms. NBER Working Paper no. 12192.

Baldwin, R., R. Forslid, P. Martin, G. Ottaviano, and F. Robert-Nicoud. 2003. *Economic Geography and Public Policy*. Princeton: Princeton University Press.

Bartelsman, E., J. Haltiwanger, and S. Scarpetta. 2009. Measuring and analyzing cross-country differences in firm dynamics. In *Producer Dynamics: New Evidence from Micro Data*, ed. T. Dunne, J. B. Jensen, and M. J. Roberts, 15–76. Chicago: University of Chicago Press.

Bernard, A., J. Eaton, B. Jensen, and S. Kortum. 2003. Plants and productivity in international trade. *American Economic Review* 93:1268–1290.

Bernard, A. B., J. B. Jensen, S. Redding, and P. Schott. 2007. Firms in international trade. *Journal of Economic Perspectives* 21 (3):105–130.

Bernard, A. B., J. B. Jensen, S. Redding, and P. Schott. 2011. The empirics of firm heterogeneity and international trade. NBER Working Paper no. 17627.

Bohnstedt, A., C. Schwarz, and J. Suedekum. 2012. Globalization and strategic research investments. *Research Policy* 41 (1): 13–23.

Chor, D. 2009. Subsidies for FDI: Implications from a model with heterogeneous firms. *Journal of International Economics* 78:113–125.

Combes, P. P., Th. Mayer, and J-F. Thisse. 2008. *Economic Geography: The Integration of Regions and Nations*. Princeton: Princeton University Press.

CreditReform. 2007. Insolvenzen in Europa, Jahr 2006/07, Verband der Vereine Creditreform e.V. http://www.creditreform.at.

CreditReform. 2009. Insolvenzen in Europa, Jahr 2008/09, Verband der Vereine Creditreform e.V. http://www.creditreform.at.

Demidova, S. 2008. Productivity improvements and falling trade costs: boon or bane? *International Economic Review* 49 (4): 1437–1462.

Demidova, S., and A. Rodríguez-Clare. 2009. Trade policy under firm-level heterogeneity in a small economy. *Journal of International Economics* 78 (1): 100–112.

Dinopoulos, E., K. Fujiwara, and K. Shimomura. 2011. International trade and volume patterns under quasilinear preferences. *Review of Development Economics* 15 (1): 154–167.

Dixit, A., and J. Stiglitz. 1977. Monopolistic competition and optimum product diversity. *American Economic Review* 67:297–308.

Del Gatto, M., G. Mion, and G. I. P. Ottaviano. 2006. Trade integration, firm selection and the costs of non-Europe. CEPR Discussion Paper 5730.

Falvey, R., D. Greenaway, and Z. Yu. 2011. Catching up or pulling away: Intra-industry trade, productivity gaps and heterogeneous firms. *Open Economies Review* 22 (1): 17–38.

Felbermayr, G., B. Jung, and M. Larch. 2012. Optimal tariffs, retaliation, and the welfare loss from tariff wars in the Melitz model. *Journal of International Economics* 89 (1): 13–25.

Flam, H., and E. Helpman. 1987. Industrial policy under monopolistic competition. *Journal of International Economics* 22:79–102.

Helpman, E., and P. Krugman. 1985. *Market Structure and Foreign Trade*. Cambridge, MA: MIT Press.

Helpman, E., and P. Krugman. 1989. *Trade Policy and Market Structure*. Cambridge, MA: MIT Press.

Helpman, E. 2006. Trade, FDI, and the organization of firms. *Journal of Economic Literature* 44 (3): 589–630.

Helpman, E., M. Melitz, and S. R. Yeaple. 2004. Export versus FDI with heterogeneous firms. *American Economic Review* 94 (1): 300–316.

Ikeda, Y. and W. Suoma. 2009. International comparison of labor productivity distribution for manufacturing and non-manufacturing firms. *Progress of Theoretical Physics Supplement*, no. 179: 93–102.

Keller, K. 2004. International technology diffusion. *Journal of Economic Literature* 42 (3): 752–782.

Martin, P., and C. A. Rogers. 1995. Industrial location and public infrastructure. *Journal of International Economics* 39:335–351.

Mayer, T., and G. I. M. Ottaviano. 2007. Happy few: The internationalization of European firms. New facts based on firm-level evidence. Open Access publications (Sciences Po) nr: info:hdl:2441/10147.

Melitz, M. J. 2003. The impact of trade on intra-industry reallocations and aggregate industry productivity. *Econometrica* 71 (6): 1695–1725.

Melitz, M., and G. Ottaviano. 2008. Market size, trade, and productivity. *Review of Economic Studies* 75:295–316.

Ossa, R. 2011. A "new trade" theory of GATT/WTO negotiations. *Journal of Political Economy* 119 (1): 122–152.

Ottaviano, G., and J-F. Thisse. 2002. Integration, agglomeration and the political economics of factor mobility. *Journal of Public Economics* 83:429–456.

Ottaviano, G., T. Tabuchi, and J-F. Thisse. 2002. Agglomeration and trade revisited. *International Economic Review* 43 (2): 409–436.

Pflüger, M., and S. Russek. 2013a. Trade and industrial policies with heterogeneous firms: The role of country asymmetries. Forthcoming in *Review of International Economics*.

Pflüger, M., and S. Russek. 2013b. Business conditions and exit risks across countries. *Open Economies Review*. doi:10.1007/s11079-013-9277-5.

Pflüger, M., and J. Suedekum. 2013. Subsidizing firm entry in open economies. *Journal of Public Economics* 97:258–271.

Redding, S. 2011. Theories of heterogeneous firms and trade. *Annual Review of Economics* 3:77–105.

Ricardo, D. 1821. *On the Principles of Political Economy and Taxation*. London: John Murray.

Tabuchi, T., and J-F. Thisse. 2006. Regional specialization, urban hierarchy, and commuting costs. *International Economic Review* 47:1295–1317.

Venables, A. 1987. Trade and trade policy with differentiated products: a Chamberlinian-Ricardian model. *Economic Journal* 97:700–717.

Yeaple, S. R. 2005. A simple model of firm heterogeneity, international trade, and wages. *Journal of International Economics* 65:1–20.

Contributors

Laura Abramovsky   Institute for Fiscal Studies & University College London

Carlo Altomonte   Bocconi University

Sjoerd Beugelsdijk   University of Groningen

Bruce Blonigen   University of Oregon and the National Bureau of Economic Research

Pamela Bombarda   Université de Cergy-Pontoise and THEMA

Steven Brakman   University of Groningen

Julia Darby   University of Strathclyde

Rodolphe Desbordes   University of Strathclyde

Filippo Di Mauro   European Central Bank

María García-Vega   University of Nottingham, School of Economics

Harry Garretsen   University of Groningen

Elena Huergo   GRIPICO (Group for Research in Productivity, Innovation, and Competition) and Universidad Complutense

Florian Mayneris   Université catholique de Louvain, IRES, CORE

Quyen T. K. Nguyen   Henley Business School, University of Reading

Verena Nowak   Mercator School of Management, University of Duisburg-Essen, Germany

Cheyney O'Fallon   University of California Santa Cruz

Gianmarco Ottaviano   LSE and Bocconi University

Michael Pflüger University of Passau, DIW Berlin and IZA

Filomena Pietrovito Università degli Studi del Molise

Sandra Poncet Paris School of Economics

Alberto Franco Pozzolo Università degli Studi del Molise, Centro Studi Luca

Alan M. Rugman Henley Business School, University of Reading, D'Agliano and MoFiR

Armando Rungi University of Warsaw

Stephan Russek University of Passau

Davide Sala University of Southern Denmark

Luca Salvatici Università degli Studi Roma Tre

Christian Schwarz Mercator School of Management, University of Duisburg-Essen, Germany

Roger Smeets Rutgers Business School

Jens Suedekum Mercator School of Management, University of Duisburg-Essen, Germany

Hans van Ees University of Groningen

Vincent Vicard Banque de France

Ian Wooton University of Strathclyde and CESifo

Erdal Yalcin Ifo Institute, University of Munich

Index